Essentials of Annuities

Financial Advisor Series

Walter J. Woerheide, Editor

Sales Skills Techniques

Techniques for Exploring Personal Markets

Techniques for Meeting Client Needs

Techniques for Prospecting: Prospect or Perish

Product Essentials

Essentials of Annuities

Essentials of Business Insurance

Essentials of Disability Income Insurance

Essentials of Life Insurance Products

Essentials of Long-Term Care Insurance

Essentials of Multiline Insurance Products*

Planning Foundations

Foundations of Estate Planning

Foundations of Financial Planning: An Overview

Foundations of Financial Planning: The Process

Foundations of Investment Planning

Foundations of Retirement Planning

* Course under development

Financial Advisor Series: Product Essentials

Essentials of Annuities

Richard A. Dulisse
Johni R. Hays

The American College Press/*Bryn Mawr, Pennsylvania*

This publication is designed to provide accurate and authoritative information about the subject covered. While every precaution has been taken in the preparation of this material, the author and The American College® assume no liability for damages resulting from the use of the information contained in this publication. The American College is not engaged in rendering legal, accounting, or other professional advice. If legal or other expert advice is required, the services of an appropriate professional should be sought.*

Library of Congress Control Number 2008921901
ISBN 1932819614

Printed in the United States of America

Contents

Preface

The mission of this book is to develop your professionalism as a financial advisor counseling clients and prospects about the uses of annuities in their retirement and financial planning. We intend to do this by teaching you about annuity product essentials, by enhancing your marketing and sales skills, and by stressing the importance of planning foundations in shaping your performance as a successful advisor. It is our hope that this book has the right blend of sales skills techniques, product essentials, and planning foundations to accomplish this mission.

While much of the text material will be new to you, some will, no doubt, refresh knowledge you acquired in the past. In either case, all of the text material is both valuable and necessary if you aspire to be a successful financial advisor. The benefits you gain from studying the text material will be directly proportional to the effort you expend. So read each chapter carefully, and answer both the essay and multiple-choice review questions for the chapter (preferably before looking in the back of the book for the answers); to do less would be to deprive yourself of a unique opportunity to become familiar with the selling/planning process and all that it entails.

The book includes numerous pedagogical features designed to help you focus your study of annuities. Among the features found in each chapter of the book are

- an overview and learning objectives
- a chapter outline, examples, quotations, and lists
- key terms and concepts
- review questions (essay format)
- self-test questions (multiple-choice format)

Features located in the back of the book are

- a glossary
- appendixes
- an answers-to-questions section
- an index

Finally, all of the individuals noted on the acknowledgments page made this a better book, and we are grateful. However, in spite of the help of all of these fine folks, some errors have undoubtedly been successful in eluding our eyes. For these we are solely responsible. At the same time, we accept full credit for giving those of you who find these errors the exhilarating intellectual experience produced by such discovery.

Richard A. Dulisse
Johni R. Hays

The American College

The American College® is an independent, nonprofit, accredited institution founded in 1927 that offers professional certification and graduate-degree distance education to men and women seeking career growth in financial services.

The Center for Financial Advisor Education at The American College offers both the LUTCF and the Financial Services Specialist (FSS) professional designations to introduce students in a classroom environment to the technical side of financial services while at the same time providing them with the requisite sales-training skills.

The Solomon S. Huebner School® of The American College administers the Chartered Life Underwriter (CLU)®; the Chartered Financial Consultant (ChFC)®; the Chartered Advisor for Senior Living (CASL)™; the Registered Health Underwriter (RHU)®; the Registered Employee Benefits Consultant (REBC)®; and the Chartered Leadership Fellow (CLF)® professional designation programs. In addition, the Huebner School also administers The College's CFP Board-registered education program for those individuals interested in pursuing CFP® certification.

The Richard D. Irwin Graduate School® of The American College offers the master of science in financial services (MSFS) degree, the Graduate Financial Planning Track (another CFP Board-registered education program), and several graduate-level certificates that concentrate on specific subject areas. It also offers the Chartered Advisor in Philanthropy® (CAP) and the master of science in management (MSM), a one-year program with an emphasis in leadership. The National Association of Estate Planners & Councils has named The College as the provider of the education required to earn its prestigious AEP designation.

The American College is accredited by the Commission on Higher Education of the Middle States Association of Colleges and Schools, 3624 Market Street, Philadelphia, PA 19104; telephone number: (215) 662-5606. The Commission on Higher Education is an institutional accrediting agency recognized by the U.S. Secretary of Education and the Commission on Recognition of Postsecondary Accreditation.

The American College does not discriminate on the basis of race, religion, sex, handicap, or national and ethnic origin in its admissions policies, educational programs and activities, or employment policies.

The American College is located at 270 S. Bryn Mawr Avenue, Bryn Mawr, PA 19010. The toll-free number of the Office of Student Services is (888) AMERCOL (263-7265), the fax number is (610) 526-1465, and the Web address is www.theamericancollege.edu.

Acknowledgments

Publication of this book required the collaborative efforts of the author as well as many other individuals. We gratefully acknowledge the generosity of the organizations and especially the individuals who assisted in developing this course with their advice, suggestions, and/or contributions of material.

This book would not have been possible without the joint efforts of numerous people. I would like to thank them for what is worthwhile about the book while holding none of them responsible for any of its shortcomings.

Specifically, a debt of gratitude is owed to the following people at The American College: Walt J. Woerheide, vice president and dean of the faculty at The American College and editor of the Financial Advisor Series, who encouraged the production of this book and course for use by LUTC financial advisors. These persons, in their administrative capacities, helped shepherd the book through its peaks and valleys and through the various departments involved in its production. Editorial assistant/permissions editor Patricia Cheers worked with outside organizations to allow us to cite their publications for key text references. Special thanks also to Evelyn Rice, production assistant, for her invaluable production assistance throughout this project.

Very special thanks to the following two people who gave a great deal of their time and expertise to advise on the writing of this book:

Ben G. Baldwin, Jr.
Shawn R. Hooper

The College would also like to thank the following individuals for their substantial contributions to this book:

Barbara N. Filippelli
Philip M. Giambri
Gail B. Goodman
Patrick Hutchinson
Craig Lafferty
Romeo Rabbe
James A. Robertson III
Eric T. Sondergeld
Enrico R. Sorrentino
Larry Wanek

To all of these individuals, without whom this book would not have been possible, The College expresses its sincere appreciation and gratitude.

Richard A. Dulisse

About the Authors

Richard A. Dulisse, LUTCF, CLU, ChFC, CASL, CFP, RHU, REBC, is an author/editor and assistant professor of financial planning at The American College. His responsibilities at The College include writing and preparing text materials for the LUTCF and FSS programs. He also teaches insurance and financial planning courses at The College.

Mr. Dulisse is author of *Essentials of Disability Income Insurance* and *Foundations of Retirement Planning,* coauthor of *Techniques for Prospecting: Prospect or Perish, Marketing Financial Services to Women,* and *Foundations of Financial Planning: The Process,* and a contributing author to *Financial Decisions for Retirement.* In addition, he edited *Ethics for the Financial Services Professional.* Mr. Dulisse also contributes articles to *Advisor Today,* the national magazine distributed to members of NAIFA.

Before joining The American College, Mr. Dulisse worked in the life insurance industry from 1979 through 2001. His experience includes five years as a life insurance agent, initially with Metropolitan Life and then with New York Life. He also served as a sales manager before becoming a training manager in 1985 at New York Life, where he helped implement the company's training curriculum to teach agents product knowledge and selling skills.

Johnine (Johni) R. Hays is the executive director of the Greater Des Moines Community Foundation's Planned Giving Institute. She coauthored the book *The Tools and Techniques of Charitable Planning,* published by the National Underwriter Company. Johni serves as the charitable planning author of Steve Leimberg's electronic newsletter service, LISI, found at www.leimbergservices.com, and is a contributing author for The Stelter Company.

Johni frequently lectures to groups on estate and charitable planning, probate, living wills, annuities, life insurance, and pension and IRA distributions, as well as income, estate, and gift taxation. She has been engaged in the practice of law with an emphasis on charitable and estate planning since 1993.

She previously served as the director of advanced markets for AmerUs Life Insurance Company in Des Moines, Iowa, and as advanced markets counsel for ManuLife Financial in its U.S. headquarters in Boston. In addition, Johni practiced estate planning with Myers Krause and Stevens, Chartered, law firm in Naples, Florida, where she specialized in life insurance as a part of the overall estate plan. She was also with Principal Mutual Life Insurance Company in Des Moines, Iowa, in sales and marketing for nine years.

Johni graduated cum laude with a Juris Doctor degree from Drake University in Des Moines, Iowa, in 1993. She also holds a bachelor of science degree in business administration from Drake University, where she majored in insurance and graduated magna cum laude in 1988.

Johni is a member of the National Committee on Planned Giving, the Mid-Iowa Planned Giving Council, and the Mid-Iowa Estate and Financial Planners Council. She is a Chartered Life Underwriter and has been a member of both the Iowa Bar and the Florida Bar since 1993. Johni can be reached by email at JohniJD@mchsi.com.

Special Notes to Advisors

Text Materials Disclaimer

This publication is designed to provide accurate and authoritative information about the subject covered. While every precaution has been taken in the preparation of this material to ensure that it is both accurate and up to date, it is still possible that some errors eluded detection. Moreover, some material may become inaccurate and/or outdated either because it is time sensitive or because new legislation will make it so. Still other material may be viewed as inaccurate because your company's products and procedures are different from those described in the book. Therefore the author and The American College assume no liability for damages resulting from the use of the information contained in this book. The American College is not engaged in rendering legal, accounting, or other professional advice. If legal or other expert advice is required, the services of an appropriate professional should be sought.

Caution Regarding Use of Illustrations

Any illustrations, fact finders, sales ideas, techniques, and/or approaches contained in this book are not to be used with the public unless you have obtained approval from your company. Your company's general support of The American College's programs for training and educational purposes does not constitute blanket approval of any illustrations, fact finders, sales ideas, techniques, and/or approaches presented in this book unless so communicated in writing by your company.

Use of the Terms "Financial Advisor" or "Advisor"

Use of the term "financial advisor" as it appears in this book is intended as the generic reference to professional members of our reading audience. It is used interchangeably with the term "advisor" so as to avoid unnecessary redundancy. "Financial advisor" takes the place of the following terms:

Account Executive	Financial Planning	Producer
Agent	Professional	Property & Casualty Agent
Associate	Financial Services	Registered Investment
Broker (stock or	Professional	Advisor
insurance)	Health Underwriter	Registered Representative
Employee Benefit	Insurance Professional	Retirement Planner
Specialist	Life Insurance Agent	Senior Advisor
Estate Planner	Life Underwriter	Tax Advisor
Financial Consultant	Planner	
Financial Planner	Practitioner	

Answers to the Questions in the Book

The answers to all essay and multiple-choice questions in this book are based on the text materials as written.

About the Financial Advisor Series

The mission of The American College is to raise the level of professionalism of its students and, by extension, the financial services industry as a whole. As an educational product of The College, the Financial Advisor Series shares in this mission. Because knowledge is the key to professionalism, a thorough and comprehensive reading of each book in the series will help the practitioner-advisor to better service his or her clients—a task made all the more difficult because the typical client is becoming more financially sophisticated every day and demands that his or her financial advisor be knowledgeable about the latest products and planning methodologies. By providing practitioner-advisors in the financial services industry with up-to-date, authoritative information about various marketing and sales techniques, product knowledge, and planning considerations, the books of the Financial Advisor Series will enable many practitioner-advisors to continue their studies so as to develop and maintain a high level of professional competence.

The books that make up the Financial Advisor Series are spread across three separate subseries, each with a special focus. The first subseries, *Sales Skills Techniques,* focuses on enhancing the practitioner-advisor's marketing and sales skills but also covers some product knowledge and planning considerations. The second subseries, *Product Essentials,* focuses on product knowledge but also delves into marketing and sales skills, as well as planning considerations, in many of its books. The third subseries, *Planning Foundations,* focuses on various planning considerations and processes that form the foundation for a successful career as a financial services professional. When appropriate, many of the books in this third subseries also touch upon product knowledge and sales and marketing skills. Current and forthcoming titles are listed earlier in this book.

Overview of the Book

Essentials of Annuities provides a comprehensive overview of the uses of various annuity products both prior to and following an individual's retirement. Chapter 1 examines what an annuity is and the various ways annuities are classified. It also discusses how important annuities are to our society today. This chapter introduces the eight-step selling/planning process (or sales cycle), which is covered in more depth in other American College publications, including how to select, approach, and meet prospects. Finally, it introduces the various age-based market segments for deferred and immediate annuity products.

From there, the book examines both the nonqualified and qualified annuity markets. The discussion includes charitable planning, business planning, and estate planning opportunities using annuities. Demographic factors that affect the annuities marketplace, methods for preapproaching and approaching prospects, along with techniques for conducting successful seminars, are also explored. Next, there is a discussion of the fixed-interest deferred annuity policy, including annuity contract provisions and how interest is credited. Withdrawals, surrenders, and policy riders are also discussed. There is then a review of the objectives of meeting with the prospect within the context of the selling/planning process and a look at ways to qualify a prospect for annuity products.

The book explores the basic structure of equity-indexed annuities, and it examines the most common indexing methods used to measure interest earnings. It also explains in detail how to conduct meaningful fact- and feeling-finding to ascertain a prospect's retirement income needs and motivation to purchase annuities. Then it examines the variable annuity and its unique product design and investment features, including professional management, dollar cost averaging, and asset allocation. The book explores considerations involved in the analysis of a prospect's need for annuities, as well as how to develop product solutions that represent a client-focused selling approach. In addition, the book helps advisors gain an understanding of the latest immediate annuities products and riders offered today and the various types of payout options individuals may choose. It also examines annuity-plan presentation techniques and how to manage prospect resistance.

The final chapters of the book focus on the tax and regulatory issues regarding annuities. The book addresses the income, estate, and gift tax implications of annuities. In addition, it discusses IRC Sec. 1035 exchanges for nonqualified annuities, as well as rollovers and transfers for qualified annuities. The book explores the implementation, servicing, and relationship of annuity products to other aspects of financial planning. In chapter 8, the book concludes with an examination of the regulation of annuity contracts at the federal and state level, covering both fixed annuities and variable annuities, which are subject to intense regulation from the Securities and Exchange Commission and the

Financial Industry Regulatory Authority (FINRA). The chapter also addresses market conduct, suitability, and creditor protection issues.

Essentials of Annuities

1

Introduction to Annuities

Learning Objectives

An understanding of the material in this chapter should enable you to

---

1-1. Identify several definitions for the word "annuity.

1-2. Explain the reasons why people purchase annuities today.

1-3. Describe the difference between nonqualified and qualified annuities.

1-4. Identify the three parties in an annuity contract.

1-5. Identify the various classifications of annuity contracts.

1-6. Explain why immediate annuities help clients feel financially secure.

1-7. Identify the eight steps in client-focused planning.

1-8. List and describe six sources of annuity prospects.

Chapter Outline

This chapter examines what an annuity is and the various ways annuities are classified. It also describes the age-old problems that annuities attempt to solve and explains how annuities have been used over the years. Finally, the chapter discusses how important annuities are to our society today.

INTRODUCTION

annuity

The American Heritage Dictionary and *Webster's Third New International Dictionary* define the word *annuity* as follows:

- the annual payment of an allowance or income
- the right to receive this payment or the obligation to make this payment
- an investment on which a person receives fixed payments for a lifetime or a specified number of years. Derivation: Latin; annus, year[1]
- a contract or agreement under which one or more persons receive periodic payments in return for prior set payments made by themselves or another (as an employer)[2]

These definitions focus on how money is paid from an annuity contract. Annuities that provide current payments to an annuitant are commonly called "immediate annuities" or "payout annuities." Normally immediate annuities are purchased with a single deposit, and income payments begin within one year; the insurance and financial services industry commonly refers to these annuities as single-premium immediate annuities or SPIAs.

The above definitions do not focus on the more common type of annuity, which is one where the income payments are not paid until some time well in the future. These contracts are referred to as deferred annuities because the income payments are deferred until at least one year has elapsed after the purchase date. Today, purchasers of deferred-annuity contracts generally focus on the accumulating values of their annuities, not the future income.

This textbook will concentrate on both types of annuity contracts—immediate annuities for paying income and deferred annuities for accumulation and growth. Annuities will be referred to throughout this textbook as annuity contracts or annuity policies. Either term is correct. The owner of the annuity will be referred to interchangeably as the annuity owner, the policyowner, or the contract owner.

Why Individuals Purchase Annuities

One of the most prevalent reasons individuals purchase annuity contracts is to accumulate funds for retirement and then, once in retirement, to manage distributions of those funds. Annuities compete for investment funds that would otherwise be in currently taxable investments. Fixed deferred annuities, which guarantee principal and some level of interest earnings, compete for money that would otherwise be in vehicles like savings accounts or certificates of deposit. Variable annuities compete for money that might otherwise be in taxable mutual funds. Investments in which earnings are subject to income taxes each year may be placed in nonqualified annuities and enjoy tax-deferred growth until withdrawal.

This brings up the distinction between qualified and nonqualified annuities. Nonqualified annuities are annuity contracts into which investors put their after-tax funds. Qualified annuities are funded with pretax (or before-tax) funds. Both qualified and nonqualified annuities will be discussed in greater detail later in this chapter.

Primary Objective of an Annuity Contract

The primary objective of an annuity contract is to pay financial benefits to the persons who receive the annuity payments during their lifetimes. Its primary objective is not to pay a death benefit, like its cousin, the life insurance contract.

There are three important distinctions between an annuity contract and a life insurance contract:

- An annuity contract has no significant mortality charges. In other words, the insurance company does not have to build a cost into the annuity to protect itself against the early death of the annuitant. No medical underwriting is required. The insurance company is not insuring against early death.
- An annuity has no net amount at risk whereas life insurance does. The death benefit that is payable is nothing more than the value of the annuity. The insurance company does not suffer a financial loss at the death of the annuitant.

- An annuity contract is not tax efficient in paying benefits at the annuitant's death. The beneficiary of an annuity will have to pay income taxes on any gain in the value of the annuity over the principal paid by the annuity owner. Life insurance, on the other hand, is almost always 100 percent income tax free to the beneficiary.

The deferred-annuity contract is used to accumulate money for some future date. It is most efficiently used to accumulate money to be used in the future either as a lump sum or as a stream of payments. Annuitization is the surest way to provide systematic payments from a specific sum of money over a specified period or for the duration of a single life or the lives of two people; this is because the payments are guaranteed by the insurance company.

Parties to an Annuity

The parties to the annuity include the insurance company that issues the annuity, the owner of the annuity, the annuitant, and the beneficiary. Each of the parties has a different set of obligations, rights, and responsibilities.

Within the annuity contract itself, the person who purchases the annuity must name the owner of the contract, the annuitant, and the beneficiary. Often the same person may assume the role of both owner and annuitant, but this is not always the case.

Insurance Company

It is the insurance company who issued the annuity contract and, in doing so, assumes a number of financial obligations to the owner, the annuitant, and the beneficiary. A discussion of the typical contract provisions of a nonqualified deferred annuity appears in Chapter 3 of this book.

The insurance company that issues a deferred-annuity contract promises to invest the owner's premium payments responsibly (or according to the owner's directions in variable annuities) and credit interest (or capital growth) to the funds placed in the annuity. How the premium payments are invested and how much, if any, control the owner retains over the investment decisions affecting his or her funds varies depending upon which type of nonqualified annuity is purchased. See Chapter 3 for information on fixed-interest deferred annuities, Chapter 4 for information on equity-indexed annuities, and Chapter 5 for information on variable annuities.

In addition to investing the owner's premium payments and crediting the funds with interest, the insurance company also promises to pay the contract death benefits in the event of the death of the owner (or in some cases the annuitant) prior to annuitization of the contract and to make benefit payments according to the contract settlement options selected by the contract owner. By fulfilling these contractual obligations, the insurance company, through the annuity contract, helps the owner to avoid outliving his or her financial means.

Owner

owner

The annuity contract *owner* is a person or legal entity who enters into the contract with the insurance company to purchase the annuity. The owner of the contract is the person or entity with all the legal rights to the contract. This is an important distinction from the annuitant. The owner is the person who pays the premiums, chooses which optional policy features or riders are to be included in the contract, and has the right to withdraw or surrender the annuity.

Furthermore, the policyowner is the person with the authority to communicate with the insurance company about the annuity's values and to determine who will receive the annual or quarterly statements from the company.

Annuitant

annuitant

The *annuitant* is the person whose life is the measuring life for the annuity. The annuitant must be a living person. It cannot be a legal entity because a legal entity has no measuring life. For example, a corporation cannot be an annuitant because a corporation has no age and has no death. The annuitant has no legal rights in the contract. Therefore the annuitant has no right to surrender or withdraw funds from the annuity or to change the beneficiary.

Beneficiary

beneficiary

The *beneficiary* is the person or legal entity who normally inherits the annuity proceeds at the death of the annuitant. The annuitant and the beneficiary should not be the same person because the beneficiary is to receive the funds at the annuitant's death. It would not be sensible to name the beneficiary as the same person whose death triggers the distribution.

The beneficiary, like the annuitant, has no legal right in the contract before the annuitant's death. Once the annuitant has died, the beneficiary does have a legal right to receive the death proceeds. However, the owner may generally change the beneficiary at any time prior to the death of the annuitant—even right up until the time of the annuitant's death. This is why the beneficiary is presumed to have only an "expectancy" in the annuity, but no legal rights arise until the annuitant's death.

Example: Jerry Jones purchases a $100,000 deferred annuity on the life of his wife, Janine. Jerry names himself as the beneficiary. Jerry is the annuity owner and the annuity beneficiary. Janine is the annuitant. Janine has no legal rights in the annuity contract. She serves as the measuring life only. If Janine wants to change the beneficiary to her son, she will not be able to do so. Jerry, as the owner of the annuity, is the only one with the legal right to change the beneficiary.

Upon Janine's death, Jerry is now entitled to receive the proceeds of the annuity as the beneficiary. Jerry has a legal right to receive those funds once the annuitant has died. Prior to Janine's death, Jerry as the beneficiary did not have any legal rights.

Chapter 7, "Taxation, Plan Implementation, and Servicing Annuity Products," will cover in more detail some of the tax traps that annuity owners can get themselves into, depending on whom they name as the owner, annuitant, and beneficiary of an annuity.

Types of Annuities

Annuities may be classified in several different categories. Table 1-1 shows the various classifications of annuities based on the following:

- single-premium or flexible-premium annuities
- immediate or deferred-payment annuities
- qualified or nonqualified annuities
- fixed-interest, indexed, or variable deferred annuities

TABLE 1-1
Annuity Classifications

	Single-Premium Deferred Annuity	Flexible-Premium Deferred Annuity	Single-Premium Immediate Annuity
Qualified Annuity	Fixed-interest annuities Indexed annuities Variable annuities	Fixed-interest annuities Indexed annuities Variable annuities	Fixed payments Variable payments
Nonqualified Annuity	Fixed-interest annuities Indexed annuities Variable annuities	Fixed-interest annuities Indexed annuities Variable annuities	Fixed payments Variable payments

Single-Premium or Flexible-Premium Annuities

single-premium annuity

First, annuities can be classified by how many deposits the consumer pays into the annuity. For example, annuities are classified as either single-premium or flexible-premium annuities. A *single-premium annuity* is structured to allow only one contribution in the contract. Subsequent contributions are usually not allowed into these types of policies. If the policyowner envisions making additional contributions into an annuity contract, the policyowner should consider purchasing a flexible-premium annuity. A *flexible-premium annuity* allows additional contributions at any time from the policyowner.

flexible-premium annuity

Note that immediate annuities generally fall only under the category of single-premium annuities. This is due to the nature of the contract in which a policyowner will give one deposit into the immediate annuity in return for a fixed amount of income. Immediate annuities, by their very nature, do not accept additional deposits. To purchase a second income stream, the policyowner will need to buy a second immediate-annuity contract. Whether the policyowner foresees making additional contributions later into a deferred annuity is a question both the financial advisor and the policyowner should discuss prior to the purchase of the annuity to make sure that the proper annuity is chosen.

Immediate or Deferred Annuities

immediate annuity

deferred annuity

An annuity is a contract between a purchaser and an insurance company in which the insurance company promises to make periodic payments to the purchaser starting immediately or at some time in the future. This definition gives us our next classification of annuities, immediate or deferred, regardless of whether they contain qualified or nonqualified money. An *immediate annuity* is a contract with an immediate payment or one with payments that begin within one year of the contract date. A *deferred annuity* is a future-pay contract with payments to begin at some later date beyond the first contract year.

Chapter 6, "Immediate Income Annuities; Plan Presentation Techniques," will cover immediate annuities in more detail.

Qualified or Nonqualified Annuities

Annuities are also classified based on the type of money placed in the annuity contract. The annuity may be funded with monies accumulated within employer-provided qualified retirement plans such as pensions, profit-sharing plans, 401(k)s, 403(b)s, Keogh or HR-10 plans, SEP IRAs, and SIMPLE IRAs, or other plans that allow the investor to put pretax money into the plan such as a traditional IRA. Because each of these plans is

qualified annuity

designed to meet regulatory qualifications in order to allow pretax investments and tax deferral on earnings, the plans are referred to as qualified plans. An annuity that accepts these types of funds is referred to as a *qualified annuity*.

To illustrate, an annuity purchaser who recently changed employment decides to use funds from his or her previous employer's 401(k) account to purchase a rollover IRA annuity. Because the employee has never paid income tax on the funds inside the 401(k) account, it is considered funded with pretax or qualified money.

Obviously, the tax-deferral feature that is a part of all annuity contracts is redundant when dealing with qualified money that already enjoys the advantage of tax deferral. As a result, when the decision is made to invest qualified money into annuities, it should be because of the features that annuity contracts offer rather than for the redundant tax deferral.

nonqualified annuity

If the money placed in the annuity has already been subject to income tax, the annuity is classified as a *nonqualified annuity*. The benefit of tax deferral in nonqualified annuities can be a great value for nonqualified money that does not enjoy tax deferral in the vehicle in which it is currently invested. Tax deferral allows money that would otherwise be paid out in income taxes to remain invested in the annuity contract and to continue to earn a return. This increases the size of the annuity that one day will be used to generate income.

For example, an individual takes $1,000 from his or her savings account at the local bank and deposits it into an annuity contract. Because the $1,000 had already been taxed to the individual (we will assume it was money from his or her employer's paycheck), it is considered nonqualified money. For that reason, nonqualified annuities are also referred to as after-tax annuities.

The issue of accumulating money over the long term can be approached by addressing the question of how long it will take money to double or triple. Taxation reduces part of an investor's return. For example, note in table 1-2, if money is earning 4 percent but the investor has to pay 25 percent of those earnings in income taxes, instead of doubling in 18 years, it will take 24 years. (The 4 percent return is reduced by 25 percent from the income taxes owed on the interest earned. This equals a net return of 3 percent. The table indicates that a 4 percent return will take 18 years to double, and a 3 percent return will take 24 years to double.) This shows one-third more time for the money to double as a result of netting, after taxes, just 3 percent instead of 4 percent.

Moreover, if an 8 percent return is subject to a 25 percent tax, the time to double is not 9 but 12 years—again, one-third longer. The deferral of income taxes on money available in qualified plans and nonqualified plans gives people time to accumulate more money for retirement.

The decision to use annuities for qualified money is quite different from the decision to use annuities for nonqualified money. The taxation of distributions differs also. Accordingly, we will explore the taxation of both qualified and nonqualified annuities in Chapter 7, "Taxation, Plan Implementation, and Servicing Annuity Products," and examine qualified and nonqualified annuities in Chapter 2, "Annuity Markets."

TABLE 1-2
Time Required for Money to Double or Triple

Growth Rate	Approximate Years to Double (Divide Growth Rate Into 72)	Approximate Years to Triple (Divide Growth Rate Into 115)
3%	24.0	38.3
4%	18.0	28.8
5%	14.4	23.0
6%	12.0	19.2
7%	10.3	16.4
8%	9.0	14.3
9%	8.0	12.7
10%	7.2	11.5

However, because annuity contracts, whether for qualified or for nonqualified money, are virtually identical in contract language, classifications, features, and associated costs and regulation, the chapters that deal with those issues, such as this one on annuity classifications, will not generally distinguish between qualified and nonqualified annuities.

Fixed-Interest, Indexed, and Variable Deferred Annuities

Deferred annuities are classified by the method the insurance company uses to determine how interest is credited to the annuity contract (that is, fixed interest rate, indexed annuity, or variable annuity).

fixed-interest annuity

A *fixed-interest annuity* is the simplest type of deferred annuity. It generally offers the annuity owner a guaranteed interest rate for a certain period of time. That time frame may be one year or 5 to 10 years, depending on the annuity contract. Once the initial guarantee period for the interest rate is over, companies generally set renewal interest rates in conjunction with the interest rate environment at the time of the renewal. Therefore annuity purchasers will have no idea when they buy the annuity what level of interest the annuity will earn once the guarantee period is over.

However, fixed-interest deferred annuities do have a guaranteed minimum interest rate by which the company must abide. This guaranteed minimum serves to provide some level of comfort to the annuity purchaser. Fixed-interest deferred annuities are covered in detail in Chapter 3, "Fixed-Interest Deferred Annuities; Effective Interviewing Techniques."

Indexed annuities, which are rather new to the industry and generally became popular in the 1990s, are another type of deferred annuity. They were developed as a response to the rising equity markets and the need for insurance advisors who were not licensed to sell variable annuities to have a product to offer their clients that could generate higher returns than a traditional fixed annuity.

indexed annuity

An *indexed annuity* ties the earnings in the annuity contract to the performance of an outside index of securities. Therefore the true earnings of the insurance company are not an indicator of the earnings for the annuity contract. The most popular type of indexed annuity is one tied to the Standard and Poor's (S&P) 500 Index. This type of annuity is meant to assist clients who want more growth potential than a fixed-interest deferred annuity can offer but who may not be ready for the full risk of a variable deferred annuity. Chapter 4, "Indexed Annuities; Fact Finding," will cover these types of deferred annuities in detail.

variable deferred annuity

A *variable deferred annuity* is a deferred annuity that allows the annuity purchaser to participate in the investment of the annuity funds by determining how much of the contribution will be invested in a series of accounts. These accounts range from a general account to a series of subaccounts tied to various financial markets.

Variable annuities are the most complex and most regulated of the three types of deferred annuities. Variable deferred annuities are covered in detail in Chapter 5, "Variable Annuities; Developing Product Recommendations."

Licensing Qualifications to Sell Annuities

Annuities are insurance products. Therefore the sale of these products comes under the jurisdiction of the various state insurance departments. Each state has its own set of rules, regulations, and licensing requirements designed to protect its citizens. Anyone who sells annuities must be licensed and must maintain the qualifications required by each of the states in which he or she does business. In some states, just giving advice about annuities requires licensing. The objective of state licensing is to ensure that only those people of good character who are knowledgeable about annuities can sell them in that respective state.

Generally before an advisor can sell annuities to the public, he or she must pass a state licensing exam. In most states, after the exam is successfully completed, the advisor must apply to various insurance companies to sell his or her products. Once all the paperwork has been submitted, each company will perform a background check on the person. If everything is in order, the advisor will be appointed as an agent by each of these companies to sell fixed annuities and many types of equity-indexed annuities.

To sell variable annuities, the licensed agent must also be a registered representative. A registered representative must register with the Financial Industry Regulatory Authority (FINRA), submit the required background information, and pass a FINRA examination. The FINRA examinations needed to sell variable annuities are either the Series 6 or the Series 7. The Series 6 examination limits a representative to selling mutual funds, unit investment trusts, and variable annuities. The Series 7 is more extensive and qualifies the individual to sell stocks and bonds as well as mutual funds and variable annuities.

FINRA is the largest nongovernmental regulator for all securities firms and registered securities representatives doing business in the United States. It sets rules for member brokerage firms and registered representatives, and hosts most of the arbitrations between investors and member firms. FINRA was created in July 2007 and took over the duties of the old National Association of Securities Dealers (NASD).

Agents who sell registered products, such as variable annuities, are also accountable to the various state securities departments. A broker-dealer is responsible for the representative's registration process and his or her compliance with the Securities and Exchange Commission (SEC) and FINRA rules and regulations.

Another aspect of the sales process and the qualifications needed for selling annuities involves the advisor's capacity for dealing with clients. Is the salesperson an agent or an advisor? The latest trend in the financial services community is for companies to change the names of their salespeople from agent to advisor. Clients expect *agents* to have allegiance to their companies and products while the same clients expect their *advisors* to hold allegiance to them. Regulators favor allegiance to clients, as do companies that recognize that satisfied clients are their most profitable customers.

This brings a new level of responsibility to the advisor. An advisor is one who gives advice, who informs, who offers opinions, and who provides counsel. This requires a broader base of knowledge than is needed just to sell annuities. Consequently the overall objective of this book is to help you become competent in advising your clients about annuities and how they fit into their financial plans. This requires the advisor to explain the selling/planning process to the client, as discussed in the next section of this chapter.

CLIENT-FOCUSED PLANNING

Because of the nature of the client-advisor relationship, it is both ethically required and financially wise for the financial advisor to thoroughly understand the client's needs and act to fulfill those needs as much as possible. There must be what is known as *consultative* (*client-focused*) *planning or selling*. Such an approach requires the advisor to gather as much information as possible from the client about the client's needs, goals, interests, and assets in order to put together an investment or insurance package that will best meet the client's needs. Consultative planning or selling is a sound approach to building good relationships with clients.

The sale of products is essentially client driven. Advisors must approach clients with a willingness to listen carefully. Clients can best provide the information regarding their own needs and goals. Clients may also think that they know which product best fits those goals, but advisors should keep the client focused on articulating needs and goals so the advisors can find the best product or service to match those goals.

Marketing annuities requires the same step-by-step procedure that is necessary for financial advisors to be successful in marketing any other personal financial product. Identifying and selecting prospects for individual planning is the first step in a chronological procedure that you need to identify, adhere to, and understand in order to enhance your competency in all financial services endeavors. In this regard, it would seem appropriate to provide an overview (perhaps for some of you a review) of the universally recognized components of what is generically referred to as the "selling process" or "planning process."

Eight Steps in the Selling/Planning Process

The selling/planning process is based on a planning philosophy. Over the years, many authors have written about selling and planning the "right" way. In doing so, they have used many terms to describe the right way: relationship, client centered, counselor, consultative, needs based, values based; the list goes on and on. We do not recommend any one method. Instead we attempt to examine those principles and concepts involved in cultivating a long-term, mutually beneficial relationship with a client.

We have divided the selling/planning process into eight steps. The selling process encompasses the (financial) planning process. Within each sale, the advisor should conduct some type of planning. The first two steps are preliminary marketing steps you must complete prior to actual planning. Steps 3 through 8 are the (financial) planning process. These next six steps involve interaction between you and your client. They will be repeated many times because they are the basis for your ongoing working relationship.

Knowing what you also want to accomplish and why you want to accomplish it will guide your actions in each step of the process. We will briefly explore the necessary actions in the successful completion of the selling/planning process from the financial advisor's perspective.

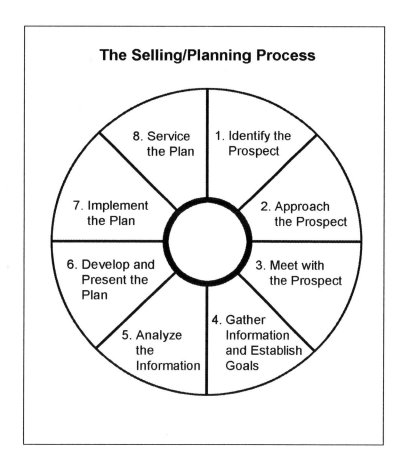

1. Identify the Prospect

Effective planning begins with getting in front of the right prospect. Not only do you want to identify prospects who have a high probability of needing, wanting, and affording your products, but you also want to find people who will value you and become a source for repeat business and, more important, referrals. A systematic approach to prospecting that utilizes various preapproach methods can help you find target markets of potential clients and enable you to market efficiently and effectively.

2. Approach the Prospect

This step involves getting appointments. You can do this either on the telephone or face to face through seminars. If you are successfully cultivating relationships, you will generate more referral-based business. With the negative feelings people have toward telemarketers, cold calling becomes more difficult, and referrals become that much more critical.

3. Meet With the Prospect

This is where you establish rapport, explain your business purpose, ask some thought-provoking questions, and listen, listen, listen. The importance of listening cannot be overstated; it is essential when building any relationship. You need to gain prospects' trust and agreement to gather pertinent information about them. You must also let prospects know what you can do for them (in general terms) and help them to see your value. You must answer the prospect's question: Why should I do business with you? Your final objective in meeting with the prospect is to gain acceptance to proceed to the information-gathering step.

4. Gather Information and Establish Goals

When you think of the word *interview*, you think of someone asking someone else questions. That is exactly what you want to do with your prospect. Questions help you uncover the prospect's current planning needs, goals, desires, values, and attitudes. It is helpful to discover as much about the prospect's financial priorities as you can. For example, long-term care insurance may be important to the prospect, but just how important is it? Is it more important than deferring a summer vacation? If it is not and you do not know that, you could be wasting your time.

The key skills in the fact-finding interviewing process are as follows:

- Questioning—ask open-ended questions to probe for individual needs, goals, attitudes, and values. Ask confirming questions to clarify.
- Listening—actively listen, rephrase, and reflect to ensure that you and the prospect are on the same page.
- Uncovering—provide information or ask open-ended questions designed to help the prospect see the reality of the situation. Be fair and honest, not manipulative.
- Taking notes—jot down numbers, goals, needs, priorities, and feelings.
- Summarizing—review what the prospect has told you and confirm that you have clearly understood him or her.

- Acting—gain acceptance to work together to achieve goals.

5. *Analyze the Information*

Once you have a good idea of the prospect's needs, goals, priorities, and attitudes, analyze his or her current financial situation. Consider the weakness(es) in the client's current plan. Then begin to formulate concepts and products that might best enhance that situation, and organize these into a potential plan, no matter how basic or sophisticated it is.

If your products do not fit the situation correctly, send the prospect where the prospect can get what he or she needs. For example, if the person has the money to systematically invest but is not doing so, advise him or her about the benefits of such a course of action. Because of your focus on the long-term relationship, even though the prospect may not do business with you today, he or she will remember that you had his or her best interest at heart. People want to do business with those they trust!

6. *Develop and Present the Plan*

Develop your product recommendations based on the information that you gathered in the fact-finding interview. Explain the applicability of as many relevant products' features and benefits as you can that address the individual prospect's financial goals. Confirm throughout the presentation that the prospect is in agreement with you so that you can handle any questions or concerns that arise. Clarify any miscommunications or misunderstandings thoroughly. Obtain the prospect's agreement to proceed toward implementing the plan.

7. *Implement the Plan*

Guide and assist the prospect in acquiring the financial products and services to put the plan into action. Complete the necessary paperwork and applications, and submit them to your company. Advise the prospect of the time frame and any responsibility he or she may have (such as taking a medical exam when applying for life insurance). Use this opportunity to proactively discuss any additional questions or concerns that the prospect may have.

Once the prospect is a policyowner or account holder, your goal is to convert him or her into a client. That process begins with delivery of any planning documents or policies. Delivery can also be accompanied by an explanation of the financial strategy and recommendations that you have assembled for your client. At delivery, review the benefits you are providing and how they address the applicant's financial needs. Reinforce the concept of comprehensive planning and the necessity to periodically monitor the applicant's situation to ensure that changes that may occur as time passes and lives evolve are addressed. You can do this by offering a periodic review—annually or at some other agreed upon time frame.

8. Service the Plan

This is the step in which you convert policyowners into lifetime clients. Ongoing service cements your relationship with each new policyowner, giving you the opportunity to make additional sales and obtain referrals. Even in the course of performing minor service transactions such as a beneficiary change, you should render excellent service. What differentiates one financial advisor from another is the proactive element of his or her service strategy. Many clients purchase products and never hear from their advisors again. Proactive servicing strategies, such as monitoring the plan through periodic reviews and sending regularly scheduled newsletters to clients, allow you to stay in touch with them. It is this high-contact service that helps you to build lasting client-advisor relationships. It will also lead to cross-selling opportunities and future referrals.

Summary

Practicing and perfecting the skills necessary to execute each of the eight steps in the selling/planning process is an evolutionary work in progress. It is something that you will do over and over again throughout your financial services career. Making the client the focus of your efforts greatly improves your chances of success.

PROSPECTING IN THE ANNUITIES MARKETPLACE

Introduction

This section discusses the application of conventional prospecting concepts to identify prospects for annuities. It begins with a look at the overall potential for earnings in the annuities marketplace. We will then discuss opportunities to sell annuities as they relate to changing demographics, longevity, and retirement planning readiness. Then we will proceed to a prospecting overview, which defines the objective and means for successful prospecting. Finally, we will examine the characteristics of a qualified prospect for annuities, identify some issues related to prospect needs, and review some age-based market segments. The information discussed here will help you get started in identifying prospects. Marketing and prospecting topics are explored further in Chapter 2.

The Increasing Opportunity for Annuities

The annuities marketplace offers the potential for bountiful earnings and sales opportunities for today's financial advisors. A look at some of the statistics regarding the volume of premiums deposited into annuities in 2002, and the numbers of people who own these products, makes it evident that the annuities marketplace is strong and growing.

Consider some of the following figures from LIMRA International's study, "2006 Individual Annuity Market: Sales and Assets." Total annuity sales in 2006 amounted to $238.7 billion, which represents an increase from 2005 of nearly 10 percent, when sales totaled $216.4 billion. The volume of variable annuity sales even increased slightly from $136.9 billion in 2005 to $160.4 billion in 2006, probably due in part to the upturn in the stock market during those years. Fixed annuity sales decreased by $1.2 billion, which accounts for the overall decrease in total fixed-annuity sales from $79.5 billion in 2005 to $78.3 billion in 2006.[3] Table 1-3 summarizes these findings.

TABLE 1-3
Individual Annuity Sales

	2005	2006	Volume Increase/Decrease	Percentage Increase/ Decrease
Total Annuity Sales	$216.4 billion	$238.7 billion	$22.3 billion	10%
Variable Annuities	$136.9 billion	$160.4 billion	$23.5 billion	17%
Fixed Annuities	$79.5 billion	$78.3 billion	($1.2 billion)	(2%)

The total assets under management within all annuities products totaled $1.916 trillion in 2006. This consisted of $1.379 trillion in variable annuity products and $537 billion in fixed annuity products. Furthermore, at the end of 2006, there were more than 36.3 million deferred-annuity contracts in force. The average contract value of all in-force contracts was just over $49,000. Approximately 14.8 million of them were fixed annuities and 21.5 million were variable annuities. Also, at the end of 2006, there were more than 3.9 million immediate annuities in force.[4]

While it is interesting to look at the numbers that account for the current size of the annuities marketplace, it is even more important to focus on the people who will be potential purchasers in the future and to understand why they will buy annuity products.

Annuities in Retirement Planning

By 2011 the leading edge of the baby boomer generation of 77 million individuals will turn 65. This unique group of people, characterized by their self-reliance, independence, and indulgence, will undoubtedly reflect these traits in their retirement-related choices and lifestyles. But will they have adequate savings to fund their desired lifestyle during retirement? Will they acquire a state of financial independence where decisions are made based on choice and not on economic necessity? Will this generation, which hopes to retire earlier and will probably live longer in an environment of reduced Social Security benefits and diminished pension plan guarantees, be able to live comfortably in a retirement that may last another 20 to 30 years?[5]

Let us examine the most prominent factors that contribute to the need for annuities: (1) the relationship between retirement income and aging, and (2) the changing demographics.

The Relationship Between Retirement Income and Aging

Regardless of the fact that people of all ages purchase annuities, the greatest single factor that motivates people to buy either deferred or immediate annuities is their need for retirement income. For preretirees, there is a genuine incentive to accumulate funds for retirement; for postretirees, there is a psychological need to guarantee that those accumulated funds will outlast their lifespans.

There is a direct correlation between aging and the amount of money needed to fund retirement. As we will see later in this chapter, the longer a person lives, the more acute the need becomes to accumulate and conserve financial resources for retirement. The purchase of annuities is not about saving money on taxes; it is about a universal, history-spanning concern about running out of money before we run out of breath. As the saying goes, "The good news is that we are living longer. And the bad news is that we are living longer."

Changing Demographics

In light of the correlation between aging and the need for retirement income, consider the following demographic changes.

Increased Longevity. People are living longer because advances in medicine, nutrition, and so forth have developed preventions, cures, and treatments for diseases and conditions that were once fatal. Consider that the average life expectancy in 1900 was 47 years; in 2000 it reached 76.9 years. That is a 29.6-year increase in the average life expectancy. Perhaps more

Good Line for annuities

significantly, people who survive to age 65 can expect to live to age 83; in 1900 they could expect to live only to age 68.

Unfortunately, while medical advances mean people will live longer, such advances have compounded the problem of funding retirement income. As lifespan increases, the length of time people will need financial resources during retirement certainly increases as well. Consequently the amount of money needed to fund a secure retirement will present unprecedented challenges to future retirees.

Many individuals fear they may run out of money, and with good reason. Medical advancements have increased life expectancy. But life expectancy is just half of the story. Life expectancy means that, statistically, half of men will die by age 74 and half of women by age 79. The other half will still be alive and more concerned than ever about outliving their money. We all tend to focus on life expectancy, but we would be wise to focus also on the potentially devastating financial impact of 50 percent of the people who live longer than life expectancy.

Psychologist and gerontologist Ken Dychtwald put it this way: "We have completed a century of incredible improvements in healthcare, which has dramatically elevated our life expectancy. While we have managed to increase our life spans by almost 30 years since 1900, we haven't yet focused properly on our health spans."[6]

As we enter a new age of biology, experts say the most profound effect may ultimately be a stunning ability to slow the aging process, perhaps allowing the healthiest and strongest among us to live 125 years or more. Even the most cautious scientists now believe that in the coming decades, many people may be biologically capable of surpassing what is, as this book is being written, the oldest person's age of 122. Some say that a very select few may even reach age 150. For others, seeing 95, even 100, may become routine.

One piece of the picture is already clear: As table 1-4 shows, there is tremendous growth in the number of people reaching age 100. The U.S. Census Bureau estimates that as of 2000, there were 75,000 Americans older than 100. That is about 23 times the number in 1960, and their ranks are growing every year. The bureau projects that there will be 214,000 centenarians by 2020 and 834,000 by 2050.

It seems apparent that the need to accumulate enough money to provide lifetime income has never been greater. The increase in the number of centenarians from 1990 to 2000 was 38,000. The increase in centenarians from 2000 to 2010 is projected to be 95,000.

Baby Boomers. Within the next few decades, the baby boom generation with retirement years between 2011 and 2030 will significantly swell the population in the postretirement age categories, which are ages 65–84 and over age 85. A few statistics using the population projections in figure 1-1 make the case dramatically.

TABLE 1-4 Centenarians in the United States	
Year	Number of Centenarians
1960	3,300
1970	4,800
1980	15,000
1990	37,000
2000	75,000
2010	170,000*
2020	214,000*
2050	834,000*
*Projected data provided by the U.S. Census Bureau.	

- In the year 2000, there were approximately 35 million people over age 65, constituting nearly 13 percent of the country's population of 282.1 million; by 2030, when the last of the baby boom generation (those born between 1946 and 1964) turn age 65, there will be 71.5 million seniors, constituting nearly 20 percent of the population (363.6 million).
- Individuals aged 85 and older are the fastest-growing segment of the senior population and are expected to increase from 4.3 million, or 1.6 percent of the population, in 2000 to 9.6 million by 2030, when they will represent over 2.6 percent of the population.
- By 2050, when the full effect of the baby boom retirees is felt, the age-85-and-over category will exceed 20.8 million and comprise almost 5 percent of the population (419.8 million).

Increased longevity already means that more people will reach ages that will require comprehensive retirement planning strategies. The baby boom phenomenon will further accentuate this due to the sheer numbers of those associated with this demographic group. Today's baby boomers can expect to live longer, healthier lives than any generation before them. The bottom line is that more people will require larger retirement funding resources in the not-so-distant future, and they will require them for a longer period of time.

FIGURE 1-1 Projected Growth in U.S. Elderly Population (in millions)

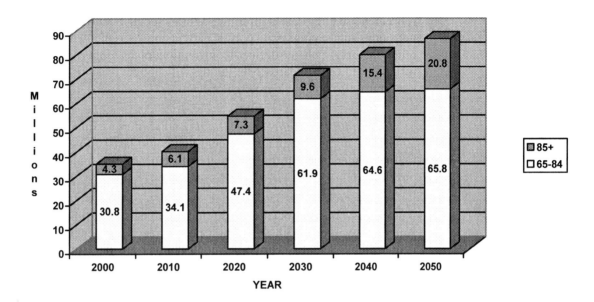

Source: U.S. Interim Projections of Total Population by Age Groups, U.S. Census Bureau, Washington, D.C., July 1, 2004.

The Three-Legged Stool of Retirement Income

A generation ago, Social Security and pensions took care of most people's needs during retirement, which lasted an average of only 12 years. With people retiring earlier and living longer, many may spend as much time in retirement as they did in the work force. Traditionally, the American retirement savings system has rested on three legs: Social Security, employer pensions, and personal savings.

But times are changing. The three-legged stool which for decades served as the model for a secure retirement income is no longer valid in today's environment. The future stability of Social Security is in question, traditional company defined-benefit pensions are rapidly being replaced with defined-contribution plans, and savings as a percentage of personal income are at an all-time low.

A Comprehensive Approach to Retirement Planning

Retirement planning today is a complex puzzle with a vast array of interlocking pieces that fit together in different ways for each individual. In order to create an effective retirement income strategy, each person must take a holistic approach that considers all the options for both accumulating assets before retirement and carefully managing those assets during retirement so they last a lifetime. While Social Security, defined benefit pensions, and savings still play a part in the retirement income equation, other factors, such as defined-contribution plans, inheritance, debt load, inflation, and healthcare costs, along with longevity and financial market risk, must also be considered.

Pieces of the Retirement Puzzles. In order to quantify how ready Americans are to live in a retirement that could last 20 to 30 years, it helps to first understand the current state of some of the major pieces of the puzzle.

Social Security. Social Security today protects an estimated 162 million American workers, with 49 million people receiving benefits. While many people think Social Security tax contributions are held in interest-bearing accounts to be used for payments to future retirees, in reality taxes paid by today's workers are used to fund benefits for today's retirees. Currently, Social Security is taking in more taxes than it is paying out in benefits, with excess funds credited to the Social Security Trust Fund. By 2017, however, tax revenues are projected to fall below program costs; by 2041, unless changes are made, trust fund accumulated reserves will be exhausted.[7]

In 1945, 10 years after the Social Security Act was signed into law, there were 41.9 workers for every beneficiary. In 2006 there were 3.3 workers paying into the system for each person collecting benefits. This is expected to drop to only 2 workers per beneficiary in less than 35 years. When this happens, there will be only enough money coming in to cover 75 percent of scheduled benefits at current tax rates.[8]

But even at current rates, the average monthly Social Security benefit for all retired workers in 2007 is only $1,044; for a couple with both receiving Social Security, the amount is $1,713[9] (These figures are not too far removed from the federal poverty guidelines of $850 per month for an individual and $1,140 for a couple.) The age of entitlement for full benefits has already risen to age 67 for those born in 1960 and later, premiums for Medicare Part B (which covers physician services) may soon increase, and it is predicted that more people will have to pay taxes on their benefit. Given these factors, plus the assumption that in order to remain solvent Social Security may have to both raise taxes and decrease benefits, clearly preretirees today will need to look beyond Social Security as a major source of retirement income.

[handwritten margin note: Average Social Sec monthly benefit is $1,044.00]

FIGURE 1-2: Percent of Retirement Income by Source

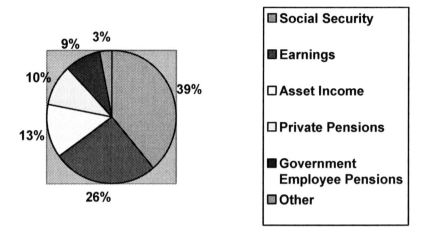

Source: Fast Facts and Figures About Social Security 2006

Pensions. Many current retirees rely on company pensions, also known as defined benefit (DB) plans, for financial support in retirement. Under these plans, the employer typically promises a lifetime stream of income to retirees based on salary, years of service, and age at retirement. The employer guarantees these payments no matter how well the underlying investments perform or how long the retiree lives, thus shouldering both the investment and the longevity risks.

But many company pension plans are on shaky ground. More than 700 plans have collapsed in the past 5 years. During this time, the Pension Benefit Guaranty Corporation (PBGC), the federal program that guarantees payment of basic pension benefits, has gone from a $10 billion surplus to a $23 billion deficit. Private pension plans, which cover 44 million Americans, are estimated to be underfunded by $300 billion to $450 billion.

During the past 20 years, while coverage in DB plans has steadily declined, participation in defined contribution (DC) plans has grown. With a DC plan, the employee makes contributions (which may be matched by the employer up to a set percentage) and controls investment decisions. Final retirement benefits depend on how much was contributed and how the investments performed over the years. The employee is responsible for both investing wisely and making sure the money lasts as long as he or she lives. The most common types of DC plans are 401(k)s and 403(b)s.

In 1983, 62 percent of eligible wage and salary workers were covered solely by a DB plan; 12 percent participated only in a DC plan. By 2004, those numbers had reversed with 63 percent of workers covered by a DC plan and only 20 percent covered by a DB plan.[10]

Figure 1-3: Percent of Wage and Salary Workers With Pension Coverage

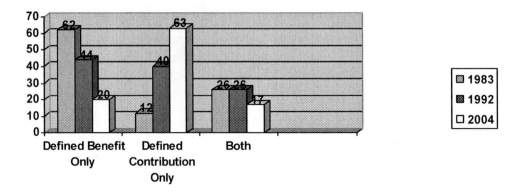

Source: Center for Retirement Research at Boston College

Although participation in DC plans is increasing, 21 percent of eligible workers still do not take part in their plan, and only 11 percent contribute the maximum. This is particularly distressing considering that a person who begins working at age 30 and retires at age 62 with a salary of $58,000 and who consistently contributed 6 percent to a retirement plan with an employer match of 3 percent should have approximately $380,000 saved. In reality, the median 401(k)/IRA account balance of individuals nearing retirement (55 to 64 years old) is only $60,000. To make matters worse, 45 percent of workers changing jobs cash out of their DC plans rather than rolling the balances into IRAs or new employer plans.[11]

Savings. With traditional pension plans slowly disappearing and Social Security becoming far less secure, it is easy to see why most Americans are concerned about their financial readiness for retirement. One has only to look at how much they are saving to see that many of these fears are well founded.

In 1982, Americans saved 11.2 percent of their disposable personal income. By 2005, this number had fallen to negative .5 percent—the lowest savings rate since the Great Depression. Savings continued their downward slide in 2006, reaching a new 74-year low of negative 1.2 percent in December.[12]

Americans not only spent all their after-tax income but took money from savings or borrowed to finance their purchases. A double-digit increase in home prices has been credited with making some consumers feel wealthier and thus more comfortable with spending beyond their means. But a year into a housing market slowdown, Americans have yet to restrain their spending. In 2006, consumers actually increased their purchases of goods and services at an inflation-adjusted annual rate of more than 3 percent—just as they have for the past 2 years.[13] The results of this disturbing trend can be seen in the amount of savings and investments that workers have amassed. Figures from the 2007 Retirement Confidence Survey[14] indicate that 71 percent of workers and 66 percent of retirees have less than $100,000 in savings and investments.

TABLE 1-5
Americans' Total Savings and Investments
(Including the Value of Primary Residence and DB Plans)

Savings and Investments	Share of Workers	Share of Retirees
Less than $25,000	48%	44%
$25,000–$49,000	10	10
$50,000–$99,00	13	12
$100,000–$249,999	15	20
$250,000 or more	14	14

Source: 2006 Retirement Confidence Survey, Employee Benefit Research Institute, and Mathew Greenwald & Associates Inc.

Debt

Another alarming development that adversely impacts retirement readiness is the massive debt many people have accumulated. The cost of borrowing on credit has tripled in real terms since the 1980s. While the average credit card debt now stands at over $9,000, when the 40 percent of households that pay their balances each month are subtracted from the equation, the amount approaches $13,000.[15] According to the Federal Reserve, Americans now owe more than $2.15 trillion in consumer debt (not including real estate loans). With liabilities increasing faster than asset accumulation, family debt as a percentage of total assets rose from 12.1 percent in 2001 to 15.0 percent in 2004 according to the latest Survey of Consumer Finances. If families without debt are excluded, the figure jumps to 19.9 percent.[16]

Clearly many Americans have a long way to go before they will be financially ready for retirement.

Inheritance

Along with the diminishing role of Social Security, a decline in DB plans, historically low savings rates, and growing debt, baby boomers may be hit with one more reality check—lower than expected inheritances.

The amount of money that will be passed down from older Americans to baby boomers has been debated for many years. Despite forecasts of the largest intergenerational transfer of wealth in U.S. history, a recent study based on data from the Federal Reserve indicates that an overwhelming majority of baby boomers (80.8 percent) have yet to receive an inheritance. Only 14.9 percent expect to receive an inheritance in the future, down from 27.3 percent in 1989. Of those boomers who received an inheritance by 2004, the median amount received was $49,000.[17]

There are many reasons for the discrepancy between wealth transfer predictions and actual inheritance. With people living longer, more of their money is spent on living expenses and healthcare, leaving less to pass on to their children. Money is also used for estate taxes and donations to charity.

With less than 20 percent of boomers yet to receive an inheritance, it is unlikely that a windfall from the previous generation will provide the answer to retirement security for most Americans.

Retirement Readiness

Many financial experts suggest that today's retirees will need between 66 percent and 75 percent of their preretirement income to maintain their current standard of living in retirement. This is based on the assumption that spending on such items as commuting, clothing, and other costs associated with working will decline when they retire. However, although some costs, such as shelter, traditionally decline in retirement, others, such as healthcare, often dramatically increase. There is also evidence to indicate that a dichotomy exists between the expected increase in spending during retirement and a decrease in the savings rate as a percentage of income among preretired workers. This has many current and prospective retirees fearing, especially in light of the volatility of the performance of financial markets, whether an accelerated depletion of retirement resources will reduce their standard of living, or perhaps cause them to exhaust their money entirely. This has to do with the simple fact that many people underestimate the amount of money they will need to retire securely.

Financial preparation for retirement presents a challenge to workers, plan sponsors, and the federal government. The future financial well-being of a large and growing segment of our population rests on finding a way to close the gap between the current level of inadequate retirement readiness and what will be necessary for the millions of individuals who will be retiring over the next 20 years.

The information, guidance, and financial advice provided by professionals within the financial services industry will be a key factor in assisting future retirees both to accumulate sufficient wealth during their working years and to move those funds into retirement income that will last as long or longer than they live.

Annuities can play a vital role in helping investors achieve financial security during retirement. There are exciting marketing opportunities for those who are willing to pursue the financial rewards that exist within this lucrative market, and it simultaneously provides a valuable financial product to retirees both today and tomorrow.

Financial and Emotional Retirement Needs

For your clients to achieve financial success in retirement, it has to be planned. The decision to retire does not mean that people should stop planning. Retirement planning is a continuous process that can be facilitated by the use of annuities. While the planning strategies after retirement may differ from those that you suggest to your prospects and clients who are planning and saving for retirement, they are no less important. However, an individual's planning perspective usually changes in the years before and after retirement occurs. Nevertheless, the older a person gets, the greater the probability that he or she will need annuities as a financial vehicle either to accumulate tax-deferred dollars for future use in retirement or as a source of guaranteed income that provides unique financial security features during retirement. In retirement planning, there are not only financial considerations but also dynamic psychosocial factors involved.

Preretirement. When preretirees in their twenties and thirties are just starting out in their careers, they tend to see retirement as a far-off, elusive concept that they will probably have to deal with someday. These workers are too busy climbing corporate ladders, establishing their own businesses, and starting their families to give the illusory concept of retirement too much thought or too many financial resources.

However, as people enter their forties and fifties, retirement takes on a much higher priority. The picture of retirement begins to crystallize in their minds as the possibility of living to old age becomes an increasing reality to them. It is during these decades of life (usually ages 45 to 64) that workers are demographically classified as *preretirees*. They develop a growing concern about their well-being beyond their working years. Many people become obsessed with the need to accumulate enough money to maintain and enjoy their lifestyle during their golden years. Accordingly they begin to allot greater resources into their qualified and nonqualified retirement plans, despite their contemporary financial obligations concerning education funding for their children, long-term care for their parents, and their own personal living expenses. Their sense of urgency regarding retirement funding is typically at its peak during their middle years.

This *preretirement mentality* is evidenced by anxiety about ensuring a comfortable retirement. Financial planning goals are geared toward amassing a large sum of money. The objective is to save as much money as possible to fill (metaphorically) a large bag of money. Preretirement mentality is greatly focused on building and accumulating money in an effort to allay the increasing fear of financial destitution in old age.

Deferred annuities that are inherently tax deferred are ideal to help accomplish this financial goal of the preretiree. This is because deferred annuities offer flexibility in making contributions into them, and nonqualified deferred annuities allow virtually unlimited deposits. Furthermore, there is a choice of three types of deferred products (fixed-interest, equity indexed, and variable) that accommodate any individual's risk tolerance and investment objectives.

Postretirement. Not all of your prospects will be emotionally comfortable with their financial outlook during retirement. As a matter of fact, there is some concern on the part of retirees that no matter how much money they have accumulated over their lifetimes for use in retirement, they cannot properly enjoy its use because they fear that they may exhaust it before they die. This concept can be referred to as the *postretirement mentality syndrome*. The main focus in postretirement is not how full the retirement bag of money has become but, rather, that the bag never becomes empty. This paradigm shift often evidences itself in behavior that results from the natural insecurity associated with becoming poor. This fear, like many others, may have little rational basis. Nonetheless, after 40 working years of conditioning themselves to be thrifty and put something away for tomorrow, many retirees never abandon this tendency. They may deprive themselves of modest luxuries and reasonable indulgences even if they truly can afford them. This, in part, accounts for some retirees whom we might consider well-to-do taking part-time jobs to bolster their incomes. Although we as advisors can attempt to alleviate their feeling of financial insecurity during retirement, we also need to be sensitive to its reality.

This is where immediate annuities can help. Immediate-annuity buyers generally purchase for one obvious financial reason: to provide guaranteed income in retirement. However, the reasons for purchasing annuities are not strictly financial. For instance, some of the more common reasons for purchase other than income are to cover specific expenses, to avoid becoming a financial burden on their children, to benefit from a variety of income and estate tax reasons, and to ensure the payment of life and long-term insurance premiums.[18] Thus the motivation to purchase immediate annuities depends on how the prospects perceive both the financial and the emotional aspects of what the product can do for them.

Once you have an understanding of why and when people will need annuities, it makes sense to identify prospects for annuities and to determine where these prospects can be found. In the next section, we will discuss prospecting factors and age-based markets for annuities products.

Reasons to Buy Immediate Annuities*

- To provide a guaranteed income in retirement
- To cover specific essential expenses in retirement
- To avoid being a financial burden on your children
- To satisfy IRS minimum required distributions
- To pass an estate onto heirs and/or reduce estate taxes
- Other tax advantages
- To provide temporary income until Social Security or other retirement income begins
- To spread out tax liability on a highly appreciated asset
- To pay long-term care insurance policy premiums
- To avoid IRS penalty taxes
- To pay life insurance policy premiums
- To spend down an estate
- To shelter assets from Medicaid to receive nursing home benefits
- To fulfill legal or financial obligations (e.g., alimony, business buy-sell, etc.)

* Multiple responses allowed
Printed with permission from *Annuitization Study: Profiles and Attitudes,* a 2003 report. © 2003, LIMRA International, Inc.

A Prospecting Overview

The objective of annuities prospecting is the same as prospecting in any personal market, which is to continuously find potential clients. Reaching that goal calls for the same type of organized, day-to-day action as you have used in your personal markets.

prospecting

Successful *prospecting* requires that you establish organized and systematic procedures to achieve specific and definable activity goals. It means following these procedures methodically, thoroughly, and regularly. It entails disciplining yourself well enough and consistently enough so that the procedures become habitual for you.

Successful prospecting is a continual process that you should integrate into all of your sales and service activities. Being alert to prospecting opportunities at every phase of the sales process will help you maintain a consistent inventory of high-quality prospects.

Need to establish this as a goal for 2013

Once you establish the habit of prospecting, you should be able to spend less time on poorer quality prospects. As you move toward working with wealthier and more qualified prospects (described below), you will find that your financial rewards will be simultaneously larger and easier to achieve. The result is that you will earn more money in proportion to the work and time you expend.

Qualified Prospects

The process of selling any insurance or financial product begins with creating a profile of the typical person who will believe in you and buy your products and services. In other words, you need to define the characteristics of qualified prospects.

qualified prospects

Generically, *qualified prospects* are people who

- need and value your products and services
- can afford to pay for your products and services
- are insurable or financially suitable
- can be approached on a favorable basis

Let us apply this definition to create a profile of a qualified annuity prospect.

Need and Value Your Products and Services

Who needs annuities? Although people in their fifties and sixties have a greater probability of needing annuities than people in their twenties do, poor planning can seriously jeopardize the financial well-being of many individuals during their retirement years. Furthermore, if a person runs out of money during retirement due to inadequate wealth accumulation, he or she will most likely experience a reduction in the quality of life during those golden years.

However, no matter how logical the financial reason for buying annuities, prospects must have a strong emotional reason to buy. They must value the future financial security and peace of mind that come from adequate retirement funding involving annuities more than they value other competing wants, needs, and desires. In other words, does the prospect *feel* that it is worth the price he or she must pay for annuities?

Emotional needs are not easily observable. However, there are some characteristics that may indicate that a prospect will value annuities. We suggest you compile your own list of characteristics, starting with these few examples. Look for people who

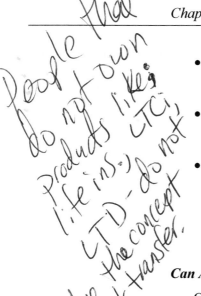

People that do not own products like (life ins., LTC, LTD) do not value the concept of risk transfer.

- are implementing a retirement plan or seriously considering one. People who have bought annuities believe that annuities are a major component of their retirement plan.
- own other insurance products such as life, disability, or long-term care insurance. People who own these types of insurance products demonstrate that they value the concept of risk transfer.
- work for an employer that offers contributory qualified plans such as SEPs, SIMPLE IRAs, or 403(b) plans that may involve annuities. In general, people who work for employers who offer such plans involving annuities are more familiar with the roles they play in retirement planning than the general public is.

Can Afford to Pay for Your Products and Services

One of the biggest obstacles to the annuities sale is cost and commitment. Note that cost and value are interrelated. For example, a middle-aged couple may say that they cannot afford annuities because they cost too much. You may discover, however, that they own a vacation home. What this couple is really saying is that they value the commitment of funds to annuities as an important component in a comprehensive retirement plan less than they value committing funds to their other current needs, wants, and desires.

If you have not done so already, identify the income and net worth ranges you will target in order to avoid affordability issues. Describe any characteristics you will look for that may indicate a prospect's ability to pay annuity premiums. For example, you might look for the prospect who

- owns a home.
- owns a business.
- has supplemental property insurance policies in place, such as a personal articles floater policy on fine jewelry.
- has high liability limits on property and casualty insurance.
- owns a personal liability umbrella policy.

Are Insurable or Financially Suitable

There are many people who want annuities and can afford to pay for them but are unsuitable for one or both of the following reasons:

- They have a greater need for asset and/or income protection products.
- The particular annuity product you are marketing does not match their risk tolerance and investment objectives.

good points

financial pyramid

build the base or foundation first, then other investment financial vehicles

For example, if you encounter a married annuity prospect who wants to purchase a deferred annuity but has insufficient life or disability income insurance coverage, you may be risking financial catastrophe for that prospect or family. Many advisors would also argue that long-term care insurance should be in place before annuities are purchased. Of course, these higher-priority needs present an opportunity to cross-sell the asset or income coverage that is lacking.

On the other hand, you may encounter an annuity prospect who is unsuitable for a variable deferred annuity because he or she has a low risk tolerance and very conservative investment objectives. It would be just as unsuitable to sell a variable deferred annuity to such a prospect as it would be to sell any deferred annuity to someone who needs insurance coverage first. The best defense against making this mistake is to use the proper risk tolerance and investment objective assessment tool as part of the fact-finding process. Fact-finding techniques will be discussed in Chapter 4.

The worst thing for everyone involved is for a prospect to purchase an annuity product that is detrimental to his or her future financial security and your business relationship with the prospect. As a proactive step to prevent this from happening, many successful advisors recommend prequalifying the prospect over the phone. This may avoid an embarrassing situation or at least better prepare you for your interview with the prospect. We will discuss prequalifying in Chapter 2 when we cover the topic of approaching the prospect.

Can Be Approached on a Favorable Basis

The first three aspects of qualified prospects are helpful in categorizing a prospect's readiness to purchase annuities. It is best to work on the assumption that all prospects see the need and value, can afford to buy, and are suitable until proven otherwise. In fact, by the time you are ready to meet with a prospect, you will have usually discovered this is true. Age is seldom a critical factor either.

Perhaps, however, the most significant factor in deciding whether someone is a qualified prospect is whether you can meet with this person on a favorable basis. Just what is involved in this concept?

The concept is easier to explain by example than by definition, but in general terms, *favorable* basis means a situation where the advisor is perceived as appropriate (or competent) in the prospect's eyes. It is largely a matter of acceptance and usually implies a good measure of respect, trust, and confidence in the advisor's professionalism. It often evidences itself by the prospect's being at ease with the advisor. It is certainly characterized by a willingness to grant you sufficient and exclusive time to meet him or her in an environment that is free of distractions.

Rapport with prospects is important even before your face-to-face meetings with them. For example, if you are making calls on the telephone, you need to be able to project a warm and professional image. If a good reputation precedes you in your target markets, prospects will be more responsive to your request to meet with them.

Once you have established a positive atmosphere and a comfortable working environment with mutual respect for each other's time, the stage is then properly set for the initial interview.

Prospecting Sources

prospecting sources

There are many different *prospecting sources.* We will provide a brief overview of some of the more popular ones that successful advisors have used to sell annuities including:

- existing clients
- referrals from clients/prospects
- centers of influence
- networking
- seminars
- lists

How about buying annuity leads from All web?

Existing Clients. Most of your existing clients who are in their late fifties and sixties are good candidates for retirement planning. Senior clients who are about to retire or have been retired for a while are good potential clients for annuities as retirement fund distribution vehicles. If these people are your clients, you already have a professional relationship with them, so it stands to reason that most will be receptive to working with you to further explore their planning needs as they move toward or into their retirement.

Almost every outstanding producer has a systematic procedure for contacting existing clients to find out if anything in their financial situation has changed, to follow up on previously discussed cross-selling opportunities, or to discuss additional needs. Turn these periodic reviews into opportunities to explore retirement planning issues for seniors who are still working—update the facts on their current retirement plans, do an analysis, and offer annuities if they fit a need you uncover.

Referrals From Clients/Prospects. It is advisable to pave the way for referrals early on in the selling/planning process, preferably during the initial meeting. Create the expectation of receiving referrals if the prospect appreciates what you do for him or her.

Bill or Bonk

April Health Insurance Renewals & Bring BOR's — to transfer new accounts

Example: "Mr. and Ms. Prospect, as we work together, if you find what we are talking about to be important and valuable, then give me the opportunity to meet with people you know and care about so that I may help them, too."

Then when you ask for referrals it will not surprise the prospect. The best time to ask is when the prospect indicates an appreciation for you and/or annuities. It could be as simple as "I'm so glad you showed me that. I always thought paying taxes on my Social Security retirement benefits was unavoidable." Obviously if the prospects purchase annuities from you, they have demonstrated an appreciation for the product. However, even if prospects do not buy an annuity, ask them about the value of the process. If they have a favorable opinion of you and the process, ask for referrals.

Example: "Ms. Prospect, I know you have decided that you do not need annuities. May I ask what, if anything, in this process you found to be of value?" [Wait for a response.] "That's great. I am glad I could help you clarify some of the income and healthcare concern issues of retirement planning. May I ask who you know who might also benefit from this type of advice?"

Of course, if your prospects have parents who may be in the market for annuities, you can specifically ask for their names.

Example: "Mr. Prospect, although I disagree with your waiting to buy an annuity at this time, I respect your decision. I am glad, however, that you see the need for retirement planning. I was wondering, do you think your parents may benefit from owning annuities to either defer their taxes or guarantee a lifetime income? Do they live in this state? Would it be okay if I met with them?"

As always, remember to follow up on referrals by providing an update to the referrer to let him or her know how the meeting went.

Satisfied clients can also be an excellent, yet often overlooked, source of referrals. Be sure to put a system in place to regularly ask existing clients for the names of people who may be interested in using annuity products in their retirement planning as well.

Centers of Influence (COI). By definition, a *center of influence* is an influential person who knows you, has a favorable opinion of you, and agrees to introduce or recommend you to others. A client may become an effective center for you, just as a center may become a client, but this is not necessary to the relationship you need to establish. In general, you will find that COIs

- are active in a community or sphere of influence.
- are sought out for advice by those within their sphere of influence.
- seek to communicate with others.
- are givers, not takers.

Good COIs know the people in your target markets regardless of their occupation or profession. However, some occupations and professions deal directly with your target markets, and finding COIs in these occupations and professions could prove very profitable. Examples include the following:

- elder law attorneys
- CPAs
- fee-based financial planners
- advisors who sell noncompeting lines of financial products (for example, a property and casualty agent)
- healthcare providers
- clergy
- members of a volunteer organization

Also keep in mind that sometimes your best COI is simply a friend or close relative who comes into contact with a lot of people on a regular basis and is personally interested in helping you to succeed in the financial services business.

Once you have identified some possible COIs, you will need to set up meetings with them. Write and practice a script if you do not know them very well.

One strategy for you is to approach the COI by explaining how the meeting will benefit him or her. For example, you might approach a noncompeting advisor as follows.

Example:	"Pat, you have a great reputation in the community, and I would feel comfortable referring clients to you. I would like to get together with you to brainstorm ways we can help each other build successful practices. Would breakfast sometime next week work for you, or would a lunch be better? My treat."

Your meeting with a COI is as important as a sales appointment. Therefore plan your presentation. Keep it brief and consistent with your approach. For example, if you are meeting with a community leader, the goal of your presentation is to show the COI just how he or she can help others by referring them to you. Your approach to accomplish this objective may include the following steps:

- Share the impact that poor retirement planning will have on people needing it and upon society in general.
- Illustrate the impact with any personal stories.
- Demonstrate how annuities can help prevent this for many people by providing tax-deferred cash accumulation and guaranteed income.
- Give the COI some practical actions that he or she can take to help.

You will probably want to ask the COI for names of qualified prospects. If so, have a brief written description of how to identify qualified prospects. Although referrals are important, you may find other ways the COI can help you. For example, if the COI is a leader for a senior community service organization, you can approach him or her about doing an educational presentation for the rest of the organization. Be creative.

Networking. Networking is the process of continuous communication and sharing ideas and prospects with others whose work does not compete with yours. In turn, their clients might also be shared with you and become your clients.

Most networking groups have the same general rules. Membership is limited to one person from each type of sales background, whether insurance, real estate, mortgage brokerage, or some other sales profession. Each person who attends the meeting is required to bring a prescribed number of names. For example, the real estate agent member of the group just sold a house located in an over-age-55 community that she represents exclusively. She gives you the name of that person as a prospect who may be interested in annuities for retirement planning. On the other hand, your client may have expressed a desire to live in an independent-living or retirement community and thus would be a good prospect to share with the real estate agent.

If you can find an existing networking group in your community, it might be worthwhile to investigate joining it to provide you with a steady stream of prospects.

Seminars. Some advisors have found that seminars are an extremely effective way to prospect, especially in the senior market. Seminars enable advisors to accomplish two key objectives. First, seminars are a means to present annuities in the context of retirement planning to several prospects at one time, resulting in less time needed to conduct one-on-one interviews. Second, seminars cast advisors as the experts, especially if they play a significant role in the presentation.

Seminars are not only a source of prospects but also a method for prospecting and marketing annuities. Many successful advisors in the annuities market use seminars as their main prospecting tool. Therefore we will comprehensively discuss the use of seminars as both a prospecting and marketing tool in the next chapter.

Lists. Many experienced advisors use this prospecting tool with excellent results. Advisors who have had success with lists note that the key is to select lists that will contain prospects who would likely have an interest in annuities. For example, a list of American Association of Retired Persons (AARP) members would certainly contain people who are age 50 or older. Some companies provide lists to their advisors through market segmentation programs; check with your company to see if one is available. Otherwise, you will want to buy a list from a reputable list vendor.

When dealing with a vendor, exercise caution. Here are some points to keep in mind:

- Select lists that reflect your target markets.
- Check to see how recently the data were collected.
- Make sure that the list has current phone numbers.
- Verify the source of the leads.
- Make sure that the list has been "scrubbed." This means that any "do not call" and undeliverable names have been eliminated.
- Check to see if duplicate entries or incomplete names have been deleted.

One final thought on lists: Keep good records so you can evaluate the quality of the leads, and compare different vendors until you find the one that gives you the best return on your investment.

Markers

You have probably been in the financial services industry long enough to know that success in the business comes from finding groups of prospects with common needs and characteristics, a process known as *segmenting*. The ultimate goal is to find a segment that is large enough so you do not run out of prospects and one that has a communication system that will facilitate the process of identifying prospects. Such a segment is known as a *target market*. Target marketing will be discussed further in Chapter 2.

Nevertheless, because of the relationship between aging and the need for retirement income, we will first segment the markets for annuities in terms of product type—deferred and immediate—and then by age. The age groups for deferred annuities we will explore are under age 45, ages 45 to 64, and age 65 and older. For immediate annuities, the age groups are under age 65 and age 65 and older. To assist you in the process of segmenting your current clientele and/or prospects according to both their age and their annuity product need, we will provide a brief overview of these market segments.

Age Distribution of Deferred Annuity Owners		
	Fixed	Variable
Under age 45	9%	18%
Ages 45 to 64	38%	52%
Ages 65 and Older	53%	30%

Source: *Deferred Annuity Buyers and Owners Profiles, A 2007 Report.* © 2007 LIMRA International Inc.®

Deferred Annuities

Under Age 45 (Providers). People under age 45 typically do not feel the need for buying annuities or retirement planning as keenly as those who are older than age 45. This segment is a little more resistant because there are many other needs that have more immediate importance to them. For example, many are still worried about saving enough for their children's education and protecting their incomes from the risks of death and disability.

According to a 2007 LIMRA study, only 18 percent of all variable deferred-annuity owners and 9 percent of all fixed-interest deferred annuity owners fall within the under-age-45 group.[19]

Nonetheless, you will find several distinct opportunities in this market for selling annuities. The first opportunity is that you can sell these people a qualified deferred-annuity contract through such vehicles as 403(b) plans offered through their employers. The second opportunity for you is to motivate this under-age-45 group to begin an individual retirement annuity

segmenting

target market

(IRA) or a nonqualified annuity in order to take advantage of compound interest over the longer period of time that they have until their retirement.

Ages 45 to 64 (Preretirees). While many in this market segment who are parents may still have other financial concerns (such as saving for children's education and the life and disability insurance mentioned in the under-age-45 segment), a greater emphasis is now being placed on their retirement needs. According to the same 2007 LIMRA study, 52 percent of all variable deferred-annuity owners and 38 percent of all fixed-interest deferred annuity owners fall within the ages of 45 and 64. Retirement for these people is no longer an abstract far-away concept but is, instead, one that is very real and that they are approaching quickly. This is the bread-and-butter market segment and will be for several years to come because baby boomers (born 1946 to 1964) comprise a growing percentage of this market.[20]

Age 65 and Older (Retirees). This market segment is formidable in size in terms of total owners (30 percent variable and 53 percent fixed), and it will continue to grow due to the aging and increased longevity of the baby boomer generation. While the average age of single-premium fixed-interest deferred annuity buyers is 64 overall, the average age of fixed-interest deferred annuity owners is 65.[21] While people in this age bracket represent a large cohort of prospects for deferred annuities, they are also the most prolific buyers of immediate annuities, as discussed below. This naturally leads to the conclusion that people in this age group own both types of annuities. There is no shortage of evidence to support this conclusion. A majority of all annuity owners (54 percent) state that their household owns at least one other annuity. On average, owners of multiple annuities own 2.7 contracts. The average combined balance held in all annuities is $133,000.[22]

Immediate Annuities

Under Age 65 (Preretirees). People under age 65, which was the traditional Social Security retirement age, largely do not see the need to purchase immediate annuities. According to the most recent Immediate Annuity Buyer Study published by LIMRA International Inc., only about 1 in 5 (22 percent) of all immediate-annuity buyers fall into this age bracket. Of these, nearly half (10 percent) are between the ages of 60 and 64.[23] A person's decision to purchase an immediate annuity has also traditionally meant that the liquidation of a single sum of money in exchange for a periodic income stream that is usually guaranteed for life irreversibly excluded access of those premiums in any other format. Recently, however, as discussed in Chapter 6, some companies now offer limited access to lump sums of cash or accelerated payments from within immediate annuities after normal annuity payments have commenced; this may increase future sales potential within this age group. Nonetheless, the likelihood of prospects in this age segment is small because the vast majority of these people are still working and preoccupied with the accumulation of wealth, not the liquidation of it. In fact, only 20 percent of immediate-annuity owners are either employed or not unemployed, while 80 percent of them are retired.

Age 65 and Older (Postretirees). This age group, by far, represents the biggest potential source of prospects for immediate-annuity products. Seventy-eight percent of all immediate-annuity buyers are 65 or older. Among them, 61 percent are over age 70; the average immediate-annuity buyer is 70 ½ years old, and age 70 is the most common age at purchase for male and female buyers and qualified market buyers.[24] Those people in retirement are extremely concerned about conserving financial resources and maintaining the lifestyle they enjoyed while working. Retired immediate-annuity buyers receive income from a variety of sources, on average more than 3.4 sources.[25] Annuities rank second, behind Social Security. This suggests that many retirees who purchase immediate annuities view them as an important source of income.

CONCLUSION

There is a tremendous opportunity for financial advisers to shape millions of Americans' retirement security through the annuity products discussed in this book. The need for both deferred and immediate annuities is evident, based on these products' current statistics regarding buyer and ownership trends. Because of the increased longevity of the American population in general, and the baby boom generation in particular, the annuities marketplace will continue to grow steadily over the next 25 to 30 years.

Now you have a basic idea of what annuities are, what they do, who the prospects for them are, and why people buy them. In the next chapter, we will examine additional markets for annuities, along with various methods for approaching prospects within each of those markets.

CHAPTER ONE REVIEW

Key Terms and Concepts are explained in the Glossary. Answers to the Review Questions and Self-Test Questions are found in the back of the book in the Answers to Questions section.

Key Terms and Concepts

annuity
owner

annuitant
beneficiary

single-premium annuity   indexed annuity
flexible-premium annuity   variable deferred annuity
immediate annuity   prospecting
deferred annuity   qualified prospects
qualified annuity   prospecting sources
nonqualified annuity   segmenting
fixed-interest annuity   target market

Review Questions

1-1.   What is the definition of an annuity?

1-2.   Describe the difference between qualified funds and nonqualified funds.

1-3.   Explain how annuity payments can provide security to a consumer.

1-4.   Identify the four classifications of annuities.

1-5.   Explain the difference between an immediate annuity and a deferred annuity.

1-6.   Describe why tax deferral is a redundant feature for qualified annuities.

1-7.   List the eight steps in the selling/planning process.

1-8.   Identify the trend in life expectancy since the early 1900s.

1-9.   List six sources for obtaining annuity prospects.

1-10. Identify the three age-based market segments

Self-Test Questions

Instructions: Read Chapter 1 first; then answer the following questions to test your knowledge. There are 10 questions. Circle the correct answer; then check your answers with the answer key in the back of the book.

1-1.   Which of the following features distinguishes an annuity contract from a life insurance contract?

   (A)   Annuity contracts have no significant mortality charges.
   (B)   Annuities have no net amount at risk.
   (C)   Annuities are not as tax efficient to beneficiaries as life insurance.
   (D)   All of the above distinguish an annuity contract from a life insurance contract.

1-2. A client has money in his 401(k) plan with his employer. He is retiring and would like to place this money in an annuity contract. The best contract would be a

    (A)   single-premium nonqualified annuity
    (B)   single-premium qualified annuity
    (C)   flexible-premium qualified annuity
    (D)   flexible-premium nonqualified annuity

1-3. What is the surest way to provide systematic payments from a specified sum of money over a specified period?

    (A)   death of annuitant
    (B)   annuitization
    (C)   withdrawals
    (D)   full annuity surrender

1-4. The greatest single factor that motivates people of all ages to purchase either deferred or immediate annuities is which of the following?

    (A)   desire to save income taxes
    (B)   need for retirement income
    (C)   need for investment diversification
    (D)   quest for guaranteed interest rates

1-5. Which of the following party or parties to the annuity contract serves as the measuring life?

    I.   owner
    II. annuitant

    (A)   I only
    (B)   II only
    (C)   Both I and II
    (D)   Neither I nor II

1-6. An advisor is already licensed to sell fixed annuities but now wants also to sell variable annuities. The advisor must pass which additional exam?

     I.   FINRA Series 6 exam
    II.   FINRA broker-dealer exam

    (A)   I only
    (B)   II only
    (C)   Both I and II
    (D)   Neither I nor II

1-7. A client purchases an annuity with after-tax dollars and wishes payments to begin in eight months. The client is purchasing which type of annuity?

    I.   immediate annuity
    II.   nonqualified annuity

    (A)   I only
    (B)   II only
    (C)   Both I and II
    (D)   Neither I nor II

1-8. Each of the following is an age-based market segment for annuities identified in the text EXCEPT

    (A)   under age 45
    (B)   ages 45 to 64
    (C)   ages 55 to 65
    (D)   age 65 and older

1-9. Each of the following is a classification of annuities EXCEPT

    (A)   multiple-premium annuities
    (B)   immediate annuities
    (C)   qualified annuities
    (D)   fixed-interest annuities

1-10. All of the following are acceptable definitions of the term "annuity" EXCEPT

  (A) the single payment of an allowance or income
  (B) the right to receive this payment or the obligation to make this payment
  (C) an investment on which a person receives fixed payments for a lifetime or a specified number of years
  (D) a contract or agreement under which one or more persons receive periodic payments in return for prior set payments made by themselves or another

NOTES

1. *The American Heritage Dictionary*, 2d College ed., 1985, Houghton Mifflin Company.
2. *Webster's Third New International Dictionary*, 1971, G&C Merriam Co.
3. *The 2006 Individual Annuity Market Sales and Assets, A 2007 Report* © 2003 LIMRA International Inc. ®
4. Ibid.
5. *2007 Annuity Fact Book*, 2nd ed., p. 9, © National Association for Variable Annuities (NAVA).
6. Ken Dychtwald, PhD, president and CEO, Agewave LLC.
7. The 2007 Annual Report of the Board of Trustees of the Federal OASDI Trust Funds.
8. Ibid.
9. "2007 Social Security Changes," http://www.ssa.gov/pressoffice/factsheets/colafacts2007.htm.
10. "An Update on Private Pensions," by Alicia H. Munnell and Pamela Perun, An Issue in Brief, August 2006, Number 50, Center for Retirement Research at Boston College.
11. "401(k) Plans Are Still Coming Up Short," by Alicia H. Munnell and Annika Sunden, An Issue in Brief, March 2006, Number 43, Center for Retirement Research at Boston College.
12. Bureau of Economic Analysis, U.S. Department of Commerce, New Release, February 1, 2007.
13. "As Housing Prices Cool, Americans Keep Spending," by Christopher Conkey, *The Wall Street Journal*, October 2, 2006.
14. *2007 Retirement Confidence Survey*; Employee Benefit Research Institute (EBRI) and Mathew Greenwald & Associates Inc. 2007.
15. "Consumer Debt Grows at Alarming Pace," by William Branigin, MSNBC.com, January 12, 2004.
16. "Recent Changes in U.S. Family Finances: Evidence from the 2001 and 2004 Survey of Consumer Finances," *Federal Reserve Bulletin*, February 2006.
17. "In Their Dreams: What Will Boomers Inherit?" by John Gist and Carlos Figueiredo, AARP Public Policy Institute, May 2006.
18. Immediate Annuity Buyer Study: Profiles and Attitudes, A 2000 Report. © 2000, LIMRA International Inc.
19. Deferred Annuity Owner Study: Profiles, A 2007 Report. © 2007, LIMRA International Inc. ®
20. Ibid.
21. Ibid.
22. Deferred Annuity Owner Study: Characteristics and Attitudes, A 2003 Report. © 2003, LIMRA International Inc. ®
23. Immediate Annuity Buyer Study: Profiles and Attitudes, A 2000 Report. © 2000, LIMRA International Inc.
24. Ibid.
25. Ibid.

2

Annuity Markets

Learning Objectives

An understanding of the material in this chapter should enable you to

---

2-1. Identify marketing opportunities for annuities in retirement planning.

2-2. Identify the three demographic generations into which most annuity prospects fall.

2-3. Explain the concept of a stretch IRA.

2-4. Identify marketing opportunities for annuities in charitable planning.

2-5. Explain the most commonly used methods for preapproaching and approaching a prospect for annuities.

2-6. Identify the main benefits of and aspects involved in conducting a successful seminar.

Chapter Outline

This chapter examines both the nonqualified and qualified annuity markets and explores IRAs, Roth IRAs, tax-sheltered annuities. and other qualified annuity plans. The discussion includes business planning opportunities for annuities, as well as college funding and charitable planning. Methods for preapproaching and approaching prospects are also discussed, along with techniques for conducting successful seminars.

MARKETING CONCEPTS

This section examines the use of conventional marketing concepts in the sale of annuities. First, we will identify the age-based market segments most applicable to deferred and immediate annuities, respectively. We will discuss how to target market to prospects for annuities and explore the sales opportunities and concepts within the nonqualified and qualified annuity markets, as well as additional markets in which annuity products may be useful. A review of these concepts will help you to put together your plan for marketing annuities.

Identifying Market Segments

market segments

After determining the profile of a qualified prospect, the next step is to find groups of qualified prospects, or *market segments*. We will begin by reviewing the age-based market segments summarized in Chapter 1. Age-based segments are an appropriate place to start because they currently play a more important role in marketing and selling annuities than any other demographic factor.

Once we have established the common characteristics and needs of the age-based market segments, we will then look at some other useful ways to segment the annuities marketplace.

Age-Based Market Segments

age-based market segments

From the definition of a qualified prospect described in Chapter 1, it is easy to conclude that an effective way to segment the annuities market is by age. It is only reasonable to assume that you will have greater success with prospects in the age ranges where they typically see the need for annuities in retirement planning, can afford to pay for them, are suited to buy them, and can be approached on a favorable basis. Fortunately these age ranges can be easily identified: Statistics show that currently most deferred-annuity sales fall into two categories: ages 45 to 64, and age 65 and older.

FIGURE 2-1

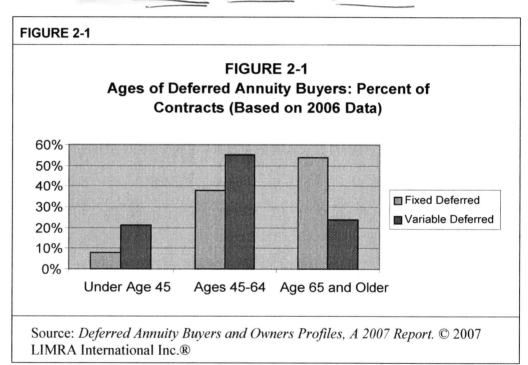

FIGURE 2-1
Ages of Deferred Annuity Buyers: Percent of Contracts (Based on 2006 Data)

Source: *Deferred Annuity Buyers and Owners Profiles, A 2007 Report.* © 2007 LIMRA International Inc.®

Because of the general acceptance of age 65 as the traditional or normal retirement age (even though for Social Security purposes, this will eventually increase to age 67), we have slightly modified the age ranges used with the statistics. Under our methodology, the age groups are separated into three market segments:

- prospects who see retirement as a distant goal (those under age 45 years old)
- prospects who see retirement as a more immediate concern (those ages 45 to 64)

- prospects who are enjoying retirement or semiretirement (those age 65 and older)

(Throughout this discussion of market segments, you will see material and discussion on the various American generations, as commonly used by demographers. One word of caution: These generations do not exactly match up with our age-based market segments. For example, baby boomers can be found in both the under-age-45 and the ages-45-to-64 market segments.)

Under Age 45. As mentioned in Chapter 1, traditionally prospects in the under-age-45 market segment have been much less receptive than prospects from the other two market segments to purchasing deferred annuities. Probably the most universal reason for this reluctance to buy deferred annuities is that people in this market segment consider other needs and wants to be more important. Examples include saving for a house, buying a new car, saving for a child's education, and securing life and/or disability income and long-term care insurance. There is only so much income to spend.

Another reason for the lack of receptivity to buying deferred annuities is that prospects in the under-age-45 market segment perceive deferred annuities to be a need for people much closer to or actually in retirement. They may believe that they still have plenty of time to plan for retirement. In fact, many of these prospects feel that they will never need deferred annuities.

According to a 2007 LIMRA study, only 21 percent of all variable deferred-annuity buyers and 8 percent of all fixed-interest deferred buyers fall within the under-age-45 group.

This is not to say that you should not approach prospects from this market segment. Obviously people with the discretionary income to pay for deferred annuities may be good prospects. Their income notwithstanding, however, you should look for prospects who

- know a friend or family member who has purchased deferred annuities
- are in their 40s
- are single or divorced with no dependents
- have high liability limits on their property and casualty insurance
- own a personal liability umbrella policy

One of the major needs common to prospects in the under-age-45 market is asset protection in the context of retirement and/or estate planning. The primary goal of retirement planning is to build a nest egg that will last. One of the major risks we all face is outliving our resources. This risk dramatically increases when we factor in inflation and the possibility of needing long-term care. Prospects with whom you have actually done retirement planning make logical prospects for discussing deferred annuities. The same holds true for prospects with whom you have done estate planning to maximize the value of their estates. Large estates can suffer severe shrinkage from taxes and estate administration costs. This is especially true in situations where the bulk of the estate assets are tied up in illiquid assets such as real estate or closely held business interests. A deferred annuity with proceeds payable at the death of its owner to a named beneficiary can provide probate-free assets directly to the heirs of the estate owner. Therefore deferred annuities should always be at least a part of any discussions about retirement and/or estate planning.

Selling to the Under-Age-45 Market

The under-age-45 market may not be your target market, but you should take advantage of the opportunities for selling annuities to this market. Specifically, educate prospects about the risks of waiting too long to start planning for retirement and the associated high costs. Stress to them the power of compound interest, tax deferral, and within qualified plan products, tax deductibility. The information can result in a sale or plant the seed for a future sale.

EXAMPLE: "Mr. and Ms. Prospect, I understand that you feel that you cannot afford to save for retirement right now. However, I would like to give you some information about how annuities can help when you are ready. Would you have any objection to my staying in touch with you from time to time so that when you are ready to take action, you might consider doing it with me?" (No)

"Great, I will contact you periodically to see if your financial situation changes, and when you feel that you are ready to start planning for retirement, we can get together and discuss how tax-favored annuities can fit into such a strategy. Does that seem fair enough to you?" (Yes)

Then put them in your call-back file for future contacts.

Ages 45 to 64. Fifty-five percent of all variable deferred-annuity buyers and thirty-eight of all fixed-interest deferred annuity buyers fall within this relatively short age range. This market segment will be the bread-and-butter market for deferred annuities for the next several years for a variety of reasons.

First, recall that the baby boomers represent a bulge in the population. Over the next several years, the baby boomer population bulge will dominate the ages-45-to-64 market segment, making it the segment with the most prospects by sheer numbers alone.

Second, people in this market segment typically are at their peak income levels. Thus prospects in the ages-45-to-64 segment typically have the means to afford annuity premiums. Therefore the chances of their qualifying to buy annuities and their willingness to act are much better than at the younger ages.

Third, the public generally views annuities as a retirement planning component, and ages 45 to 64 are when planning for retirement becomes a front-burner issue. Thus prospects in this segment generally have a greater sense of urgency about planning for retirement than those in the under-age-45 market segment.

Another important need among this group is their desire to preserve independence during retirement. When people have self-reliant attitudes, they want to avoid having to depend on government welfare programs and/or their children. You will find this independent, self-reliant attitude among the middle class, especially those who have worked hard to accrue a nest egg for retirement. They are the people who have planned for their retirement and take great pride in having done so. Again, as previously indicated, the purchase of annuities should be a part of any retirement planning discussion.

Individuals in the ages-45-to-64 market who might make good prospects are those

- who are saving aggressively for retirement
- who are skeptical about the future solvency of Social Security
- with few or no dependent children in the household (so-called empty nesters)

Be aware that many people in this market segment are under pressure to save both for retirement and for their children's postsecondary education. In this regard, they face the same challenges as their under-age-45 counterparts. The difference is that they probably have a higher income and thus a greater ability to pay for annuities.

Age 65 and Older. As Figure 2-2 shows, the age-65-and-older market segment has generated the vast majority of immediate-annuity sales. Also immediate-annuity owners are generally over 70 years old, and they are usually retired; only 9 percent of immediate-annuity owners are under the age of 60. Thus 91 percent of immediate-annuity owners are over age 60, and 74 percent are age 70 or older. [1]

Although studies show that the current trend is toward more deferred annuity sales for the age-45-to-64 market, there are still many prospects in the age-65-and-older market segment who purchase deferred annuities (24 percent of variable deferred and 54 percent of all fixed-interest deferred annuity sales overall), especially for the transfer of assets from employer-sponsored qualified retirement plans that are distributable to employees when they terminate their employment.

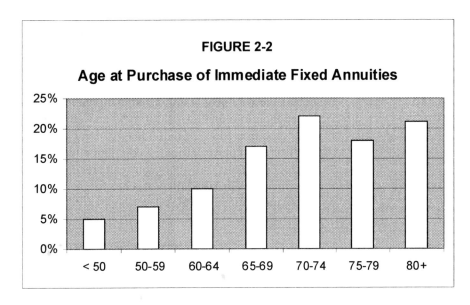

Prospects in the age-65-and-older market segment generally have the same retirement planning needs as those in the age-45-to-64 market segment except that prospects aged 65 and older are definitely more sensitive to healthcare issues, especially those related to Medicare and long-term care. In addition, because the majority of people in the age-65-and-older segment are no longer employed, they have a heightened fear that their monthly income and assets are not going to be sufficient to pay for everything they may want or even need. They fear that a lack of money will force them to depend on relatives, friends, or public assistance and will limit their access to quality long-term care.

Because of their age and retirement status, prospects from the age-65-and-older market are much more concerned about protecting and conserving their assets than younger prospects are. As retirees, these prospects are generally not able to add to their retirement nest egg. Consequently they readily relate to the risks involved in outliving their assets. Therefore, as consumers, they are more inclined to purchase fixed-interest deferred annuities than variable products, and they are also by far the largest segment of buyers (78 percent) of immediate annuities.

This market segment is largely composed of retirees, who have more spare time. Thus they are more deliberate in their decision making and very receptive to seminars. One topic that makes a great seminar is long-term care. If you sell long-term care insurance, a seminar could serve a dual purpose: The topic of financing long-term care insurance could effectively also sell immediate annuities. This concept will be discussed further in chapter 6.

Demographers often divide the population into age-based segments known as generations. The process is not an exact science, so you will find that dates for when a generation begins and ends vary slightly from source to source.

The basis for a demographic generation is the theory that the general population's psyche and behavior are shaped by significant life experiences, such as the way people are raised, national and world events, wars, the social and economic climate of the times, and so forth. While each prospect will need to be treated as an individual, generalizations allow you to be aware of the different types of attitudes you may encounter from members of each of these generations so that you can recognize them quickly and make adjustments. Virtually all prospects for annuities will fall into one of the three American generations described below.

American Generations

The Silent Generation—There are over 60 million members of this population segment who were born prior to 1946. The Silent Generation is sometimes referred to as the GI, Swing, or Mature Generation. This generation falls into three groups: preretirees, new retirees, and long-time retirees.

Older members of this generation fought in and lived as adults during World War II. Many helped to shape the socioeconomic direction of America after the war, have been able to accumulate comfortable wealth, and may be remembered as the affluent senior generation. Younger members of this generation are called Depression-era or war babies.

Generally, these people have discretionary income, and their children are grown. They often grew up as children in households with one wage earner, and they have retired or will retire as senior adults in households that have two wage earners. They tend to be

Hard-working—They equate success with hard work.

Frugal—The Great Depression and their parents instilled this value in them. This frugality has translated into the unprecedented wealth that they carry into their elderly years.

Cautious—As children of the Great Depression parents, they were taught not to take risks.

Self-reliant—They want to be independent and self-reliant and do not want to trust others for their security.

As a whole, they benefited from two decades of economic growth following World War II, large increases in Social Security benefit rates between 1968 and 1972, and the boom in real estate and the value of housing. Members of this generation have deep concerns regarding access to quality healthcare and asset preservation. These characteristics make them receptive to purchasing annuities.

Baby Boomer Generation—Over 78 million people born between 1946 and 1964 will reach age 65 from 2011 through 2029. Because its size so large, this generation can be divided in to two subgroups: Older Boomers (born from 1946 through 1954) and Younger Boomers (born from 1955 through 1964).
The members of the Baby Boom Generation often married later, divorced more often, and had fewer children than the generations before them. Baby Boomers have higher real incomes than their parents did, but as a group they are poor savers. Many are educating their children and taking care of aging parents. Because of this dual role, they are sometimes referred to as the sandwiched generation. They are

Spenders—Although Baby Boomers have more money than preceding generations in the middle years, they tend to spend it. It is not that they do not save at all, but they save less percentage-wise.

Inheritors—It is predicted that they will be collecting over $16 trillion in inheritances between 1990 and 2030.

Image-conscious—Cosmetic surgery, designer clothing, and luxury cars exemplify their passion for image.

Youth-oriented—Health, fitness, and laser eye surgery exemplify their desire to remain young forever.

The Baby Boomers will enter retirement with money saved from their working years and inheritances. They will be able to afford premiums for annuities. Their preoccupation with image makes annuities an appealing product because annuities are designed to help them preserve their dignity and independence. Baby Boomers face increasing healthcare costs, uncertainties about the Social Security system, and fewer adequately funded pension or retirement plans to sufficiently meet their income needs.

Generation X—Born from 1965 through 1981, the Generation Xers are the children of Baby Boomers or the younger members of the Silent Generation. There are about 59 million of them. Sometimes referred to as the Baby Bust Generation, they are

Risk-takers—They are ambitious, and entrepreneurial opportunities appeal to them.

Self-oriented—They want to know what is in it for them.

Practical—They want something that works; they want a plan with specific steps and a well-defined result.

Because of their self-orientation and practical nature, expect them to encourage their Silent Generation and Baby Boomer parents to take individual responsibility for retirement, healthcare, and asset-preservation planning. Also, in the future, look for them to take action regarding their own retirement needs, making them excellent candidates for variable deferred annuities.

Targeting a Market

Market segmentation is a powerful marketing strategy that allows you to customize your approach and presentations based on the common needs and characteristics of the prospects in the segmented market. If you can find a market segment that has a communication or network system, then you have a target market. The communication system can be formal, such as a newsletter or regular meeting, or it can be informal, such as word of mouth within a tightly knit ethnic community. Either way, the communication system or network provides the means by which your reputation as a professional advisor can precede you. In other words, before you personally meet with any prospects in a target market, they will know about your abilities as a financial advisor.

[handwritten: Important concept + term "Target market"]

Targeting Markets for Annuities

Because of the nature of retirement planning, annuities can be marketed successfully using age-based market segments as "makeshift" target markets (age-based market segments are very broad and lack a communication system and for that reason do not technically qualify as a target market). Many successful advisors do this by targeting narrow but specific age ranges. For example, one successful advisor targets prospects ages 55 to 65 because most of them are probably empty nesters who are focused on funding for retirement.

An extension of the age-based target market theme is when advisors target people in a specific, but narrow, age range who are also members of an association, service organization, or club. The ideal situation occurs when the majority of the membership is in the chosen age range. For example, if an advisor wants to target prospects ages 45 to 64, he or she may consider targeting a service organization (such as the Rotary, Jaycees, Kiwanis, and so forth) or club (such as a VFW, Elks, or a country club) in the community that has a large membership of people in the desired age range. Besides age range

[handwritten: Steve Dellelo 55 + Age bracket]

and membership, other common characteristics of the prospect group, such as income range, could help in establishing a new target market. If you use this method for targeting a market, you will need to develop a list of desirable characteristics that you want the prospects to possess to guide you in the process of establishing the new target market.

For many advisors, annuities are just one of several insurance and financial products they sell, so they position annuities in a manner consistent with their current target market's view of them as advisors. For instance, if an advisor works as an estate planner for business owners making $100,000 to $500,000 per year, he or she will want to position annuities as an estate liquidity and preservation tool.

Likewise, if an advisor's target market is teachers in a large city, he or she will want to position annuities, especially within a 403(b) plan, as part of a strategy for safeguarding the teachers' retirement nest eggs. Similarly, multiline advisors selling property and casualty insurance will want to position annuities as a piece of their prospect's overall financial plan.

Target markets enable you to focus on the unique needs of your prospects. This focusing will not only foster your reputation within the target market as an expert in annuities exclusively or in retirement planning products in general, but it will also allow you to better understand your prospect's needs. With this knowledge, you will soon discover the efficiencies of tailoring a marketing strategy for a large number of prospects with common characteristics and needs.

NONQUALIFIED RETIREMENT PLANNING

nonqualified retirement planning

As individuals look to the three-legged retirement income stool, they see more and more that they have to take control of their retirement future. They realize the need to focus on the third leg of the stool, which is their own personal savings. With the uncertainty over the long-term existence of Social Security and with employers cutting back on their contributions to pension plans, it has become more apparent than ever that the third leg of the stool may be the only leg they can control and count on for long-term retirement security.

One technique that consumers can use to control their own personal retirement savings is a deferred annuity. Whether a flexible-premium or single-premium policy is desired, the market for nonqualified annuities in retirement planning is enormous.

In 2006, nonqualified annuities totaled $100.1 billion—42 percent of the $238.7 billion total annuity sales. Approximately 43 percent ($43 billion) of those sales were fixed annuity products while 57 percent ($57.1 billion) were variable. Furthermore, 95 percent were deferred annuities, and only 5 percent were immediate. This brought the total amount of nonqualified annuity assets in force to $850 billion in that year.[2]

Flexible-premium deferred annuities are ideal for consumers who want to systematically save for retirement with small contributions at frequent intervals. Single-premium deferred annuities can be used to fund a retirement plan when a person has a lump sum of money to invest such as from the sale of a business, an inheritance, a salary bonus, and so forth.

Deferred annuities are designed to allow consumers to save money for retirement. Because they offer tax-deferred growth, consumers can set aside dollars for retirement and watch the values grow year after year. Deferred annuities can help provide significant retirement nest eggs, and depending on which type of annuity the policyowner chooses—fixed, variable, or equity-indexed—the risk to those retirement funds can be little or nothing.

Deferred annuities are encouraged for use in saving for retirement because tax laws discourage annuity owners from taking money out early. The government imposes a 10 percent penalty tax on certain amounts withdrawn from annuities prior to age 59 ½, and the insurance company imposes surrender charges.

Deferred annuities, as retirement planning tools, offer clients such important features as

- income tax deferral
- probate avoidance*
- guaranteed lifetime income at annuitization
- limited liquidity using free-corridor withdrawal amounts
- the ability to take partial surrenders without having to surrender the entire annuity
- flexibility in making contributions as needed
- no limits on the amount of premiums that can be invested
- surrender charges that discourage clients from withdrawing funds prior to retirement age
- low cost (typically annuities do not charge an annual fee, but if they do, it is relatively modest)

* In order to avoid probate, the beneficiary must be a named beneficiary other than the estate of the deceased. If the estate is the beneficiary of the annuity, then the proceeds are deposited with the executor of the estate. The annuity becomes an asset of the probate estate and is subject to the claims of creditors. The annuity funds are also subject to lengthy red tape prior to distribution to beneficiaries.

Annuity Buyer Profiles

To succeed in today's competitive world, it takes a keen awareness and a thorough understanding of the underlying market forces. Transforming data into valuable insight helps you identify trends and understand annuity buyer and owner characteristics, which allows you to leverage the knowledge necessary to develop realistic marketing strategies.

According to Eric T. Sondergeld, Corporate Vice President and Director, Retirement Research, LIMRA International, "The most significant opportunity available in the financial services industry today is the retirement market—those people nearing retirement. They are increasingly burdened with financing a growing share of their retirement. Much of this burden relates to the many risks they will face in retirement. Financial services providers, especially life insurers, are uniquely positioned to capitalize on this because they can offer risk-transfer solutions through annuities, life insurance, long-term care insurance, and other products."

Research organizations, such as LIMRA International, frequently conduct studies of nonqualified deferred annuity buyers to determine profiles of their demographic characteristics. LIMRA studies have compiled information on hundreds of thousands of annuity contracts from numerous insurance companies. LIMRA collects demographic, attitudinal, and financial product ownership information from annuity buyers and owners; participating companies represent a mix of large, midsize, and small annuity writers, with in-force contracts sold in both retail and employer-sponsored markets.

These reports investigate how owner characteristics (such as age, retirement status, household income, and investable financial assets) relate to attitudes, behaviors, and product features. Consider this information extracted from LIMRA's recent *Deferred Annuity Owner Study: Profiles Reports:*

- Older owners are far more likely than younger owners to have nonqualified annuities.[3]
- The average age of a fixed-interest deferred nonqualified annuity purchaser is 64 (50 percent are age 70 or older).[4]
- Sixty-three percent of owners are married, 20 percent are widowed, 10 percent have never married, and 6 percent are divorced.[5]
- According to product type, 56 percent of nonqualified deferred-annuity buyers bought variable products, and 44 percent of them bought fixed annuities.[6]

These statistics are a jumble of useless numbers unless you interpret them to provide guidance in your annuity target marketing efforts. For example, if you want to purchase a list of prospects for nonqualified deferred annuities—or to describe to a center of influence the ideal profile of the type of prospect you seek for the sale of nonqualified deferred annuities—you can make the following conclusions from the information above to target the type of prospect you seek: You would want prospects who are older, and it would be wise to start with those who are near or in retirement, and married. Also you would improve your chances of receptivity if you gear your approach to these older prospects by discussing fixed-annuity products. This will not guarantee your success in selling annuities, but it will increase your chances of marketing the right product to the most receptive prospects. This will also enable you to more effectively allocate your time and financial resources into your nonqualified deferred-annuities prospecting and marketing strategies.

QUALIFIED RETIREMENT PLANNING

qualified retirement planning

Because an annuity is already a tax-deferred investment vehicle, investing qualified plan dollars in an annuity may appear somewhat redundant. Nevertheless, annuities have consistently been a popular vehicle for qualified plan dollars.

Qualified annuities comprised $132.7 billion, or 56 percent, of the $238.7 billion total annuity sales in 2006. Of the $132.7 billion in qualified plan annuity sales, $103.3 billion (78 percent) went into variable products while only $29.4 billion (22 percent) went into fixed annuities.[7]

Within the qualified annuities category, there are two broad market subcategories—the IRA, and employer-sponsored plans including 403(b) and "other plans" such as 401(k), profit-sharing, Keogh, deferred compensation (IRC Sec. 457 plans), and pension trusts. Of these markets, IRA sales were $95,9 billion (72.2 percent) of all qualified plan annuities sold in 2006. Employer-sponsored plans accounted for $36.8 billion (27.8 percent) of all qualified plan sales.[8]

Each insurance company will have its own set of policies, or riders to nonqualified policies, for the various types of qualified annuities the insurer chooses to offer. Each type of qualified annuity requires a specialized endorsement or policy. For example, an IRA annuity will be different from a Roth IRA annuity, which will be different from a tax-sheltered annuity. The financial advisor must first determine which types of annuities are offered by the insurer because not all insurers offer all types of qualified annuities.

For Individuals

Individual Retirement Account (IRA)

individual retirement account (IRA)

Annuities have long been a solid retirement planning solution for people who want to save for retirement using tax-deductible contributions. The maximum *individual retirement account (IRA)* contribution per year is shown in Table 2-1.

TABLE 2-1
Maximum Combined Contributions to All IRAs per Year

Calendar Year	Taxpayer < Age 50	Taxpayer Age 50+
2008	$5,000	$6,000
2009	Indexed for inflation	Base contribution amount plus $1,000
2010	Indexed for inflation	Base contribution amount plus $1,000

An amount less than $5,000 (or the larger amounts shown in Table 2-1) may be contributed as long as the minimum premium is met, as determined by the insurance company, to issue the policy.

Whether or not the IRA contribution is *tax deductible* by the taxpayer depends on a number of items:

- The taxpayer must have earned income equal to the contribution.
- The taxpayer must be less than age 70 ½.
- The taxpayer must not be an active participant in an employer's retirement plan for any part of the calendar year. (An active participant is an individual who makes voluntary contributions to or for whom employer contributions are made or accrued benefits exist within a qualified corporate, Keogh, pension, profit-sharing, stock bonus, or annuity plan, or in a simplified employee pension, 403(b) tax-sheltered annuity, SIMPLE IRA, or government plan.)
- If the taxpayer is an active participant, then the taxpayer must have adjusted gross income (AGI) below a specified level to deduct the contribution. See the filing status tables (Tables 2-2 and 2-3).

Note: Adjusted gross income as used for determining eligibility for an IRA deduction is calculated before the IRA deduction. That is, modified adjusted gross income (MAGI) is generally equal to the total income on the individual's Form 1040 tax return, minus adjustments to income other than for IRA deductions.

The deduction for contributions will be phased out for active participants whose MAGI or MAGIs exceed the applicable dollar limits described in Tables 2-2 and 2-3.

Table 2-2 indicates the applicable dollar amount in the case of a taxpayer whose tax filing status is single or head of household.

TABLE 2-2 **Filing Status: Single or Head of Household**		
For taxable years beginning in	The "applicable dollar amount" is	The IRA deduction is totally phased out if MAGI exceeds
2008 Years thereafter	$53,000 Indexed for inflation	$63,000 Indexed for inflation

Table 2-3 indicates the applicable dollar amount for the spouse who is an active participant in the case of taxpayers whose filing status is married filing jointly when either both or only one spouse is an active participant.

TABLE 2-3 **Filing Status: Married Filing Jointly**		
For taxable years beginning in	The "applicable dollar amount" is	The IRA deduction is totally phased out if MAGI exceeds
2008 Years thereafter	$85,000 Indexed for inflation	$105,000 Indexed for inflation

- Those individuals who are not active participants in a qualified plan can contribute the maximum contribution to an IRA regardless of how much income they earned that year (that is, there is no ceiling on their income for deductibility).
- If the spouse of an active participant wishes to make an IRA contribution under the spousal IRA rules, then the total AGI for both taxpayers must be below a stated level for that calendar year.

  The joint filer who is not an active participant in a qualified plan will not have his or her IRA deductibility phased out until combined AGI exceeds $159,000 (2008).
- A taxpayer can make an IRA contribution that is not tax deductible as long as the first two bullet points on page 2-15 are met. However, the appeal to taxpayers in making nondeductible contributions has greatly faded because of the Roth IRA.

The trade-off for a traditional IRA owner's receiving a current income tax deduction for contributions that go to the IRA is that when distributions are taken from it, all funds contained within it that are not rolled over or redeposited within 60 days are subject to income taxation. Thus there is no tax-free recoverable cost basis in a traditional IRA.

If a client chooses to fund an IRA using a deferred annuity, the client will be listed as both the owner and annuitant of the IRA. Joint owners or joint annuitants are not available on any type of IRA plan. The IRA owner can name any person, trust, or entity as the beneficiary of the IRA.

Flexible-premium deferred annuities allow taxpayers to continually invest every year into the same IRA annuity. For contributions made during the months of January through April, it is important for the IRA owner to clearly mark on the check to which tax year the IRA contribution applies (that is, the current year or the prior year).

IRA owners are prohibited from borrowing against their IRAs. Therefore regardless of what vehicle a client chooses to fund his or her IRA, the IRA will not allow the client to borrow against the fund values.

Chapter 7 will describe in detail the income taxation rules as they apply to qualified retirement plans and IRAs, including the 10 percent penalty tax for distributions prior to age 59 1/2 and the required minimum distribution (RMD) rules at age 70 ½.

Spousal IRA. A person can make an IRA contribution on behalf of his or her spouse if that spouse does not have the required amount of earned income to fund his or her own IRA. The couple must file a joint income tax return, however. The IRA policy is set up in the name of the nonworking spouse with that spouse as the annuitant. There is no special rider for a spousal IRA. The traditional IRA endorsement is used. *Spousal IRA* just means, from a tax standpoint, that the IRA is funded by the working spouse.

spousal IRA

Rollover IRA

rollover IRA

Rollover IRAs are the largest market for qualified single-premium annuities. A participant in a qualified retirement plan (a pension, profit-sharing, or 401(k) plan, or a tax-sheltered annuity) or in an IRA who receives a distribution can take those funds and deposit them into a rollover IRA to avoid taxes on the distribution. The following events will trigger the opportunity for the plan participant to roll over his or her distribution into an IRA:

- death of the plan participant (spousal or nonspousal rollover)*
- termination of employment+
- termination of the pension plan+
- retirement from the employer+

* Beginning with distributions in 2007 pursuant to the death of a qualified plan participant, the Pension Protection Act of 2006 permits a nonspouse designated beneficiary of a qualified retirement plan to roll over qualified plan proceeds but only by means of a direct trustee-to-trustee transfer into an inherited IRA.

+ Beginning with distributions in 2008, the Pension Protection Act of 2006 permits taxpayers to directly transfer (and thereby convert) money from a qualified retirement plan, an IRC 403(b) tax-sheltered annuity, or an eligible IRC Section 457 plan into a Roth IRA, thus eliminating the need for a conduit traditional IRA.

As more employees move from one job to another, the opportunity for financial advisors to help these employees invest in rollover IRAs is increasing. Financial advisors may consider building relationships with human resource managers in local companies to assist their terminating or retiring employees in rolling over their distributions.

Certain employer distributions cannot be rolled over into an IRA. Those distributions include

- any distribution made to avoid the penalty tax for people under 59 ½ who are using the "substantially equal periodic payment" method (see chapter 7 for a complete description)
- any after-tax contribution
- any required minimum distribution made after the person is age 70 ½

A rollover IRA is not a special type of policy but is the same as the traditional IRA. It is merely called a rollover IRA to designate what type of funds came into the policy. The distinction is made to differentiate a rollover IRA contribution from a traditional IRA contribution.

Stretch IRA

stretch IRA

The *stretch IRA* has been a popular retirement planning concept in the last few years. A stretch IRA is not a specific type of IRA product or policy. It is a marketing concept that allows beneficiaries of IRAs to avoid taking a lump-sum death benefit by instead taking only the required minimum distribution and thus avoiding a huge income tax liability. The beneficiary can stretch out the required distributions from the death benefit over a long period of time, usually over the life expectancy of the beneficiary.

Stretching out the proceeds simultaneously stretches out the income tax liability. It also allows the remaining balance to continue to grow on a tax-deferred basis. The end result is that over time the beneficiary ends up with a much larger inheritance than he or she would have had if the IRA were taken as a lump-sum distribution at the time of death. The following examples illustrate the concept.

Example 1: Let us say you are the owner of a retirement account in which your daughter is the primary beneficiary. When you reach 70 ½, you elect to take only the required minimum distribution each year, in effect choosing to "stretch out" the retirement account. Your daughter, upon inheriting the account, would then be able to step in and resume taking the RMD. However, once the account passes on from one generation to the next, the life expectancy changes as well.

The distribution will then be made on your daughter's life expectancy instead of yours. The significance is a substantially lower distribution, letting the account be spread out over a longer period of time. This allows the retirement account to continue to earn deferred interest while the distributions are taken. If your daughter had been forced into a lump-sum settlement, as much as one-third or more could possibly have been consumed in income taxes.

Example 2:   The following example shows how a payout might work under a multigenerational distribution option. In year one, we will assume Husband is 65 and has an IRA. Wife is age 55, Daughter is 22, and Grandson is 2. We will also assume that Husband will live to be 73 and that Wife will live to be 72. Let us also assume that over the entire period that the IRA is paying out, it will be earning a 6 percent interest rate. (The examples are hypothetical and all withdrawals shown are before taxes.).

Year	Husband's Age	Beginning of Year	RMD Life Expectancy	Interest	RMD With-drawal	End-of-Year Accumu-lation
1	65	$300,000	N/A	$18,000	---	$318,000
2	66	318,000	N/A	19,080	---	337,080
3	67	337,080	N/A	20,225	---	357,305
4	68	357,305	N/A	21,438	---	378,743
5	69	378,743	N/A	22,725	---	401,468
6	70	401,468	27.4	24,088	$14,652	410,904
7	71	410,904	26.5	24,654	15,506	420,052
8	72	420,052	25.6	25,203	16,408	428,847
9	73	428,847	24.7	25,731	17,362	437,215

Husband leaves $437,215 at his death to Wife. She inherits the IRA account, and she begins to take RMDs based on her life expectancy at age 70 ½.

Year	Wife's Age	Beginning of Year	RMD Life Expectancy	Interest	RMD With-drawal	End-of-Year Accumu-lation
10	64	$437,215	N/A	$26,233	0	$463,448
11	65	463,448	N/A	27,807	0	491,255
12	66	491,255	N/A	29,475	0	520,731
13	67	520,731	N/A	31,244	0	551,974
14	68	551,974	N/A	33,118	0	585,093
15	69	585,093	N/A	35,106	0	620,199
16	70	620,199	27.4	37,212	22,635	634,775
17	71	634,775	26.5	38,087	23,954	648,908
18	72	648,908	25.6	38,934	25,348	662,495
					$135,865	**$798,360**

Wife leaves $662,495 at her death to Daughter. She continues RMDs based on her life expectancy using the beneficiary life expectancy table following the year of her mother's death.

Year	Daughter's Age	Beginning of Year	RMD Life Expectancy	Interest	RMD With-drawal	End-of-Year Accumu-lation
19	40	$ 662,495	43.6	$39,750	$ 15,195	$ 687,050
20	41	687,050	42.6	41,223	16,128	712,145
21	42	712,145	41.6	42,729	17,119	737,754
22	43	737,754	40.6	44,265	18,171	763,848
23	44	763,848	39.6	45,831	19,289	790,390
24	45	790,390	38.6	47,423	20,476	817,337
25	46	817,337	37.6	49,040	21,738	844,640
30	51	956,127	32.6	57,368	29,329	984,166
35	56	1,093,691	27.6	65,621	39,626	1,119,686
40	61	1,212,357	22.6	72,741	53,644	1,231,454
45	66	1,281,914	17.6	76,915	72,836	1,285,993
50	71	1,252,358	12.6	75,141	99,393	1,228,106
55	76	1,041,724	7.6	62,503	137,069	967,158
60	81	510,456	2.6	30,627	196,329	344,754
61	82	344,754	1.6	20,685	215,471	149,968
62	83	149,968	0.6	8,998	158,966	0
					$3,401,188	

Payments will continue to Daughter for the remainder of her life or until the account balance is depleted. In summary, Husband's initial premium of $300,000 totaled a payout of $3,401,188 over Husband's, Wife's, and Daughter's lifetimes. This can be compared to Daughter's electing to take a lump-sum settlement at Wife's death, which would have resulted in a payout of $798,360—the accumulation value at Wife's death ($662,495) plus the total of all RMDs previously taken by both Husband and Wife ($135,865).

Now let us take the scenario a step further and assume that Daughter, instead of inheriting the IRA, chooses to disclaim it. It would then pass to the next in line, which for this illustration is Grandson. At the time of inheritance, Grandson is age 20 and is the sole contingent beneficiary. Again, we assume that the IRA is paying 6 percent.

Year	Grandson's Age	Beginning of Year	RMD Life Expectancy	Interest	RMD With-drawal	End-of-Year Accumulation
19	20	$ 662,495	63	$ 39,750	$ 10,516	$ 691.72
20	21	691,729	62	41,504	11,157	722,075
21	22	722,075	61	43,325	11,837	753,563
22	23	753,563	60	45,214	12,559	786,217
23	24	786,217	59	47,173	13,326	820,064
24	25	820,064	58	49,204	14,139	855,129
25	26	855,129	57	51,308	15,002	891,435
30	31	1,049,460	52	62,968	20,182	1,092,246
35	36	1,276,730	47	76,604	27,164	1,326,169
40	41	1,536,648	42	92,199	36,587	1,592,260
45	46	1,824,776	37	109,487	49,318	1,884,944
50	51	2,129,637	32	127,778	66,551	2,190,864
55	56	2,428,248	27	145,695	89,935	2,484,007
60	61	2,679,257	22	160,755	121,784	2,718,228
65	66	2,812,325	17	168,739	165,431	2,815,634
70	71	2,711,313	12	162,679	225,943	2,648,049
75	76	2,185,691	7	131,141	312,242	2,004,591
80	81	906,479	2	54,389	453,240	507,628
81	82	507,628	1	30,458	538,086	0
					$7,650,240	

All the assumptions for the first 18 years until the death of the Wife occurs are identical to those above.

Wife again leaves $662,495 at her death to Daughter. However, Daughter now disclaims the retirement account, and it passes to Wife's contingent beneficiary, Grandson. Grandson then continues RMDs based on his life expectancy using the beneficiary life expectancy table following the year of his grandmother's death.

Payments will continue to Grandson. In this example, Husband's initial premium of $300,000 totaled to a payout of $7,650,240 "stretched" over multiple generations. This can be compared to Grandson's electing to take a lump-sum settlement at his grandmother's death, which would have resulted in a payout of $798,360—the accumulation value at the grandmother's death ($662,495) plus the total of all RMDs previously taken by both Husband and Wife ($135,865).

It is critical for the financial advisor to discuss with the particular insurer if the insurer has the administrative capability to handle stretch IRAs. The insurer must be able to take multiple beneficiaries of an IRA and administer each beneficiary with his or her own account, tying the distributions to the particular life expectancy of that beneficiary. Because the administrative requirements are critical to the success of the stretch IRA plan, it is crucial to know the insurer's capability before recommending this type of plan.

As a final note, a stretch IRA is normally suited for beneficiaries in the high net worth categories. Beneficiaries who are likely to request the full death benefit regardless of the income tax liability will not make use of the intended benefits of the stretch IRA. If the beneficiary feels he or she needs to withdraw the entire death benefit in a lump sum, the stretch IRA plan will be pointless.

Roth IRA

Roth IRA

A *Roth IRA* is a special type of IRA plan with contributions that are made only on an after-tax basis. In other words, Roth IRA contributions are never tax deductible. The participant must have earned income equal to or greater than his or her contribution. Unlike the traditional IRA, an individual may still contribute to a Roth IRA after age 70 ½ as long as he or she is still earning wages. The maximum contribution per year is illustrated in Table 2-4.

TABLE 2-4
Maximum Contributions to Roth IRAs

Calendar Year	Taxpayer < Age 50	Taxpayer Age 50+
2008	$5,000	$6,000
2009	Indexed for inflation	Base contribution amount plus $1,000
2010	Indexed for inflation	Base contribution amount plus $1,000

A participant can contribute the maximum amount to either a traditional IRA or a Roth IRA or a portion into each. A person cannot contribute the maximum to both a Roth and a traditional IRA in the same calendar year. For example, if Lucy wants to contribute $5,000 to a Roth IRA in 2008, she would be prevented from also depositing $5,000 to a traditional IRA in the same tax year.

Even though Roth IRA contributions are not deductible, taxpayers still have to have modified adjusted gross incomes below certain levels to contribute to a Roth IRA. The IRS has established maximum income levels applicable in 2008 for single taxpayers, married taxpayers, and married filing separate taxpayers, as shown in Table 2-5.

TABLE 2-5
Maximum Roth IRA Contribution

If you have taxable compensation and your filing status is	You can contribute up to $5,000 in 2008 (under age 50) and up to $6,000 (over age 50) to a Roth IRA if modified AGI* does not exceed	The $5,000 contribution ceiling in 2008 for someone under age 50 and the $6,000 contribution ceiling for someone over age 50 is phased out up to a modified AGI of
Married filing jointly	$159,000	$169,000
Married filing separately—and you lived with your spouse during the year	$0	$10,000
Single, head of household, or married filing separately—and you did not live with your spouse at any time during the year	$101,000	$116,000

*Modified AGI is adjusted gross income as shown on your tax return, minus any income resulting from a conversion of a traditional IRA to a Roth IRA, plus certain items such as any traditional IRA deduction and tax-free foreign earned income.

The most beneficial aspect of the Roth IRA is that if certain conditions are met, all the funds withdrawn from the Roth IRA by the participant or the surviving spouse are completely income tax free. Unlike their traditional IRA counterpart for which distributions are almost always 100 percent taxable, Roth distributions can provide tax-free retirement income.

Furthermore, "qualified distributions" from Roth IRAs are not included in the recipient's gross income for federal income tax purposes, regardless of whether or not the recipient is the participant or a beneficiary. A qualified distribution is one that is made after the 5-year holding period beginning with the first taxable year for which the contribution was made to the Roth IRA. In addition to satisfying the 5-year period, the distribution must meet one of the following four criteria:

- It is made on or after the date the client reaches age 59 ½.
- It is made after the owner's death.
- It is attributable to the owner's being totally disabled.
- Up to $10,000 is used for certain purchases of a "first home."

Additionally, Roth IRAs do not have minimum distributions required at age 70 ½. The owner and annuitant must be the same person for a Roth IRA. No joint ownership arrangements are allowed. The beneficiary of the Roth IRA does not have to be the spouse of policyowner.

For Businesses

SEP IRA

SEP IRA

A *SEP IRA* is a simplified employee pension plan for business owners or self-employed persons. SEP IRAs can be funded with annuity contracts. Each participant is the owner and annuitant of his or her SEP policy. The employer must meet nondiscrimination requirements and therefore cover all eligible employees. No employee deferrals are allowed.

SARSEP

Although no longer available for newly issued policies, a SARSEP (salary reduction simplified employee pension) allowed participants of employers with fewer than 25 employees to defer some of their own income into the plan. The plans in existence before January 31, 1997, are grandfathered to allow continued employee deferrals.

SIMPLE IRA

SIMPLE IRA

A *SIMPLE IRA* (savings incentive match plan for employees) is a relatively new type of IRA account. The first SIMPLE IRAs were established in 1997. The SIMPLE IRA was designed to replace a specialized SEP plan called the SARSEP in which the employee was able to make contributions along with the employer. (New SARSEPs can no longer be established although contributions can still be made to existing SARSEPs.)

Employers with 100 or fewer employees may establish a SIMPLE IRA. Table 2-6 shows the maximum employee contribution per year.

The employer must also make a matching contribution up to 3 percent of the employee's salary or a flat 2 percent for all eligible employees.

TABLE 2-6 Maximum Contributions to a SIMPLE IRAs		
Calendar Year	Taxpayer < Age 50	Taxpayer Age 50+
2007	$10,500	$13,000
2008	Indexed	Indexed
2009	indexed	indexed

The benefit of a SIMPLE IRA is that the employee can contribute up to the lesser of annually specified maximum dollar amounts or 100 percent of his or her income. For example, if an employee had $10,500 of compensation in 2007, that employee would be able to contribute his or her entire salary to the SIMPLE plan.

If a client establishes a SIMPLE IRA, the owner of the IRA and the annuitant will be the employee. The employer will not be listed as the owner of the annuity.

To establish a SIMPLE IRA, the insurance company must first have a special policy or a special rider to specifically allow SIMPLE IRA contributions. Before recommending a SIMPLE IRA to an employer, the financial advisor should determine if the insurer offers this type of plan.

TSA/403(b) Plan

tax-sheltered annuity
(TSA)
403(b) plan

A *tax-sheltered annuity (TSA)* is also called a *403(b) plan*, derived from the Internal Revenue Code section from which it was enacted. TSAs are primarily for public school employees and those employees of 501(c)(3) organizations. Each employee will be the owner and annuitant of his or her annuity contract.

TSA plans vary from the traditional IRA in several aspects:

- TSAs have different rules with respect to accessing funds and determining when required minimum distributions must begin.
- TSAs may have loan provisions in the annuity agreement.

- Transfers of TSA accounts between insurers do not occur under the rollover IRA/transfer rules but are transferred in accordance with Revenue Ruling 90-24.

401(k)/Pension/Profit-Sharing Plan

If the financial advisor works with an employer to establish an annuity as a possible investment inside the pension plan, the owner and beneficiary of the annuity will be the trustee of the particular pension plan. Each individual employee will normally be the annuitant. Upon the employee's death, the insurer will pay the death benefit to the trustee. The trustee will, in turn, look to the beneficiary designation the employee has on file with the qualified plan and pay the death benefit accordingly. Therefore it is imperative that the employee have his or her beneficiary on file with the trustee of the pension plan. The employee will not have the beneficiary designation filed with the insurance company.

The beneficiary of the 401(k) or pension plan must be the spouse of the employee. If the spouse signs a valid waiver, the employee can name someone other than the spouse as the beneficiary of the plan.

Normally a deferred annuity might be just one of many options the employee has for investing his or her retirement funds. The annuity should not be the only option available to employees.

ADDITIONAL MARKETS FOR ANNUITIES

Structured Settlements

Frequently, the courts seek lifetime financial support for the injured party in a lawsuit or throughout the minority of dependent heirs. Consequently it is usually acceptable to the court for the award to be paid as a *structured settlement*, in which there are periodic payments instead of, or in addition to, a single lump-sum payment. Insurance companies issue immediate annuity contracts that guarantee the payments over the required lifetime or over the mandated support period. Structured settlements, a category separate from either qualified or nonqualified annuity sales, comprised $5.9 billion, or roughly 2.5 percent, of the $238.7 billion in total annuity sales in 2006. These contracts are specifically tailored to the needs of the claimants, who are the injured or wronged parties.

Since the 1970s, the number of cases using structured settlement contracts to satisfy plaintiffs' claims has grown substantially. The most frequent cases in which structured settlements are applicable involve general liability, medical malpractice, defective products, automobile accidents, or workers' compensation injuries.

Personal injury claims adjusters and/or defense attorneys work together with a structured settlement specialist to arrange appropriate settlements. Suitable structured settlements provide an adequate amount of immediate cash for liquidity needs, as well as reimbursement for past expenses, legal fees, and other cash needs. If the recipient is unable to work, an income stream can be designed to fund his or her normal living expenses, custodial and medical services, rehabilitation costs, and, where appropriate, tuition for educational programs.

How Annuities Work in Structured Settlements

The customary structured settlement uses an immediate annuity to provide periodic payments that meet the recipient's financial needs as much as possible. The periodic payments of income are typically received tax free by the claimant during his or her life and by the claimant's beneficiaries thereafter for the balance of any guarantee period.

An example of a structured settlement is a fixed-period annuity with a payment of $1,000 per month for 5 years and $2,000 per month during years 6 through 10. This is also referred to as a step-rate annuity. Annuity benefit payments can generally be increased on a compound annual rate, ranging from 3 percent to 6 percent.

Generally, this kind of annuity can be purchased only by defendants or their insurers in personal injury and wrongful death cases, and the number of insurance companies that issue such contracts is rather small.

Business Planning

Annuities can be useful tools in business planning. For example, a sole proprietor of a business may choose to sell the business in his or her retirement years. One way the buyer may choose to fund the purchase price is with an immediate annuity. The immediate annuity can be used to fund the buyer's payments to the seller.

The seller of the business might require as part of the negotiations that the buyer purchase this immediate annuity. The seller has a better guarantee that funds will be available each year in the future to make the installment payments.

If the buyer and seller agree to a 10-year installment plan, the buyer could purchase a 10-year fixed-period immediate annuity to cover the installment payments. The buyer of the business would be the owner and the annuitant of the immediate annuity. If the buyer dies before the end of the 10-year period, the seller could be named as the beneficiary of the remaining payments.

The buyer would receive the annuity payments, pay the necessary income taxes due on a portion of each payment, and take the remaining amount and use it to fund the installment obligation to the seller.

An installment payment may be more suitable to the seller of the business than receiving a lump-sum payment. With installment payments, the seller is able to spread out the income taxation on the sale over several years.

Example: Fred owns the Dust Bunny Cleaning Corporation. Joe is the prospective buyer. The sale price is $100,000. If Fred does not require a lump-sum payment but agrees to an installment sale of $10,000 over 10 years, Joe can purchase an immediate annuity for a 10-year fixed period to help make the payments. (For ease of explanation we'll ignore any interest due Fred over the 10-year period.) This plan gives Fred the security of knowing that Joe will have the resources to make the payments long after the agreement is signed.

The arrangement benefits Fred because Fred will not have to declare $100,000 of sale proceeds in the year of the sale. Instead, Fred will have to declare only $10,000 per year over the 10-year period.

Joe likes the idea too because due to the interest the funds will earn from the insurance company, Joe will have to come up with less than $100,000 in a lump sum today to fund $10,000 for 10 years.

Charitable Planning

Annuities can be a solid financial tool in the charitable planning market. The key to successful marketing is to know in what situations annuities are strong tools and in what situations annuities may be inappropriate.

Bequest of Annuity Proceeds to Charity

As a client works with his or her professional advisors in the estate planning process, the client must make sure that the beneficiary designations on his or her annuities, life insurance, retirement plans, and so on match his or her intended estate plan. This means if the client wants to leave half of his or her assets to the spouse and the other half to charity, the client must align beneficiary designations with those wishes.

Sometimes when dealing with estate taxes, professional advisors will help determine how to distribute assets based on tax-efficiency considerations. In other words, they will ascertain how to distribute tax-heavy assets to charities while keeping the least taxable assets for the client.

In this context of planning, one of the best assets a donor can leave to his or her favorite charitable organization is a deferred annuity. Whether this is a nonqualified or qualified annuity, leaving the death proceeds to a tax-exempt charity is a win-win proposition for both the charity and the policyowner.

What makes this type of plan a win-win proposition is that normally the proceeds from the annuity will be taxable to the extent that they are larger than the policyowner's cost basis. Consequently the beneficiary must pay the income tax on the gain in the annuity. If a charity inherits the annuity, because the charity is a tax-exempt organization, it will inherit the annuity and not have to pay a dime in income taxes. So if the choice is between giving a taxable asset or a tax-free asset to charity, the planner will always suggest giving the potentially taxable asset.

Lifetime Charitable Gift

We have just explained how well charitable gifts of deferred annuities work upon death, but the opposite is true about lifetime gifts of annuities. As chapter 7 will explain in detail, a lifetime gift of a deferred annuity will result in a taxable event to the donor. This is true whether the gift is made to a person or to a charity. Therefore making a lifetime charitable gift of an annuity will cause a taxable event to the donor and is therefore generally not a good idea.

Charitable Gift Annuity

charitable gift annuity

A *charitable gift annuity* is a type of planned gift that is frequently confused with a commercial annuity product. A charitable gift annuity is a legal agreement between a charity and a donor. There is no insurance company involved. It is an agreement in which the donor gives the charitable organization an asset, and in exchange, the charity pays the donor a lifetime income from the charity's assets.

The amount of the income the charity pays the donor is typically much higher than the rates on certificates of deposit or savings accounts. Whatever is left from the gifted asset when the donor dies is then available for the charity to spend on its operations. The income paid to the donor is normally based on the premise that at the donor's life expectancy, 50 percent of the amount contributed to the charity should be left in the gift annuity.

Example: A donor makes a cash gift of $100,000 to her favorite charity. The donor is aged 73 and will receive level income for the rest of her life. If invested properly, upon the donor's life expectancy, the amount left in the gift annuity should be $50,000. If the donor lives longer, there will be less money in the account left over for charity. If the donor does not live to her life expectancy, there should be more than $50,000 left over for charity.

Even though a charitable gift annuity is not an annuity available from an insurance company, there is a market for you to sell immediate annuities with charitable gift annuities. The sale potential comes into play with smaller charitable organizations. These small charities may not have the financial strength to stand behind their guarantee to pay a fixed amount of income for the donor's entire life, especially if the donor lives well beyond his or her life expectancy. In these cases, the charitable organization may "reinsure" its financial obligation to the donor by purchasing an immediate annuity.

The charitable organization purchases the immediate annuity on the life of the donor. The charitable organization is the owner and beneficiary. The insurance company pays the immediate annuity to the charity that, in turn, pays the donor. The benefit to the charity is that no matter how long the donor lives, there will be no financial hardship to the charity.

Charitable Remainder Trust (CRT)

charitable remainder trust

A second type of charitable planning technique is the *charitable remainder trust*. An actual trust is constructed into which the donor contributes assets and out of which the trustee pays income to the donor (or someone else the donor names). When the trust ends, the balance of the money in the trust is paid to the donor's chosen charities.

Two types of charitable trusts are available: a charitable remainder annuity trust (CRAT) and a charitable remainder unitrust (CRUT). The CRAT will pay the donor a flat dollar amount; the CRUT will pay a varying dollar amount (a minimum of 5 percent is required to be paid annually), depending on the value of the trust assets each year.

Although the word "annuity" shows up in the charitable remainder annuity trust, immediate annuities are seldom used to fund the payments made to the donor of this type of charitable trust.

Deferred annuities are not proper assets to use to *initially fund* the charitable trust. In other words, the donor must use either cash or assets to fund the charitable trust at the inception. Then the trustee will often sell the assets inside the charitable trust and reinvest the proceeds into other investments. It is at the point of reinvesting that deferred annuities are often an ideal investment.

Deferred annuities are popular investments inside a CRT. The deferred annuity is sold to the trustee of the CRT. The trustee is the owner and beneficiary. The annuitant is the income beneficiary and is also usually the donor.

Net Income With Make-up Charitable Remainder Unitrust. A special type of charitable trust exists, called the net income with make-up charitable remainder unitrust, or NIMCRUT for short. This type of trust is an excellent retirement planning tool for young successful professionals, such as doctors, executives, and so forth. Because of the special nature of this type of charitable trust, it is the ideal charitable trust in which to use a deferred annuity.

A NIMCRUT works as follows: The grantor of the trust deposits property that has appreciated into a charitable remainder unitrust, and the trust then sells the assets and reinvests the proceeds. Under the trust shelter, no capital gains tax is assessed at this point. In addition, the donor receives a current tax deduction on the full value of the charity's remainder interest in the assets that have been placed in the trust. There is a higher deduction for a shorter-duration trust. If the trust is for life, the older the income beneficiary is and the lower the income payout, the greater the deduction.

The trust income beneficiary will receive either a set percentage of the trust assets (at least 5 percent under the unitrust rules of IRC. Sec. 664(d)) or the total income generated by the trust investments, whichever is less. This schedule protects the trust principal from being depleted. If there is a year with low yields, only the total income generated needs to be distributed, and principal does not need to be invaded. Shortages in one year can be made up in a following year. At the end of the trust's duration or the death of the beneficiary, the balance remaining in the trust goes to the designated charity.

The use of a variable annuity to fund such a trust can yield interesting results.

Example: A married couple in their fifties decide to set up a NIMCRUT, which, in addition to a charitable donation, would provide retirement income and might also fund the purchase of a retirement home. They use a variable deferred annuity, which distributes no current income, to fund the NIMCRUT. Ten years later, at retirement time, the couple begins to receive income from the fund, and they decide to purchase a retirement home. The trustee distributes to them the funds for the home purchase and their regular income payment for that year. Because the annuity has been accumulating the funds for the previous 10 years, there is enough cash to meet the couple's needs. The key to this arrangement is the use of the annuity because regulations mandate that charitable trust ordinary income must be paid out in the year that it is earned. The IRS has accepted the position adopted under some state trust laws that the build-up within an annuity is not distributable income until the trustee removes funds from the annuity. Thus it allows the deferral of income from the charitable remainder trust until some later date.

Be sure to consult with your advanced underwriting and compliance departments and the appropriate legal and tax advisors for proper counsel and guidance before recommending a CRT to anyone.

College Funding

The cost to send a student to college for 4 years keeps escalating every year. With the high cost of education and the equally high demand for children to attend college, more parents are making funding their children's education a high planning priority.

Nonqualified deferred annuities can be used to fund a student's college education. However, due to surrender charges and potential penalty taxes, annuities have fairly limited use as a college funding vehicle. Other college funding solutions such as Coverdell Education Savings Accounts (CESAs) and Section 529 plans offer greater flexibility, particularly when it comes time to withdraw the funds to pay college expenses.

The significant advantage that deferred annuities offer as tools for college funding plans is tax-deferred growth. This allows each year's growth to continue without having to surrender some of the annuity values to cover any tax due on the growth. However, interest earned on funds contributed to CESAs and Section 529 plans are also income tax deferred, and withdrawals from these plans can be nontaxable if used for qualifying education expenses.

As mentioned, the downside of using a deferred annuity for college funding is the taxation of withdrawals. Chapter 7 will cover taxes in detail, but as a quick overview, withdrawals out of most newly funded annuities are income taxable to the policyowner to the extent that there is any gain in the annuity. Therefore it is most likely that the policyowner will have to pay ordinary income tax on part or all of the money withdrawn.

Furthermore, the Internal Revenue Service generally imposes a 10 percent penalty tax for withdrawals taken by policyowners who are under age 59 ½. If the parents will be in their 40s or 50s when their children are in college, it may not make sense for them to own annuities for college funding, at least from a tax perspective.

An alternative approach, which may avoid the penalty tax, is to consider any grandparents of the college student as potential owners of the annuity. As long as the grandparent is over age 59 ½, the 10 percent IRS penalty tax will not be an issue. It will not, however, change the income taxable nature of the withdrawals. However, when the grandparents give the money to the grandchild, there could be gift tax implications for them.

Ownership of a deferred annuity by the grandparents for college funding allows them control over the funds until the time the grandchild begins college. The funds could not be used by the parents for expenses other than college. If the grandchild's parents divorce, the funds will not be dissipated in a divorce property settlement. The grandparents should also name a trust established on the child's behalf as beneficiary of the proceeds so that the funds in the deferred annuity can be used specifically for the child's education expenses.

Estate Planning

When a financial advisor conducts a fact-finding meeting with a prospective client, the financial advisor may notice that the client has already accumulated plenty of retirement funds and assume that a nonqualified annuity might not be a solution for that client. However, some clients purchase nonqualified annuities as a vehicle through which they leave assets to their heirs. Using nonqualified annuities in the estate planning process has both upsides and downsides.

The upside of using a nonqualified annuity to pass assets from one generation to the next is that the annuity generally bypasses the probate process. Bypassing probate is a benefit because the annuity values are not subject to the claims of the deceased's creditors. Also the beneficiary will receive the proceeds much faster than if the death benefit goes through the probate process. Often probate assets are not distributed for many months until the probate process is complete. Nonqualified annuities, on the other hand, are payable to the beneficiary as soon as the paperwork, including proof of death, is submitted to the insurer.

The downside of using a nonqualified annuity to pass money from one generation to the next is the taxation of annuity death benefits. When a beneficiary inherits nonqualified deferred annuity death benefits, the beneficiary must pay ordinary income taxes on any gain in the annuity. Therefore the beneficiary does not receive the proceeds on an income-tax-free basis, as is usually the case with life insurance. In addition, the annuity is included in the estate for estate tax purposes.

Example: Belle owns a nonqualified annuity worth $150,000; she paid $40,000 in premiums. When Belle dies, her beneficiary will have to pay income tax on the gain (which is the cash value less the premiums paid) or $150,000 – $40,000 = $110,000.

On the other hand, had the beneficiary received shares of stock worth $150,000 instead of annuity values, the shares of stock will pass to the beneficiary with a cost basis equal to the value at death, or $150,000. If the beneficiary sells the stock immediately, he or she will not have to pay income taxes on any gain because the cost basis is now equal to its current value.

The taxation of nonqualified annuity death benefits makes a valid argument against leaving assets to heirs through annuities. One way to overcome this argument is to consider leaving the proceeds of a nonqualified annuity as a bequest to a specified charity.

Example: Helen has a deferred nonqualified annuity worth $100,000. She originally paid $25,000 into the annuity several years ago. Helen has plenty of retirement funds and really has no need for this annuity. She is trying to decide whether to name one of her favorite charities or name her nephew Adam as the beneficiary. If Adam receives the proceeds, he will have to pay ordinary income taxes at his marginal income tax bracket on the $75,000 untaxed gain in the contract.

If Helen chooses to name her favorite charity as the beneficiary of the annuity, the charity will still receive a $100,000 check. Technically, the charity receives the nonqualified deferred annuity with $75,000 of taxable gain, but the charity is a tax-exempt organization; therefore it does not have to pay any income taxes. Instead, the charity receives the entire $100,000 free and clear.

From an estate tax perspective, because the beneficiary of the annuity is a tax-exempt organization, Helen's estate will receive a charitable estate tax deduction of $100,000. In the end, the net effect of this second option is to eliminate all estate and income taxes.

Private Annuities

private annuity

A *private annuity* is not a product sold by a commercial insurance company. Rather, a private annuity is a contract between two people. One person, the transferor, transfers assets to the other person, the transferee, in exchange for a lifetime income stream. The payments cease when the transferor dies.

Private annuities are usually established between family members. They are particularly appropriate for parents who want to transfer property to their adult children but are afraid that by giving up the property, they may not have enough assets to generate the retirement income they need for their lifetime.

The transferee immediately receives title to the asset, but the asset cannot be used as collateral to back the payments. For this reason, the private annuity concept is not normally established between unrelated parties.

PREAPPROACH AND APPROACH STRATEGIES TO MARKET ANNUITIES

Once you have identified a few target markets or market segments, the next step is to select some general preapproach strategies that you can use to identify yourself and to precondition prospects so that you can approach them about annuities. First we will explore various preapproach and approach strategies and techniques that create interest and enable you to set appointments with prospects for annuity products. The section concludes with a closer look at seminars, a prospecting and marketing method that has proven to be effective in the annuities market.

What works effectively for you will depend on your specific market, as well as your individual personality and skills.

Preapproaches

preapproach

The purpose of a *preapproach* is to create awareness of who you are and to generate an interest in your products. You want to precondition your prospects to meet with you when you call them. They will be less apt to do so if they have no idea who you are and what you can do for them.

How do you feel when you receive a cold call? If you react like most people, you are suspicious and defensive and do not listen to what the caller says. You are too busy thinking, "Who is this, how did he get my number, and how can I get rid of him?" Compare this scenario to receiving a call from a CPA you met briefly at a wedding or who sent you a postcard introducing herself as "a CPA for financial advisors, helping them to maximize their income tax deductions." Would you listen? Use the preapproach to make your prospect curious; this can be done in many different ways. We will discuss some of the more standard preapproaches. The ones you use will depend on your target market, your prospecting methods, and your creativity.

Direct Mail

Direct mail is a systematic way to reach large targeted groups of prospects. Many companies offer direct mail programs that automatically send out a set number of compliance-approved letters each month to the market segments you have chosen. Most direct mail includes a response card for potential clients to return if they want more information on the products or services described in the letter. Check with your product carriers to find out how they will assist you with direct mail. If you choose to write your own letters, be sure to have the appropriate compliance department approve them.

Direct mail is one of the more common preapproaches because it is an easy and relatively inexpensive way to precondition prospects to be receptive when you call them. It allows people to see your message who otherwise might not be looking for your name in the telephone book or for your billboard advertisement. Furthermore, you can use direct mail to customize your message to different target markets. For example, you may send prospects aged 45 to 64 a postcard that talks about annuities as a major component of a retirement plan. For prospects aged 65 and older, you may instead send a postcard that talks about the uses of immediate annuities to provide a guaranteed stream of income.

Your company may have a direct mail program that requires you to supply the list of prospects you want to approach, select the particular letter you wish to send, and choose a giveaway offer if desired. Although the giveaway offer could be a remembrance item, such as a road atlas or a coffee mug, a better choice would be a booklet, book, or video on retirement planning that includes descriptions of annuities.

As mentioned when we discussed lists in chapter 1, many companies also offer market-segmentation programs that allow advisors to create a list of prospects who meet specific criteria. Examples of often-used criteria include marital status, age range, income level, zip code, home ownership, and phone

(See Insphere)

number. Consider a reputable vendor if you are dissatisfied with your company's options or if your company does not offer this service. Some vendors also have customizable direct mail pieces that they will send for you. Whether you use a direct mail piece from a vendor or one of your own, remember to have it approved by your company's compliance area before you send it out.

Here are some additional tips for a direct mail campaign:

- If you are working with a list of prospects you have generated through referrals, centers of influence, and casual meetings, make sure the names are spelled correctly.
- Before you purchase a list, check the undeliverable rate. Also check to see if the vendor uses a five- or nine-digit zip code (five digits have a greater chance of being undeliverable).
- Select a letter that matches the type of prospects on your list. Be conscious of both the content and the layout. For example, some companies use larger fonts for seniors.
- Keep the letter short. The main paragraph that creates interest should be no more than three or four sentences; otherwise, people will not read it.
- Try using postcards. Many people do not open "junk mail" but they will take time to read a postcard.
- Use stamps rather than metered mail (no stamp). Metered mail to most people is perceived as junk mail.
- Try the "wave" mail technique, which involves sending several pieces of mail to the prospect over a period of time. For example, you may send three or four mailing pieces over a 3- or 4-week period, or perhaps over a 12-month period. Direct mail results show that people often respond between the third and sixth time they have seen a letter or an idea.

  Drip Marketing

- Always include a postage-paid reply card that is easy for prospects to complete.
- Follow up direct mail with a phone call; it gives you an excuse to call. In the wave mail technique, wait to call after the prospects have received a few mailings from you. The mailings will help the prospects feel that they know who you are, and as a result, they will be more receptive to your call.
- Track your leads to monitor the effectiveness of your direct mail and other preapproach efforts.

Reputation-Building Strategy

Prestige, or reputation, is your personal public relations campaign. It is your standing in the eyes of others; it is the position or influence you command in people's minds. A good reputation increases the probability of your ability to approach prospects on a favorable basis. Therefore take great care in *building prestige* and maintaining it. Make professionalism a priority. Here are a few guidelines:

building prestige

- Dress professionally but not in a showy way.
- Be approachable and personable.
- Keep your car and office clean and organized.
- Consider earning an industry-recognized designation.
- Build your knowledge of annuities.

Furthermore, implement a strategy that will publicize your reputation, especially to your target markets. You want as many people as possible in your target market to know you as the expert on annuities. For example, if you target the seniors market, sponsoring a little league team would not be part of your strategy. Teaching a personal finance class at the local senior center, however, would be an excellent reputation-building activity.

Here are some other prestige-building ideas:

- Advertise on local radio stations. Select shows and stations that appeal to your target market. For example, "Sunday with Sinatra" would be a good radio show on which to advertise if you are targeting prospects over age 55.
- Advertise in local community-based newspapers.
- Make yourself available to the local media. Alert journalists that you are knowledgeable about retirement planning issues and willing to provide expert information.
- Give back to your community in ways that both you and your target market value such as volunteering activities.
- Leave annuities brochures (with your contact information on them) in places where people from your target markets frequently obtain free information—for example, doctors' offices, train stations, and credit unions.
- Educate key advisors, such as attorneys and CPAs who work with your target markets.
- Work with a local newspaper to publish achievements such as receiving your LUTCF, CLU®, ChFC®, or CFP® certifications.
- Join a local organization that will have a positive impact on the community.

professional brochure

Professional Brochure. Some advisors develop a *professional brochure* as one of their preapproach methods. The brochure is a self-promotional piece that introduces the advisor. Some advisors create their own brochures and then reproduce them using a local printing company. Other advisors use a vendor to design and print the brochures. The goal is to impress potential clients, so do not let price be the only consideration.

The self-promotional piece includes such information as

- name and contact information
- your mission statement
- a short biography
- credentials (designations, experience, and so forth)
- services
- products

Some advisors send brochures to referred leads, along with a cover letter that tells them to expect a phone call. A promotional brochure is also an appropriate handout to give new prospects when you introduce yourself to them, especially at an event you are hosting such as a seminar. The brochure should also become a part of your sales presentation binder.

As with other materials, the brochure will need to meet your company's compliance standards.

approaches

Approaches

Generally, advisors use the telephone to approach prospects for sales appointments. This section will review some of the basics of effective telephone approaches and methods to prequalify prospects during the appointment-setting call. Many advisors view annuities as one of several products they use to meet a client's financial and insurance needs; therefore this section also looks at directing clients to annuities after selling another financial product.

Before we discuss aspects of telephone approaches, it is necessary to address the reality of the FCC's do-not-call rule, which is applicable to all financial advisors. For many, this is seen as a major obstacle to their prospecting efforts, but for others it is seen as an opportunity to explore avenues of marketing that play within the exceptions to the do-not-call rule.

Telephoning Compliance

Do Not Call (DNC) Regulations

The Federal Communications Commission (FCC), the Federal Trade Commission (FTC), and the majority of states have adopted rules regarding unsolicited telemarketing calls without the consumer's prior consent, or sales calls to persons with whom the caller does not have an established business relationship. The FCC rule makes use of the Do Not Call Registry established by the FTC and sets forth the ways that telemarketers must check the list to ensure compliance. The term "telemarketer" refers to any person or entity—including a financial advisor—making a telephone solicitation.

The regulations under the Do Not Call Law are designed to protect consumers from telemarketing abuses. Generally a telemarketer's call to a person on the national or state DNC list is subject to a fine of $11,000 or more per violation.

There are many restrictions placed on telemarketing. Some of the important ones are as follows:

- Sales calls to persons who have placed their residential or mobile phone numbers on federal or state DNC lists are prohibited.
- Calls cannot be made before 8 a.m. or after 9 p.m.
- Stiff penalties are placed on violators.
- Sellers must maintain an in-house DNC list of existing customers who do not want to receive sales calls.
- Sales callers must, at the beginning of every sales call, identify themselves, the company they represent, and the purpose of the call.
- Telemarketers may not intentionally block consumers' use of caller identification.

For many, these restrictions are seen as a major obstacle to their prospecting efforts. For others, however, the restrictions are viewed as an opportunity to explore avenues of marketing that play within the exceptions to the Do Not Call Law.

These exceptions apply when there is

- *an established business relationship.* A business relationship exists when there is a product or service in place, and it continues for 18 months after that product or service is no longer in effect or active. Several states have stricter requirements. If a consumer contacts an advisor, whether by phone, mail, or in person, to inquire about a product or service, an existing business relationship exists for 3 months after that inquiry. (Referrals do not satisfy the established business relationship exceptions and are not a basis to call someone on the list.)
- *prior express permission.* Advisors may make calls to a person on the DNC lists if they have a signed, written agreement from the consumer in which he or she agrees to be contacted by telephone. Written permission if it is received prior to the call is valid indefinitely unless revoked by the consumer.
- *a business-to-business relationship.* The DNC regulations do not apply to business-to-business calls.

- *a personal relationship*. Calls may be made to people with whom an advisor has a personal relationship, including family members, friends, and acquaintances.

Because of the DNC regulations, you need to capitalize more effectively than ever on the opportunity to make telephone appointments with prospects who are not on the national DNC Registry. For prospects who are on the registry, you must think creatively and utilize every opportunity within the law to make appointments with them.

In addition to the federal Do Not Call Law, most states have rules that must be observed regarding solicitations using the telephone. It is your responsibility to know how they apply to you in your everyday business activities.

A Professional Phone Skills Trainer's Viewpoint*

Many advisors have expressed frustration because of the Do Not Call Law. They have called me, lamenting, "What should I do?" since the passing of this new legislation.

Here are some ideas for making calls to "easier" leads:

- Seminars are a terrific forum for getting interested people to sit and listen to you talk.
- You can also canvass a business area and introduce yourself to local business owners. Make sure you have a good, short face-to-face introductory presentation that will lay the groundwork for the appointment-setting phone call that follows.
- Try calling the people in your natural market such as friends, family, and acquaintances whom you have been too afraid to call. Those folks will accept your phone call, won't they?

I am sure that, overall, this Do Not Call Law will help the truly professional financial advisors to rise to the challenge.

* Gail B. Goodman, president, ConsulTel, Inc./www.phoneteacher.com

---

Also be aware that telemarketing by charitable organizations is exempt from the Do Not Call Law. Furthermore, people can be solicited at their place of employment because business phone numbers are also exempt from the law.

Last, all financial advisors are responsible for knowing and following the compliance rules of the company or companies with which they do business. Accordingly any advisor who uses the telephone scripts or techniques for handling prospects' questions and problems presented in this text must get approval from his or her company's compliance department and/or manager prior to using them.

Telephone Approach

You need to capitalize more effectively than ever on the opportunity to make telephone appointments with prospects who *are not* on the national do-not-call registry.

Objective. Your objective is to introduce yourself to the prospect and set the appointment. Obviously you will not need to introduce yourself to an existing client, but you will want to re-establish rapport if you have not spoken to him or her for some time.

Sometimes a prospect or client may ask you a question related to the product. One you probably hear often is, "How much does it cost?" Some advisors cannot resist the temptation to answer these questions over the telephone. It is more productive to save such answers for the interview; for now, you simply want to get the appointment.

Follow-up to a Mailing to Preretirees

"Hello, this is Tom Smith from DEF Insurance. I recently sent you some information on the tax advantages of deferred annuities.

"As a specialist in retirement planning, I would like to get together with you and explain how tax-deferred annuities can enhance your retirement income. Regardless of whether tax-deferred annuities are appropriate for you, people in situations similar to yours have found it useful for them to take the time to learn some of the facts about how they work.

"Are evenings good for you, or do afternoons work better?"

System. You may already have a system for setting appointments. If you do not, now is a good time to develop one. A system is critical to ensure that appointment setting is done effectively. It provides you with clear expectations and a game plan that will increase your confidence and improve your results. Here are some points to consider as you create or modify your system:

- *Use a telephone script.* Write and practice your telephone script. Your script should reflect the needs and characteristics of your target markets. The script should vary depending on the source of the prospect and the preapproach, if one was used. For example, if you approach a referred lead, you will want to mention the referrer's name.

- *Coordinate logistics.* Plan a specific time to make your calls. Have a goal for the number of appointments you will make based on your sales and commission goals. Maintain a prospect list of names, telephone numbers, and addresses (to confirm where the appointment will be).

- *Follow the laws.* Follow federal and state laws concerning telemarketing. For example, observe the do-not-call rules established by the Federal Communications Commission, and abide by the call curfews set by your state.
- *Use good telephone techniques.* Smile, project your voice, and enunciate your words. These are just a few of the many suggested techniques.
- *Track your results.* Record keeping enables you to evaluate your prospect list and target markets. Without adequate records, you may miss a target market because you are relying on "feel" to measure results rather than objective numbers.
- *Confirm the appointment.* Send a letter or postcard and/or call the prospect to confirm the appointment to prevent being stood up.

Script. Many advisors balk at the words *telephone script*. They feel a script will restrict them or make them sound mechanical. Actually the opposite is true. Scripts help you feel more comfortable and enable you to project a more confident phone personality. They free you to focus on the prospect and listen for clues to gauge his or her level of interest. In addition, they help you repeat success and diagnose failure.

A good script is short and creates interest.

Example:

Good Approach

"Good afternoon, Prospect, this is Joe Advisor from ABC Insurance. I will only take a moment of your time. The reason for my call is that I specialize in helping senior citizens (and retirees) increase the fixed rate of return on their retirement savings. I've been working with a lot of retirees and have found that many of them are not happy with the current rates of interest that they're earning on their money. So I am offering information that shows some alternatives on how you could earn a higher rate of interest on a tax-deferred basis. Some ideas offer a guaranteed interest rate that may also reduce your total income taxes. What I'd like to do is meet with you to share ideas that may help you. Would some time during the morning work for you, or are afternoons better?"[9]

If you do not have a script, here are some of the basic elements of a good script. As always, remember to follow company guidelines and obtain any necessary compliance approval.

Greeting. You want to make a good first impression.

- Open your conversation with something upbeat like, "Good morning/Good evening."
- Identify yourself and the company you represent.
- Consider adding a phrase that demonstrates you are sensitive to the prospect's busy schedule: "Good afternoon, this is Jane Advisor with XYZ Company. I'll only take a moment of your time."

Creating Interest. Remember, you are trying to motivate the prospect to see you.

- Tell why you are calling and state your credentials (areas of expertise).
- Offer information.
- Give a unique benefit statement that describes the results you create for people like the prospect (your target market).
- Explain the purpose of the meeting in terms of the personalized results you hope to achieve for the prospect: "I'm calling because my area of expertise is in retirement funding for preretirees like you and your husband/wife. I offer individual plans tailored to meet your retirement income needs. I would like to get together with both of you and show you some basic principles to prepare for your future financial security. Many of my clients feel that after meeting with me they were much better prepared to meet their retirement income needs."

Close for the appointment. This is why you are calling.

- *Avoid using the word appointment.* Use "meet," "see," or "get together."
- Use the word "share."
- Keep your close as a choice between two large concepts of time, such as mornings or afternoons, evening or daytime, or beginning or end of the week: "What I'd like to do is get together with you to share some ideas that may help you. Are evenings convenient for you or is the daytime better?"

Conclusion—This ends the call and confirms the appointment.

- Give or get directions, depending on where you will meet for the appointment.
- Reconfirm the appointment and affirm your desire to meet the prospect.

Asking Prequalifying Questions. Many successful advisors prequalify prospects once they have agreed to an appointment. Whether you prequalify your prospects depends on your type of practice and personal views on this matter. For example, if you have multiple products, prequalification before the initial interview may not be crucial because you have other products that you can turn to in order to satisfy other needs the prospects may have. However, prequalifying before the initial interview will allow you to prepare for a smooth transition to the other needs and products.

If you do wish to prequalify before the initial interview, the next step is to decide what information you need to know and build a script. Choosing what questions you ask is based on your philosophy of prequalification. For instance, one advisor prequalifies for age only. His philosophy is that although annuities are his main products, they are not his only products. He can switch to a discussion of the prospect's possible need for long-term care or life insurance. Even so, he cannot help anyone over the age of 85 who may need these products. Therefore, as a matter of practice, he asks people for their date of birth. If they ask why he wants to know it, he simply tells them that all annuities (as well as life or long-term care insurance products) have age limits that restrict their issuance.

The transition from getting the appointment to asking the prequalifying questions needs to be smooth; that is why a script is important. One commonly used transition is, "I know your time is valuable. So to make our time together as productive as possible, it would help for me to know some basic information about you." Then pause and begin to ask three to five brief and simple questions.

Some advisors include questions to identify other people who will influence the prospect's decision such as children or a CPA. If these advisors find that there are other people involved in the decision-making process, they often suggest having them present at the interview. Here are a few of the questions successful advisors ask:

- What is your date of birth?
- What is your occupation?
- What is more important to you, saving income taxes or preserving your assets?

- Would you consider yourself a risk-taker or a conservative investor?
- Do you rely on anyone to help you make decisions about financial products?

Besides the actual answers to these questions, the prospect's willingness to answer them and the tone of voice and spirit of cooperation will give you valuable preliminary insight into how well he or she meets the four criteria of a qualified prospect discussed in chapter 1. You will also begin to formulate ideas about the prospect's income, his or her buying attitudes, and what products to discuss.

Finally, have a short script prepared that you can use to let the person down gently if you know he or she will not qualify. This requires the utmost care and sensitivity. You do not want the prospect to feel bad.

Example:	"Prospect, I am really sorry, but according to your date of birth, we will not be able to help you at this time. I highly recommend that you consider seeing an attorney or financial planner who specializes in alternative strategies for meeting your estate planning needs. I can provide the names of several attorneys if you would like."

pivot approach

Pivot Approach

An effective pivot or transition from one product to another uses previously shared information as the context for asking a question relevant to another product. Pivoting can occur from any type of product sale. Most likely, you will discuss annuities as part of retirement or estate planning. But if you are a property and casualty advisor or a life advisor who is working in the income replacement market, you will have the opportunity to pivot as well.

How and when to pivot are going to depend on such factors as what type of product the prospect bought from you (or did not buy from you), your personality, and so forth. Try to use something from the previous discussion to lead into annuities. Pivot when there is closure to the previous discussion. For instance, one of the best times to pivot is when you deliver and review a policy.

Example:	"Prospect, you have made a great choice to buy this life insurance policy. You are really thinking and planning ahead. Since you seem to be the planning

> type, I was wondering—have you thought about your plans for retirement? Do you know about how annuities can bolster your retirement income and save you income taxes before and after you retire"?

If your prospect responds with curiosity or wants to know more about how annuities can serve dual purposes, you can simply ask for the appointment so that you can discuss annuities further. For example, you might say, "Can we get together next week or another convenient time to discuss your current situation in more detail?" If the prospect asks you to tell him or her more now, keep it very general and brief; then ask again for the appointment.

Summary

Successful selling begins with effective marketing. Defining target markets for a product enables you to create efficient and effective preapproach and approach strategies that are customized to appeal to your prospects' needs. As you begin to market annuities, treat them like other products you sell, and take the time to define your target markets and strategy, including details like your telephone and pivoting scripts. The execution of a well-thought-out plan will enable you to take advantage of the marketing opportunities in annuity sales.

SEMINAR MARKETING

Seminars: What Are They and Why Use Them?

A seminar is a prospecting method in which you, alone or as part of a team of professional advisors, conduct an educational and motivational meeting for a group of people who are interested in the topic being presented.

Seminars are a form of mass marketing. Although classified in this textbook as a prospecting method, seminars do more than help you identify prospects. Seminars are a proven strategy for prospecting in the annuities marketplace. They create awareness and interest in your products and services, and they serve to establish and build your reputation as an expert in annuities, especially within the context of retirement planning. In these ways, seminars also function as a preapproach vehicle.

Think of seminars as live infomercials that educate people about the retirement planning need and motivate them to want to know how annuities can help them. Because of the educational and motivational aspects of seminars, they are an effective way to obtain appointments. The objective is *not* to make an immediate sale. The only selling that takes place in the seminar is selling yourself and your ideas.

Seminars as a Prospecting Source

One advisor conducts 12 to 15 seminars a year for groups that include both preretirees and postretirees. He uses such facilities as hotels, firehouses, churches, and retirement communities. Topics include

- how to make money in a down market
- asset allocation strategies
- safety of investments while making money

He uses a company that mails 5,000 invitations and calls the prospective attendees who responded the day before the seminar to remind them of the time and location. Seminars are his primary source for obtaining annuity prospects.

Not surprisingly, in one study, advisors who were classified as "high earners" ranked seminars as the third most effective marketing tool for reaching targeted prospects, just behind referrals or centers of influence and the effective use of newsletters and brochures. — *Andy Pynnen create it.*

The general success of seminars and, specifically, the success that advisors have had using them to sell annuities are why we are looking in depth at this prospecting method. This section will discuss the advantages of seminars, some planning considerations, presentation tips, and the most important aspect—follow-up.

Advantages of Seminars

Seminars are a popular prospecting method for annuities because they appeal to the demographic age groups most interested in annuities: people aged 45 to 64, and people aged 65 and over. This appeal has much to do with the fact that typically seminars appeal to prospects who need information and have the time to seek it out—a description that fits prospects in the seniors market.

But there are other reasons why you should consider using this prospecting method.

Other Advantages of Seminars

In addition to being tailor made for the age-45-and-over annuities market, seminars offer some of the following advantages:

- Seminars enable you to maximize your time. They represent an opportunity to educate and motivate many prospects at once. Consider seminars to be a group version of the first appointment.

- Seminars create a nonthreatening environment in which you can build rapport and credibility with prospects. What other prospecting method allows you to demonstrate your knowledge of the financial problems prospects face and the solutions that you can provide?

- Seminars help you identify qualified prospects. If you use a questionnaire or feedback form, you can identify whom you should call first. In addition, answers to questions can give you insight into prospects' concerns, needs, and questions before you meet them for follow-up appointments.

- To some extent, seminars prequalify prospects. Although you initiate the seminar by inviting the prospects, they confirm their interest by attending and represent a much better prospect pool than a cold-call list. If you can bring together the right people, ask the right probing questions, present the right solutions, and project yourself as the professional source for a specialized area of expertise, such as retirement planning, your seminar will be tremendously successful.

Planning a Seminar

Arrangements, program content, and follow-up are critical to the success of a seminar. If a seminar is not well planned, you risk losing credibility with the people who attend. Therefore developing a well-thought-out plan is essential.

It is helpful to have a written game plan—a step-by-step description of what you need to do and when you need to do it. A checklist, such as the one provided at the conclusion of this section of the chapter, lets you see at a glance where you are and what remains to be done.

Your Objective

The first step in the planning process is to set your goal or objective. Before you do anything else, ask yourself what the seminar will accomplish. Your goal should be specific, attainable, and measurable. For example, you may set a goal of making 10 appointments with seminar attendees. Or your goal may be to provide an informational seminar for 15 of your best clients. The goal you set is important because it will affect other decisions regarding the seminar details.

Budget

It is especially helpful to establish a budget and work to stay within this constraint. Food is generally not served, but if you wish to provide refreshments, keep them simple and inexpensive. If you are using a hotel or restaurant, you may need to resist the pressures for lavish meals. Remember, you are selling your services and knowledge; you are not offering free food.

The Audience

Seminars Involve Target Marketing. The people you invite should have a common interest or need. This allows you to focus on the specific needs of the audience. For example, you could present a seminar that covers Social Security retirement benefits and annuities, which would generally appeal to prospects over age 65. A seminar that focused on annuities as they relate to planning for retirement, on the other hand, would generally appeal more to prospects under age 65.

Sometimes the audience will be from a preselected group and is determined by the purpose of the seminar. For example, if your purpose is to create centers of influence, your audience will be made up of other professionals who work with prospects in your target market. You will probably invite such professionals as attorneys, CPAs, and fee-based financial planners. If your objective is to improve retention in your multiline book of business, you will invite a market segment from your current client base. Finally you may want to expand your client base. In that case, you will invite new prospects (not current clients) from a specific market segment or target market. The point is that you need to make a list of invitees who have some common characteristics and needs.

To determine how many people to invite, begin by setting a goal for the number of attendees you wish to have. Initially aiming for 15 to 20 prospects is reasonable. If 15 to 20 prospects attend, you can justify costs. At the same time, the group will be small enough to allow interaction between the speaker and attendees. You will learn from experience how many people to invite to have the desired number of attendees. A good rule of thumb is to invite at least 10 people from a preselected audience for each desired attendee. The ratio of invitees to attendees will improve as your seminars become better known.

Once you have created a list of invitees, your next step is to determine how to invite them to your seminar. Individual invitation letters are the most effective way. However, newspaper ads may be effective for attracting new prospects. Regardless of how you communicate your invitation, you need to determine how you want your prospects to respond. You may want to send a return card with your invitation letters. Another method is to ask for phone reservations from those who are interested. You may even want to plan follow-up phone calls in the event that your responses fall below your expectations.

Lists

Many advisors who host public seminars consistently draw their audiences from mailing lists that are available from list vendors. Review the information about lists in the section under "Preapproaches."

One word of caution: Lists have short lifespans. Today, our society is increasingly mobile. People move more frequently. Make sure to ask your list broker for the source of the list and how often it is updated.

A list broker will also be able to give you guidance on how many invitations must be mailed to obtain the desired number of attendees. These numbers can vary, depending on the targeted audience, the topic, the time of year, and the geographic location. A conservative approach is to expect a response rate of one-quarter of one percent. This means that for every 10,000 invitations sent, there will be 25 attendees.

Evaluating Vendor Lists

Use the following series of questions to evaluate your sources of lists:

- What is the source of the list?
- How often is the list updated?
- What selections are possible within the list?
- What is the history of successful usage of the list?
- What is the minimum quantity of names you must purchase?
- What addressing formats are available?
- Is the list in zip code sequence?
- What is the delivery time?
- What will it cost?
- Why is this particular list being recommended?

Topics

The content of your seminar should be a blend of technical information and motivational material. How much of each depends on the needs of the prospects you invite. The program should be technically accurate and informative. If you give too much information, however, you may bore your prospects or they may have no need to make an appointment with you. In addition to being educational, the program should motivate attendees to meet with you for more information.

After you decide on a topic, your next step is to figure out whether the material is available or if you must develop it yourself. Many companies have seminar material for their advisors and require advisors to use it. If your company allows it, you can purchase seminar presentation material. If you decide to develop and write your own seminar material, allow enough time to research your topic thoroughly, and make sure you have adequate resources to produce it. Be sure to allow time for a compliance review by the financial services company or companies you represent.

Alternatively, you may decide to use the services of a professional presenter or advisor such as a broker, CPA, or attorney. You may even decide to help organize and cosponsor seminars where other advisors are the seminar leaders. This may be a good choice until you have some experience under your belt. If you pair up with another advisor, you will need to agree on some form of compensation such as a split in the commission. If you both invite prospects, you could offer to pay for the cost of the seminar since the other advisor is doing the majority of the speaking.

Whether you present the seminar or someone else does it for you, the seminar should establish you as an expert and a professional who can be trusted. Remember to follow your company's compliance procedures for situations in which you bring in an outside speaker.

Time Dimension

The time dimension of seminars has a couple of different meanings. First, effective seminars require a great deal of time to prepare, execute, and follow up. Many advisors who are successful in seminars contend that a seminar is not a single event but a continual process. All elements of the process must be carefully planned and implemented, which takes a great deal of time. The good news is that once the elements are satisfactorily developed, the seminar can be repeated time after time, frequently with increasing productivity.

Second, the time aspect of seminars also means selecting the best day and time to hold a seminar. The optimal day and time will depend on the needs of your audience. For example, it may be foolish to hold a seminar for your working prospects during working hours. Similarly, it may not be wise to hold a seminar for seniors late in the evening.

There are other factors to consider when choosing a date for your seminar. You need to be sensitive to holidays, holy days, and competing events. You may plan a terrific seminar, but if it competes with the NBA finals or the county fair, attendance may be adversely affected. You must keep all of this in mind as you look at the available dates and times for the facility where you will hold your seminar and examine your own schedule.

Preparing and Presenting a Professional Program

Presenting a successful seminar for the annuities marketplace involves the following steps:

- selecting the site
- announcing the seminar
- confirming attendees
- checking the facilities
- addressing miscellaneous details
- preparing the presentation
- presenting the seminar

Selecting the Site. Whether or not your seminar is being sponsored, try to have as much input as possible in site selection. A site that is inviting will result in a higher response rate. Thus it is generally recommended that you not use your office. Attendees fear high-pressure selling. If prospective attendees think a seminar will be high pressured, they will stay away. An outside meeting space creates an air of objectivity and reduces perceived pressure to buy.

The site you select should be convenient for the members of your targeted group. Parking may be a critical consideration in urban and suburban areas.

The accommodations you select should match the size of your group. A small group in a large room gives the appearance that a lot of people decided not to come. On the other hand, too small a room may cause some people to leave your seminar because they feel crowded in too small a space.

Announcing the Seminar. The seminar announcement and/or invitation literature should clearly inform prospects that the seminar will be educational in nature. It should also provide information regarding the topic, date, time, and length of each session. The seminar title should be clear and relate to the areas of prospects' identified needs such as maximizing retirement income, lowering taxes, financing healthcare, and facilitating estate planning. If your seminar will include workbooks or other written information, the announcement should highlight the benefits of these materials. You may also wish to plant the seeds for follow-up work by indicating that each attendee will be entitled to a no-cost consultation regarding his or her personal financial situation.

Some financial advisors suggest that the announcement or invitation list the advisor's credentials. If the seminar is part of a team effort, the list should include the names and accomplishments of everyone who will be sharing the platform. It is important that the intended audience perceive that a quality seminar is being offered.

There are some cases where your audience will be drawn primarily from an announcement in a publication such as an association bulletin. Be sure that the announcement clearly lists the date, location, and time of your presentation. Many financial advisors include a telephone number so that prospective attendees can call to reserve a seat. Some also tie their presentations to other association business such as normally scheduled monthly meetings. This association tie-in increases the potential for higher attendance.

Confirming Attendees. The success of any seminar depends on who attends it. Therefore it is important to monitor the mailing of invitations and equally important to monitor the response rate. Careful monitoring will allow time for you to make corrections, if necessary. The mailing itself should usually begin at least 4 weeks prior to the seminar date. When large numbers of invitations are being sent, it is best to seed the mailing with your name and those of a few trusted friends or colleagues. This gives you a mechanism to determine whether or not invitations have reached their intended destinations.

In addition to the invitation itself, your letter should contain a response mechanism—for example, a telephone number to call. Another approach is to include a stamped, self-addressed postcard as well as a number to call to reserve a seminar seat. You should also provide an e-mail address. Some financial advisors send a second (reminder) mailing.

Many advisors also suggest that if your presentation is being announced in an association bulletin, a familiar association telephone number or e-mail address should be used for seat reservations.

For best results, follow up replies with calls confirming attendance a day or two prior to the presentation.

Checking the Facilities. Checking and rechecking the facilities you have chosen will help your meeting run smoothly. If possible, try to visit the facility while another meeting is in progress. This will allow you to evaluate the lighting, the sound system, and the visibility of any screens you will use with an overhead, LCD, or slide projector. You can assess how well everyone in the room can see the speaker and judge whether the ambiance of the room reflects the feeling you wish to convey to your audience.

Consider what audiovisual equipment or visual aids, such as an easel or whiteboard, you will need before you begin calling facilities. If the facility does not provide audiovisual equipment, check that there are ample outlets for computers, projectors, or audio equipment. Double check all equipment prior to the seminar to be sure everything is in working order.

Check with the facility about refreshments, and if you serve them, keep them simple. A basic guide is to serve something wet and something dry. For example, coffee and cookies are usually a hit.

Addressing Miscellaneous Details. Consider providing name tags, pencils, paper, and handouts. These may seem like small details, but it is important to pay attention to details. They send your prospect a message about you. For example, handouts of the highest quality that include your name and address convey the message that you are professional and that you are willing to put your name on the work you do. Having paper and pencils available sends the message that what you say is important enough to write down.

You also want to plan a feedback mechanism. Some seminar presenters ask attendees to sign in, giving their names, addresses, and phone numbers. Others design an evaluation form that asks the attendees for this information, as well as for feedback on the quality and usefulness of the presentation.

Preparing the Presentation. An integral goal of seminar marketing to preretirees and retirees is to enhance your image in that marketplace. Therefore it is important to take all steps possible to heighten the professionalism of your presentation. We suggest that you use a written script and rehearse it in preparation for the seminar. (However, when conducting the actual seminar, it looks more professional if you speak from an outline or note cards, not a script.) This is particularly important if there are several presenters. A written script provides a framework for the presentation, familiarizes the presenters with the materials, and helps presenters develop answers to potential questions that may arise from the audience.

If you are working as part of a team, be sure that each speaker is aware of the overall scope of the program in order to achieve a cohesive program and avoid repetition. If possible, have each team member submit a draft of his or her presentation a month before the seminar. This allows time for necessary revision if the presentation does not match the seminar content.

Presenting a Seminar. If properly presented, a seminar helps to sell you as a competent professional. The following list gives you a few pointers that may help you make an effective seminar presentation:

- Begin and end on time.
- Speak to your audience.
- Get to the point and stay focused. Your audience wants to know what you can do for them. They do not want to hear war stories.
- Keep your goal in mind during your presentation. If you keep your goal in mind, you will stay focused.
- Speak from an outline or note cards, but do not read or memorize your speech.
- Be conversational, friendly, and enthusiastic.
- Use visual aids, if appropriate, but keep them simple.

- Avoid offensive jokes, stories, comments, or language.
- Move around as you speak. Do not remain in one spot the whole time.
- Relax, smile, and enjoy yourself. People like to work with professionals who enjoy their work.
- Ask for feedback during your presentation in the form of questions and after your presentation in the form of a critique.

Conducting an Effective Follow-up Campaign

Seminars typically serve to present you as a knowledgeable professional to a group of potential prospects. Most effective seminars are low key and avoid overt attempts to sell products or specific services. Any one-on-one selling typically occurs after the seminar. It is for this reason that the follow-up phase of the seminar takes on such significance. In fact, many advisors who use seminars end their presentation by telling their audience that the advisor will contact each attendee to answer any questions that might have resulted from the seminar.

Send each attendee a thank-you letter with an invitation to contact you to discuss any of the seminar topics. A letter offers a margin of safety for both you and your senior prospects. Some prospects are difficult to reach by phone. Moreover, some seniors are so afraid of scams that they will not conduct business over the phone unless they initiate the call. The written invitation reminds them to take action and gives them your name and telephone number.

Telephone. Following your seminar, contact the attendees by telephone or in person to schedule appointments for discussing individual needs. Ideally this follow-up should occur within one or two days of the seminar.

Some advisors try to learn more about the specific interests or needs of the prospective attendees by asking them to complete a confidential fact-finding questionnaire prior to attending the seminar. Among other things, the questionnaire asks attendees about their health and financial situation.

Follow-up Phone Script

"Hello, this is Tom Smith from ABC Advisors. Thank you very much for attending our meeting. We covered a lot of details about how annuities can enhance your retirement income. I would like to sit down with you (and your spouse if you are married) on a one-to-one basis and review some of the material that would be very important to you and your family. Are the evenings or mornings more convenient for you?"

Questionnaire. Other advisors rely on postseminar questionnaires to determine interest. A postseminar questionnaire can be a very useful tool for determining which of the attendees is most likely to be interested in learning more about your services. (See the accompanying sample postseminar questionnaire.)

The mere fact that an attendee takes the time to complete a postseminar questionnaire is a sign of interest. You can use the attitudinal questions at the end of the survey to gauge each prospect's interest and possible motivations for buying annuities.

Observation. Still other advisors rely on observation and target those people who have asked questions during the seminar presentation for a follow-up call. These advisors mix with the audience during breaks and identify those who seem to be most interested in the presentations. They also ask each of the seminar speakers to give them the names of attendees who asked them questions after the seminar. (Remember that name tags for all attendees will help you and your speakers in this process.)

Contact. Whatever technique you choose to determine which attendees will be your best prospects, try to capitalize on the goodwill and credibility you have cultivated at your seminar by scheduling a personal visit with each of the attendees. Many financial advisors recommend that you contact nonattendees as well, especially those who previously indicated that they would be in your audience.

Even when they are unable to schedule an appointment with the nonattendees, astute advisors keep these prospects on their mailing lists for a specified time. The advisors then stay in contact with them regularly, sending them newsletters or bulletins on ideas that might be of interest. They invite these prospects to their next seminar and generally get a positive response. Many financial advisors find that these prospects become clients after the second seminar.

Here are some approaches you might use when you follow up on each seminar attendee on the telephone or in person.

Example 1:   "John, at the seminar you recently attended, we had a question-and-answer period. Since the time allocated for this purpose was fairly brief, I am calling to schedule a time when we could discuss your specific questions or concerns. Would the evening or daytime be more convenient for you?"

Example 2:   "Ann, several of the speakers from the seminar you attended this week indicated that you had some excellent comments regarding some of the areas discussed. I'd like to spend some time with you covering those areas. Would the a.m. or p.m. hours best suit your schedule?"

Postseminar Questionnaire

We would very much appreciate your assistance in answering the following questions. Your responses will guide us in improving future seminars and in determining if our organization may be of assistance to you in the future.

1. Which speaker did you find the most helpful?

   _____

   _____

   _____

2. Which subject covered during the seminar was of most interest to you?

   _____

   _____

   _____

3. Briefly list any subject areas that were not covered in the seminar but which you think should have been covered.

   _____

   _____

   _____

4. You may have some questions that you did not have an opportunity to raise during the question-and-answer session. Please briefly list these questions below. We will make every effort to answer these questions for you or to find experts who can provide responses.

   _____

   _____

   _____

Name _____

Address _____

_____

Phone _____

Summary

Finally, for seminars to be a cost-effective prospecting tool, you must repeat programs regularly. Only with repeat seminars will you be able to justify the heavy commitment of time that is required to develop a viable seminar process and an effective seminar program. If your seminars acquire the reputation for being informative and valuable, they will be well attended by qualified prospects.

For your convenience, we've included a checklist of the details and logistics that need to be considered and planned for in order to make your seminar successful.

Seminar Checklist

Meeting Room
- Confirm the meeting room.
- Determine your contact. Meet this person, if possible.
- Examine the facilities in person.
- Ascertain how easy it is for your guests to find the meeting room.

Guest List
- Know who is coming.
- Determine if anyone from your organization will be there.
- Resolve budgetary concerns.

Seminar Promotion
- Arrange a schedule for printing promotional material and handouts. (Include time to proof printed material to avoid errors.) Make sure the schedule takes into account the possibility of delays at the print shop.
- Send announcements to the local newspaper, radio station(s), or other media outlets.
- Send letters or formal invitations at least two weeks before the seminar.
- Call the invitees to confirm their attendance prior to the seminar.

Getting There
- Make sure your guests know the date and precise time of the seminar.
- Give them directions to the meeting room.
- Inform guests if they will have to use a special entrance.
- Ask the hotel or office complex for directional signs, if necessary.
- Determine whether you will have a check-in desk.
- Decide how early arrivals will be handled.
- Make sure there are adequate provisions for parking.
- Determine whether your prospects will require a means of identification such as name tags.
- Decide who will look for late arrivals.

Seminar Checklist (Continued)

Meeting Facilities
- Determine how the room will be arranged.
- Resolve whether you want chairs only or chairs and tables.
- Ascertain if you will need reserved seat signs.
- Evaluate the lighting in the room. Make sure there are spare light bulbs.
- Decide if you are supplying paper, pens, and pencils.
- Find out if the speakers will need help with any equipment during the presentation.
- Determine if you will need a microphone. If so, make sure to bring one in case one cannot be located at the meeting facility.
- Determine if you will need an overhead or LCD projector.
- Find out if presenters will need a projection screen. If so, also find out whether the main room lights must be shut off and who will handle this.
- Determine if a lectern, flip chart, writing pad, or magic markers are necessary for presenters.
- Make sure to supply water and glasses for the speakers.
- Decide whether or not there will be a coffee break. If so, also decide on refreshments, and delegate someone to be responsible for obtaining them.

Seminar Content/Speakers
- Select the topics that will be covered.
- Determine who the best speakers are to address each area.
- Decide how much compensation (if any) speakers should be offered.
- Identify the most appropriate format for the presentation (for example, lecture, roundtable discussion).
- Figure out how long each person should speak.
- Choose the person who will introduce the speakers.

Problems
- Find out whom to contact if there is a problem.
- Determine whether or not the house audiovisual technician will be available.
- Have a plan in place in case someone becomes ill.
- Know where the exits and fire escapes are located.
- Be cognizant of any required security measures.
- Assign someone to deal with any incoming phone calls.
- Determine how you will handle people's use of cell phones during the seminar.
- Appoint a reliable assistant to help you run the meeting, if necessary.
- Anticipate possible problems and resolutions to those problems.

CHAPTER TWO REVIEW

Key Terms and Concepts are explained in the Glossary. Answers to the Review Questions and Self-Test Questions are found in the back of the book in the Answers to Questions section.

Key Terms and Concepts

market segment	401(k) plan
age-based market segment	pension plan
nonqualified retirement planning	additional markets for annuities
qualified retirement planning	structured settlement
individual retirement account (IRA)	charitable gift annuity
spousal IRA	charitable remainder trust
rollover IRA	private annuity
stretch IRA	preapproach
spousal rollover	direct mail
Roth IRA	building prestige
SEP IRA	professional brochure
SARSEP	approach
SIMPLE IRA	telephone approach
tax-sheltered annuity (TSA)	pivot approach
403(b) plan	

Review Questions

2-1.   Identify the features of a nonqualified deferred annuity that make it an ideal retirement planning tool.

2-2.   Describe the concept of a stretch IRA.

2-3.   Identify the income tax benefits of distributions from a Roth IRA compared to a traditional IRA.

2-4.   Explain how an immediate annuity can be used to "reinsure" a charitable gift annuity between a charitable organization and its donor.

2-5.   Describe how a deferred annuity can be purchased by the trustee of a net income with make-up charitable remainder unitrust (NIMCRUT) to build retirement assets for the donor.

2-6.   Describe the income tax consequences of a death benefit payable to the beneficiary of a nonqualified deferred annuity.

2-7.   List three ways to preapproach a prospect.

2-8.   Identify the four elements of an effective telephone approach script.

2-9.   Describe four advantages of using seminars as a marketing and prospecting tool.

Self-Test Questions

Instructions: Read Chapter 2 first; then answer the following questions to test your knowledge. There are 10 questions; circle the correct answer, and then check your answers with the answer key in the back of the book.

2-1.   The average age of a fixed-interest nonqualified deferred annuity buyer is

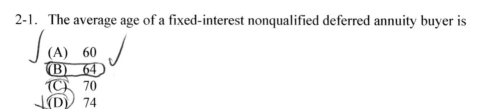

(A)   60
(B)   64
(C)   70
(D)   74

2-2.   IRAs can accept contributions up to $5,000 per year in 2008 as long as the client

(A)   has up to $5,000 of earned income for the same tax year
(B)   is under age 70 ½
(C)   is named the owner and annuitant of the IRA
(D)   is all of the above

2-3.   A client can contribute $5,000 in 2008 on behalf of his or her nonworking spouse (called a spousal IRA) plus $5,000 to his or her own IRA as long as

(A)   the nonworking spouse has $5,000 of earned income
(B)   the contributing spouse has $10,000 of earned income
(C)   the contributing spouse is the owner and annuitant of the spousal IRA
(D)   the spouse is not an active participant in a pension plan

2-4.   Which market segment contains the highest percentage of deferred annuity buyers?

(A)   age-65-and-older market segment
(B)   age-45-to-64 market segment
(C)   under-age-45 market segment
(D)   business owners market segment

2-5.   Which of the following statements regarding seminar marketing is (are) correct?

   I.   There is a constant need to stay current on the subject matter to remain credible.

   II.   Financial advisors should seek to establish postseminar individual appointments with attendees.

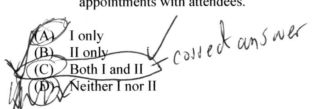

   (A)   I only
   (B)   II only
   (C)   Both I and II
   (D)   Neither I nor II

2-6.   Nonqualified deferred annuities are excellent charitable planning tools to accomplish which of the following?

   I.   Reinsure a charity's financial obligation to a donor.
   II.   Give to a charitable remainder trust.

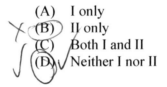

   (A)   I only
   (B)   II only
   (C)   Both I and II
   (D)   Neither I nor II

2-7.   A deferred annuity is an ideal asset to leave to a charitable organization upon death for which of the following reasons?

   I.   The nonprofit organization is not subject to income tax on the built-in gain because of its tax-exempt status.

   II.   The estate of the deceased will receive an estate tax charitable deduction for the value of the deferred annuity.

   (A)   I only
   (B)   II only
   (C)   Both I and II
   (D)   Neither I nor II

2-8. A deferred annuity can be used to fund the premiums for a life insurance policy in all of the following cases EXCEPT

(A) The client must be insurable for life insurance purposes.
(B) The event will occur based on an IRC Sec. 1035 tax-free-exchange basis.
(C) The annuity owner will have to pay income tax on the gain in the annuity if surrendered to fund the life insurance.
(D) The life insurance death benefit must be larger than the annuity's value to make it a worthwhile planning tool.

2-9. All of the following are advantages of prospecting using seminars EXCEPT

(A) Seminars are an efficient use of time.
(B) Advisors can meet prospects in a nonthreatening way.
(C) Seminars can be used to prequalify prospects.
(D) Seminars require less planning and effort than other prospecting methods.

2-10. A distribution from a pension or profit-sharing plan is eligible to be invested in a rollover IRA for all of the following reasons EXCEPT

(A) death of the participant
(B) termination of the participant's employment
(C) retirement of the participant
(D) withdrawal due to illness

NOTES

1. *Immediate Annuity Buyer Study: Profiles and Attitudes, A 2000 Report.* © 2000, LIMRA International Inc.
2. The *2006 Individual Annuity Market: Sales and Assets, A 2007 Report.* © 2007 LIMRA International Inc. ®
3. *Deferred Annuity Owner Study: Profiles, A 2003 Report.* LIMRA International Inc.
4. *Deferred Annuity Owner Study: Profiles, A 2007 Report.* © 2007, LIMRA International Inc. ®
5. *Deferred Annuity Owner Study: Profiles, A 2003 Report.* LIMRA International Inc.
6. Ibid.
7. *The 2006 Individual Annuity Market: Sales and Assets, A 2007 Report.* © 2007 LIMRA International Inc. ®
8. Ibid.
9. Printed with permission of Gail B. Goodman, president, ConsulTel Inc.

Fixed-Interest Deferred Annuities; Effective Interviewing Techniques

---

Learning Objectives

An understanding of the material in this chapter should enable you to

3-1. Identify the basic contract provisions in a fixed-interest deferred annuity.

3-2. Explain the liquidity features of fixed-interest deferred annuity policies.

3-3. Describe the main provisions for crediting interest in single-premium and flexible-premium fixed-interest deferred annuity policies.

3-4. Identify several methods for the payment of death benefits from a deferred annuity.

3-5. Describe the features and impact of several riders often found in deferred annuity contracts.

3-6. Describe the purpose and goals of the initial interview with the prospect.

3-7. Identify the sections and techniques of an effective fact-finding interview.

3-8. In general terms, identify a strategy to explain the need for retirement planning.

Chapter Outline

This chapter examines the fixed-interest deferred annuity policy. It discusses the annuity contract provisions, including how interest is credited. It also discusses withdrawals, surrenders, and policy riders. The chapter ends with a review of the objectives of meeting with the prospect within the context of the selling/planning process.

FIXED-INTEREST DEFERRED ANNUITIES

Annuity contracts that guarantee principal and some amount of interest are referred to as fixed-interest deferred annuities. They are marketed under all sorts of names to appeal to the client: guaranteed growth annuity, ultra provider, the dominator, and select guarantee, to name a few. The client basically buys the quality of the insurance company's guarantee of principal and the interest rate over the period selected.

Fixed deferred annuities may be purchased with single investments as single-premium deferred annuities (SPDAs) or with flexible investments in contracts referred to as flexible-premium deferred annuities (FPDAs). The insurance company's profit over time is the difference between what the company earns on the invested money and what it pays out to the policyowner. The company's objective is to earn at least 1.5 percent—preferably 2 percent—more than it passes on to the consumer. The company can usually do this if the policyowner holds the contract for a long enough period of time. If the policyowner chooses to terminate the contract early, the insurance company protects itself from the lost income by imposing surrender charges.

Typically, fixed-interest deferred annuities are marketed with guaranteed interest rates from one to 10 years. Higher credited interest rates, longer surrender charge periods, and higher surrender charge percentages can be found in even longer-term contracts or bonus annuities. Longer-term contracts also may incorporate a market value adjustment in addition to, or in lieu of, the contractual surrender charge.

Interest-rate-driven deferred annuities compete for the client's money based on the following factors and in approximately the following order:

- interest rate
- duration of interest rate period
- minimum guaranteed interest rate
- bonus interest rates, premium bonuses, or deferred credits
- minimum premium required
- liquidity issues, including
  - surrender-free withdrawals
  - surrender charges
  - surrender periods
  - surrender waivers such as death, long-term care, terminal illness, unemployment, and annuitization
  - market value adjustments, if any

One advantage of the fixed-interest deferred annuity is its perceived simplicity. The insurance company guarantees the principal and interest rate for a specific period of time. If the interest rate is competitive with other alternatives and also tax deferred, the annuity is very appealing.

Investment decisions over the years have to do with the interest rate offered by the insurance company—how high the rate is and how long it is guaranteed. If interest rates are at a peak and going down, locking in the higher current interest rates for the longest period available would be the best choice. The 1980s is an example of a period when this strategy was profitable. Alternatively, if interest rates are low and the likelihood is that they will increase rather than decrease, a short guarantee period is preferable so the contract owner can renew the contract at a higher interest rate as soon as possible. The years 2003 to 2005 are an example of a period in which this latter strategy would have been profitable.

Single-Premium Deferred Annuity

single-premium
deferred annuity

The *single-premium deferred annuity* is a fixed-interest annuity contract that competes for the client's investment by offering competitive current interest rates and tax deferral on the interest earnings within the contract. Typically this type of annuity is attractive to those who have invested in certificates of deposit or those who seek high-interest-rate investments. Like a certificate of deposit, it accepts a single deposit with a current interest rate that is guaranteed to some future date. At that time, the insurance company will offer a new interest rate for the next period of time. The policy's maturity may be at a date after the end of the interest guarantee period, such as age 90.

Flexible-Premium Deferred Annuity

flexible-premium deferred annuity

A *flexible-premium deferred annuity* is a tax-deferred fixed-interest annuity contract that accepts periodic premiums and typically offers a minimum guaranteed interest plus excess interest, reflecting the general interest rate marketplace for shorter periods of time. Because the insurance company has the ability to adjust interest rates, it can allow individuals to make additional contributions to the contract without unacceptable interest rate risk. An important client concern in these flexible-premium contracts is the measurement period for any surrender charge. The time period for the surrender charge may be measured from the original date of the contract or from the date of each deposit, referred to as a rolling surrender charge. This will be explained in more detail when we cover contract provisions. However, the existence of a rolling surrender charge means that the contract owner has to consider the risk this puts on each future deposit into the annuity contract. The policy's maturity may be at a future retirement or postretirement date such as age 65 or 90.

Insurance Company Financial Strength

Annuities are guaranteed by the insurance company that issues the contract, making the financial strength of the insurance company a fundamental issue the client must consider.

It is particularly important for purchasers of annuities to choose a company that will last as long as they will. Life expectancy increased to 77.8 years for the general population—75.2 years for males and 80.4 years for females in 2004.[1] As stated earlier in this textbook, it is important to understand that life expectancy indicates the age at which half of that population is no longer living. The other half is still living and may need annuity income. Annuity actuaries assume longevity in annuitants to be greater than that of the general population.[2]

As a result of increasing longevity and the long period of time an annuity contract needs to be productive for contract owners, it is prudent for individuals to purchase annuities from financially stable insurance companies. Insurance companies have failed in the past. For example, from 1979 to 1983 the Baldwin United Companies, National Investors Life, and University Life sold over $3 billion in fixed annuities. They were touted as risk free, promising interest rates of up to 15 percent and paying commissions of 5 percent. The total promised payout in year one was 20 percent! Then these companies had problems with their investments. In May 1983 the Arkansas and Indiana insurance commissioners put the companies into receivership. For more than 3 ½ years, the proceedings dragged through the courts while policyowners suffered. Some commentators did not understand what the policyowners endured during those years. They said that policyowners were made whole when Metropolitan Life assumed the contracts. For over 3 years, those annuitants agonized over what the final outcome would be. They did not know if any company would be there to stand behind their contracts. During all that time, contracts were not earning the returns that had been promised.

Benefits of Tax Deferral

tax deferral

Tax deferral for money in an annuity contract is granted by the federal government under tax law. This concept allows for the accumulation of money in a deferred-annuity contract to be free of income taxation until the funds within it are withdrawn. Tax deferral is the first feature that most people think of when they consider deferred annuities. It is a crucial aspect of nonqualified annuities. However, when annuity contracts are used for qualified plan money that already has the benefit of this feature, tax deferral is redundant as a result of the qualified plan structure. The typical complaint is that a person who puts qualified money into an annuity is paying for something he or she does not need. The annuity itself may have annual charges and expenses, but the truth is that there is no cost for the tax-deferral feature.

The federal government encourages people to leave the money in the deferred annuity until their retirement by making preretirement, nonperiodic distributions less tax efficient. The bottom line is that the income tax deferral on money inside annuities is granted by the federal government and can be changed or taken away by the federal government.

The good news about income tax deferral in deferred annuities is that the downside of paying income taxes on the earnings does not happen every year nor does it reduce the funds that a contract owner otherwise would have available to invest.

The bad news is that income taxes eventually will have to be paid. Deferring income taxes during an individual's high income-earning preretirement tax years and paying the taxes in lower post-age 59 ½ tax years is profitable. Doing otherwise is less tax efficient. Deferred annuities are usually purchased for the purpose of accumulating money for retirement. To accomplish this, the client needs time for compound interest to multiply the retirement money that will be used as an income generator during retirement.

The deferral of income taxes on money available within qualified plans and nonqualified annuities gives people time to accumulate a block of money that is intended to be used to provide income in the future. The larger the retirement fund base, the greater the income. Figure 3-1 illustrates the accumulation and distribution of annuity funds.

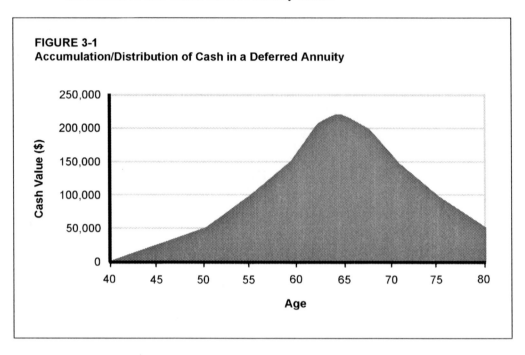

FIGURE 3-1
Accumulation/Distribution of Cash in a Deferred Annuity

ANNUITY CONTRACT PROVISIONS

Insurance companies develop and sell annuity contracts. The contract between the insurer and the client describes what happens during the accumulation and distribution phases of the contract. It sets forth the rights and obligations of the contracting parties. Generally speaking, the client agrees to be a purchaser and to place money into an annuity contract in order to have the rights offered under the contract. The insurance company agrees to the obligations because it has the capacity to meet those obligations and is in the business of doing so as a for-profit enterprise. Although insurance companies are regulated by the individual states, and contract forms have to be acceptable to each state, in the interest of efficiency, there is a great deal of standardization in all annuity contracts.

The annuity contract's general provisions include a statement defining the document as a contract between the insurance company and the contract owner. The documentation of the agreement is the contract, the application, and any riders or endorsements attached to it. The application identifies the contract owner and successive owners (if named), the beneficiary and any successive beneficiaries, and the annuitant or annuitants. The general provisions also include the premium payment arrangement—such as single or flexible—and define the accumulation value of the contract.

Policyowner

The contract owner is the person or entity that applies for and purchases the annuity, who has all legal rights in the policy, and whose Social Security number or tax identification number is shown in the contract. The IRS uses the term *holder* and, although the IRS does not specifically define the term, it generally means whoever is holding the income tax liability, no matter what other title that holder might have.

Entity/Non-natural Person Owner

It also is possible to have an entity or a nonnatural person, as opposed to a natural person, own an annuity. However, if an irrevocable trust, corporation, or other nonnatural person is not simply acting as an agent for a natural person, all tax deferral in the annuity contract will be lost and current earnings will be taxable.[3]

Joint Owners

joint owners

It is possible to have co-owners or *joint owners* of an annuity contract. This means that all owners will have to agree on any changes to the contract, or the insurance company will have to refuse the change.

Annuitant

Because the annuitant(s) provides the measuring life (or lives) for the annuity contract, the annuitant must be a living natural person and not an entity. Owners and beneficiaries can usually change during the lifetime of an annuity contract (although there may be adverse tax consequences with a change of owner), but annuitants may not change.

The contract owner may also choose to add, if allowed, contingent annuitants, such as a spouse, to become the annuitant should the primary annuitant die.

The insurance company's promise to pay annuity payments is calculated based on the age and sex of the annuitant. Although provisions normally are not made for a change of annuitant, they are made in the contract for the changes required if the age or sex of that annuitant has been misstated on the application.

Joint Annuitants

joint annuitants

Some policies may also allow *joint annuitants*. Normally joint annuitants are named when joint owners are named and generally should be restricted to use for spouses only. The effect of naming joint annuitants is to allow the annuity policy to continue to stay in force and not pay a death benefit until the death of both annuitants.

Beneficiary

As with the owner and annuitant, the annuity policy must also provide a designation for the beneficiary, who will generally receive the death benefits payable from the annuity upon the death of the annuitant. Although there are normally only one or two owners and annuitants, there can virtually be any number of beneficiaries listed in the policy. Beneficiaries can be living people or entities such as trusts, businesses, or other entities. In addition, a revocable beneficiary designation can be changed as frequently as the owner wishes as long as the insurance company receives the necessary paperwork to properly record the transaction.

Annual Fees

Some deferred annuities may charge a nominal annual contract maintenance fee such as one percent of the cash value not to exceed $20 to $50. These fees are usually deducted from the annuity cash values, and they will often expire when the contract accrues a certain amount of cash value such as $5,000 or $10,000. Recent competition among annuity products, however, has made this contract provision less common in newly issued annuity contracts.

Minimum Initial Premium

Each annuity contract will designate a minimum premium that the policyowner must pay to purchase an annuity. Normally these amounts are in the $5,000 to $10,000 range for single-premium policies and $25 to $50 per month for flexible-premium policies. Insurance companies may designate a different minimum amount, depending on the type of funds the client places inside the annuity. For example, a policy might show a minimum premium of $1,000 for a qualified single-premium annuity but still keep the nonqualified annuity minimum premium at $5,000. Lower premium amounts are common for qualified contracts so that the annuity can accept small annual IRA contributions.

Issue-Age Requirements

Each annuity contract will have a provision for the minimum and maximum age of the owner or the annuitant who can purchase the contract. Generally the insurance company is more interested in the age of the annuitant for purposes of mortality. But the issue age of the owner is also important because of legal issues related to minors who purchase the contract. Normally an insurance company does not want a minor to own one of its policies because of the minor's legal right, upon reaching the age of 18, to rescind a purchase made while he or she was a minor. For our purposes, we will consider the issue age of the annuitant. Usually annuity contracts allow annuitants between the ages of 18 and 85. Some companies may stop issuing annuities at age 70 or 75; other companies will issue annuities up to age 90.

In addition, the insurance company may limit the issue age based on the type of funds in the annuity. Qualified annuity contracts typically carry a maximum issue age of 70 while nonqualified annuities will be issued to age 85 or 90. The reason for the qualified funds' limitation is based on the minimum distribution requirements for qualified annuity contracts. The tax code stipulates that qualified plans distribute a certain percentage of the account after the owner reaches age 70 ½. The insurance company does not want to accept new policies with these types of funds at the same time the policyowner will be forced to take immediate distributions. This tax code distribution requirement goes against the fundamental principle of the insurance company's desire to have a long-term investment from the policyowner. Minimum distributions will be explained in Chapter 7.

Crediting Interest

The amount of interest the annuity product earns is of primary importance to the owner of the policy. In addition, because the initial interest rate is guaranteed for some period of time, the length of the guarantee period is critical. Furthermore, the owner needs to know how the insurance carrier has typically treated its policyowners in terms of renewal interest rates—that is, the interest rates declared once the initial guaranteed interest rate period has expired.

Interest Rates and Guarantee Periods

When individuals consider purchasing a deferred annuity, they are most interested in two areas: (1) What is the current interest rate available, and (2) what length of time is that interest rate guaranteed? Is it for one year only, for 2 years, for 5 years, or longer? The length of time the annuity will pay the initial interest rate is important. Policyowners need to know how long they can count on the insurance company to pay the specified interest rate. Often the *interest rate guarantee period* is tied to the length of the annuity's surrender charge period.

Minimum Interest Guarantees

Fixed-interest deferred annuity contracts will also provide a minimum interest rate, and the insurance company guarantees that it will never credit an interest rate less than this percentage to the annuity. Until recently this rate has typically been about 3 percent. Even if the economy or market is at an all-time low, this provision allows policyowners to feel comfortable, knowing that they will earn at least 3 percent per year, no matter what the economy is doing.

However, many insurance companies have lowered the guaranteed rate on new contracts below these levels due to a prolonged period of historically low market interest rates.

Some annuity contracts now offer a guaranteed minimum rate as low as 1.5 percent. Other companies have adopted the practice of determining the guaranteed rate referenced to an index. This index approach has been sanctioned by several states and may be adopted by more. Under the index method, the rate determined by reference to the index can change as often as every calendar quarter. However, the use of the index to determine an annuity's guaranteed interest rate does not mean the rate on an individual annuity can change every quarter. Rather, an individual annuity contract takes as its guaranteed rate the rate in effect in the quarter it is purchased and then retains that guaranteed rate for the life of the contract. Thus an annuity purchased in the fourth quarter of the year could have a guaranteed rate of 2 percent for the life of the contract while another annuity purchased a few weeks later in the first quarter of the next year could have a guaranteed rate of 2.2 percent for the life of the contact. Generally states that have adopted the index method for minimum guaranteed interest rates for fixed-interest deferred annuities provide that the guaranteed rate will always be more than 1 percent but less than 3 percent.[4]

Bonus Interest Rates

Bonus interest rates are extra amounts of interest granted to new purchasers of fixed-interest deferred annuities that are paid in addition to the normal stated current interest rate. These amounts are usually based on the total dollars contained in the contract during its first year and are added to the current interest rate credited at the end of the first year. Bonus-plan annuities are designed to attract money from existing annuity contracts, which still may be subject to a surrender charge, by paying extra interest in the first year. This extra interest (the bonus) is designed to offset some of the loss caused by the termination of the old annuity policy. Clients must understand that these bonuses have an indirect cost behind them. Thus the financial advisor must be sure to tell prospects of any circumstance in which the bonus will not be paid, such as early termination or surrender.

Both the client and advisor should be well informed regarding any bonus interest rates. Bonus rates are enticements to get the individuals to purchase an annuity. Bigger enticements usually mean bigger constraints on when that bonus will be applied or earned. Any forfeiture and possibly even a withdrawal prior to the end of the surrender charge period could void the bonus.

Unfortunately, interest rate bonuses often encourage replacement of annuities. The policyowner is lured by the high interest rate and a bonus above the normal current interest rate; the annuity owner may feel that the bonus will help to offset any surrender penalties he or she may incur. Bonus annuities will bear much higher surrender charges than a nonbonus product, putting the policyowner at a still greater disadvantage.

Example: A policyowner is currently in the sixth year of a 7-year fixed-interest deferred annuity, and an advisor proposes the policyowner move the annuity to a bonus-interest product paying 5 percent annually with a 2 percent additional bonus. If the surrender charge period is 1 percent on an account value of $10,000, the surrender charge equals $100. By receiving an extra 2 percent on $10,000, the policyowner earns $200. This technique therefore could be used to persuade the policyowner to move her funds now instead of leaving the funds with the original carrier—or at the very least waiting until the surrender charge period is over. Moving the annuity now will subject the client to a new surrender charge period within the replacement annuity contract.

When interest rate bonuses are used, the bonus is usually offered for 1 year to 5 years, after which the subsequent current interest rate may be reduced. Clients need to understand this and to know that the insurance company will seek to keep their money for a longer period of time with surrender charges or penalties so that these products remain profitable.

Deferred credits, a variation of a bonus, may not be paid unless the contract is still in force for periods of time up to 10 to 12 years. A typical example might be an insurance company that offers a 5 percent bonus interest rate, but it is not guaranteed until the policyowner keeps the annuity in force at the insurance company for the specified period of years.

Premium Bonus

premium bonus

A *premium bonus* is similar to an interest rate bonus incentive found in deferred annuities except that the percentage of bonus interest granted by the issuing insurance company is applied to the premium when it goes into the contract, not added later to the current interest rate paid on total dollars accrued after they were deposited into the contract. Using the above example, a 3 percent premium bonus would pay $300 (3% x $10,000 = $300), and this amount would be immediately added to the client's policy. Check the contract provisions to determine how much, if any, of this premium bonus is actually guaranteed and what the additional surrender charges are to have a premium bonus applied to the policy.

Renewal Interest Rates

A critical area for a prospective purchaser to consider is how the company treats its policyowners regarding the interest rate it declares it will pay when the guarantee period is over. For example, if an annuity owner purchases a policy with a one-year interest rate guarantee period of 5 percent, at the end of the first year the insurance company will declare what interest rate the company will credit for the second policy year. The prospect should know if the rate for the second year will be competitive with what other annuities are paying at that time. Will the *renewal interest rate* equal the same rate the insurance company is giving to newly issued policies? Will the renewal rate drop to the guaranteed policy minimum?

renewal interest rate

A problem that can crop up in fixed-interest deferred annuities is that their renewal interest rate, especially in times of decreasing interest rates, may be less than what most people desire. This is not very different from what happens with certificates of deposit with banks. However, it often feels to individuals that insurance companies and banks attract their attention with higher first-year teaser interest rates in which companies may give up some of their spread or profit. Later, when the rates are up for renewal, the companies lower renewal rates to increase their spread.

Whether true or not, this feeling is most prevalent during times of falling interest rates and is most annoying to clients if their annuity contracts have surrender charges that prevent them from moving their money to a more profitable place. This has led some annuity purchasers to think of fixed annuities as "trust me" contracts because buyers are forced to rely on the insurance company to provide a competitive rate. Purchasers are put in the position of having to trust that the insurance company will not take advantage of them by providing exceedingly low interest rates during the period in which they are locked into the contract by a surrender charge.

To avoid the ill will that this perception may cause, a few insurance companies have designed fixed-interest deferred annuity contracts with renewal interest rates tied to some outside index that is not controlled by the insurance company such as 5-year Treasury note rates. Insurers have also created annuities that mimic the renewal process of certificates of deposit. That is, when the renewal interest rate is announced, annuity holders may move their money without the imposition of a surrender charge if they do so within 30 days. After that 30-day window, contract owners will receive the renewal interest rate for the period specified, and early withdrawal prior to the maturity date will result in a withdrawal charge.

Liquidity

Deferred annuities are purchased with long-term accumulation in mind and particularly as retirement savings tools. In accordance with those goals, annuities are not structured to be liquid investments. Nevertheless, policyowners need to know how they can access the funds, if needed, in the annuity product they are buying.

Withdrawals or Surrenders

Deferred annuities are retirement planning financial tools. Because the goal is to have an annuity as a long-term investment, the insurance companies design deferred annuities to be illiquid investments during the early years of the policy. The length of the period of illiquidity is concurrent with the period of time the company needs the policy to stay on the books to be profitable.

In the event the policyowner needs to access funds prior to maturity, the owner has the option of requesting a *withdrawal*, also called a *partial surrender*. Withdrawal provisions in deferred annuity contracts allow the policyowner limited withdrawal of funds prior to maturity of the contract.

If the owner needs to access all of his or her annuity values, the owner can request a full *surrender* of the policy. A full surrender provision in a deferred annuity contract allows the policyowner total withdrawal of funds prior to maturity of the contract, which results in termination of the contract.

The surrender or withdrawal, if made during the *surrender charge period*, is normally subject to a surrender charge. If the withdrawal is requested after the policy is beyond its surrender charge period, the policyowner should be able to access the withdrawal without any charges imposed by the insurance company. Withdrawals are not expected to be repaid to the annuity contract. In fact, with single-premium deferred annuities, the policyowner cannot reinvest the withdrawn funds even if he or she is able to. With flexible-premium policies, the withdrawal can later be paid into the annuity policy as new premiums, but the policyowner should

withdrawal

partial surrender

surrender

surrender charge period

make sure the policy does not inflict a new set of surrender charges on those funds.

Most nonqualified annuity contracts do not make loan provisions available to the policyowner. This is probably due to the fact that loans taken from annuity contracts entered into after August 13, 1982, are taxable to the extent that the cash value of the contract immediately before the loan exceeds the investment in the contract. Therefore, in terms of access to annuity values, our discussion will be in the context of withdrawals or surrenders.

Surrender Charges

surrender charge

Surrender charges are used by the insurance company to encourage purchasers to make long-term investment commitments. If contract owners want to take money out of their annuity contracts prior to the end of the period to which they committed when they invested in the contract, the insurer imposes a charge. In fixed annuities, the period during which the insurer can impose a surrender charge typically lasts 5 to 10 years, depending on the company that issues it.

A surrender charge is paid from the annuity values. It is usually highest within the first years of the contract or within the first years after money is put into the contract, and it decreases and is eliminated over the years.

Example: A 7 percent, 7-year surrender charge decreasing 1 percent per year means that any amount withdrawn is subject to a 7 percent charge in year 1, a 6 percent charge in year 2, and so on until the money has been in the contract for a full 7 years. Money that has been in this contract for 7 years can be entirely withdrawn without a surrender charge. See Table 3-1 for a comparison of two different surrender charge schedules that both start with 7 percent and end in 7 years. As the table shows, one schedule is much more liquid than the other.

---

accumulation value

surrender value

The annuity value before any surrender charges is usually called the *accumulation value*; the account value after surrender charges have been deducted is called the *surrender value*. The surrender value is the actual amount the owner would receive upon a complete and total surrender of the policy.

A "rolling" surrender charge begins with each additional investment into the contract. This means that the surrender charge is applicable to each contribution to the contract for the full surrender charge period from the date money is put into the contract. In the example above, if the surrender charge was a rolling one, any money added to this contract in the eighth year would have to remain in the contract for 7 full years before it would be free of surrender charges. Typically the older money, which is free of surrender charges, plus the free-corridor amount (described below) would be withdrawn first to avoid the surrender charge on the new money in this contract.

TABLE 3-1
Annuity Surrender Charges

Policy Year	Company A Surrender Charge Percentage	Company B Surrender Charge Percentage
1	7%	7%
2	6	7
3	5	7
4	4	5
5	3	5
6	2	3
7	1	1
8	0	0

Rolling surrender charges can sometimes be a source of client confusion and complaints. In our example, it would be understandable that after the first 7 years the contract owner would remember only that there was an 7-year surrender charge but not remember that putting more money into the policy would create constraints on that amount of new money for another 7 years. It is possible that the contract owner could lodge a complaint merely because he or she did not understand what rolling surrender charges entail. Such charges may also influence clients not to put additional funds into their contracts. For those reasons, rolling surrender charges can be counterproductive.

Example: Let's assume that an annuity owner has a $15,000 annuity accumulation value. The annuity owner requests a $1,000 withdrawal from the annuity policy. The annuity has a 5 percent surrender charge in the year of withdrawal. The company must be sure to ask if the annuity owner wants $1,000 before or after the surrender charge has been applied. The difference is important. If the client needs $1,000 after all surrender charges have been subtracted, the company must subtract both the $1,000 withdrawal and the 5 percent surrender charge from the annuity cash value. The insurance company accomplishes this by dividing $1,000 by 1 minus the surrender charge.

The formula is $1,000 / .95 = $1,053.

Therefore to net $1,000, the client must withdraw $1,053.

If, on the other hand, the client wants to withdraw only $1,000 before surrender charges have been deducted, the insurance company will deduct $1,000, keep $50 for the surrender charge, and pay the owner $950 ($1,000 − $50 = $950). Chapter 7 will explore the income tax implications of surrenders and withdrawals.

Misconception About Penalty Tax. A misconception sometimes occurs about the surrender charge the insurance company imposes against the policyowner and the penalty tax the Internal Revenue Service imposes against the withdrawn annuity cash value. The surrender charge is paid by the policyowner from the annuity cash value. The 10 percent penalty tax for premature distributions is a tax the policyowner pays on his or her annual income tax return, along with any income tax owed on the gain in the annuity proceeds.

Example: A policyowner aged 52 withdraws $10,000 from an annuity with an accumulation value of $82,000, all of which is considered taxable income. The policyowner will be subject to a surrender charge of 6 percent, or $600 ($10,000 x 6% = $600). Therefore the policyowner will actually receive $9,400 ($10,000 − $600 = $9,400).

Because the policyowner is under age 59 ½, the withdrawal is subject to a 10 percent penalty tax against the $9,400 net proceeds.[5] The penalty tax is equal to $940 ($9,400 x .10 = $940). And the $9,400 is subject to income tax that is payable at the owner's marginal tax bracket.

The annuity owner receives $9,400, and the insurance company keeps $600. The penalty tax of $940 is paid by the annuity owner to the IRS on his income tax return, and he may use part of $9,400 to pay the penalty, as well as the income tax due on the $9,400.

---

free-corridor amount

Free-Corridor Amount

To accommodate a contract owner's unforeseen need for money, practically all companies provide a free withdrawal corridor. A free corridor is some maximum amount of money that a contract owner can withdraw from the contract each year without incurring a surrender charge.

If a contract owner elects to make an early withdrawal of just part of the funds in an annuity contract before the end of the surrender charge period, there is likely to be a free-corridor amount that he or she can withdraw without any charge. Normally this amount is about 10 percent of the last year's accumulation value or 10 percent of the initial premium paid. However, some contracts do not allow any withdrawals without charge; the most generous allow withdrawals of up to 15 percent per contract year without charge. Amounts in excess of the free corridor amount are subject to proportional surrender charges.

Examine surrender charges and free-corridor provisions carefully. A client should be confident that there are no foreseeable situations that will result in withdrawing funds prematurely and incurring a surrender charge. If the client makes a withdrawal and incurs a surrender charge for a situation that he or she should have foreseen, nobody wins.

Bailout Provision

Generally a bailout provision allows the contract owner to fully surrender the annuity contract without incurring any surrender charges imposed under the annuity contract if the new current interest rate drops by a certain percentage from the current interest rate of a previous period. Another name for a bailout provision is an escape clause.

For example, an annuity might offer a bailout provision that allows the contract to be surrendered if the current interest rate drops 2 percent below the current interest rate of a previous period. Assuming that the previous current interest was 6 percent, if the current interest rate for the next crediting period falls below 4 percent, the annuity owner may surrender the contract completely and not be subject to any contract surrender charges. However, the 10 percent IRS penalty and general income taxation of interest received from the contract would still apply to a surrender made under the bailout provision.

Waiving Surrender Charges

Almost all fixed annuities waive surrender charges or market value adjustments at the death of either the contract owner or the annuitant—but not both. In addition, some, but not all, annuities will waive the surrender charges if the policyowner wants to annuitize his or her values into a guaranteed income stream.

In some cases, there are waivers of surrender charges for withdrawals or full surrenders due to admittance to a long-term care facility, terminal illness, disability, and even unemployment of either the contract owner or the annuitant. Owners of contracts in which the annuitant and the contract owner are different individuals need to know whether these waivers-of-surrender-charge provisions apply to the annuitant's or the contract owner's condition.

One important issue with respect to penalty-free withdrawals that must be examined for any contract issued with qualified funds is whether or not the insurance company will waive surrender charges for any required minimum distributions.

Example:	An annuity owner purchases a qualified annuity on March 1, using $55,000 of annuity funds from another policy she is exchanging. Her required minimum distribution for the year is 6 percent. She must take the distribution by December 31 of the same year. Because this particular insurance company imposes a 7 percent surrender charge for withdrawals in the first year, she might be boxed into a corner. On the one hand, she must take the distribution to be in compliance with the tax code; on the other hand, the insurance company will impose a penalty against her for taking the distribution from her annuity to comply with what the tax law mandates.

She can resolve this dilemma by taking the distribution before the annuity is exchanged. That way, her distribution is taken from the old policy and she will not need a distribution from this policy until the next year when (ideally) she is eligible for a free-corridor amount. Clients and advisors need to fully understand the consequences of minimum distributions and how they interact with the particular policy's surrender charges.

Market Value Adjustments

Market value adjustments are features added to some deferred annuities to discourage surrenders prior to the expiration of their initial contractually guaranteed current interest rate. Their intent is for insurance companies to share some of the risk of interest rate changes in the economy with the annuity's contract owner. If, during this type of annuity contract's initial interest rate guarantee period, money in excess of any free-corridor amount is withdrawn, it is subject to a *market value adjustment (MVA)*. The MVA is an increase or decrease in the annuity's value, depending on the level of the general economy's interest rates relative to the interest rates of the contract from which the withdrawal is taken. Annuities with MVA features often offer a slightly higher current interest rate than a comparable fixed annuity without MVA features.

market value adjustment (MVA)

The MVA works in the annuity contract in a manner similar to the way individual bond prices fluctuate. For example, if a contract owner has a deferred annuity with an initial contractually guaranteed interest rate of 8 percent for a term of 7 years, and similar contracts after 3 years into the term are being issued with 4 percent interest rates, the contract owner can expect some gain upon early surrender before the 7-year term has expired. This is because the surrender will relieve the insurance company from its 8 percent obligation in a market where interest rates have decreased to 4 percent. On the other hand, if the opposite occurred and the existing initial contractual interest rate obligation was for 4 percent in a current interest rate market of 8 percent, the contract owner can expect a negative MVA and therefore will receive a smaller surrender value.

Death Benefits

Deferred annuities are traditionally purchased to build retirement nest eggs for the policyowner. However, if the entire annuity value is not consumed during retirement, when the annuitant dies, the annuity will still be in force. Therefore deferred annuities must have provisions for a beneficiary or some other party to legally receive the values at the annuitant's death.

death benefit

Deferred annuity contracts can be classified in one of two ways depending on how the *death benefit* is payable in the policy: Policies are either annuitant driven or owner driven. In an annuitant-driven contract, the death of the annuitant causes the payment of the death benefit. However, if the annuity contract specifies a death benefit free of surrender charges at the death of an owner, it is referred to as an owner-driven contract. Regardless of the distinction, depending on the contract, the insurance company may still apply surrender charges at death.

The majority of annuity contracts are annuitant driven. That is, the death-benefit provisions become effective when the annuitant dies, and other provisions become effective based on the annuitant's age, health, and so on. If the contract owner and the annuitant are the same person, the only question to be resolved is the best legal way to distribute the money to the beneficiary.

If the death occurs prior to the time that annuitization payments have begun and an individual who is not a spouse is the beneficiary, the contract proceeds payable to that nonspouse beneficiary must either be distributed (1) within 5 years of the death of the annuitant/owner or (2) as an annuity based on the life expectancy of the beneficiary, as long as payments begin within one year of the date of the owner's death (or such later date as the Secretary of the Treasury may, by regulations, prescribe).[6]

Spousal Beneficiary Options

Under the tax code, the spouse as the beneficiary of a deferred annuity contract may choose not to accept the death benefit and instead may choose to continue the annuity contract with the insurance company. The insurance company will change the owner from the deceased person's name to that of the surviving spouse. The surviving spouse now has the right as the owner to name a new beneficiary. This right exists whether the policy is a nonqualified annuity or a qualified deferred-annuity contract.

Example: Suppose Larry purchases a deferred annuity and is the owner and annuitant, and he names his wife, Laura, as the beneficiary. Upon Larry's death, Laura has two choices: She can either keep the policy in force in her own name (the insurance company will then change the owner and annuitant designation to Laura's name, and she will need to name a new beneficiary), or she can accept the proceeds as a death benefit.

Settlement Options

Deferred annuity contracts also include provisions for taking the money out of the contract at some future contract-owner-determined date—called annuitization—or at the insurance company's designated maximum age at which distributions must begin—also known as the *maturity date*.

maturity date

These optional modes of settlement may be taking a lump-sum withdrawal, leaving the proceeds in the contract at interest, choosing fixed-period or fixed-amount payments, or selecting the various life-contingent or joint-life-contingent options described in Chapter 6. People sometimes paid little attention to these contractual provisions in the past because the guarantees were thought to be too low to be of consequence. This is no longer true. As interest rates have fallen and longevity has increased, the guaranteed lifetime annuitization factors and interest rate guarantees of 3 percent or 4 percent have real value in comparison to the guarantees in new annuity contracts.

The minimum payout rates for settlement options are listed in the annuity policy. In a normal economy, these rates are much lower than what the annuity company can afford to pay. Therefore it is important for the owner to look at the guaranteed settlement option rates in the policy and compare those rates to the current offerings from the insurance company to be sure to obtain the best rates available.

Annuity Riders

Annuity policies can have riders attached to them to add various features to the annuity. The following describe some of the more common annuity riders.

Terminal Illness

terminal illness rider

A *terminal illness rider* generally makes annuity values available to the policyowner if the annuitant becomes "terminally ill." Terminally ill is commonly defined as having 12 months or less life expectancy as determined by the annuitant's doctor. The rider usually allows the owner to access up to 75 percent of annuity values without a surrender charge. Generally the owner and annuitant are the same person, but in a situation where they are two different people, it is important to check the policy to determine if the terminal illness provision is applicable to the owner or the annuitant.

The rider should specify the definition of terminally ill and what evidence the annuitant/owner must provide to the insurance company for this option to be activated. Also the insurance company may have a provision that if the annuitant becomes terminally ill in the first 12 months of the insurance contract, the owner will not be able to activate this provision. Therefore this type of provision is usually not helpful to those who are already ill at policy issue.

Long-Term-Care Benefit

long-term care benefit rider

A *long-term-care benefit rider* generally provides the owner of the contract access to cash values if the annuitant has to enter a long-term care facility. This rider typically allows the owner to access 50 to 100 percent of annuity values without a surrender charge. The purpose of the rider is to provide peace of mind so that if annuity owners have to go to long-term care facilities, they will have access to funds to pay for these costs without incurring high surrender charges. Additional benefits may be offered such as eldercare resources, referral and consultation services, and discounted long-term care services from a specified group of providers.

Most riders will state at policy issue a maximum age the annuitant can be and still have this rider made available to the owner. It is important when a policy is replaced to be sure the policy being exchanged does not contain significant benefits, such as a long-term-care benefit rider, that could be lost if the new policy does not make the same features available to the owner, or if the annuitant is too old to have this rider on the new policy.

Effect of the Pension Protection Act of 2006. With the enactment of the Pension Protection Act of 2006, new hybrid products that combine annuities with LTC insurance are being introduced. Beginning January 1, 2010, tax-free distribution status will be given to both annuity assets and LTC insurance rider benefits used for a qualified LTC purpose. Under prior law, withdrawals taken from the annuity to pay the LTC insurance premiums were taxable and subject to the 10 percent IRS penalty prior to age 59 ½.

LTC Insurance Riders Permitted for Annuities. The act allows annuities as well as life insurance contracts to contain LTC insurance riders. As with life insurance contracts, the portion of the annuity that provides the LTC insurance coverage is treated as a separate contract, preserving its qualified status (except as otherwise provided by regulation).

Charges Against Cash Value to Pay LTC Insurance Premiums Are Excluded From Gross Income. Under the act, charges to pay LTC insurance premiums against the cash surrender value of the life insurance policy or cash value of the annuity that contains the qualified LTC insurance rider are not includable in income. That is, it is possible under the act to pay for LTC insurance out of the cash value of the insurance or annuity contract, and such payments will not be treated as taxable distributions from the embedding policy [§ 72(e)(11)(A)]. The investment in the contract is reduced by such charges though not below zero. Moreover, such charges (being tax favored already) cannot be deducted as medical expenses.

Qualified Plan Riders

Depending on how the annuity policy is drafted by the particular insurance company, it may provide for the acceptance of qualified funds through the addition of riders to the policy. Riders are normally provided to allow IRA funds, 403(b)/tax-sheltered annuity funds, and IRC Sec. 457 funds into otherwise nonqualified annuity policies. Alternatively, the annuity policy may have specific versions drafted for each of the qualified plan types. It is important that the financial advisor knows how the specific company handles the qualified plan provisions to ensure that he or she applies for the correct type of annuity.

SELLING FIXED-INTEREST DEFERRED ANNUITIES

Replacements

To determine a prospect's financial needs, the advisor may often develop a list of the prospect's assets. When reviewing the client's assets, the advisor should determine if the client owns any annuity policies. But beware: This review can lead to unnecessary replacement of existing annuity contracts, and the insurance industry has been criticized heavily for this part of the selling process. Policies should not be replaced unless doing so is in the best interest of the client. Clients must clearly understand that new surrender charges will apply, new commissions will be earned, and other benefits may be lost before they can make an informed decision to change insurance carriers. Replacements and necessary disclosures will be addressed in detail in Chapter 8.

Illustrations

Most insurance companies have computer systems that will generate an illustration for a fixed-interest deferred annuity. Although signed illustrations are not required in most states (as they are with life insurance illustrations), they are generally helpful in the sales process because they give the prospect a visual description. The illustrations may show the prospect columns displaying the guaranteed minimum values with 3 percent growth, the accumulation value at the then-current interest rate, and the respective surrender values under each scenario year by year. All this data helps to show the client how the annuity product works.

Commissions

Fixed-interest deferred annuity commissions paid to advisors are determined as a percentage of the money the client invests in the contract. Commissions are typically from 1.5 percent to 11 percent of the premium. Generally speaking, the higher the commission, the more constraints there will be on the policyowner's ability to surrender the contract.

Fixed-interest deferred annuity commissions are quite a bit less compared to life insurance commissions, which normally are approximately 50 percent of the first year premium. However, this is an apples-to-oranges comparison because with most annuities, the policyowner generally pays just one premium. With life insurance, future premiums are expected for many years from which the advisor will continue to earn commissions.

Competition With Certificates of Deposit

Fixed-interest deferred annuities often compete for dollars from long-term investors with other investment alternatives that generate taxable interest. Interest-bearing investments compete on the basis of return and safety. Investors who agree to invest their money for longer periods of time demand to be paid more interest than those who invest their money for shorter periods of time. The long-term investor is taking more risk because of the longer amount of time money is at risk and the loss of the right to invest those proceeds elsewhere.

Fixed-interest deferred annuities are considered long-term investments because the pricing structure usually includes a surrender charge. Ideally the investor should be sure he or she will not need to access the funds prior to age 59 ½ and/or until after the surrender charge is no longer applicable. Therefore these annuities do not compete for the client's short-term money, which belongs in checking accounts, savings accounts, money market funds, or even short-term bond funds, which provide instant liquidity with little, if any, market risk.

A certificate of deposit is one of the main investment alternatives that typically competes with fixed-interest deferred annuities. The basic issue that concerns these investors is safety. Unlike certificates of deposit, fixed-interest deferred annuities are not insured by the federal government under the Federal Deposit Insurance Corporation (FDIC). When banks sell annuities, the banks will explicitly point out that annuities are not bank deposits, are not FDIC insured, are not insured by any federal government agency, have no bank guarantee, and may lose value.

FDIC Versus Guaranty Associations

A Life and Health Guaranty Association operates in each state under the supervision of the state insurance commissioner. It is the regulatory structure that protects its resident contract owners, insureds, beneficiaries, and annuitants against losses from failing insurance companies. Each state determines the maximum amounts it may reimburse contract owners under various types of insurance contracts; these maximums can range from as low as $100,000 in one state to as high as $500,000 in another.

The states do not wish to be relied upon by the client as the insurer of last resort, and therefore state laws typically prohibit insurers and advisors from using the existence of the guaranty association to sell annuities. That is, it is not only false but also illegal to assure clients that they need not worry about the financial strength of the insurance company because the state provides a guarantee. The bottom line is that the financial viability of the insurance company is important to individuals, particularly regarding fixed-interest deferred annuity products, in which all promises by the company are entirely secured by the insurance company's general account.

Once an acceptable level of safety is determined, the next question that the prospect typically asks is about the rate of interest to be received and how the interest rate compares to similar investments. Table 3-2, for example, compares a single-premium fixed-interest deferred annuity to a certificate of deposit. Comparisons of alternatives should be presented to prospects before a purchase decision is made.

TABLE 3-2
Single-Premium Fixed-Interest Deferred Annuity Compared to CD

Type of Investment	How Liquid Is the Investment?	How Safe Is the Investment?	Current Interest Rate*	Income Taxation Attributes
1-year certificate of deposit	Interest penalty applied if withdrawn early	FDIC insured up to $100,000, including other deposits	4.45%	Taxed as interest is earned
Fixed-interest deferred annuity with a 1-year rate guarantee	Surrender charge during early years	Backed by full faith and credit of insurance company	4.55%	Tax-deferred interest
5-year certificate of deposit	Interest penalty applied if withdrawn early	FDIC insured up to $100,000, including other deposits	4.46%	Taxed as interest is earned
Fixed-interest deferred annuity with a 5-year rate guarantee	Surrender charge during early years	Backed by full faith and credit of insurance company	5.00%	Tax-deferred interest

*As of December 2007

Interest rate competition depends on the current market and the ability of the individual company to profitably reinvest the investment dollars it receives as annuity premiums. The straightforward competition rewards larger deposits committed for longer periods of time with higher interest rates.

MEETING WITH THE PROSPECT

In this section, we will return to the third component in the selling/planning process as it applies to the sale of annuities, especially within the context of retirement planning. We will explore effective techniques for interviewing prospects, along with methods for explaining the need for annuities in retirement planning. Finally we will discuss alternative retirement funding sources, as well as several approaches for qualifying prospects.

Preparing for the Interview

What to Expect in the Annuities Sales Process

The annuity sales process is much the same as that for any other individual product sale. That is, you need to identify and approach prospects, meet with them, and conduct effective fact finding to establish a financial need. Then you should schedule a second interview in which you recommend the appropriate financial product(s), such as some type of annuity, to help solve that problem. Annuities should be addressed within the context of retirement planning and/or as a component of a broader, more comprehensive financial plan.

Annuities Selling/Planning Process

Part of your job as a financial advisor is to guide prospects through the selling/planning process by executing the same due diligence that you would expect if you were the buyer. This process, as it relates to the sale of annuities, involves (but is not limited to)

- meeting personally with the prospect
- explaining the need for (annuity products in) retirement planning
- discussing the potential inadequacy of traditional retirement funding sources
- discussing annuity products as part of the retirement funding solution
- qualifying the prospect
- gathering information
  - fact finding
  - financial information
  - feeling-finding
- identifying the need
- securing a discovery agreement
- analyzing the information
- formulating a potential annuity product design
- developing and presenting the product or plan
- addressing the prospect's concerns and objections

In the remainder of this chapter, and in the second parts of chapters 4, 5, and 6, we will address each of these topics in the order listed above.

Initial Interview

The purpose of the initial interview is to establish the foundation for a collaborative relationship with the prospect, not to make a sale. In fact, many successful advisors have said that if you collect the information from the prospect during the initial interview, including his or her needs, values, feelings, goals, and objectives, as well as facts and figures, this will result in much less resistance to making a sale and implementing the solution. The systematic process of building a lasting client-advisor relationship begins with this initial meeting and is made up of the following four steps:

- establishing rapport and credibility
- utilizing effective communication techniques
- identifying the prospect's needs, wants, qualifications, and concerns*
- reaching an agreement to work together to address the prospect's needs, wants, and concerns*

* These topics will be addressed in the next chapter.

Establishing Rapport

Client building begins with establishing rapport. People want to work with professionals who create meaningful relationships with them and listen to what they want to accomplish. If rapport and credibility are developed in the process of exchanging information, then the product options and amounts you recommend will more likely reflect the prospect's real needs and values. In order for prospects to buy any products from you, they must first trust you. Trust is the intangible aspect of selling that must be gradually cultivated and earned. You must prove that you are there to help them, not simply there to sell them something. Thus your objective in the initial interview is to establish rapport by creating an environment that promotes prospect openness by

- alleviating the prospect's concerns
- responding to the prospect's social style
- communicating effectively with the prospect
- mutually agreeing to an agenda for the interview

Alleviating the Prospect's Concerns. Various barriers that can create tension between you and your prospect during an initial meeting must be removed if rapport is to be established. These barriers can be divided into four major categories:

(1) *Distrust of Salespeople.* Many people have a negative image of salespeople and avoid meeting with them for fear of being talked into buying something they do not want or need.

(2) *Fear of Making a Decision.* Decisions involve risk, and many people avoid risk, especially when money is involved. Also fear of making the wrong decision or potential buyer's remorse can cause avoidance of stressful decision-making situations.

(3) *Need for Status Quo.* Often people are complacent and resistant to change because they prefer familiarity.

(4) *Time Constraints.* At today's increasingly hectic pace of life, busy prospects are reluctant to commit their time.

Being aware of prospect tension can help you identify opportunities to alleviate it and to establish rapport. Here are some tips:

- *Do not impose.* Schedule your initial meeting at times that are convenient for prospects.
- *Watch your verbal pace.* Talk in an unhurried, businesslike manner. Never interrupt when prospects speak. Listen carefully to what they say. As we will discuss shortly, listening is your best tool.
- *Remember nonverbal behavior.* You might be surprised to learn that as little as 7 percent of a first impression is based on what is actually said. The remaining 93 percent is based on nonverbal behavior, such as physical appearance, body language, voice quality, and tone.
- *Encourage prospects to talk.* Having prospects talk is not only a great tool for getting feedback, but it is also a common way for them to relieve stress. Encourage prospects to do most of the talking.
- *Control your anxiety.* Several studies have shown that a person who is already anxious becomes even more so when talking with someone who displays nervousness or anxiety.

social styles

Responding to the Prospect's Social Style. Establishing rapport is your responsibility. This means you should be able to detect what each prospect wants in a sales relationship and to use your versatility to shape the discussion and your responses to his or her respective needs. Psychologist Dr. David Merrill described the characteristics of four different *social styles*:

- driver
- expressive

- amiable
- analytical

According to Dr. Merrill and Roger H. Reid, "We all say and do things as a result of certain habit patterns, and people make predictions about us because they come to expect us to behave in a particular way—the fact is that even though each of us is unique, we tend to act in fairly consistent, describable ways. All of us use habits that have worked well for us, habits that make us comfortable, and these habits become the social style that others can observe."[7]

The American population is approximately evenly divided among the four social styles listed above. Each person has a dominant social style, and that style influences the way he or she behaves. People will tend to seek out social situations that reinforce their behavior and avoid situations that cause discomfort. Figure 3-2 illustrates the four social styles.

FIGURE 3-2
The Four Social Styles

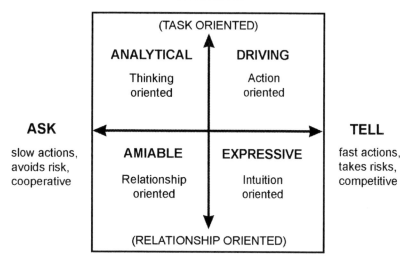

People are like thermostats; they are constantly seeking to reach a state of equilibrium or comfort. As soon as another person enters the picture, tension results, and each person must re-establish his or her balance and comfort zone. The challenge for each of us is to determine the right amount of tension and stress that will provide the proper balance.

As advisors, we can achieve better communication when we understand the other person and treat him or her the way he or she wants to be treated. Table 3-3 offers some suggestions for ways to establish more effective communication and a better relationship with prospects.

When you adapt to a prospect's social style, you make him or her feel more at home and less threatened. Listening closely and observing carefully during the first few minutes of the initial interview gives you an idea of how to treat the prospect. Table 3-4 summarizes the characteristics of each social style. The first six rows at the top of the table highlight the basic attributes and personal needs of each style. The five rows at the bottom indicate how you can best establish rapport and maintain a good working relationship with a person who has that style. Listen carefully and observe your prospect to determine which set of characteristics most closely describes him or her; then establish rapport by responding in an appropriate manner throughout the interview.

Example 1:	If your prospect, Jane Weston, enthusiastically talks at length about the plans she has for the new business she is starting, she would be classified as an Expressive. To establish rapport, respond to her by taking time to listen and ask about her plans.
Example 2:	If your prospect, Ben Hammer, tells you where to sit when you enter his office and looks at his watch when you ask about the photograph of the sailboat on his wall, he would be classified as a Driver. To establish rapport, respond to him by immediately getting down to business and explaining the purpose, process, and benefits of the appointment.

TABLE 3-3
Communication Guidelines

Guidelines for Communicating With Analyticals		Guidelines for Communicating With Drivers	
Communicate	**Avoid**	**Communicate**	**Avoid**
• in a straightforward, direct manner; stick to an agenda • your support of their principles; establish your credibility by enumerating the positives and negatives to any suggestions you make • your intention to be available for long-term management of their financial needs • your understanding of their desire to be thorough	• being disorganized, casual, informal, or loud • rushing the decision-making process • being vague about what is expected of either of you; don't fail to follow through • using testimonies of others or unreliable sources • being clever or appearing manipulative • pushing too hard or being unrealistic with deadlines	• clear, specific, brief, and to-the-point information in a business-like manner • all requirements and objectives, have available all support material in a well-organized package • logical, efficient treatment of information • when possible, facts and figures regarding the probability of success or effectiveness of options	• rambling conversations and/or nonessential information; i.e., don't waste their time • trying to build personal relationships • disorganized presentation of facts • open-ended issues or asking rhetorical questions • appearing to have made the decision for them; i.e., don't give autocratic advice or opinions
Guidelines for Communicating With Amiables		Guidelines for Communicating With Expressives	
Communicate	**Avoid**	**Communicate**	**Avoid**
• your concern and interest in them as people; find areas of common involvement; be candid and open • patience and interest in their personal goals and how you will work with them to help achieve these goals; listen and be responsive • in a soft, nonthreatening manner • by asking questions that draw their opinions • in a casual, informal manner • personal assurances that their decision will minimize risks; provide them with maximum guarantees	• rushing the interview, yet do not lose sight of the goals by being too personal • being domineering or demanding; reduce your position power • pressuring them into agreement because they will probably not risk the discomfort of confrontation • patronizing or demeaning them by using subtlety or invective • being abrupt and rapid or offering assurances and guarantees you cannot fulfill • deciding for them or they will lose initiative	• interaction that supports their dreams and intentions • that you have planned time for relating and socializing • your intent to formalize the details of their plan in a written report, if necessary • with questions that draw out their opinions/ideas • that you can provide testimonials from people they see as important and prominent	• being perceived as curt, cold, or autocratic • leaving decisions hanging in the air • impersonal, judgmental, task-oriented behavior when possible • "dreaming" with them or you will lose time • talking down to them or being dogmatic

TABLE 3-4
Social Styles Summary

	Analytical	Amiable	Driver	Expressive
Primary Asset	Systematic	Supportive	Controlling	Energizing
Back-up Behavior	Avoiding	Acquiescing	Autocratic	Attacking
For Growth Needs to	Decide	Initiate	Listen	Check
Is Motivated by a Desire for	Respect	Approval	Power	Recognition
Needs Climate That	Describes	Processes	Responds	Collaborates
Seeks to Save	Face	Relationships	Time	Effort
Make Effort to Be	Accurate	Cooperative	Efficient	Interesting
Support Their	Principles and thinking	Relationships and feelings	Conclusions and actions	Visions and intuitions
Explain to Them	How problem is solved	Why solution is best	What solution will do	Who else has used these products
For Decisions Give Them	Evidence and service	Assurances and guarantees	Options and probabilities	Testimony and incentives
Follow Up With	Service	Support	Results	Attention

Here are two more examples to review.

Example 3:   If your prospect, Bob Hinds, greets you with a worried smile, apologizes for being 15 minutes late, and says that he could not get away from his last meeting where they were planning a retirement party for his administrative assistant—a wonderful woman who has been with him since he started the company—he would be classified as an Amiable. To establish rapport, respond to him by taking time to ask about his retiring administrative assistant.

Example 4:	If your prospect, Dr. Patricia Gibbons, stands to greet you from behind her desk when you are ushered into her office, waits for you to take a seat, and immediately asks you what the maximum gift is that she can give tax free to each of her grandchildren, she would be classified as an Analytical. To establish rapport, respond to her by taking the time to answer her question with a detailed and documented reply.

If you can readily identify and respond appropriately to a person's social style in a sales situation, you will be able to establish rapport more quickly and will facilitate the relationship-building process. How can you distinguish among the styles with people you have just met? A simple guideline involves the following: Refer to Figure 3-2 titled "The Four Social Styles." Notice the words "ask" and "tell" on the left and right sides of the box, and the words "control" and "emote" at the top and bottom. Of the social styles within the four quadrants, those on the left side (analyticals and amiables) tend to make requests to other people by *asking* them for things. Those on the right side (drivers and expressives) tend to make requests to other people by *telling* them what they want. Furthermore, those with social styles in the top two quadrants (analyticals and drivers) tend to be unanimated, unemotional, and reserved or self-controlled in interview situations. Those in the bottom two quadrants (amiables and expressives) tend to be much more outgoing, loud speaking, animated, and emotional.

Example:	If you meet a couple, and in the course of getting settled into the interview, you observe that the male asks his wife to help find his pen, then asks his child to take his homework up to his room, there is a high probability that he is either an analytical or amiable. If, later, the male prospect sits rather still before you while taking notes during your interview, you can safely assume that this person has an analytical social style. You should then employ the tips in Table 3-3 for "Guidelines for Communicating with Analyticals," and be aware of the basic characteristics and how to respond to them found in Table 3-4.

Communicating Effectively With Prospects

**effective
communication**

To help solve prospects' problems, advisors must be effective communicators. Some advisors think *effective communication* means only that they have to be able to explain financial products to prospects. Obviously that is important, but one of the most critical aspects of being an effective communicator is learning also to be an effective listener. Failing to hear what your prospect is really saying can cost you dearly. Developing good listening skills will result in increased sales and the sense of a job well done.

Moreover, your ability to be a good listener is vitally important in personal communications. Your prospects are more likely to accept your recommendations if you demonstrate an interest in them as individuals, listen to their hopes and dreams, and help them prioritize their goals. In other words, the most important part of communication is listening.

active listening

Active Listening. Your goal as an advisor should be to become an active, understanding listener—one who attempts to understand the prospect from the prospect's perspective. If you can state in your own words what the prospect has said and meant to communicate, and the prospect accepts your statement as an accurate reflection of what he or she said and felt, *active listening* has occurred. If you develop this skill, you will be in the best position to solve the prospect's problems with a plan or sale.

Active listening is hard work and requires intense focus and concentration. Years of not listening have made most of us poor listeners. We as salespeople often spend too much time talking and not enough time listening. We cannot listen to what the prospect is saying if we are too busy talking. It is easy to become distracted or to prejudge the prospect's meaning before the prospect is finished speaking. It is also too easy to form a response before hearing the prospect's question or comment. Thus we can easily miss the prospect's message.

Effective listening is a genuine skill worth developing. To become an active listener, you must believe in the importance of each prospect's needs. Then you must commit to hearing and understanding what each prospect is saying. If you put aside your prejudices, opinions, and preconceived notions about a subject and the prospect, you can be objective and open-minded.

It should be obvious to you that a successful fact-finding session requires you to be an effective listener to learn essential information about your prospect in order to make the best recommendations. Yet how often do you find yourself asking questions but not listening to the prospect's responses? You may have decided what is best for the prospect based on your own thinking. By critically listening to the prospect's answers to your questions, you will not be as likely to mistake your preconceived ideas for the prospect's wants or needs.

Learning the difference between sympathy and empathy is also important for an advisor. Despite the general use of the word "empathy," most people still do not fully recognize the difference between sympathy and empathy and the application of the words in the world of selling. Sympathy means you feel like another person feels; you share the same feelings. By contrast, empathy means you understand how the other person feels though you do not feel the same way. While you cannot sympathize with all of your prospects, you can learn to be empathetic.

Body language is another aspect of active listening. Gestures that are made in silence can often give you, the listener, more of an indication of what the prospect is communicating than words can. A person's facial expressions, posture, and body stance can be informative to the observer. By watching people's eyes and hands, you can often determine what signals they are conveying.

Questioning. In any fact-finding session, you will ask questions and your prospects will answer them. If you can help your prospects feel comfortable talking about themselves, you will learn what is important to them. The more you know about your prospects' feelings, the better job you can do. Asking questions and being an active listener allows you to control the direction of the fact-finding conversation without being too obvious about it. Prospects then feel they are a part of the process.

In fact-finding interviews, you will want your prospects to communicate facts and figures. To be effective, however, you must also know your prospects' feelings. Feelings are often difficult to uncover in a question-and-answer format where you are cast into the role of the interviewer. Although your goal should be to listen more than talk, there are times when only a well-phrased question will elicit the information you are seeking.

Finally it is important to keep in mind that the primary reason for gathering data from prospects is to make suitable recommendations. Each time you meet with your prospects, it is important that your communication be directed at uncovering as many facts and feelings as possible so that you can assure your prospects of the suitability of the products you recommend.

The intangible by-product of establishing rapport, tuning into and responding to the prospect's social style, and actively listening during the interview process is the enhancement of your credibility to the prospect. Your credibility combined with your compassion and understanding will eventually lead to trust. Once a prospect trusts you, he or she will be willing to do business with you. Winning a prospect's trust does not come easily. You have to work hard to achieve it, so be patient.

Interviewing Your Prospect

Your job as a financial advisor involves you in an ongoing process. You will spend considerable time with your prospects to determine their financial goals and objectives—their needs. Once this is complete, you will use the information gathered—the facts and feelings that you have discussed—to make recommendations. Each meeting with prospects should be productive and accomplish specific objectives.

The beginning of the initial interview with the prospect sets the tone for the entire meeting by establishing expectations for both you and the prospect. Three specific topics must be addressed in the introductory phase of the interview:

- establishing an agenda
- identifying the decision makers
- setting the stage for referred leads

Establishing an Agenda

It is a good idea to follow a predetermined agenda for each fact-gathering session. This lets the prospects know what is expected of them and reduces anxiety and discomfort concerning what will happen during the meeting. It is wise to involve your prospects in setting the agenda.

Setting proper expectations for the meeting helps establish rapport and gets the initial interview off to a positive start. You can reduce any early tension in an interview with a prospect whom you have never met before by outlining your approach to retirement planning. Explain the following steps of the planning process:

- Assist the prospect in forming goals and objectives.
- Help the prospect identify existing resources for meeting goals and objectives.
- Analyze the gap between goals and objectives and existing resources.
- Develop a plan for bridging the resource gap.
- Implement the plan.
- Service the plan.

You should have an agenda for every sales meeting. To present the agenda you should do the following:

- Communicate what you intend to accomplish during the meeting.
- Explain how you will work with the prospect.

- State the benefit for the prospect.
- Check for acceptance.

In the initial planning session, you might propose the agenda by saying something like this to the prospect:

Purpose	*What You Say*
Communicate what you intend to accomplish during the meeting.	During this meeting, we will discuss some retirement planning issues that may concern you.
Explain how you will work with the prospect.	First, I'll tell you a little about who I am and the company I represent.
	We'll also talk about the need for adequate retirement funding. Then we'll talk about your concerns, goals, and desires regarding retirement planning.
	Next, we will look at your current financial status in regard to your current cash flow, current savings and investments, and potential sources of retirement income.
	Finally, I'll identify any problems or gaps in your current retirement plan.
State the benefit for the prospect.	That way, you can determine whether it will be of value for us to move ahead and develop a retirement planning strategy tailored for you.
Check for acceptance.	How does that sound?

By proposing the agenda in this way, stating the benefit to the prospect and checking for acceptance, you are sharing control of the interview with your prospect, which helps to establish rapport. It may be advisable to reassure the prospect of your continuing commitment to the process.

Example:	"If in the course of our work together we should discover that you have a need for financial products within a plan for funding retirement, I'll assist you in devising a customized plan that addresses your individual concerns. I'll then help you to implement that plan and promise to monitor and service it in the future."

After you present your agenda, ask for any other concerns that your prospect wishes to discuss. Write them down, and be sure to cover these concerns in your discussion. Do so even if the concerns fall under categories you had on your agenda. Your prospect's input is an important step in the open exchange of data and feelings.

Identifying Decision Makers

The next step you will want to take in the interview is to attempt to identify the decision makers in addition to the prospect who may be involved in the purchase of any financial products. This could include professional advisors, such as the prospect's attorney, or other immediate family members such as siblings or adult children. Ask the prospect if there are any advisors that he or she will consult before making the buying decision. If so, it is best to try to get them personally involved as soon as possible. From a sales standpoint, you cannot deal effectively with objections or concerns that may arise unless you are able to speak directly with the person to whom they apply. There is far too much technical language and professional jargon used in the annuities selling/planning process that the prospect might be unable to explain or interpret for these other decision makers. There is also too much at stake for you not to ask the prospect at least to arrange for open lines of communication with his or her other professional or personal advisors. Ideally have the prospect invite them to participate in the interview.

Setting the Stage for Referred Leads

Many financial advisors use the early part of their initial interviews with new prospects to prepare them to be asked later for referred leads. If the prospects are pleased with the service you have given them—whether or not they actually do business with you—you will have earned the right to ask them for referrals at some point during the selling/planning process because you performed a valuable service by educating them about retirement planning needs.

Good Referral Technique

Example: "One of the ways that I am compensated for the work I do is by receiving personal introductions from people like you to others you know. Now I wouldn't expect you to have any idea whether these people are in the market for annuities or, for that matter, any insurance or investment-related products. However, if you are pleased with my professionalism, I would appreciate it if you could refer me to several people you know so that I may have the opportunity to help them also. Does this seem reasonable to you?"

Explaining the Need for Retirement Planning

The transition from the exchange of amenities and acknowledgment of the agenda to the qualification portion of the interview is during a relatively short section in which you describe your company, yourself, your services, and the general problems facing individuals today in financing the increasing costs of retirement.

This part of the initial interview deals with explaining, in general terms, the need for adequate income during retirement. Various methods are used to accomplish this objective. Here is where you can discuss the universal financial problem of the need for sufficient retirement funding. You can caution against depending too heavily on financing alternatives like government programs and qualified plans to solve the problem, pointing out how low-yielding taxable investments may hamper prospects' cash accumulation goals during their working years and noting that postretirement employment may not be desirable or even possible. You can then describe briefly how either deferred or immediate annuities can help to alleviate the looming retirement funding problem. You should select some appropriate concept papers to give to the prospect to reinforce these points if you have not already done so.

Clarifying Motives and Goals

Your first meeting with a prospect is both an opportunity and a challenge. The opportunity is to address the prospect's interest in retirement planning. The challenge is to develop a climate of cooperation so you can learn enough about the prospect's financial planning goals and buying motives in order to individualize a plan of action that best addresses his or her circumstances.

In setting the stage to explain the need for retirement planning, you may want to take time to establish what prospects know and what they think they know about annuities. For example, one advisor simply asks, "What does the word 'annuity' mean to you?" Asking this or a similar question is a great way to begin a discussion of annuities to establish certain definitions used for such concepts as tax deferral, the cost of retirement, and what various government and pension programs do and do not provide. It also requires uncovering the prospects' assumptions about the myths and misunderstandings of what annuities are and how they work, especially tax-deferred annuities. You have to ask questions to establish a common baseline in the language of annuities.

You also have to elicit feedback from prospects regarding their level of knowledge about annuities and seek corroboration of their understanding of retirement planning goals. Only when you are speaking the same language with prospects can you begin to comprehend their objectives in potentially purchasing annuities as a component of a retirement plan.

Methods

To enhance your credibility with your prospects, it is important that you explain why they may need to consider an annuity. This discussion often leads to the use of other tools and techniques (which, of course, must be approved by your company's compliance department) that you as an advisor can draw upon to help you. These various tools and techniques are contained in the annuity sales presentation binder that you should consider developing for your use.

Visuals. Visuals are a compelling presentation technique. People tend to listen actively to what is being said when they are involved in the communication; it is your responsibility to ensure that your prospects are involved and actively listening throughout the data-gathering process. Asking questions and soliciting prospects' opinions while they look at visuals keep them involved in the process. The physical act of placing visuals in front of them helps to direct the discussion and focus prospects' attention.

Keep in mind that any materials presented to prospects must have your company's prior approval. Because of this requirement, it is a good idea to have one or two prepared presentations that you use consistently with all your prospects. This consistency helps to ensure your compliance with the applicable regulations.

Third-Party Substantiation. In addition to simple pictures, your company probably has preapproved annuity marketing brochures, product fact sheets, and even third-party testimonials available for your use. Become familiar with these and selectively decide which ones to include in the annuities presentation binder you are developing.

Statistical Evidence. Many advisors use charts, graphs, and statistics about the cost of retirement funding in light of increasing longevity in the United States today. Other relevant resources are magazine articles and slides or Powerpoint presentations. You need to develop and update your own inventory of useful materials that are designed to appeal to the prospect's emotions regarding financial security and his or her potential need for annuities.

Real-Life Stories. Some advisors also find it useful to develop a repertoire of real-life stories and case histories that they can draw upon to illustrate the usefulness of annuities in retirement planning. Although this technique may not be appropriate for every advisor—some are better storytellers than others—it is one more resource in your inventory of tools and techniques for marketing annuities. Recounting an actual situation where the need for emergency funds arose suddenly prior to retirement, or how an annuity provided guaranteed income or premium dollars after retirement, can help to heighten a prospect's personal awareness about the need for proper planning.

The Problem: Ensuring Adequate Retirement Income

As mentioned in Chapter 1, the greatest single factor that motivates the purchase of deferred or immediate annuities is the need for retirement income. The greater longevity that Americans enjoy has increased the need for adequate funding of their income during retirement. People in this country who live to age 65 can expect to live an average of 18 more years. With increased longevity comes the greater probability of depleting the personal financial reserves accumulated over a lifetime of saving. How will adequate retirement funding be accomplished?

As we will see below, the answer for most individuals (and their families) depends on the level of income prior to retirement.

Sources of Retirement Income

A helpful technique to begin a general discussion about the need for retirement planning is to ask this question: How much money will you need to accumulate to enjoy a comfortable retirement? Many prospects have a total lack of knowledge on this topic. It may take $1 million or more to provide a comfortable retirement for many of your prospects and clients. This seems like an enormous amount of money, but it really is not if you think about it. Consider that a couple that needs an income of $50,000 a year for 20 years needs $1 million, assuming no inflation or interest earnings.

There are many misunderstandings regarding retirement income and the resources available for financing it. As a financial advisor, you must be prepared to educate prospects on the shortcomings of the various personal, employer-sponsored, and government financing alternatives for retirement income. This process will often require you to discuss the misconceptions regarding the effectiveness of these alternatives as adequate retirement funding vehicles. Most individuals believe that retirement income will come from one or more of the following sources:

- Social Security
- pensions
- personal savings

Of course, there are other sources of retirement income. For example, any one of us can inherit a large sum of money. But we cannot plan with any certainty if we rely on the chance or the timing of such an event.

Some planners use the analogy of a three-legged stool when they speak of retirement income because they feel that approximately one-third of retirement income should come from each of the three traditional sources above. This analogy has been a simple and useful starting point for discussions about retirement planning.

The majority of your prospects and clients will continue to rely on some combination of Social Security, pensions, and personal savings to fund their retirements. However, the assumption that one-third of retirement income will come from each of the traditional sources may no longer apply. According to a study done by the Social Security Administration, the *four* main sources of income for those aged 65 and older are as follows:

- Social Security
- retirement plan benefits
- asset income
- earnings from wages

A small percentage of aggregate income comes from other sources. (See Table 3-5.)

TABLE 3-5		
Income Sources of People Aged 65 and Over		
Source of Income	Percentage of Aggregate Income (2005)	Percent Receiving Income from Each Respective Source (2005)
Social Security	37%	89%
Retirement plans	19%	44%
Asset income	13%	55%
Earnings	28%	24%
Other (public assistance and veterans benefits)	3%	8%
Source: Fact and Figures about Social Security, 2007.		

Many preretirees are less than optimistic about the future. Many believe Social Security benefits will be delayed, cut, and fully taxed. Some have failed to make maximum use of their company-sponsored pension plans. And few have saved enough money. As a matter of fact, the median annual income for retirees depends on age, as Figure 3-3 shows.

FIGURE 3-3
Median Income, by Age, 2004

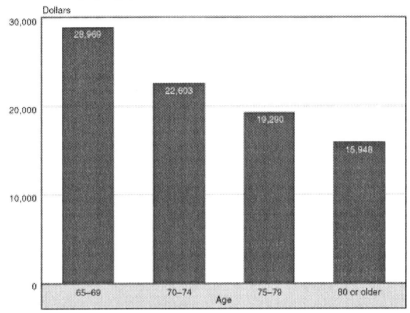

Source: Income of the Aged Chartbook, 2004, Social Security Administration

Rather than looking forward to comfort and leisure in retirement, many people are understandably concerned that they will outlive their resources. They realize that there is a huge gap between what they need and expect in retirement income and what they will actually receive. You need only examine the current status of each of the three traditional sources of retirement income to understand their concerns.

Social Security. Almost everyone has a retirement plan—Social Security. Traditionally, for nearly 70 years, even people who reached retirement age with no financial assets could generally rely on Social Security. For most Americans, it is the largest single source of retirement income. For low-income families, it may be the only source. (See Table 3-6.) Yet it was never intended to be the sole retirement funding mechanism. Rather, it is and has been the retirement safety net.

Although 37 percent of the aggregate income of those 65 and older comes from Social Security, actual reliance on Social Security is highly dependent on income. As you can see in Table 3-6, if you divide those 65 and over into quintiles of income, those in the lowest quintile receive over 82 percent of their income from Social Security while those in the highest quintile receive only about 19 percent from Social Security. Those in the highest quintile depend as much or more on retirement plans, asset income, and earnings as they do on Social Security.

TABLE 3-6
Shares of Aggregate Income by Quintiles of Total Income, 2004

Source	Lowest	Second	Third	Fourth	Fifth
Social Security	**82.6%**	**83.4%**	**66.6%**	**47.5%**	**18.9%**
Retirement plans*	3.5%	7%	16.6%	25.7%	21.2%
Asset income	2.3%	3.8%	6%	8.4%	17.8%
Earnings	1.2%	2.8%	7.1%	15.7%	40.1%
Public assistance	8.4%	1.6%	.9%	**	**
Other	2%	1.5%	2.7%	2.6%	1.9%

NOTE: Quintile limits are $10,399, $16,363, $25,587, and $44,129 .

* Includes private pensions and annuities, government employee pensions, Railroad Retirement, and IRS Keogh and 401(k) payments.
** Less than 0.5 percent.
   Percentages may not equal 100 due to rounding.

Source: Income of the Population 55 and Older, 2004, Social Security Administration, May 2006.

However, the future of the current Social Security program of contributions and payments is the subject of much public policy debate. Any suggestion that the government raise taxes to make up the entire shortfall fails to recognize the magnitude of the problem. Increased longevity and the size of the aging baby boom generation, combined with lower birth rates for generations that follow, will strain the solvency of the Social Security system.

As planners, we should approach the topic of Social Security objectively. You should be knowledgeable about the shortcomings of this government program and be prepared to discuss them. It is likely that in the future, Social Security as we know it will change. It is equally likely that Social Security will be part of your prospects' and clients' retirement income. Although Social Security will most likely remain a viable source of retirement funding, it is now and always was intended only to be a safety net designed to provide subsistence in the absence of other retirement financial resources.

Perhaps the approach your prospects can take is to understand the role of Social Security and its potential benefits but to plan and save so that they do not have to rely on it.

Pensions. Pensions and retirement plans are the second leg of the traditional retirement planning stool. Although Social Security is the mainstay of most people's retirement income, retirement plan benefits make up 19 percent of the aggregate income. Retirement plans include private and public pensions, 401(k) plans, IRAs, and Keoghs.

Although coverage rates in employment-based plans have not changed much in the last several decades, what has changed dramatically are the types of plans employers are offering. The trend is away from the guaranteed income defined-benefit plans (DB) and toward less secure, higher risk defined-contribution (DC) plans. In many cases, employers make retirement plans available but do not even contribute to the plans.

During the past 20 years, while coverage in DB plans has steadily declined, participation in DC plans has grown. In 1983, 62 percent of eligible wage and salary workers were covered solely by a DB plan; 12 percent participated only in a DC plan. By 2004, those numbers had reversed with 63 percent of workers covered by a DC plan, and only 20 percent covered by a DB plan.[8]

The implications of these statistics are significant: Risk and responsibility of retirement income from employment-based retirement plans have shifted from employers to employees.

This may be difficult for some prospects. Some employees have never been covered by employer-sponsored plans. Many others have not taken full advantage of them. It may be too late for some of your prospects to save enough to help meet their retirement income expectations.

Personal Savings. A discussion about the inadequacy of saving in the United States was presented in Chapter 1. It is likely that most of your prospects are going to need more money for retirement than they are now saving. There is little evidence that Americans are saving enough to preserve their preretirement lifestyles in retirement. According to a recent study by Aon Consulting and Georgia State University, workers in all income and age groups have saved 5 percent or less of their preretirement income.

According to the Committee for Economic Development, all kinds of savings have fallen over the recent decades. Savings continued their downward slide in 2006, reaching a new 74-year low of negative 1.2 percent in December. Savings had been less than 2 percent of gross domestic product in 2002, down from 4 percent in the 1980s and 8 percent in previous decades. Misperceptions about retirement and investments may be contributing to the low saving rates. Common mistakes include overestimating investment returns and consequently overwithdrawing funds in retirement, underestimating the needed income to preserve an active lifestyle, expecting too much from Social Security, depending on an inheritance or a spouse's pension, and underestimating their own longevity.

Those who are saving may not be saving effectively, as noted in the lump-sum savings accumulation figures from the 2007 Retirement Confidence Survey conducted by Employee Benefit Research Institute (EBRI) cited in Chapter 1. There is often a large gap between the income before retirement and the income after retirement. Unfortunately, many retirees may have to rely on their most valuable financial asset, which is the equity in their home, to make up the needed retirement income shortfall. Others may be forced to continue working.

Earnings. According to the Social Security Administration study cited above, 28 percent of the aggregate income of those 65 and older comes from earnings; approximately 23 percent comes from wages, and 5 percent comes from self-employment. What has happened to the three-legged stool for funding retirement? The irrefutable demographic phenomenon of the twenty-first century is that retirees are working.

People are not simply employed one day and retired the next. They are making the transition to retirement through "bridge" jobs or phased retirement. A recent AARP survey confirmed that most baby boomers (80 percent) plan to work at least part time in retirement. Some of the reasons for retirees to continue to work include

- concerns about continued health care coverage because there has been an erosion in employment-based retiree healthcare coverage
- increased longevity and the fear of running out of money
- the gradually increasing Social Security retirement age
- the elimination of the Social Security earnings test for those who reach full retirement age

The harsh reality of aging is that many people are or will become physically unable to work during their retirement years. Many others will simply be unwilling to work. Thus counting on employment income after retirement can be a serious strategic planning mistake. In any event, whether a person works or does not work during retirement should be a decision of personal preference, not one of financial necessity.

Annuities as Part of the Solution

Your Role. Your prospects are likely to need more money than they are saving, so they must evaluate and plan for the things that can go wrong. If retirement were their only goal, planning might be easier. But your prospects may also need to fund college costs for children or long-term care costs for long-lived parents who underestimated their longevity. Prospects are also facing their own medical and long-term care costs, which are increasing at much higher rates than inflation in general.

Planning has to occur at all levels. Although policymakers are working to restructure Social Security and pensions, your prospects should be taking greater responsibility for themselves. They should be planning and saving more for their futures. Retirement security is primarily the culmination of a series of personal decisions (or nondecisions) over the course of an individual's lifetime. The most effective retirement savings education will make it clear to people that they hold retirement security in their own hands; it will help to motivate them to develop and live by their own personal retirement savings strategy.

You can play a vital role if you understand your market and the issues people in it face. Advisors must do a better job of educating the public— employers and individuals alike—about the importance of saving and the tools available to ensure that their clients can afford to retire and remain financially independent.

The features that annuities can offer your clients were listed in Chapter 2 under the heading "Nonqualified Retirement Planning." In addition, annuities provide numerous benefits as an important component of a diversified and comprehensive retirement:

- Annuities are the only financial instruments available today, other than Social Security and defined benefit pension plans, that can guarantee a lifetime stream of income during retirement.
- Annuities help to enable your clients to preserve their sense of dignity by enhancing their financial independence.
- They allow your clients to partake in more recreational activities in retirement due to the increased income from reduced taxation of the earnings in their deferred annuities and their Social Security retirement benefits.
- They provide the peace of mind of knowing that assets that have accumulated are available when needed for an emergency or a large unforeseen expense.
- They offer policy options that address specialized liquidity concerns such as long-term care or terminal illness.
- By helping to provide financial security during retirement, annuities alleviate the fear of running out of money.

In addition, as evidence of the opportunity for you to affect your clients' retirement planning and market annuities in the process, consider the following facts from a recent LIMRA study of annuity characteristics and attitudes:[9]

- Only 32 percent of all annuity owners have a formal written plan in place for meeting their financial goals.
- However, 60 percent of respondents have someone they consider to be their personal financial advisor, and 71 percent of these respondents purchased their annuity from this person.

The information above is valuable to use in the early stages of your meeting with a prospect. It may also help you approach prospects and clients regarding the need to begin the retirement planning process. Most of you want to build long-term relationships with your clients. Therefore you will want to be the advisor who plans, reviews, and periodically performs updates with them.

In approaching prospects about retirement planning, you may want to say something like this: "Mr./Ms. Prospect, have you started to plan a strategy for your retirement?" Or "Are you saving enough to control the decision to retire when you want to and to enjoy the lifestyle that you desire?"

Qualifying the Prospect

After you have discussed the need for retirement planning in general, you should make sure that your prospect and his or her spouse, if applicable, will qualify for an annuity either before you proceed to personal information gathering or while you are performing it. In the ideal scenario, qualified prospects are identified before private face-to-face meetings are established. As was mentioned in Chapter 2, many successful advisors prequalify prospects on the telephone once they have agreed to an appointment. It is advisable to ask the kind of questions that will preliminarily qualify the prospect for the appointment. However, in many instances, a face-to-face meeting occurs before you know for certain whether or not you are dealing with a *qualified* prospect. These meetings take time. The more time you spend with qualified prospects, the greater the number of them you will convert into clients. Therefore you can use one of three methods that are discussed below to qualify your prospect.

Remember, in order to increase the amount of time you spend with qualified prospects, keep in mind the four characteristics of a qualified prospect that we mentioned in Chapter 1. Qualified prospects for annuities have these four basic characteristics. They are people who

- need and value your products and services
- can afford to pay for them
- are financially suitable for the product
- can be approached on a favorable basis

If these four conditions are satisfied, then you have a potential client. If at any time during the interview you discover that these four conditions are not satisfied, you should have a contingency strategy either to pivot to another product, outline a plan for future contact with the prospect when he or she is better qualified, or gracefully exit the interview and move on. Some pivoting ideas are discussed later in this chapter.

By virtue of the fact that you have obtained the interview, let us assume that you approached the prospect and are meeting with him or her on a favorable basis. Whether or not the prospect satisfies the remaining three criteria of being qualified has yet to be determined. Thus it is helpful for you to have a sense of whether the prospect perceives the need for retirement planning that may involve purchasing an annuity product and whether he or she is equipped to purchase one. You must have a barometer of the prospect's finances to determine if there are sufficient funds to pay for an annuity. Whether or not the prospect satisfies these three qualifying criteria will become apparent as you gather information from the prospect. You will need to remain alert so that you are aware of when each qualifying criterion is fulfilled. As each one is satisfied, you should mentally check it off so that you will know that the prospect is qualified to purchase an annuity product that you may recommend as part of the retirement plan.

Regardless of the extent of the information you acquire, you must keep several points in mind regarding your professional responsibility. You should always complete a fact finder of some sort within the context of an annuity sale. At the same time, you need to maintain a certain degree of flexibility, depending on the circumstances under which you made the appointment with the prospect. This is because most, but not all, annuities are sold as retirement planning vehicles. For example, you could be meeting with a client to discuss using an immediate annuity as a guaranteed funding vehicle for long-term care insurance. In this case, a guaranteed income for funding retirement is not the prospect's concern, so only the relevant segments of a comprehensive retirement planning fact finder would have to be completed in order for you to adequately know your client.

The first method we will explore for qualifying a prospect involves the use of the Personal Retirement Planning Review that is discussed in the next section.

Personal Retirement Planning Review

After you have discussed in overall terms the need for retirement planning, consider the following approach to increase the amount of time you spend with current qualified prospects:

- Begin qualifying your prospect with a general retirement planning qualifying form.

- Attempt a preliminary discovery agreement or trial close before conducting a full retirement planning analysis.

Afterwards you would then conduct a comprehensive retirement planning fact finder that will be discussed in detail in the next chapter.

The Personal Retirement Planning Review is a short and simple qualifying fact finder designed to uncover a prospect's predisposition or potential objections to retirement planning. It can also serve as an additional motivator to purchase annuities. The use of this mini fact finder is optional, but you may find it helpful.

A copy of this fact finder is included here for your use, but please be sure first to obtain your company's approval.

The answers to these questions in the Personal Retirement Planning Review will help you discern whether the prospect feels motivated to take action to improve retirement security and meet financial goals. In other words, the answers give you enough information to make an initial judgment about whether you should proceed with the prospect into the more detailed retirement planning fact finder.

Some of the reasons that prospects cite for buying financial products such as annuities have to do with their perceptions of the benefits associated with owning them, as discussed in Chapter 1. It is important to remember that the purchase of any financial product is not always just about dollars and cents; it is often also emotional. Consequently this is something about which you need to be sensitive as you ask these types of feeling-finding questions in the interview.

Preliminary Discovery Agreement. By the time you have successfully discussed the need for retirement planning and asked the prequalification questions, you should expect that a qualified prospect is ready to take the next steps toward planning for retirement that may involve purchasing an annuity. These steps begin with the completion of a more thorough fact finder and feeling-finder so that you can determine a financial need and recommend an appropriate product or products. Therefore at this juncture, you may consider using a trial close or *preliminary discovery agreement.*

preliminary discovery agreement

Example:

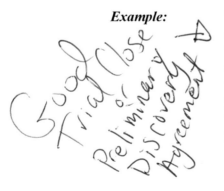

"Mr. and Mrs. Prospect, based on your answers to my questions up to this point, it is apparent that you want to take action to ensure a financially secure and comfortable retirement. You also indicated that you would consider taking appropriate action to reach your retirement goals. If I can design or formulate a plan that would enable you to accomplish the goals you've expressed at an affordable cost to you, would you be interested in working together to construct such a plan?"

(If the answer is no or not positive enough, see the section below titled "Handling Prospects Who Fail to Qualify" for optional pivoting strategies you may consider using, depending on the type of situation you encounter.)

Personal Retirement Planning Review

Prepared for _____

1. Retirement Preferences
   When do you plan to retire? (When did you retire?) ....
   Where do you plan to live when you retire? ....
   Do you expect to maintain your preretirement standard of living in retirement?   Yes   No
   Do you believe you are sufficiently preparing (prepared) financially to enjoy
      the lifestyle you prefer during retirement?   Yes   No

2. Savings and Investments
   Are you satisfied with the amount of money you currently have accumulated?   Yes   No
   Are you currently saving and investing enough to reach your retirement goal?   Yes   No
      If no, do you feel you need to increase your savings?   Yes   No
   Are you willing to increase your savings to meet your retirement goals?   Yes   No
   Have you recently been forced to dip into savings?   Yes   No
      If yes, why was it necessary?...
   Are you concerned with reducing the taxes you pay on your savings?   Yes   No

3. Risk Tolerance and Risk Coverage
   Into what risk category or categories would you consider yourself to be
      included?
   1. High risk? (Aggressive)   Yes   No
   2. Balanced risk? (Some aggressive, some conservative)   Yes   No
   3. Conservative? (Little or no risk)   Yes   No
   Do you feel you have sufficiently addressed your need for
   1. Life insurance coverage?   Yes   No
   2. Disability income coverage?   Yes   No
   3. Long-term care insurance?   Yes   No

4. Goals for Retirement Resources
   During retirement, do you want to be financially able to
      A. Leave an estate to your children?   Yes   No
      B. Provide long-term care for any dependents?   Yes   No
      C. Help pay for your grandchildren's education?   Yes   No
   Would you want to be certain that your assets are not depleted during
      retirement?   Yes   No
   Are you willing to consider purchasing additional financial products to help you
      reach your retirement goals?   Yes   No

If the answer is yes, you have a qualified prospect with whom you can proceed. You should use a transitional phrase (see below) in which you gain the prospect's permission to ask for confidential information. You should then proceed to complete the retirement planning fact finder included in the next chapter. — *Chapter 4 — Retirement planning fact Finder*

Dominant-Need Situation

A second alternative may occur in which you preliminarily qualify the prospect using the Personal Retirement Planning Review form and then proceed to an abbreviated or modified retirement planning fact finder or your company fact finder because an obvious planning concern or dominant need arises that does not require a full-blown retirement planning analysis. Thus, depending on the prospect's preconception of the purpose of your meeting or willingness to purchase an annuity product, you may find it advisable to begin to take an application for the appropriate type of product at this point in the initial interview. This situation is the exception rather than the rule in the normal annuity sales process; however, it may happen.

Example:	Suppose you meet with a very conservative retired prospect who was referred to you. This prospect, who has some money in low-yielding taxable savings and tax-free investment accounts, seeks tax deferral along with a higher return on her money. In this case, you may sell a fixed-interest deferred annuity and not explore every facet of her retirement resources. Although the prospect's main concern is a better rate of return on her money, you still need to do fact finding to determine the suitability of a fixed-interest deferred annuity in the context of the other financial products she owns. It may involve obtaining only some basic personal and financial data, but you must explore the prospect's current situation to justify the financial suitability of any product you sell.

As stated previously, flexibility is a key consideration in conducting a successful interview with potential clients. However, you still need to ask the prospect questions regarding desired areas of annuity benefits, as well as basic personal-information questions found in the fact finder that will be needed in order to complete the annuity application. Thus if the prospect clearly views an annuity as a single-product need and displays positive buying signs, then sell the product now rather than jeopardize the opportunity to make the prospect your client. If, however, based on your sales experience and judgment, you perceive that the prospect is more interested in a comprehensive retirement plan that may or may not include an annuity, then move into more thorough fact finding using a transitional phrase such as those found below.

Direct Transition

In the third alternative, immediately after a general discussion of the need for retirement planning and the possible need for annuities in that plan, instead of completing any additional qualifying questions, you could bypass the Personal Retirement Planning Review altogether and proceed directly into personal information gathering using your company's more comprehensive retirement planning fact finder or the one found in Chapter 4. Regardless of which qualifying method you use, it is always advisable to make a smooth transition from one segment of the interview into the next.

Transitional Phrase. The transition from a general discussion to actual fact finding is accomplished by asking for the prospect's permission to proceed.

Example: "In order for me to do a proper job analyzing your potential retirement (financial) well-being, I'll need to ask you some personal questions. I can assure you that the information I gather will be held in the strictest confidence. With this in mind, is it all right to proceed?"

Note that it might be necessary to schedule a second interview to complete the fact finder. This decision is a judgment call that is based on the following factors: how well you know the prospect, how well educated he or she is about retirement planning issues, how long the previous segments of the interview have taken, and how tired the prospect is.

Summary

Selling a financial product to unqualified prospects is unethical because it may cause them more financial harm than good; it may also expose you to legal liability. Thus it is in the best interest of all parties to use one of the three procedures above to make certain that the prospect is qualified before recommending a financial product.

Handling Prospects Who Fail to Qualify

You will encounter some situations where you are prepared to make the transition into completing the comprehensive fact finder only to discover that the prospect does not qualify for an annuity. There are many reasons why a prospect may fail to qualify. Whatever the reasons are, you should first attempt to pivot to another product sale using the fact finder to gather the necessary information.

The following are several categories of prospects who fail to qualify for annuity products:

- hostile or uncooperative prospects
- prospects with insufficient funds
- unsuitable prospects
- prospects shopping for a better deal

Uncooperative Prospects. If a prospect is hostile or is generally uncooperative during the prequalification process, you should move on and concentrate your efforts on people who will appreciate your expertise and assistance. There are too many qualified prospects who do not own annuities and would be more than willing to purchase them if they were properly guided through the selling/planning process. You need to spend your time with them.

Prospects With Insufficient Funds. Some prospects simply cannot afford an annuity at this time. Not everyone who needs an annuity is qualified to purchase it. The "no money" objection is one of the basic disqualifying criteria in financial services selling. The sooner you discover that the prospect cannot afford an annuity, the sooner you may be able to pivot to another product that he or she can afford. For example, someone with modest savings might be a prospect for a small life insurance policy or long-term care insurance policy. Furthermore, he or she may also become a source of leads to other prospects who may be more qualified for annuities.

Unsuitable Prospects. There are many people who may want an annuity and can afford to pay for it, but who are financially unsuitable because they have a greater need for asset and/or income protection products such as life insurance, disability income insurance, or long-term care insurance. Although we are mentioning it here, this reason that a prospect fails to qualify is usually revealed much later in the fact-finding process when you learn more specific information about what financial products the prospect

[handwritten: I like this line!!]

[handwritten: pre-approach?]

[handwritten: Unbalanced Insurance portfolios, over insured on health insurance in MA + under insured w/ life d;t]

[handwritten: foundation of any retirement plan on a pryamid is life insurance + disability insurance]

owns. Many advisors feel that these products should be in place before an annuity is purchased. Explain your concerns about the consequences to them *[handwritten: LTC;]* and their families of being exposed to the financial risks associated with not owning the coverages that life, disability, and long-term care insurance provide, and then explain how to acquire these other product lines.

Of course, whether or not prospects are uninsured or underinsured is ultimately their decision. Your job is to make them aware that they may have a financially devastating risk exposure. Higher priority needs present the opportunity to cross-sell the insurance coverage they lack. In fact, when this situation is handled tactfully, it can build your credibility in the prospect's eyes, and this can lead to the sale of these other products currently, as well as future referrals to other family members.

Prospects Shopping for a Better Deal. Many prospects have hidden objections. They are not interested in completing a comprehensive fact finder or establishing a long-lasting client/advisor relationship. They may just be shopping for the best guaranteed or bonus annuity interest rates. Sometimes they even spend years waiting for the illusive better deal. Nevertheless, these prospects can be cultivated slowly over time if you have the patience.

Education can sometimes be the solution to overcoming procrastination. These are excellent prospects to invite to a retirement planning seminar that you may be conducting. The education you provide may help them confront and overcome their reasons for procrastinating. A seminar is a low-key way for you to maintain contact with them. When they are ready to buy an annuity, your name should come to mind. In the meantime, these prospects may purchase other products from you or become a source of referrals.

Pivoting Options (if the Prospect Does Not Qualify). When a prospect does not qualify for an annuity, you must tell him or her, but you do not necessarily have to lose the prospect. *Pivoting*, as discussed in Chapter 2, involves delicately suggesting to the prospect that he or she consider alternative products or for the time being delay using annuities to finance retirement. Likewise, if the prospect is able, wants to fund the annuity, and is insurable but has higher priority needs, you can propose an alternative.

[handwritten: Get a visual for pivoting 3-Ring Binder of the above Pryamid]

pivoting

Example:

[handwritten: Great example!!]

"I feel ethically compelled to tell you that in my professional opinion, an annuity would not be appropriate for you now because of your more urgent need for life insurance to protect the financial stability of your family. However, you may be able to cushion some of the potential costs of funding your retirement by using the cash values in a permanent life insurance policy to supplement your

[handwritten: Can you see The Insphere Boys doing this in Norwell? - Hell no!!]

other retirement income resources at that time. <u>If we can construct a plan of action within your budget to cover your life insurance needs, would you be interested?</u>"

Keeping in Contact With Qualified Prospects

Do not forget to maintain contact with qualified prospects who do not buy annuity products from you initially. Also remember to stay in contact with your clients once a sale is made. Seminars, newsletters, birthday and holiday cards, and periodic reviews are all methods of maintaining contact. Your annuity clients are prospects for other products. If you are conducting a seminar on a topic other than retirement planning, invite them. A seminar is an excellent way to maintain face-to-face contact and to invite cross-selling opportunities in a time-efficient manner. Newsletters are less personal but still remind clients of your expertise. Sending birthday and holiday greeting cards also keeps your name in front of clients and prospects and can lead to repeat business and referrals, may help to build relationships, and is usually appreciated. Periodic reviews offer a way to uncover sequential sales opportunities while staying alert to your clients' changing needs.

CHAPTER THREE REVIEW

Key Terms and Concepts are explained in the Glossary. Answers to the Review Questions and Self-Test Questions are found in the back of the book in the Answers to Questions section.

Key Terms and Concepts

single-premium deferred annuity
flexible-premium deferred annuity
tax deferral
joint owners
joint annuitants
interest rate guarantee period
bonus interest rate
premium bonus
renewal interest rate
withdrawal
partial surrender
surrender
surrender charge period
surrender charge

accumulation value
surrender value
free-corridor amount
market value adjustment
death benefit
maturity date
terminal illness rider
long-term care benefit rider
social style
effective communication
active listening
preliminary discovery agreement
pivoting

Review Questions

3-1.   Describe the difference between a single-premium deferred annuity and a flexible-premium deferred annuity.

3-2.   Describe how annuity values increase on a tax-deferred basis.

3-3.   Describe a bonus interest rate and a premium bonus, and explain how the two concepts differ.

3-4.   Describe a market value adjustment feature and its application at the time of surrender.

3-5.   Describe a partial surrender, and explain how it differs from a full surrender.

3-6.   Describe a typical free corridor amount provision in a deferred annuity contract.

3-7.   Explain why companies may limit the issue age for qualified deferred annuity contracts to a younger age than that for nonqualified deferred-annuity contracts.

3-8.   Explain why a prospect would be concerned about the renewal interest rates a company typically pays to its policyowners.

3-9.   Explain the main purpose of the initial interview in a two-interview sales approach.

3-10. List the four social styles, and identify the characteristic that best explains what a prospect with a particular style is motivated to achieve.

3-11. List the steps in the retirement planning process.

3-12. Describe some of the sales presentation tools and techniques that an advisor can use to explain the need for annuities.

3-13. Explain why some prospects fail to qualify for an annuity during the fact-finding interview.

Self-Test Questions

Instructions: Read Chapter 3 first; then answer the following questions to test your knowledge. There are 10 questions; circle the correct answer, and then check your answers with the answer key in the back of the book.

3-1.   The most important part of effective communication is

   (A)   talking
   (B)   listening
   (C)   understanding
   (D)   responding

3-2. Which investment most commonly competes with a fixed-interest deferred annuity?

  (A) life insurance
  (B) variable annuity
  (C) mutual fund
  (D) certificate of deposit

3-3. Which feature or benefit about a deferred annuity do purchasers think of first?

  (A) withdrawals
  (B) death benefits
  (C) renewal interest rates
  (D) tax deferral

3-4. Which of the following options is available for a nonspouse beneficiary upon the annuitant's death?

  (A) rolling over the annuity to the annuitant's name
  (B) receiving the proceeds on an income-tax-free basis
  (C) leaving the values with the insurance company for up to 5 years
  (D) within 90 days of death, annuitizing the values without paying any income taxes

3-5. Which of the following statements regarding annuities is (are) correct?

  I. Insurance companies may establish different minimum premiums for qualified deferred annuities than for nonqualified deferred annuities.
  II. Insurance companies may limit the issue ages for qualified deferred annuities more than for nonqualified deferred annuities.

  (A) I only
  (B) II only
  (C) Both I and II
  (D) Neither I nor II

3-6. If the interest rate is 8 percent, there are 4 years remaining before the end of the surrender charge period, and newly issued annuities are paying 6 percent interest, which of the following statements regarding a market value adjustment (MVA) to the annuity surrender value is (are) correct?

    I.   The annuity owner generally receives a higher credited interest rate for the MVA feature.

    II.   The annuity owner generally receives an increase in annuity value upon surrender.

    (A)   I only
    (B)   II only
    (C)   Both I and II
    (D)   Neither I nor II

3-7. Which of the following statements regarding the payment of the contract proceeds to a nonspouse beneficiary if the death occurs prior to the time of annuitization is (are) correct?

    I.   Proceeds must be distributed within 5 years of the death of the annuitant/owner.

    II.   Proceeds must be distributed as an annuity based on life expectancy of the beneficiary, as long as payments begin within one year of the date of the owner's death.

    (A)   I only
    (B)   II only
    (C)   Both I and II
    (D)   Neither I nor II

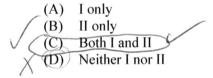

3-8. All of the following statements regarding bonus interest rates are correct EXCEPT

    (A)   Bonus rates are generally available for one year and possibly up to 5 years.
    (B)   Surrender charges are usually higher with bonus annuities than nonbonus annuities.
    (C)   Bonus rates do not encourage the replacement of annuities.
    (D)   Interest rates normally decrease after the bonus period is over.

3-9. All of the following statements regarding rolling surrender charges are correct EXCEPT

   (A)   They normally apply to flexible-premium deferred annuity policies.
   (B)   They can easily cause confusion to the policyowner.
   (C)   They do not apply to nonqualified annuities.
   (D)   They cannot be waived at the owner's discretion.

3-10. To establish rapport in the initial interview, advisors must create an environment that promotes prospect openness by doing all of the following EXCEPT

   (A)   alleviating the prospect's concerns
   (B)   responding to the social style of the prospect
   (C)   talking most of the time to the prospect
   (D)   mutually agreeing to an agenda for the interview

NOTES

1. *National Vital Statistics Reports*, vol. 55, no. 19, August 21, 2007. Deaths: Final Data for 2004, p. 6.
2. *2001 Life Insurance Fact Book*, American Council of Life Insurance, chapter 13, table 13-3. Mortality and life expectancy tables show a life expectancy of 6 months at age 99 under the Commissioners 1980 Standard Ordinary Table whereas the Individual Annuity 2000 table shows a 6-month life expectancy for a 115-year-old.
3. Title 26, Internal Revenue Code Sec. 72(u), Letter Ruling 199905015.
4. *The Annuity Handbook*. ©2005, The National Underwriter Company, P.O. Box 14367, Cincinnati, Ohio, 45250, p. 29.
5. This interpretation is in accordance with Sections 72(e)(3)(A)(i) and 72(e)(5)(E)(i) of the Internal Revenue Code.
6. Letter Ruling 200307095.
7. "Personal Styles and Effective Performance," David W. Merill and Roger H. Reid © 1999 CRC Press LLC.
8. "An Update on Private Pensions," by Alicia H. Munnell and Pamela Perun, An Issue in Brief, August 2006, Number 50, Center for Retirement Research at Boston College.
9. *Deferred Annuity Owner Characteristics and Attititudes—A 2003 Report.* © 2003, LIMRA International Inc.®

4

Indexed Annuities; Fact Finding

Learning Objectives

An understanding of the material in this chapter should enable you to

4-1. Explain the basic structure and marketing appeal of an equity-indexed annuity.

4-2. Identify the three basic methods of indexed crediting.

4-3. Explain the function behind equity-indexed annuity minimum guarantees.

4-4. Explain how insurance companies invest equity-indexed annuity premiums.

4-5. Identify the questions in a retirement planning fact-finder form.

Chapter Outline

Chapter 4 explores indexed annuities (also referred to throughout this chapter as equity-indexed annuities). The chapter covers the basic structure of equity-indexed annuities, the most common methods of measuring interest earnings, and how insurance companies invest premiums to replicate the index's actual earnings. The second part of the chapter focuses on how to conduct meaningful fact- and feeling-finding to ascertain a prospect's retirement income need and motivation to purchase annuities.

THE EMERGENCE OF INDEXED ANNUITIES

An indexed annuity or, as it is frequently referred to, an equity-indexed annuity, is a unique form of a deferred annuity that offers a middle ground between a fixed-interest deferred annuity and a variable deferred annuity. It pays interest not on what the insurance company declares but rather on the perfomance of an outside index of securities. It also provides a minimum guaranteed return.

Equity-indexed annuities (EIAs) and other indexed annuities emerged in the insurance industry in 1995. At that time, the stock market was doing very well, and lots of clients were purchasing variable deferred annuities. Nonregistered representatives could sell only traditional fixed-interest and immediate annuities. But fixed-interest deferred annuities were not looking competitive next to their cousin, the variable annuity. Because only registered representatives can sell variable deferred annuities, the nonregistered representatives were asking insurance companies to build a product that would capture some of the stock market's upside potential.

In response, the insurance industry designed a product that would offer the upside of the variable deferred annuity but would avoid SEC registration so that nonregistered representatives would have an attractive product to offer.

From this product development effort, the indexed annuity appeared. Sales have grown from $6.8 billion in 2001 to $25.4 billion in 2006, which was 38 percent of all fixed deferred-annuity sales for that year. Most indexed annuities are tied to an "equity" index, meaning a stock index. Some are tied to a nonequity index—for example, a bond index. Although this chapter will mainly use the phrase equity-indexed annuity, bear in mind that not all indexed annuities are actually tied to an equity index.

Product Design

The equity-indexed annuity is unique among annuity products. New product features and terms were created to design this new and innovative product. This section will help the financial advisor understand the various product designs available and become familiar with the terminology associated with the equity-indexed market. The section will demonstrate how the different product features work together to provide index-linked interest to annuity clients.

Equity and Bond Indexes

index

Indexing is a strategy insurance companies use to match the performance of the annuity to an outside group of securities. The outside group of securities forms an *index*. The index is a measure of the group's performance. The index's performance is then the measure of the indexed annuity's performance, which the insurance company uses as a basis for the current rates of interest that it passes on to owners of its indexed annuity products.

A recent review of the indexed annuity marketplace shows the following indexes are used for interest crediting purposes:

- S&P 500 Index®
- S&P Midcap 400®
- Dow Jones Industrial Average®
- Russell 2000® Index
- Lehman Brothers U.S. Treasury Index®
- Lehman Brothers Aggregate Bond Index
- Merrill Lynch All Convertibles Index
- NASDAQ 100 Index®
- various international indexes

This list includes both equity and nonequity indexes and thus illustrates the appropriateness of using the term *indexed annuities* as opposed to *equity-indexed annuities* when referring to these annuity policies.

Indexing Methods

To understand how the indexing methods in indexed annuities work, it helps to become familiar with the following three key terms:

contract term

- *contract term.* Interest credited to an equity-indexed annuity is based on the increases in the index that occur over a defined period of time, which is called the contract term. The term can be from one year to seven or even ten years. The term is an important concept for a prospect to understand because once the term is selected, it will usually limit the owner's free access to the funds during the term. Therefore if funds are withdrawn before the end of the term, they will usually be subject to an early surrender penalty imposed by the issuing company.

free window period

- *free window period.* The owner usually has several options at the end of the contract term, which is called the free window period, or window period, which include the following:
  - The equity-indexed annuity can be renewed for another contract term.
  - It can be exchanged for another type of annuity such as a fixed-interest-deferred or variable-deferred annuity.
  - The contract can be annuitized, and the annuitant can begin to receive the benefits under one of the available settlement options.
  - The contract's indexed account value can be partially or completely surrendered without incurring company surrender charges, and the owner will pay any income taxes that are due.

percentage change

- *percentage change.* The percentage change is the change in the index from the beginning of the contract term to the end of the contract term expressed as a percentage. For example, if the S&P 500 Index stands at 1,000 at the beginning of the term and it rises to 1,150, there is a 15 percent change.

There are various methods to measure the performance of the index from the starting point (the date the contract was originally put in force) to the end of the contract term. The three principal methods of index measurement for crediting interest to an equity-indexed annuity are the annual reset design, point-to-point design, and high water mark.

There are many variations of each of these basic designs. We will examine how the three different indexing methods affect the performance of three equity-indexed annuities by comparing the cash value growth of the three policies when applying hypothetical percentage changes in the S&P 500 Index using the three basic indexing methods to credit interest within each of them. We will assume that an investor deposits $100,000 into each equity-indexed annuity, and we will track the results of the cash value growth over a 5-year interest-crediting period. For simplicity's sake, the three scenarios ignore any cap rates, participation rates, or asset fees, which are discussed in detail later in this chapter.

To begin, look at Figure 4-1, which represents the S&P 500 Index for a 5-year period. When our investor buys the three annuities, the S&P 500 Index level, upon which the annuities' performance will be based, stands at 1,000. At the end of year 1, the index has risen 15 percent to the 1,150 level. By the end of year 2, the index has fallen back to 1,100 (a 4.35 percent decline). By the end of year 3, the index has fallen again to 1,050 (a 4.55 percent decline). By the end of year 4, the index has fallen a third time to 1,000 (a 4.7 percent decline). By the end of year 5, the index has increased to 1,100, which is a 10 percent increase.

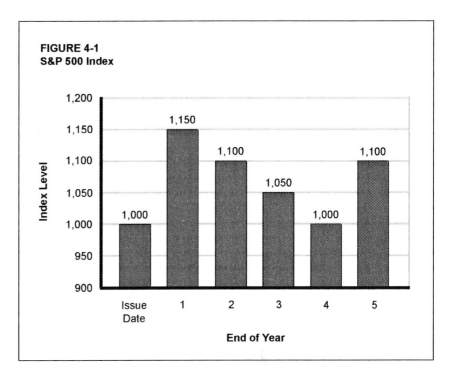

FIGURE 4-1
S&P 500 Index

We will compare how $100,000 deposited into three separate equity-indexed annuities performs when linked to the S&P 500 Index according to the changing levels in the index over a 5-year period. The three annuities will use the annual reset, point-to-point design, and high water mark indexing methods, respectively.

Annual Reset Design

annual reset

Annual reset (or annual ratchet) indexed annuities compare the positive change in the index from the beginning of the policy year to the end of the policy year. The annual reset method provides incremental protection on growth by locking in the previous year's anniversary value. Locking in the positive index returns and ignoring negative index returns preserves the contract's principal and past positive earnings. This process of building on the past positive returns is sometimes referred to as *ratcheting*. Annual resets will perform well when the index experiences moderate consistent growth; they will also perform well in choppy markets.

ratcheting

As Figure 4-2 shows, the annual reset design will credit growth as follows: from the issue date to the end of year 1, and from the end of year 4 to the end of year 5. However, no losses are subtracted or lost in the negative years from the end of year 1 to the end of year 2, from the end of year 2 to the end of year 3, and from the end of year 3 to the end of year 4. The starting point for one year is the end of the year value from the year before, hence the term annual reset.

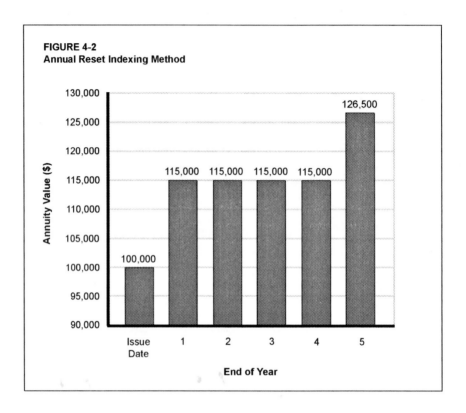

FIGURE 4-2
Annual Reset Indexing Method

Therefore in this scenario, the first annuity's contract value increased by 15 percent from the issue date ($100,000) to the end of year 1 ($115,000), then by another 10 percent from the end of year 4 ($115,000) to the end of year 5 ($126,500).

Averaging. Another strategy to bring up the value of returns in negatively moving indexes and bring down the value of returns in positively moving indexes is *averaging*. Some indexed annuities average an index's value either daily or monthly rather than using the actual value of the index on a specified date. Because averaging can reduce the amount of index-linked interest, it reduces the insurance company's risk and therefore its cost.

averaging

Table 4-1 shows the negative effect that monthly averaging can have in a *constantly rising* market. The table shows a straight 7 percent increase in the index. Note the monthly average increase compared to 7 percent.

TABLE 4-1
S&P 500 Index Growth Using Monthly Averaging Assuming a
Constantly Increasing Index Over the 12-Month Period

Purchase Date: December 1
December 1 Index = 900

Index Date	Index Value	Index Date	Index Value
January	900	July	935
February	910	August	940
March	915	September	945
April	920	October	950
May	925	November	960
June	930	December	963
		Total Index Values	11,193

The following formula is used to calculate the index average:

Total index values ÷ 12 months = Monthly index average

$$\frac{11,193}{12} = 933$$

$$\frac{\text{Monthly index average } - \text{ starting index}}{\text{Starting index}} = \text{Monthly average index earnings}$$

$$\frac{933 - 900}{900} = 3.7\%$$

Therefore the monthly average index earnings for the year are 3.7 percent, which is roughly half the straight line increase of 7 percent.
Had the annuity policy used the annual reset method without monthly averaging, the policy would credit

$$\frac{\text{End-of-year index value } - \text{ beginning-of-year value}}{\text{Beginning-of-year index value}} = \text{Index growth}$$

$$\frac{963 - 900}{900} = 7.0\% \text{ Index growth}$$

These two calculations show that while the actual index using the annual reset method increased at 7 percent for the year, with averaging, the index credits only 3.7 percent. This is a large difference in interest earnings based on the same index, simply by using different methods to calculate the interest. Clients need to understand how interest is credited on their policies to be satisfied with their annuity's performance and not surprised by the numbers on their annual statement. The importance of having the policy-owner and the financial advisor understand EIAs and how they credit interest is critical to maintaining satisfied and happy clients.

Point-to-Point Design

point-to-point

Point-to-point indexed annuities do not lock in positive growth in the index each year. Instead, they compare the change in the index at the beginning and at the ending dates of the contract term. For example, if an S&P 500 Indexed, 5-year, point-to-point contract was purchased in January 2005, the contract owner will not know if he or she will receive any indexed interest until January 2010. Therefore the client risks losing previous gains if the index declines near the end of the term. The primary benefit of the point-to-point design is that it offers the highest return to the client during uninterrupted bull markets.

Figure 4-3 shows the hypothetical performance of the second equity-indexed annuity using a 5-year point-to-point indexing method. This annuity will credit interest based on the difference between the issue date and the end of the 5-year contract term, which is a 10 percent gain in value.

Moreover, at the end of each policy year during that 5-year period, interest earnings are not credited to the policy. It is only at the end of the 5-year period that the index value is compared to the index value on the policy's issue date.

Some indexed annuity policies will also use the concept of averaging with point-to-point policies. With point-to-point products, this concept works slightly differently. The policy may choose to average the last policy year's monthly indexes and compare that year's monthly average to the policy issue index. Another alternative is to average the last 6 months instead of the last year. For example, the policy may take the index value 4 years and 6 months into the contract term and average that index value with the index as of the end of the contract term. By averaging these two index points, the annuity owner has a better chance of receiving interest earnings if the market has dropped in the last year.

Example: Assume the index as of the policy issue date is 1,000, the index at 4 ½ years is 1,050, and the year 5 index value is 980. A pure 5-year point-to-point is calculated as follows:

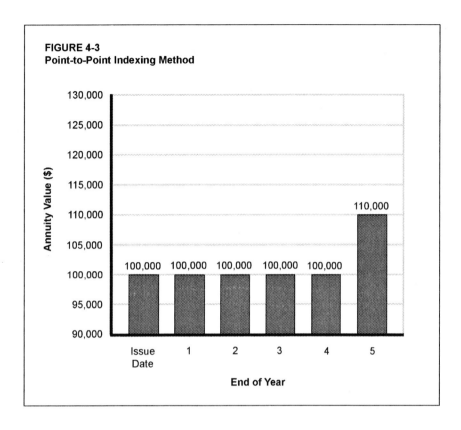

FIGURE 4-3
Point-to-Point Indexing Method

Because the ending index of 980 is less than the policy issue index of 1,000, no interest is credited for the 5-year period. However, by averaging the last 6 months, the interest earnings are calculated as follows:

$$980 + 1050 = 2030 / 2 = 1015$$
$$1015 / 1000 = 1.5\% \text{ increase}$$

This calculation shows the difference that averaging can make in how much interest is credited to the policy. Clearly, without averaging, the client would receive no interest earnings for the 5-year period. By averaging the last 6 months' indexes, the annuity would earn 1.5 percent interest.

High Water Mark Design

high water mark

The *high water mark* crediting method typically assesses the index value at each prior anniversary of the contract during the measuring period and uses the highest of these anniversary index values. The index level at the start of the contract is then compared to the highest point during the measuring period. Each year that a new high water mark value is achieved for the index, the value of the equity-indexed annuity grows. If the index level at the end of the year is below the previous high water mark, the account value does not grow, but previous gains are not lost. During periods of volatility, the index must recover to its previous highs before further gains are recorded.

Three Types of Indexing Methods

- **Annual reset method:** compares the positive change in the index from the beginning of the policy year to the end of the policy year

- **Point-to-point:** credits interest earnings by measuring from one particular index point to a second particular index point at the end of the contract term

- **High water mark:** compares the index point at the end of each policy year to the last highest anniversary point within the contract term

---

In Figure 4-4, from the issue date to the end of year 1, the contract will earn 15 percent interest because the S&P 500 Index level of 1,150 is 15 percent higher than the level at the issue date, which was 1,000. However, at the end of year 2 no interest earnings will be credited because the index level has dropped to 1,100, and it is not the highest mark so far in the policy's first 2 years. At the end of year 3, no interest earnings will be credited because the index level has dropped to 1,050, and it is not the highest mark so far in the policy's first 3 years. Again, at the end of year 4, no interest earnings will be credited because the index level has dropped to 1,000 and is not the highest mark in the policy's first 4 years. Finally, although the index increases from the end of year 4 at the 1,000 level to the 1,100 level at the end of year 5, no interest is credited to the policy because the index has not exceeded the highest water mark within the 5-year contract term, which was 1,150 at the end of year 1. Therefore the third annuity contract illustrated in this example experiences the 15 percent gain in the S&P 500 Index experienced from the issue date to the end of year 1, then remains constant at a $115,000 cash value for the remainder of the 5-year contract term.

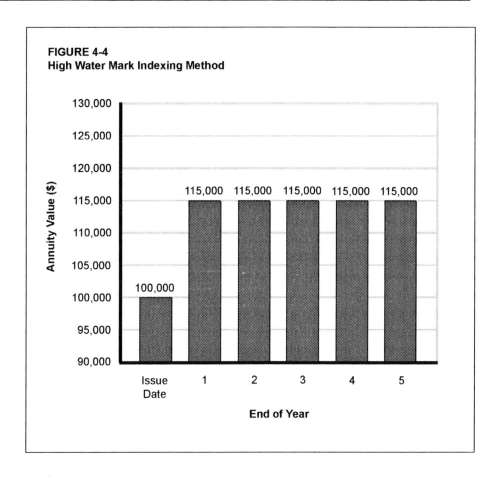

FIGURE 4-4
High Water Mark Indexing Method

With each crediting method it is crucial to know when earnings will be credited to the policy as well as when those credited earnings will be available for the client to withdraw. Some product designs may not credit interest annually, and some still might not allow the client to withdraw funds even if they are credited annually. In addition, it is important to determine how withdrawals from the policy affect interest already credited. The policyowner might forfeit any earnings if he or she withdraws funds before the end of the contract term.

 Note that during a prolonged bear market, none of these methods will offer positive results, in which case the contract will provide only its underlying guarantees.

Once the index has been identified, the next factor to consider is the length of time that must transpire before the interest will be credited. Will it be credited annually at the end of each year, biannually at the end of each second contract year, or at the end of some longer period of time? These time periods are referred to as the contract term for interest crediting, which could be as long as 10 to 15 years. It is particularly important for clients to be able to leave their money in the contract until the maturity date. Potential surrender charges and the loss of any index gains can hurt the policyowner if the funds are not held long enough

Investing Equity-Indexed Annuity Premiums

Every dollar the client pays in premiums for an indexed annuity has to be split into three pieces. First, the expenses are deducted. Second, the portion of the dollar required to provide the guarantee (for example, 90 percent of the principal will earn 3 percent) is invested. Finally, what is left over is used to purchase *options* on the index. These options are securities that an insurance company purchases, using a portion of the premium it collects from the sale of an indexed annuity, to back the interest-earning obligation it has to the owners of those contracts. By buying options, the insurance company owns the right to any gain in the index during the policy period. If the option is profitable to the insurance company, the insurance company will have the necessary profit to pass on to the annuity policy.

Table 4-2 shows the breakdown of each premium dollar. The insurance company puts 90 cents into an investment that will cover the 3 percent guarantee. Three cents is deducted to pay immediate expenses, which leaves 7 cents to invest in options. Because the cost of options for indexes can be volatile, the insurance company is constantly adjusting how much interest it can credit based on the price of the options.

options

TABLE 4-2				
Investing Equity-Indexed Annuity Premiums				
Distribution of $1	3% Guarantee on 90% of premium	Expenses	Options	Total
	$0.90	$0.03	$0.07	$1.00

The most difficult part of managing the capital in an indexed annuity is buying the options. Option buying can be expensive. In times of tranquil markets, options typically are less expensive, but as volatility increases, costs can increase.

Indexed interest earnings are subject to limits imposed by the insurance company through capped interest rates, participation rates, and asset fees, which are discussed next, so that the insurance company will have sufficient profit.

Crediting Interest

The uniqueness of the equity-indexed annuity is based on the method the insurance company uses to calculate the annuity's interest earnings. This method is what sets EIAs apart from all other annuity products. Terms, such as asset fees, participation rates, and caps, all fit together like a puzzle to calculate the interest earnings.

Asset Fees

**asset fee
spread
margin**

Some indexed annuities use an *asset fee* (also called a *spread* or a *margin*) to reduce the amount of interest credited to the policy. The asset fee is stated as a percentage such as 2 percent or 3 percent. The asset fee is subtracted from any gain in the index. For example, if the index gained 16 percent and the asset fee is 2 percent, then the credited interest will be 14 percent.

The asset fee is the company's profit on the annuity policy. If the index earns 7 percent and the spread is 2 percent, then the annuity will be credited with 5 percent interest. The company keeps 2 percent as its profit.

Typically assets fees are adjustable every year by the insurance company. The policy should state a maximum that the asset fee will never exceed. For example, the current asset fee charged by the insurance company might be 2 percent, but the contract may state a maximum asset fee of 5 percent.

Participation Rates

participation rate

The *participation rate* is the proportionate amount of the percentage change that is used to determine the actual interest rate that will be credited to an equity-indexed annuity for the contract term. The participation rate is set by the insurance company and stated in the equity-indexed annuity contract. Insurance companies offer various percentages of participation in the index, such as 100 percent, or lower rates such as 70 percent or 80 percent. A participation rate may be used in addition to, or in lieu of, an asset fee. The insurance company may set the participation rate at 80 percent, which means the annuity will be credited with only 80 percent of the gain experienced by the index. If the participation rate is used in addition to a hypothetical 2 percent asset fee, and the index rises 16 percent, the credited interest rate will be 11.2 percent.

$$16\% - 2\% = 14\% \ \text{x} \ 80\% = 11.2\%$$

Or the credited rate could be 10.8 percent if the insurance company applies the participation rate of 80 percent *before* it applies a 2 percent asset fee.

$$16\% \times 80\% = 12.8\% - 2\% = 10.8\%$$

Participation rates are adjustable by the insurance company. They are usually adjustable on each policy anniversary, but some policies may guarantee the participation rate for the length of the contract term.

Cap Rates

cap rate

The insurance company may place a *cap rate* or upper limit on the amount of interest the annuity can earn. The cap is the absolute maximum interest rate the annuity will earn. The cap rate is usually expressed as a percentage. For example, in the case above, assume the cap rate is 10 percent. We do not have to worry about whether the company applies the 80 percent participation rate or the 2 percent asset fee first. Because both credited rates are over 10 percent, the cap rate will prevail, and 10 percent will be the maximum amount of interest credited to the annuity.

Like asset fees and participation rates, caps are adjustable by the insurance company. They are normally adjusted on each policy anniversary.

Example: Assume the S&P 500 Index has grown 13 percent over the year and the annuity has

- 100 percent participation
- 11 percent cap
- 3.5 percent asset fee

If the insurance company applies the cap before the asset fee is subtracted, the annuity's growth will be calculated as follows:

Compare the actual index earnings of 13 percent to the current cap rate, which is 11 percent. Because the current cap is less than the actual index earnings, the annuity formula will use the lesser of the two figures—11 percent. Next the asset fee will be subtracted from the above figure.

$$11\% - 3.5\% = 7.5\% \text{ credited interest}$$

Alternatively, if the annuity policy's formula requires the asset fee to be deducted from the indexed earnings *before* the cap is applied, then the formula for the example above will be as follows:

$$11\% - 3.5\% = 7.5\% \text{ credited interest}$$

Compare 9.5 percent to the cap of 11 percent. The lower of the two figures is used to credit interest earnings to the policy. Because 9.5 percent is less than 11 percent, the company will credit 9.5 percent interest earnings to the annuity policy.

$$13\% - 3.5\% = 9.5\%$$

Note that not all product designs will have a cap. Caps are frequently used with annual reset methods but not with long-term point-to-point or high water mark designs.

Financial advisors might ask the question, "What happens to the profit if the index earns 13 percent and the cap is 11 percent? Does the insurance company keep the profit earned above the cap?" The answer is that normally the insurance company will buy only enough options to reach the cap. In this example, the insurance company would cover only the index up to 11 percent and not 13 percent. Therefore there would not be any profit for the company to keep.

All these examples show the importance of understanding how insurance companies credit interest and how the participation rate, cap, and asset fee are applied to the formula. Each of these factors in the interest-crediting formula is established by the insurance company to control the amount of profit the company earns and the amount of interest earnings it must credit to its indexed policies. Bear in mind that just knowing one of the elements—for example, knowing the participation rate is 100 percent—does not give the financial advisor the whole picture. Participation rates, caps, and asset fees are all part of the total package. A product could be competitive and still have a low participation rate. Likewise a product could be uncompetitive and still have a low asset fee. The bottom line is to know all the features of the indexed annuity you are recommending and how they work together.

Minimum Interest Guarantees

guaranteed minimum interest rate

The *guaranteed minimum interest rate* is the contractually stated percentage rate that will be credited to an indexed annuity during a year or over the term of the contract. This guaranteed minimum interest rate is what allows the equity-indexed annuity to be considered a fixed annuity rather than a securities product.

To address decreasing profits from equity-indexed annuities partially due to the decreasing spreads from interest rates, companies have revised their policies. Revisions include decreasing the 3 percent guaranteed minimum interest rate. When indexed annuities first came to the market, the minimum guarantee was 3 percent on 100 percent of the premium. Now some policies guarantee only 3 percent on 90 percent of the premium.

Another method to reduce interest rates—while trying to make the lower rate not sound quite so bad—is to describe it as a guaranteed minimum return of 115 percent of premium at the end of a 10-year term, which comes out to be less than a 1 percent return on 90 percent of premium paid.

A large misconception with EIAs is that many advisors, as well as clients, believe that during a down year in the index, the indexed account value will earn the guaranteed minimum interest rate. Unfortunately, that is not how equity-indexed annuities are designed. This is easily explained by the use of two separate and distinct calculations: the indexed account value and the guaranteed account value.

The indexed account value is based solely on the earnings of the index, and the guaranteed account value is based solely on guaranteed minimum interest rates. Neither calculation crosses over into the other. The indexed account value will grow based only on the indexed earnings, subject to the participation rates, caps, and asset fees. If the index has a down year, the indexed account value just stays constant, meaning it does not grow for the year but it also does not decrease. The guaranteed interest of 3 percent is not applied to the indexed account value.

The guaranteed account value might start at only 80 percent or 90 percent of the premium and earn 3 percent from that figure. An important distinction is that normally asset fees are deducted from only the indexed account value and never from the guaranteed account value. This answers a commonly asked question, "If the guarantee is only 3 percent and the asset fee is 3.5 percent, how can the client earn any interest?" The answer is that these two parts of the indexed annuity do not function together. The asset fee is deductible against only *index earnings*, not guaranteed interest.

When a policyowner decides to surrender the policy, generally the insurance company determines which of the two account values is the higher. Usually that is what the client receives, *minus any applicable surrender charges.* However, note that not all indexed policies will credit guaranteed interest if the client surrenders the policy before the end of the contract term.

Table 4-3 shows a hypothetical indexed annuity with a $100,000 single premium and a 3 percent guaranteed account value based on 100 percent of the premium. If the policy credits guaranteed interest earnings at the end of each policy year, and does not wait until the end of the contract term, the client will receive the higher of column A or column B at surrender. (During years in which the index was in a negative position, the indexed account value remained constant and did not decrease.)

Withdrawals and Surrenders

Indexed annuity surrender charges are more complicated than those for fixed-interest deferred annuities. The free withdrawal corridors are also more complicated. Depending on how the interest is calculated, both

TABLE 4-3
Indexed Account Values and Guaranteed Account Values

End of Year	S&P 500 Index Annual Earnings*	Indexed Account Value (Column A)	Guaranteed Account Value Based on 3% on 100% of Premium (Column B)
Year 1	5%	$105,000	$103,000
Year 2	0%	$105,000	$106,090
Year 3	–2.0%	$105,000	$109,273
Year 4	4.0%	$109,200	$112,551
Year 5	8.0%	$117,936	$115,928
Year 6	6.0%	$125,012	$119,406
Year 7	2.0%	$127,512	$122,988
Year 8	–2.0%	$127,512	$126,678
Year 9	4.0%	$132,612	$130,478
Year 10	–1.0%	$132,612	$134,392

*After the participation rate, cap, and asset fees have been applied

potential interest from the underlying guarantee and index-calculated interest can be forfeited. In addition, surrender charges are typically higher than in fixed-interest deferred annuities—up to 17 percent in the first year—and last longer, ranging from 7 to 16 years; 12 years is typical. The variety of surrender charges makes the decision to purchase more difficult for the client and the advisor.

If, at time of purchase, a client's time horizon for taking money out of the annuity (in excess of the free corridor) is shorter than the surrender charge period, the product, by definition, is unsuitable. However, life events can happen after purchase that unexpectedly cause people to withdraw money from their contracts. It is for this reason that companies provide a free corridor and waivers of the surrender charge for nursing home stays, terminal illness, and even unemployment in some cases.

The good news about surrender charges is that they allow insurance companies to pay a higher rate of interest than they would be able to pay if people could freely withdraw from their contracts. The existence of the surrender charge allows the insurance company to invest in longer-duration, higher-interest-paying bonds to provide better returns. Just as is typical in certificates of deposit, the longer the restricted period, the higher the interest.

Death Benefits

On Quiz Question #2

Death benefit provisions in EIA contracts have some similarities to those of declared-rate fixed-interest deferred annuities, but there also are some differences. In some EIAs, the death benefit will be the greater of the guaranteed account value or the indexed account value. In others, it will be the return of premium or the return of premium plus a minimum interest rate, regardless of index interest growth. In a very few situations, it will be the guaranteed account value only.

The second aspect of death benefits has to do with equity-indexed annuities that pay the indexed account value at death. In these contracts, the interest rate calculation method used by the particular EIA product can affect how much index interest there is. When looking at an EIA that credits the total index interest rate, it is important to know how that total interest rate is determined at the time of death. Sometimes the index level at the time of death is used; at other times, the calculation is based on the value at the last anniversary of the policy. This difference can cause great variations under certain economic conditions that may affect the index being used. It is also important to know whether a pro rata portion of the participation rate or asset fees is applied if interest is calculated as of the date of death.

There are many considerations to look at regarding death benefits. Clients and their families must have a clear understanding of what the death benefit will be at any given time. It is critical that you communicate as clearly as possible how the death benefit in an EIA is calculated so that your clients readily understand it.

Annuitization

Some EIAs provide full access to the indexed account value and also waive surrender charges during the index period if the account values are annuitized. If there is not full access and waiver of surrender charges, there is often a minimum length of time that must pass before annuitization is permitted. Typically, this is the first few contract years. In many cases, there is also a minimum time period over which the values are to be paid out. These provisions tend to work similarly to their counterparts in fixed-interest deferred annuities. Clients should carefully explore contractual options and limitations on annuitization when considering various EIA products.

Generally account values may be distributed over a period of years or for the life of the annuitant either on a single-life or joint-life basis. There are various payment options available if annuitization is chosen. These life income options and the tax advantages of annuitization are discussed in greater detail in Chapters 6 and 7, respectively.

SELLING EQUITY-INDEXED ANNUITIES

Recently, decreasing interest rates and increasing equity volatility have substantially increased costs to the insurance companies that manufacture equity-indexed annuities. The decrease in the difference between what companies were guaranteeing to the client and what they could earn on their investments occurred at the same time the cost of options increased. As a result, indexed products coming into the market today have lower guaranteed minimum interest rates than earlier versions of the product. Insurance companies have also had to place more constraints on how index-linked interest is credited.

Commissions

In 1995 and 1996, the first years for indexed annuities, the average contract term was 5 years, the average commission was 6 percent, and the products were fairly similar. Only two companies were significant providers at the time. As interest rates decreased and the equities market became more volatile, more indexed products came to market. By early 2006, some 40-plus major companies offered various designs of indexed products. Each product had features that made it different from any other product, even those issued by the same company. Now almost all of the indexed products have 10-year terms or more, constraints have been built into the crediting methods, and the commissions paid on almost all sales are 9 percent or higher.

Typically, high commission rates are a great way to get shelf space and attention when breaking into a new market, but it comes at a price, and that price is paid by the consumer. Generally speaking, the higher the commission, the less consumer friendly the product. The least consumer friendly products are those that pay inordinately high commissions, have extremely long surrender periods, and give the insurance company the right to change the product design before the end of the surrender charge period.

Commission schedules for equity-indexed annuities are, in general, higher than the commission schedules on fixed-interest deferred annuities. All else being equal, a higher commission to the insurance company means lower overall interest earnings to the policyowner.

The trend for equity-indexed annuities is to develop commission schedules to pay reduced commissions for policies on very old policyowners (or annuitants). For example, a commission schedule may pay 7 percent for policies with issue ages up to 80, 5 percent for policies with issue ages between 81 and 84, and 2.5 percent for issue ages from 85 to 90.

The reason for decreasing commissions at older ages is that the purchaser is closer to actuarial life expectancy; therefore the chance of paying a death benefit is closer, and the insurance company's ability to retain the money for a longer period of time is reduced. The company will not have the money for a long enough period to make a profit, so reducing the commissions helps the company reach its profit goal within the shorter estimated time frame.

Industry Regulation

Indexed annuities are generally considered fixed-annuity products. Most are not registered products despite their reference to equity indexes to determine how much interest the policy earns. They do not pay equity returns; they pay interest. The interest they pay is measured by the positive change in the index or the guaranteed interest rate, whichever is higher.

Some companies that have chosen to register their indexed products have done so based on the investment nature of the product and the fact that the product's complexity and link to the equity index deserve to be fully disclosed to the client. These companies maintain that full disclosure is best provided in a prospectus and that only regulated registered representatives may properly sell the product.

The distinction as to whether the indexed annuity belongs on the fixed annuity side or the registered annuity side is also important from a licensing standpoint. Individuals with an agent's license, licensed by the states in which they sell insurance products, can sell the annuities on the fixed annuity side, which is generally where indexed annuities currently reside. To sell variable insurance products, the individual must also be a registered representative and comply with SEC and NASD requirements, as well as state securities and insurance regulation.

The problem with fixed, nonregistered annuities is that their earnings, especially in times of relatively low interest rates, are less than what most people want and need. Long-term returns have not kept up with inflation.

The problem with the securities-registered variable annuities is that, although people love returns on stocks when they are positive, they do not like to see negative results. The equity-indexed annuity is a hybrid product. It is designed to trade some of the high potential return, or possibly devastating negative returns of variable products, for a product that can limit the downside but still allow some of the positive returns available from equity indexes.

In August 1997 the SEC issued a release that requested comments as to whether equity-indexed products should or should not be registered with the SEC. The SEC has taken no action as yet. However, on January 16, 2002, the NASD, now called the Financial Industry Regulatory Authority (FINRA), posted a rather extensive report on equity-indexed annuities, which was last updated on June 30, 2005, on its Web site under its "Investor Education, New Financial Products" section, at http://www.finra.org. It is unprecedented for FINRA to expend this much energy and to pay this much attention to a financial product that is not under its jurisdiction.

It is important for advisors to be aware of regulators' warnings to the public concerning the potential pitfalls of financial products. Financial advisors must be proactive in addressing those concerns. They need to make sure that their clients understand the advantages and disadvantages of all products in order to make informed decisions about the suitability of any product recommended to them.

Market Criticisms

Equity-indexed annuities have been subject to criticism since their introduction in 1995. Criticism stems from the complexity of the product and misunderstandings from clients. Some individuals assumed they were buying a product that operated and credited interest one way and then later found out it operated and paid interest quite differently.

The complexity of the equity-indexed annuity is in the way the annuity is designed. The annuity policy does not credit a flat amount of annual interest like its cousin, the fixed-interest deferred annuity. Instead, the insurance company must look to some event that happens outside the insurance industry, outside the insurance company, and outside the annuity policy itself just to credit interest. This leads to confusion.

Also the formula for determining the amount of interest can be complex to an average consumer. Furthermore, instead of directly connecting the interest to the index, the policy also compares the index earnings to yet another number (that is, the cap) before the client can figure out how much the annuity is really worth. Add the concept of "averaging" index values, and the client can become glassy-eyed. In fact, one insurance company shows a mathematical formula for crediting interest that looks like it came from a college statistics final exam. It does not stretch the imagination to see how clients can get confused.

The lack of SEC registration is another area of strong criticism against equity-indexed annuities. Critics would like to see these annuities registered with FINRA and the SEC so that consumers are given more disclosures in the sales process and also so that the product is regulated more heavily than fixed annuities.

The heavy commissions paid to the advisor to sell some, but not all, equity-indexed annuities have also brought criticism to the industry. Since traditional fixed-interest deferred annuity commissions are in the 4 percent range, to have equity-indexed annuities pay up to 15 percent commissions begs the question, "How much less competitive are these policies because of higher commissions?"

Because this product has more complexity than a traditional fixed-interest deferred annuity, insurance companies must increase the level of training they give their advisors before these products are available for sale. Critics contend that companies that have not provided the level of detailed

[handwritten margin note: 15% commission where?]

training on the product, the crediting methods, and the link to indexes have caused the industry to come under scrutiny.

The financial services industry has been criticized for the unjustified use of replacements and for subjecting the policyowner to a brand new set of surrender charges.

Equity-indexed annuities have been heavily criticized for having surrender charges that are longer than fixed-interest deferred annuity policies. Some equity-indexed annuities have surrender charges up to 15 years or more. When these annuities are sold to individuals whose actuarial life expectancy is shorter than the surrender charge period, it compounds the criticism.

Other critics contend that it is unclear with EIAs that the insurance company really is not taking the policyowner's money and investing it in the particular index. Many clients, as well as a few advisors, believe that the premium dollars are used to buy the actual index. Because this is not the case (insurance companies purchase options with policyowner premiums), confusion can easily exist. Critics want the industry to be clear that individuals are not buying shares in the actual index.

To put an end to the criticism over this product, financial advisors should determine that the client falls within all the following categories before recommending an equity-indexed annuity product. The client

- does not want a fixed-interest deferred annuity because the interest earnings are too low
- does not want a variable deferred annuity because of the possible loss of principal
- wants the possibility of higher interest than fixed-interest deferred annuities offer and will accept substantially less than the potential return of variable deferred annuities to avoid downside risk
- understands the indexed annuity structure and will not need the funds committed to the contract until after the surrender charge period
- understands and accepts the maturity date, index, and crediting method and finds them suitable
- understands and accepts the limitations on interest earnings from participation rates, spreads, and caps and finds them suitable
- understands and accepts the minimum guarantee as a trade-off for the potential interest that may be earned if the index's performance is poor
- knows what the commission is and considers it acceptable and well earned

THE FACT-FINDING PROCESS

After you have qualified the prospect and obtained a preliminary discovery agreement, the actual fact-finding and feeling-finding portion of the retirement planning process can be a continuation of the initial interview, or it can be a separate interview. This is your option. It is important, however, to remember that the prospect might be tired. The discussion of finances can be exhausting. You need to make certain that your prospect is still alert and attentive to your questions if you decide to continue the initial interview into the fact-finding process.

One approach to the financial needs analysis is deductive while the other is inductive.

Total Financial Needs Analysis to the Dominant or Single Need— the Deductive Approach

deductive approach

The *deductive approach* uses a thorough and lengthy fact-finding form that encompasses all the prospect's financial needs. This method covers life, disability income, and long-term care insurance; investment, estate, and education planning needs; and retirement income needs. The process requires quantifying these various financial planning needs and asking the prospect to prioritize them. The category of needs with the highest priority should be determined first. You should then address this most important category of needs by selling the prospect the appropriate product or products that meets that category.

Dominant or Single Need to Total Financial Needs Analysis—the Inductive Approach

inductive approach

The *inductive approach* is the converse of the broad information gathering described above. This method starts with a dominant or single need, such as the need for an annuity to reduce the current taxation of the prospect's savings. It then widens into a full-blown comprehensive financial needs analysis that identifies and prioritizes several financial planning needs. This may occur only after the dominant or single need has been covered by a particular product sale, and it could take several interviews to complete. Sometimes, however, as discussed previously under the "Dominant Need Situation," the dominant or single need product, such as a deferred annuity, may be the only product you ever sell to the prospect, and a total financial needs analysis may never transpire.

We do not necessarily endorse one approach over the other. Your company can provide you with guidance in this area that is consistent with its own marketing strategy and suitability requirements. Some companies that use the inductive or dominant-needs approach focus on preapproaching prospects for specific financial products as a door opener in the preretirement or seniors market in the hope of becoming involved in the prospect's retirement planning. Other companies that use the deductive or comprehensive financial planning approach attempt to position the sale of financial products somewhere in the sequence of financial planning needs. For purposes of our discussion, we have chosen the fact-finding and feeling-finding questions that can be used with either approach to enhance your retirement-planning sales opportunities.

Fact Finders

fact finder

There are numerous *fact finders* available for collecting data. Your company has probably already provided you with several that you are using. Nevertheless, we have included a Retirement Planning Fact Finder in appendix A that you are welcome to use with the permission of your company's compliance department. The point to remember about using a fact finder is not to limit yourself to asking just factual and quantitative questions. You should also ascertain your prospect's feelings and values. Asking only the factual questions will not involve your prospect and will not reveal his or her important feelings and values. Values are a person's beliefs and attitudes about a given subject. Feelings reflect a person's values. When you learn about your prospect's dreams and aspirations, you begin to understand him or her. Values are the basis of a person's behavior, and they influence an individual's priorities in life. Discovering your prospect's priorities is the key to understanding what he or she will spend time and money to achieve. Be sure to record the feelings and values revealed during the fact-finding process.

Involving the prospect in the fact-finding segment of the selling/planning process gives him or her an ownership interest in your financial product recommendations. The very process of discussing and examining feelings leads the prospect to self-discovery. In fact, the prospect is far more likely to spend more time and money on financial products associated with a plan that he or she played a role in designing.

Your prospect must collaborate in the process. Because the prospect is potentially buying your financial products and services, he or she should make that decision based on knowledge obtained from you during the interview. This involves more than just being told what type of product is the best one for him or her. By making a knowledgeable decision to buy, the prospect develops a sense of ownership in the planning process and will truly become your client for other products.

retirement planning fact finder

A formal *retirement planning fact finder* can be divided into four distinct components. The first three are discovery components you should complete with the prospect. The fourth section is for your use only. Whether or not you complete the fourth section in the prospect's presence or after your meeting depends on how comfortable you are using interest tables and performing retirement income need calculations. The four fact-finder components are as follows:

- personal data and retirement goals
- quantitative data
- retirement income sources
- calculations and interest tables

As you proceed through the instructions for using this fact finder, keep in mind that it is meant to be a self-contained vehicle for gathering facts, figures, and feelings from a prospect to quantify and qualify the need for financial products, especially as it relates to retirement funding. This requires eliciting personal financial information from the prospect and using several planning assumptions. So that a financial calculator or computer software that illustrates complex time-value-of-money concepts is not needed, this fact finder incorporates interest tables to calculate the prospect's retirement income need. However, because planning assumptions must take into account the inflation rate, interest rates, and the prospect's life expectancy, you should regard the resulting figures as only an estimate of what may actually be sufficient when the prospect retires. Consequently once you have estimated the retirement income need, you should meet with your client periodically to make any necessary adjustments to the plan.

Note: All page numbers referred to in the Retirement Planning Fact Finder in appendix A are the internal page numbers in the fact finder itself, not the page numbers in this textbook.

 ### *Personal Data and Retirement Goals*

Most questions in the Personal Data and Retirement Goals section of the Retirement Planning Fact Finder are closed-end and designed to learn simple information that the prospect can easily identify or remember. Many questions in this section begin with "Who is," "When did you," "When do you," and "What are" or "What is." These questions can be asked and answered rapidly. There are also several open-ended questions that require the prospect to consider what he or she would like to do in retirement or reflect on what retirement means to him or her personally.

Questions on fact finder pages 2 and 4 that are marked with an asterisk indicate, as the footnote explains, that these questions also appear on the Personal Retirement Planning Review form in this chapter. This is to remind you that if you used that form to qualify the prospect prior to using the Retirement Planning Fact Finder, you will not ask these same questions again. However, if you make the transition directly from the general discussion of the need for retirement planning to the fact finder, the questions on pages 2 and 4 are useful qualifying questions that you should ask early in the retirement planning fact-finding process.

Spaces are provided to fill in the prospect's and spouse's names, dates of birth, Social Security numbers, phone numbers, and children's names, ages, and locations. There is also a question that asks for the names, addresses, and phone numbers of the prospect's professional advisors (that is, attorney, accountant, insurance advisor, bank or trust officer, and securities broker). Additional questions ask about the documents prepared and the services performed by these advisors.

The questions in the Retirement Goals—Assumptions subsection of page 2 are important because they form the basis upon which all calculations of retirement assets and income will be based. For example, it is necessary to know whether a spouse is to be included in this plan, and if so, when the prospect and spouse plan to retire (or have retired). The question on the number of retirement years for which to plan is important because it affects all retirement income calculations regarding how long resources will be required to last. Likewise, accuracy is important regarding the average rate of inflation. You will use this percentage throughout the entire pre- and postretirement periods to ensure that the prospect's future income remains equivalent to what it is today in real or inflation-adjusted dollars. Refer to fact finder table 2 on page 13 of the fact finder for sample inflation rates in the last 3-, 5-, 10-, 15- and 20-year periods to help the prospect select a realistic rate. Approximately 2.5 percent is the average of all the rates found in that table. You and the prospect should determine an average whole number inflation rate and write it in the blank space provided in fact finder table 2. You should also write it in the space provided in question 2 on page 2 of the fact finder.

For questions 3 and 4 on page 2, you need to obtain from the prospect an average rate of compound interest before taxes that can be applied to all savings and investment vehicles before and after retirement begins. An alternative is to calculate the growth of each savings or investment vehicle individually using different rates of interest. This can be confusing to the prospect and cumbersome for you, however, so avoid it if possible. It may be easier for you to use the same interest rate before and after retirement if the prospect agrees.

For questions 5 and 6 on page 2, you have to determine the prospect's average income tax rate. This is important because, in reality, all gross income from wages, pensions, taxable savings, and investments, either before or after retirement, will be reduced by this average percentage of expense. Average tax rate is not the same as a person's marginal tax bracket. Marginal tax bracket is the percentage of income taxation applied to the last dollar of income received. Average or effective tax rate percentage is determined by dividing the actual dollar amount of income taxes paid in a year by total income received.

Example: If a single person earns $50,000 in income and pays a total of $8,000 in taxes for the year, his or her average tax rate is $8,000 ÷ $50,000 = 16 percent.

Using current rates, the individual's marginal tax bracket is probably 25 percent.

The difference in the two rates is because individuals are allowed to take reductions from gross income for a personal exemption amount, tax-qualified plan contributions, and itemized deductions. You do not have to be a tax expert to determine a prospect's average tax rate. Just find out the total income taxes the prospect paid in a recent year (from his or her W-2 form or federal income tax return), and divide it by the prospect's gross income.

There are also several questions in the Retirement Goals—Qualitative section on page 2 that ask about the prospect's recreational activities and where he or she plans to live in retirement. The questions on what retirement means to the prospect personally and the desired standard of living in retirement will give you insight into the prospect's priorities concerning his or her post-retirement lifestyle. There is also a question regarding whether or not any children will be involved in the financial decisions about retirement planning. If so, it is good to discover this early so that you can invite them to be part of subsequent interviews, if appropriate.

All these questions will take only a few minutes to answer and are a good warm-up for the more difficult questions that follow.

Transitional Phrase. You should then make the transition into the next section of the fact finder by letting the prospect know that answers to questions about personal details will help you get a clearer understanding of his or her present financial situation.

Example: "I appreciate your cooperation in providing the answers to personal details about you and your family, as well as your general retirement goals. Now with your permission, I'd like to ask you some questions about your finances that are necessary for me to get a clear picture of where you stand so that any recommendations I may make will be suitable for your situation. If you have no objection, may I continue?"

Quantitative Data

The objective of this section of the Retirement Planning Fact Finder, which begins on page 3, is to have the prospect provide information about his or her assets and liabilities, most recent cash flow statement, current financial status, investment objectives, and risk tolerance. If the prospect has not already prepared a cash flow statement, he or she may have to obtain the information by looking at income tax records, checkbook receipts, and other documents.

The questions in this section of the fact finder are mostly closed-end factual questions that ask for a number or percentage, or they are questions that require a "yes" or "no" answer that may have to be combined with an open-ended question to help clarify reasons behind the quantitative data. The answers help you to qualify the prospect and determine the motivation to buy financial products, such as deferred annuities, that will enhance the prospect's financial situation in retirement.

This section of the fact finder asks for personal financial information. Even though you have already told the prospect that you need this information and why, completing this section may take a considerable amount of time, especially if there are no existing financial statements. Meanwhile you are gradually building trust with the prospect as he or she answers each question.

A key question to ask in the Quantitative Data section is at the top of page 5, immediately after determining the prospect's net cash flow. Asking the prospect what percentage of total annual income received today he or she will require to live comfortably in retirement forces the prospect to begin to realize just how much he or she needs to accumulate from available financial resources to generate the desired income when his or her working life ceases. The percentage of income needed in retirement should then be multiplied by the total gross income today (ascertained from the cash flow statement on fact finder page 4) to calculate what amount of income will be necessary during retirement. This amount should be expressed in today's dollars before taxation.

You may have to help the prospect be realistic in setting a goal for income during retirement. A good rule of thumb is that retirement income should equal about 75 percent of preretirement income to maintain the standard of living after retirement. A goal of less than 75 percent usually means a lower standard of living; a goal of more than 75 percent usually means a higher standard of living after retirement. This will, of course, vary depending on the prospect's individual retirement plans, goals, and financial circumstances.

Obtaining a Dollar Commitment for the Amount That the Prospect Can Afford. While completing the quantitative section of the Retirement Planning Fact Finder, you should obtain a dollar amount commitment from the prospect that he or she can afford to budget to save for retirement. It does not have to be a specific dollar figure *per se*. It can be a "range of affordability" in terms of monthly or annual cost. Therefore if the prospect indicates that he or she feels the need to increase savings to reach the retirement income goal, you should discuss this need while all the financial information is still fresh in everyone's mind.

Example:	"Mr. or Ms. Prospect, assuming you have a need to increase your savings for retirement, I would like you to consider how much you could comfortably afford on a monthly basis to address that need. I don't expect you to have a specific dollar figure in mind, but if you have some idea of what you can afford, I assure you I will do everything possible to customize a plan that fits within your budget. Does this make sense to you?"

Alternatively, depending on the prospect's age and retirement status, an increase in savings may be inappropriate because saving has ceased. The prospect may be retired and interested in conserving or growing the assets he or she has accumulated, or at least improving the return on his or her money. Therefore you may want to ask this question on page 5: "Do you have any funds on hand now that you might want to invest?" If the answer is "yes," then you should ask how much the prospect would consider investing. If the answer is "no," you will have to probe further using questions on page 8 in the Current Investments subsection of the Retirement Income Sources section to uncover assets in taxable income, poorly performing savings, or investment vehicles that could be reallocated to tax-deferred financial products.

By the time you have completed the quantitative section of the fact finder, you should have set the stage for the all-important Retirement Income Sources section.

Transitional Phrase. Again you should smooth your progression into the next section of the interview with a transitional phrase. Confirm the prospect's annual and monthly cash flow amounts so that you are both in agreement on the figures. Confirmation of figures is a good way to signal the completion of this section of the fact finder. At this point in the interview, you may want to thank the prospect for his or her cooperation.

Example:	"You've been very cooperative and forthcoming with information about your personal finances, and I appreciate your help. Now I'd like to ask you some questions that explore your possible retirement income sources. This information will allow me to calculate where you stand today in relation to tomorrow's retirement income goal that you have expressed. Does this sound reasonable?"

Retirement Income Sources

This section of the fact finder is the longest and consists of the most questions. It is essential to complete it thoroughly and accurately in order to estimate the prospect's retirement income. It begins with three categories of retirement income summary sections on page 6. The first two income summary categories include inflation-indexed income derived from Social Security and the other five retirement income sources listed underneath. The third summary category includes fixed income derived from all of the retirement income sources listed below except Social Security. The summaries of inflation-indexed and fixed-income sources of retirement income are derived from information determined in the six subsections on pages 7 through 11. These subsections are

- Social Security Benefits (page 7)
- Pension and Other Funded Income Payments (page 7)
- Current Investments (page 8)
- Deposits and Earnings (page 9)
- Distribution Options (page 10)
- Income and Expenses in Addition to Living Requirements (page 11)

After completing each subsection on fact finder pages 7 through 11, you should go back to the summary sections on page 6 and fill in the correct total for each source of inflation-indexed and fixed income.

The totals of retirement income from each of the six subsections except Social Security are referred to as "sources," as in retirement income sources. The total projected Social Security retirement income is a separate category that is shown in line 1-1 on page 6. All inflation-indexed income derived from each of the remaining five subsections (lines 1-2 through 1-6) is totaled on the line SOURCE 1. All fixed income derived from each of the five subsections, excluding Social Security, is totaled on the line Total of SOURCES 2 + 3 + 4 +5 + 6. The projected income from Social Security should be expressed in today's dollars. The other inflation-indexed income and estimated fixed income from each of the other five sources should be expressed in the actual future dollars anticipated at the prospect's retirement. These five sources constitute the Total Fixed Income (total of SOURCES 2 through 6). The Total Fixed Income amount should be converted into Total Inflation-Adjusted Fixed Income. The procedure for doing this is explained in the retirement funding calculation example. This will become the category 3 retirement income source, which is the last line on page 6 of the fact finder. Later, the numbers for the prospect's estimated income from Social Security (line 1-1), the total Other Inflation-Indexed Income (SOURCE 1), and the total Inflation-Adjusted Fixed Income (SOURCES 2 through 6) can be copied into their proper boxes in the Client's

Figures column of the Retirement Income Calculation Worksheet on fact finder page 12.

Social Security Benefits. The information requested here is straight-forward. You should enter the estimated Social Security retirement benefit for the prospect and spouse, if applicable, and indicate the age at which retirement benefits will begin. This information is available from the Social Security benefits statement mailed each year to all participants from the Social Security administration. It can also be requested online at www.ssa.gov. The total of these numbers (on line 1-1 of fact finder page 7) should be in today's dollars because it will be indexed automatically to reflect changes in the CPI. You should also enter this same dollar amount on line 1-1 of the retirement income summary on fact finder page 6.

Pension and Other Funded Income Payments. This subsection consists of annual projected future income from employer-sponsored defined-benefit pension plans, deferred-compensation arrangements, or taxable trust income. The age when benefits will start and the number of years they will be paid should be entered for each separate source, if any. The income derived from this source is presumed to be fixed, not increasing. If it is indexed for inflation at retirement, it should be totaled at the bottom of this subsection (line 1-2 of page 7) and added to other inflation-indexed income dollar amounts (if any) on page 6, line 1-2, to be included as a component of the SOURCE 1 total because it is automatically inflation indexed.

Most defined-benefit plans are not indexed once payment commences, so they should be entered in the SOURCE 2 amount, which will consist of a flat dollar future figure. Many defined-benefit plans may, however, show a projected retirement income figure that will be indexed each year until the prospect's retirement, at which time it will remain fixed. You can obtain this figure from the prospect's current pension benefit statement, which will be expressed in today's dollars. To calculate it at tomorrow's dollars payable at retirement, take the payment in today's dollars and use fact finder table 1 on page 13 to increase it to the expected payment at retirement, assuming a given rate of inflation. For example, if the prospect has $1,000 per month of benefits on his or her statement and has 15 years remaining until retirement, use the factor found in fact finder table 1 assuming a 3 percent inflation rate, and multiply $1,000 by 1.558 to arrive at $1,558 of income expected from this source at retirement. Then enter $1,558 in SOURCE 2 on fact finder page 7, and also in the SOURCE 2 dollar amount of the summary of fixed income on page 6.

Current Investments. This subsection of the fact finder may be the most cumbersome for the purpose of determining the annual income generated for use in retirement. The inventory of current investments gives you a clear picture of what asset types the prospect owns, how much of each one, and what interest rate each one is earning. This can be extremely valuable information for the possible reallocation of investment or savings dollars away from poorly performing taxable investments and into a tax-deferred product such as a single-premium deferred annuity that is consistent with the prospect's risk tolerance and investment objectives. Therefore this section of the fact finder can be useful in a dominant-needs sales situation when you want to get a total picture of a prospect's current asset allocations. It will help you to better determine the prospect's investment diversification needs so that you can more responsibly recommend the most suitable annuity product. Now we will calculate retirement income from resources listed in this subsection of the fact finder.

First, notice that there are six columns. The first column is the tax category, which requires you to indicate whether the investment is taxable (T), tax free (TF), deductible tax deferred (TD), nondeductible tax deferred (ND), or a Roth IRA (R). The second column is the asset class, where you will list the type of each investment. Next ask the prospect the current value and rate of return for each investment. Using the rate of return (before taxes or after taxes, depending on the tax category of the investment) and the number of years until retirement, estimate the future value of only those investments that will be utilized in retirement to generate income. The after-tax rate of return on an investment can be estimated by reducing the pretax interest rate by the average tax rate found on page 2 of the fact finder. For example, an 8 percent pretax rate of return and a 15 percent average tax rate will generate an after-tax rate of return of about 7 percent (8% x .85 = 6.8%, rounded to 7%). The future value of a single sum is then calculated by using the fact finder table 1 factor on page 13 corresponding to the assumed interest rate and the years of accumulation until retirement. Thus if $100,000 today grows at 8 percent tax-deferred compound interest for 15 years, multiply $100,000 by the factor in fact finder table 1, which is 3.1722, to find the future value of $317,220. Then, in the last column on the right in the Current Investments section on page 8, indicate what amount of the future value the prospect will use to generate income (all of it, none of it, or only a fraction of it).

Income from investments can be calculated on either a capital-retention basis or a capital-liquidation basis. Instructions for calculating income without depleting the capital are under the heading "How to Calculate the Fixed Income from Investments." For example, if the prospect has for use in retirement $100,000 that is earning an average of 8 percent interest, it will generate $8,000 per year in income before taxes and not deplete the principal sum ($100,000 x .08 = $8,000). You should then enter this figure, $8,000, as the SOURCE 3 dollar amount on page 8 and as the SOURCE 3 dollar amount of the fixed-income summary section on page 6.

This income is fixed, meaning it will not increase. A more realistic method of calculating retirement income is to consider the need for the income to increase each year while in retirement. This involves assuming an inflation rate as well as an earnings rate. It also involves using factors from fact finder table 4 on page 15, titled "Retirement Income Multiplier/Divisor Factors."

Instructions for calculating capital liquidation on an inflation-indexed basis over a finite period of retirement are under the heading "How to Calculate the Inflation-Indexed Income From Investments" on fact finder page 8. For example, if income in real dollars is desired for a finite period of time in retirement, such as 20 years, then use the retirement income multiplier/divisor factors from fact finder table 4. Assuming an interest earnings rate of 8 percent and an inflation rate of 3 percent, to receive 20 years of income, divide the investment capital sum of $100,000 by 13.23. Thus $7,558 is the inflation-indexed (real) income amount that will be generated each year for 20 years, at which time the capital sum will become exhausted. Thus you should enter $7,558 on line 1-3 of fact finder page 8 and on line 1-3 of page 6.

What that means is that the actual dollar amount of the payment will increase by the rate of inflation each year but have the same purchasing power as when the payments began, which would usually be when retirement begins. This method is the more responsible one for calculating retirement income needs because inflation is a fact of life; therefore income in retirement must increase to keep pace with it. It is important, however, to note that this method of using a lump sum of money to generate retirement income will deplete funds that are earmarked to provide income at the end of the assumed period of time that retirement is expected to last.

Also notice that some of the totals lines in this and the next three subsections have a "+" sign to the right of them. This, as the explanatory footnote says, indicates that the totals may include tax-free income that will need to be converted to taxable equivalent amounts. In this way we can regard all income in retirement as taxable for the sake of simplification and express the shortfall of income on a uniform basis, thus making it more understandable to the prospect. Therefore any tax-free income receivable during retirement should be converted to its taxable equivalent amount using the prospect's average tax rate and the instructions and example at the bottom of page 11 of the fact finder. The conversion of any tax-free amounts marked with the plus sign should be done before transferring them to their respective SOURCE or line in the summary sections on fact finder page 6.

Deposits and Earnings. This subsection separates the prospect's deposits and earnings into five types of investments. For each type of investment, you should ask the prospect the amount of annualized deposits being made and whether the deposits will increase each year with the rate of inflation. Then, using either the annual rate of interest that applies to each type of investment or the assumed rate of interest from fact finder page 2, estimate the lump-sum value of each future sum that can be used to generate income at retirement. Use either fact finder table 3 (Annual Accumulation Factors: One Dollar Per Year in Advance) alone or in conjunction with fact finder table 1.

Example:

Assume a prospect is depositing $3,000 per year into a nondeductible tax-deferred annuity. Also assume the average earnings rate is 8 percent and that there are 15 years until retirement. If the deposits remain level, multiply the factor from fact finder table 3 for an 8 percent accumulation rate over 15 years:

29.324 x $3,000 = $87,972

However, if the deposits grow by 3 percent per year, you can use fact finder table 1 to estimate the average dollar amount of deposits for 15 years, and then multiply that figure by 29.324. The approximate inflation adjustment to $3,000 deposits for 15 years can be found using the 3 percent column of fact finder table 1. Take the factor that appears in this column that corresponds to the midpoint year between today and year 15, which is assumed to be the number of years until the prospect retires (year 8). Multiply that factor (1.2668) by $3,000. Next multiply that amount by 29.324 from fact finder table 3, which equals $111,443, the approximate lump-sum value accumulated by making deposits of $3,000 that increase by 3 percent per year for 15 years and earn 8 percent interest each year:

1.2668 x $3,000 x 29.324 = $111,443

Then determine the projected income generated at retirement from the lump sum accumulated, using either the capital-retention method or the capital-liquidation method discussed previously. Thus $111,443 multiplied by .08 will provide a level income of $8,915 every year in retirement. This number will constitute the SOURCE 4 dollar amount at the bottom of fact finder page 9, and you should also enter it as the SOURCE 4 dollar amount on page 6.

If, on the other hand, $111,443 is divided by 13.23, which is the retirement income divisor factor from fact finder table 4 for 8 percent interest, 3 percent inflation, and a 20-year liquidation period, $8,424 will be generated in inflation-indexed dollars during the 20-year retirement. You should enter this indexed income from deposits and earning on line 1-4 at the bottom of fact finder page 9 and on line 1-4 of page 6.

Distribution Options. This subsection totals the annual distributions of income from required minimum distributions, annuity payouts, and life insurance products that the prospect will receive during retirement. These income amounts can be fixed and/or level, depending on their source. Add together those distribution options that are fixed income, and write the total dollar amount as SOURCE 5 at the bottom of fact finder page 10. Also transfer the total to page 6 as SOURCE 5 in the summary of fixed income.

Total the sources of distribution-options income that may be indexed to inflation, and enter the dollar amount on line 1-5 at the bottom of page 10; also enter that amount on page 6, line 1-5, in the summary of indexed income.

Income and Expenses in Addition to Living Requirements. This subsection is a catch-all for annually received income sources that the fact finder has thus far not addressed. The exact amount of income from some of these sources may be hard to predict. For instance, the sale of a business that may take place 15 years in the future may generate a large sum of investable capital that the prospect can use to help fund retirement. However, the sale price may be impossible to determine accurately, so you will have to work with the prospect to arrive at a reasonable estimate. Other annual sources of income may be temporary. You must exercise judgment as to whether or not you can count on these sources to be consistent during retirement. Total the sources that apply as additional funds are expected per year.

From this amount, subtract any additional major expenses such as the annual mortgage payments needed to purchase a retirement home. Again, some of these expenses may also be temporary, and they may be offset by temporary additional income amounts. But identify those that are deemed to be permanent, and subtract them from additional income. Finally list the total amount of net fixed additional annual income or expenses as either a positive or negative number, and enter it on fact finder page 11 as the SOURCE 6 dollar amount. Also enter it on page 6 as SOURCE 6. For those amounts that are net-indexed additional annual income or expense amounts, list the total as either a positive or negative number, and enter it on page 11 as the line 1-6 dollar amount. Also transfer it to page 6, line 1-6.

Before concluding the interview, you should return to fact finder page 6 and confirm the amount of total Social Security benefits in today's dollars. Then total all inflation-indexed income on lines 1-2 through 1-6. This represents Other Inflation-Indexed Income from SOURCE 1. Also add fixed retirement income SOURCES 2 through 6 to find Total Fixed Income. Although it may be apparent that a shortfall in retirement income exists, depending on the prospect's situation, it is wise to refrain from discussing products or solutions until the next interview. In any event, the final section of the fact finder, Calculations and Interest Tables, is for your use only and is discussed below.

Calculations and Interest Tables

This section of the fact finder, pages 12 through 15, consists of a retirement income calculation worksheet and four tables (to which we have previously referred). Three of the tables contain interest factors used in the calculation of an additional retirement income need. This section of the fact finder can best be understood by using an example.

Calculating the Retirement Funding Requirement. Financial advisors need to show prospects the annual or monthly savings required to meet their retirement funding goal. The calculation lends itself to several time-value-of-money concepts that are simplified here to focus on the practical application of these concepts within retirement planning. A worksheet that generates a good approximation of the retirement funding required should contain the following:

- annual gross income goal at retirement in today's dollars
- annual Social Security benefits in today's dollars
- other inflation-indexed income
- total inflation-adjusted fixed income
- an assumed inflation rate
- the number of years until retirement
- the number of years in retirement
- an assumed investment rate of return

The following example describes the calculation process. The replacement-ratio method of calculating the required retirement income is demonstrated. The example illustrates the eight inputs above, and it includes an explanation of how they are derived from the Retirement Planning Fact Finder to determine the income needed at retirement. There is also a detailed explanation of the rationale and procedure for each step of the calculation.

First in this example, the prospect's current annual income ($75,000) is multiplied by a percentage of income with which he or she will be comfortable during retirement. This can range from 50 to 100 percent; 60 percent is shown in the example. This result ($45,000) will produce the prospect's gross annual retirement income goal, which must be expressed in today's dollars.

Next, from the gross annual retirement income goal, subtract the prospect's estimated Social Security retirement income ($21,200), which can be found on the prospect's annual Social Security statement. Again, this number is expressed in today's dollars because under current assumptions, the Social Security retirement benefit will increase in accordance with the CPI. The result is the adjusted annual retirement income goal—in this example, $23,800.

Multiply this figure by the appropriate inflation factor in fact finder table 1 that corresponds to the inflation rate the prospect has chosen and the number of years until retirement. As a guideline, most advisors use a rate in the 3 percent to 4 percent range. Three percent is shown in the example below; factor 1.558 is under the 3 percent column in fact finder table 1 and the row that corresponds to 15 years until retirement. The result determines the first-year retirement income needed, which is $37,080 in this example.

Example:

Current annual income	$75,000
Multiplied by percentage of income needed	x 60%
1. Annual retirement income goal	$45,000
2. Minus projected annual Social Security benefits in today's dollars	−$21,200
Equals adjusted annual retirement income goal (in today's dollars)	$23,800
Multiplied by inflation factor for 15 years at 3%	x 1.558
Equals first-year retirement income needed	$ 37,080
Multiplied by the average inflation factor during 20 years of retirement	x 1.3439
Equals the inflation-adjusted annual retirement income goal	$49,832
Future accumulation of $167,176 / 13.23 (retirement income multiplier/divisor factor from fact finder table 4) = $12,636	
3. Minus other inflation-indexed income	− $12,636
Equals preliminary retirement income shortage	$37,196
4. Minus total inflation-adjusted fixed income	$–7,441
Equals net annual retirement income shortage (approximately)	29,755
Multiplied by retirement multiplier factor for 20 years in retirement	x 13.23
Equals additional accumulation needed	$393,659
Divided by annual accumulation factor for 15 years (fact finder table 3)	÷29.324
Equals annual savings required to reach retirement funding goal	$13,424

Assumptions:
5. Annual inflation rate = 3%
6. Years until retirement = 15
7. Years in retirement = 20
8. Investment return = 8%

Next you must adjust the first-year retirement income need by the average inflation rate that is anticipated over the 20-year period of retirement. You can estimate this amount by finding the factor from fact finder table 1 that corresponds to the midpoint year of retirement. The midpoint between years 1 and 20 is 10. Thus the factor from fact finder table 1 under the 3 percent inflation column for year 10 is 1.3439; $37,080 x 1.3439 = $49,832—the inflation-adjusted annual retirement income goal.

From this figure, subtract all other inflation-indexed income (SOURCE 1) and inflation-adjusted fixed income (SOURCES 2 through 6), based on their expected values at retirement. In this example, the SOURCE 1 value is

$12,636, which is arrived at by applying several factors to certain accumulation assumptions. Specifically, assume that the prospect is depositing 4 percent of income into a tax-sheltered annuity at work and that the employer is matching it with another 2 percent of income. That means that 6 percent of $75,000, or $4,500 per year, is accumulating at an average assumed compound interest rate of 8 percent. However, this contribution is linked to the prospect's salary, so it is assumed to be increasing with the rate of inflation. There are several steps involved to estimate the approximate result (on an annual basis).

First, you must multiply $4,500 deposited for 15 years by the average 3 percent inflation rate factor for 15 years in fact finder table 1. The factor applied is for the midpoint between today, year 1, and 15 years from today, which would be year 8. This factor, 1.2668, is then multiplied by $4,500, which equals $5,701. This is assumed to be the average annual deposit that is approximately equal to $4,500 growing each year for 15 years at a 3 percent inflation rate. Next $5,701 is multiplied by the annual accumulation factor from fact finder table 3 for deposits made each year for 15 years at 8 percent interest. That factor is 29.324. Thus $5,701 multiplied by 29.324 equals $167,176. This result, $167,176, is then divided by 13.23, which is the appropriate retirement divisor factor in fact finder table 4 for an 8 percent interest accumulation rate, a 3 percent inflation rate, and a 20-year (capital liquidation) period of retirement. This results in $12,636 of other inflation-indexed income, which you should enter in the Client's Figures column on the retirement income worksheet in the box next to Other Inflation-Indexed Income (SOURCE 1). Subtracting $12,636 from $49,832 results in a preliminary retirement income shortage of $37,196.

Next you should divide the total amount of fixed income in SOURCES 2–6 on page 6 of the Retirement Planning Fact Finder by the average inflation factor for the retirement period to arrive at an estimated inflation-adjusted fixed income figure. This is necessary to ensure that all retirement income reflects the erosion of purchasing power caused by inflation while the prospect is retired. For example, if the prospect expects a fixed $10,000 per year at retirement from investments, divide $10,000 by the average inflation factor for 20 years of retirement, which is the factor in fact finder table 1 for the midpoint year (year 10). Thus $10,000 divided by 1.3439 equals $7,441, which is the 3 percent inflation-adjusted or real-dollar income equivalent of $10,000 for 20 years of retirement. Enter the $7,441 amount in the Client's Figures column, on the worksheet in the box next to Total Inflation-Adjusted Fixed Income (SOURCES 2-6 Adjusted for Inflation). Subtract this amount from the preliminary retirement shortage of $37,196 to find the net annual retirement income shortage.

Calculation Note: Table 4 in the fact finder (Retirement Multiplier/Divisor Factors) works in two ways. It shows factors for compound interest rates of 4 percent, 6 percent, 8 percent, and 10 percent, with inflation rates of 1 percent to 5 percent, for 5-, 10-, 15-, 20-, and 25-year periods. When a lump sum of dollars ($167,176) is divided by the respective factor (13.23) based on three retirement planning assumptions, (8 percent compound interest, 3 percent inflation, and 20 years of retirement, in this case), the result ($12,636) shows the annual retirement income that will be generated in real or inflation-adjusted dollars. Conversely, when a shortfall of income in real dollars must be filled with income that will not be eroded by inflation, then the desired annual income or shortfall is multiplied by the respective factor shown in fact finder table 4 to arrive at the lump sum that the prospect must accumulate to generate the desired annual retirement income. This will be demonstrated in Figure 3-3.

Thus far, in this case, there is a net annual retirement income shortage of $29,755. A calculation is needed to determine the sum of capital that must be accumulated by the beginning of retirement that will generate $29,755 in inflation-adjusted dollars throughout the 20-year retirement period. To find the capital sum required, multiply $29,755 by factor 13.23, which is the factor from fact finder table 4 that corresponds to 8 percent compound interest and 3 percent inflation for 20 years of retirement. The result is $393,659, which is the additional sum of money that the prospect needs to accumulate over the next 15 years, assuming an 8 percent compound interest rate before taxes and a 3 percent inflation rate, to produce $29,755 in constant purchasing power each year.

To determine how much the prospect must save each year to reach this $393,659 accumulation goal, refer to fact finder table 3. This table shows accumulation factors for $1.00 deposited each year in advance for a given number of years at various assumed compound interest rates. A capital sum desired at some future year can be divided by these factors based on years of accumulation and net compound interest rate to determine the annual savings required to reach the desired future sum. Thus $393,659 is divided by factor 29.324 in fact finder table 3 under the 8 percent interest column in the 15-years row. The result, $13,424, is the level annual savings amount required to accumulate $393,659 earning 8 percent for 15 years. The result of dividing $13,424 by 12, which is $1,119, is the approximate level monthly deposit the prospect must make to reach his or her desired retirement income goal based on the above cited current assumptions and inputs.

You can also include the step-up rate of savings required for the first year, beginning immediately. You can calculate this by dividing the $13,424 level annual savings required by the inflation rate factor for the midpoint between today and 15 years when retirement will begin. The factor is 1.2668 in the 3 percent column of fact finder table 1 corresponding to year 8 The result of dividing $13,424 by 1.2668 is $10,597, which would be the first year's contribution. The contribution would increase by 3 percent each year to correspond to increases in earnings that are assumed to increase at the rate of inflation.

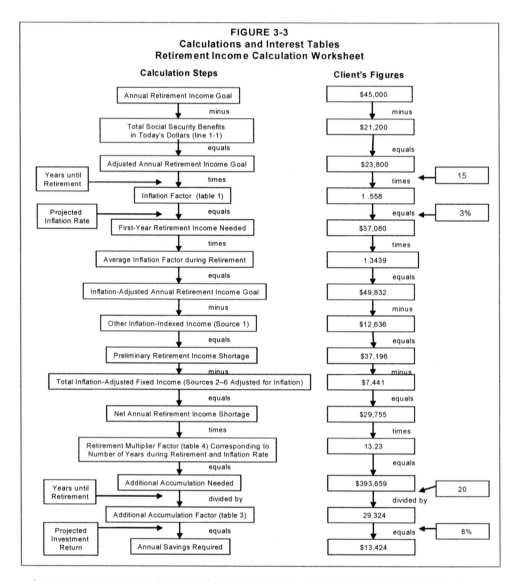

FIGURE 3-3
Calculations and Interest Tables
Retirement Income Calculation Worksheet

Assumes an average annual net rate of return on a 20-year retirement. Retirement begins at age 65. (Taxes not considered.) Rate of return is hypothetical, for illustrative purposes only, and does not represent actual performance of any product.

Conclusion and Summary

When you have completed all three information-gathering sections of the Retirement Planning Fact Finder, you should be equipped to analyze and digest the information so that you can design an appropriate plan and recommend products that are consistent with the prospect's goals and objectives.

Because an enormous amount of data may be collected during the fact-finding process, it may be a good idea to review and confirm each section as it is completed. Or you may choose the close of the interview as the best time to review all the information you have recorded.

You should review and summarize your interpretation of the prospect's feelings about retirement planning issues and give him or her a chance to agree with your assessment or to clarify any aspects you may not have accurately understood.

The point at which you complete the retirement income calculation worksheet is a matter of choice. One approach is to apply the information from the Retirement Income Sources section of the fact finder (pages 5 through 10) and use the worksheet after your meeting with the prospect. In this way, you can carefully calculate what is needed to fill the retirement income gap and make specific product recommendations at that time. However, as mentioned previously, flexibility is the key to successful interviewing, and if you feel comfortable enough to use the retirement income calculation worksheet in the presence of the prospect, then by all means do it. If you take this latter approach to quantifying the additional retirement income needed, make sure you show it to the prospect and include a reference to it in the verbal discovery agreement, which is discussed below, before you conclude the meeting.

By reviewing the facts and feelings that you have recorded, you not only check your understanding of what the prospect told you, but you also show the prospect that you were paying attention to what he or she said. Be sure that the prospect concurs with your interpretation of his or her feelings. A retirement plan or product recommendation will not be effective if it is based on inaccurate information or on assumptions that you, rather than the prospect, made.

Mutual Agreement to Work Together

The fact-finding process is often a very complex one. More than one meeting may be necessary before the entire process is complete. At the beginning of any subsequent meetings, be sure to review and confirm the information gathered at the previous meetings. Always be sure that you and the prospect are thinking along the same lines.

Discovery Agreement

discovery agreement

Finally many financial advisors conclude the initial fact-finding interview by summarizing the prospect's goals in writing. This practice, known as the *discovery agreement*, can also be done verbally. When the discovery agreement is verbal, you should ask the prospect to acknowledge that he or she has a financial need and elicit from the prospect a willingness to work together toward seeking financial solutions within the framework of his or her budget that address the retirement planning concerns discussed throughout the interview.

It is more effective, however, to send a letter subsequent to the meeting that not only acknowledges the gist of what was discussed but also provides a blueprint for proceeding through the next step(s) in the selling/planning process. This implied contract is an essential ingredient for establishing the foundation of a true client/advisor relationship. This agreement to work together toward mutually acceptable solutions to the prospect's financial concerns establishes a climate of trust and partnership.

Summary

The client-focused selling/planning philosophy is the basis for creating and building a personally rewarding clientele. The third and fourth steps in the selling/planning process outlined in Chapter 1, which are to meet the prospect and to gather information and establish goals, have been described in Chapters 3 and 4 as a way of making this philosophy practical. Contacting the right people means that you will have more appointments with prospects who are qualified. By focusing on your prospects' needs and values during interviews with them, you will build the credibility necessary to gain their trust in you and your professional ability to assist them in reaching their financial goals. Ultimately this can lead to greater acceptance of your product recommendations and generate a higher volume of sales and an ongoing supply of referrals. These are essential ingredients of a selling/planning process that will enable you to develop a thriving financial services practice.

CHAPTER FOUR REVIEW

Key Terms and Concepts are explained in the Glossary. Answers to the Review Questions and Self-Test Questions are found in the back of the book in the Answers to Questions section.

Key Terms and Concepts

index	percentage change
contract term	annual reset
free window period	ratcheting

averaging   participation rate
index average   cap rate
point-to-point   guaranteed minimum interest rate
high water mark   deductive approach
options   inductive approach
asset fee   fact finder
spread   retirement planning fact finder
margin   discovery agreement

Review Questions

4-1. Explain why an equity-indexed annuity is appropriate for individuals who would like an investment that offers a better chance of growth than a fixed-interest deferred annuity and yet does not have the downside risk of a variable deferred annuity.

4-2. Identify various investment indexes, both equity and nonequity, used in indexed products.

4-3. Identify the three major types of indexing methods that insurance companies use in the design of equity-indexed annuities.

4-4. Describe how insurance companies invest in options to credit indexed growth in an equity-indexed annuity.

4-5. Describe how a capped interest rate can limit the amount of indexed earnings credited to an equity-indexed annuity contract.

4-6. Describe what the concept of averaging in indexed annuities is and why it is used by insurance companies.

4-7. Describe how minimum interest rate guarantees protect against negative performance in an index.

4-8. Explain why a majority of equity-indexed annuities are not registered with the SEC.

4-9. Identify the four distinct components of a formal retirement planning fact-finding form.

4-10. Identify and briefly describe the implied contract that you should secure at the conclusion of the fact-finding interview that represents mutual consent between you and the prospect to continue working together.

Self-Test Questions

Instructions: Read Chapter 4 first; then answer the following questions to test your knowledge. There are 10 questions; circle the correct answer, and then check your answers with the answer key in the back of the book.

4-1. What term best describes an equity-indexed annuity policy that measures the growth of an index from one year to the next policy anniversary and uses each month in the year as a measuring point?

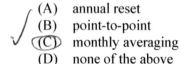

   (A)   annual reset
   (B)   point-to-point
   (C)   monthly averaging
   (D)   none of the above

4-2. If an equity-indexed annuity uses the annual reset method, which of the following occurs at the policy anniversary?

   (A)   The index is set for the upcoming policy year at the ending level of the current policy year.
   (B)   The index is ignored for the first 10 years.
   (C)   The guaranteed minimum amount is ignored over the indexed earnings.
   (D)   The indexed values are averaged over the 12 months of the policy year.

4-3. Assume the following: The S&P 500 Index rose at the rate of 15 percent during the year, the participation rate is 80 percent, the cap is 12 percent, and the asset fee is 3.5 percent (deducted after the cap and after the participation rate). How much interest will the equity-indexed annuity credit?

   (A)   8.5%
   (B)   9.0%
   (C)   9.5%
   (D)   12%

4-4. The approach to information gathering that uses a fact-finding form that first broadly covers all the prospect's financial needs and then narrows the discussion to prioritized dominant needs is the

   (A)   deductive approach
   (B)   inductive approach
   (C)   single-need approach
   (D)   dominant-need approach

4-5.   Which of the following statements regarding the strategies insurance companies use to invest equity-indexed annuity premiums is (are) correct?

     I.   Insurance companies purchase units of the S&P 500 Index to match the increase in the actual S&P 500, and these units are transferred to the annuity on an annual basis.

    II.   Insurance companies generally invest in options to back the contractual promise to help support payment of the same percentage increase to the annuity as the specific index earns.

    (A)   I only
    (B)   II only
    (C)   Both I and II
    (D)   Neither I nor II

4-6.   Which of the following statements regarding asset fees is (are) correct?

     I.   Asset fees are deducted from the growth in the index and are always deducted prior to the application of the cap rate.

    II.   Asset fees are also referred to as the spread or margin.

    (A)   I only
    (B)   II only
    (C)   Both I and II
    (D)   Neither I nor II

4-7.   Which of the following statements regarding participation rates and caps is (are) correct?

     I.   Participation rates are one of the insurance company's strategies to control the amount of interest credited.

    II.   Caps are one of the strategies insurance companies use to control the amount of interest credited.

    (A)   I only
    (B)   II only
    (C)   Both I and II
    (D)   Neither I nor II

4-8   All of the following sources of retirement income are not typically adjusted automatically to reflect the rate of inflation EXCEPT

(A)   Social Security benefits
(B)   pension payments
(C)   current investments
(D)   distribution options

4-9.   All of the following methods are commonly used to credit interest on an equity-indexed annuity policy EXCEPT

(A)   point-to-point
(B)   annual reset
(C)   high water mark
(D)   participation rate

4-10. Insurance companies use all of the following techniques to control the interest earnings on an equity-indexed annuity EXCEPT

(A)   participation rates
(B)   spreads
(C)   caps
(D)   surrender charges

Variable Annuities; Developing Product Recommendations

Learning Objectives

An understanding of the material in this chapter should enable you to

---

5-1. Identify the features of a variable deferred annuity that are also common to a fixed-interest deferred annuity.

5-2. Explain the charges and expenses associated with variable deferred annuities.

5-3. Explain the unique features of the different types of guaranteed death benefits offered in variable deferred annuity policies.

5-4. Identify the investment features and typical subaccounts in variable deferred annuities.

5-5. Compare and contrast the value of investing in variable deferred annuities versus mutual funds.

5-6. Describe important aspects of analyzing a prospect's need for annuity products.

5-7. Identify key components of designing a plan when recommending the purchase of various annuity products.

5-8. Identify the factors used to analyze the companies that compete for annuity product sales.

Chapter Outline

NOTE: The terms *variable deferred annuity* and *variable annuity* are used interchangeably to refer to the same product, which is the tax-deferred variable annuity. On those occasions when reference is made to the variable immediate annuity, it will be clearly indicated.

Chapter 5 examines the variable deferred annuity and its unique product design and investment features, including professional management, dollar cost averaging, and asset allocation. The chapter explores considerations involved in the analysis of a prospect's need for annuities, as well as how to develop product solutions that represent a client-focused selling approach

VARIABLE DEFERRED ANNUITY

Variable deferred annuities are contractually similar to fixed-interest deferred annuities. They have the same policy forms, general provisions, and nonforfeiture rights. The settlement options and option tables, actuarial principles, and mortality and expense assumptions are the same. Variable deferred annuities are subject to similar income tax treatment. The major difference between the variable deferred annuity and fixed-interest deferred annuity is the underlying investment vehicle.

Variable deferred annuities typically offer two major categories of investment selection: a general account and a separate account. The general account selection provides a guarantee of principal and interest. The separate account offers an array of diversified subaccounts that operate in a manner similar to mutual funds.

Unlike the fixed-interest deferred annuity, variable deferred annuities are considered securities and are registered products. They may be sold only by salespeople who are properly licensed by the state and as registered representatives by the Financial Industry Regulatory Authority (FINRA). Any

prospectus

potential buyer of a variable deferred annuity must be given a *prospectus* (a document that provides the complete details of the product: its investment features, options, fees, other costs, death benefits, and payout options).

A major difference between variable deferred annuities and fixed-interest deferred annuities is which party to the annuity policy assumes the investment risk. With the fixed-interest deferred annuity, the insurance company declares in advance what level of interest will be credited to the annuity policy for the year. If the insurance company declares that it will pay 5.5 percent interest for the year, the company will need to earn at least 7.5 percent on its invested assets to cover both the promised interest of 5.5 percent plus its profit spread of 2 percent.

On the other hand, with a variable deferred annuity, the investment risk lies with the policyowner, not the insurance company. The policyowner chooses the investment options for his or her premiums. The insurance company does not promise any returns except, of course, the minimum guarantee for premiums allocated into the general account. Therefore how the subaccounts perform is a risk to the policyowner, not the insurance company.

Because the investment responsibility lies with the policyowner, insurance companies generally provide the following investment features and benefits to assist policyowners with their investment responsibilities:

- professional money management, as with mutual funds
- an array of subaccount choices that offer the opportunity for investment diversification among companies of various sizes and investment management styles
- economy of investing and reasonableness of asset-based fees
- flexibility to make deposits at the contract owner's convenience, including the opportunity to dollar cost average with small deposits at minimum expense
- a variety of payout options to match future withdrawals to future needs

Product Design

The features and costs of variable deferred annuities are unique. Many policies have varying features and benefits, as well as special names and terms for the features. It is imperative that both the policyowner and the advisor consult the prospectus and the annuity contract itself for the specific features, costs, and designs of the variable deferred annuity policies under consideration.

General Account

general account

The foundation of the typical variable deferred annuity is a *general account*, which guarantees principal and some minimum fixed amount of interest, which until recently was usually 3 to 4 percent under most state insurance laws. However, many insurance companies have lowered the guaranteed interest in newly issued policies below these levels due to a prolonged period of historically low market interest rates in the first few years of this century. This will have no impact on already in-force policies.

Some companies use a sliding scale approach to determine the minimum interest guarantee that is referenced to an index. This approach gives the company the flexibility to set the minimum guarantee anywhere from 1 percent to 3 percent for newly issued policies.

Separate Account and Subaccounts

separate account
subaccounts

In addition to the general account, a *separate account* is an option for the policyowner. It is composed of various *subaccounts* from which the contract owner can select investment options that match his or her investment objectives and risk tolerance. Contract owners can continually adjust their investment choices as their circumstances change.

The general account offering is spread based, and it is priced within the normal 2 percent spread. The costs of the subaccounts within the separate account are paid for by asset-based fees, much like mutual funds. Because these subaccounts are similar to mutual funds and are priced in the same fashion, the marketplace compares mutual fund costs to variable deferred annuity costs to determine relative value. See the section on "Mutual Fund versus Variable Deferred Annuity" for a discussion of variable annuities compared to mutual funds.

Variable deferred-annuity subaccounts offer investment funds from large, medium, and small company common stock accounts. There are a range of professional investment manager styles, from value to growth, including the aggressive, blue-chip, and balanced varieties. These subaccounts also offer quality and high-yield bond funds, zero-coupon bonds, Ginnie Mae, and real-estate accounts. Contract owners have the option of moving among these funds, switching their contributions and accumulations from one fund to the other, and managing the funds in accordance with their particular objectives.

To illustrate the subaccount choices, a typical variable annuity might offer the following investments options:

- General (Guaranteed) Account
- Money Market Fund
- Government Securities Fund
- Bond Fund
- Total Return (Balanced) Fund
- Growth (Common Stock) Fund
- Growth With Income (Stock) Fund

According to Morningstar Inc., the average number of subaccounts in 1,150 annuity contracts offered by 42 insurance companies is 44.

Figure 5-1 shows the flow of premiums from the client's hands to the insurance company. The insurance company then invests those premium dollars in the variable annuity policy according to the policyowner's choices. Those choices are in two main categories: the general account, which provides fixed-interest earnings, and the separate account, which is made up of the many various subaccounts.

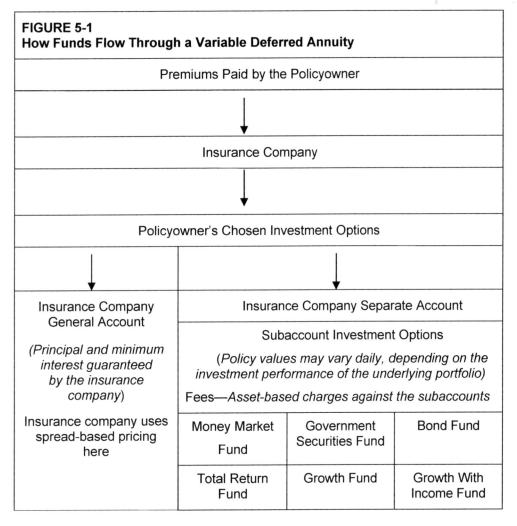

FIGURE 5-1
How Funds Flow Through a Variable Deferred Annuity

However, these subaccounts may contain restrictions on the ability to transfer funds, such as limiting the number of transfers from one account to another during a particular time period, or charging a fee for making a transfer from one account to another.

People who fear the stock market can still appreciate the variable annuity. They often put their money into the general account and then just transfer their interest earnings into the subaccounts each month. This strategy assures that they will have no loss to their principal investment, and they can still participate in the stock market.

Variable Deferred-Annuity Accumulation Units

accumulation units

A policyowner purchases *accumulation units* with the premium invested in a variable deferred-annuity subaccount. The purchase of an accumulation unit is similar to the purchase of a share in a mutual fund. Money arrives at the insurance company, and the company calculates the value of the account accumulation unit at the "closing price" on the day the money is received or the next business day of the New York Stock Exchange. The money purchases units of the fund based on that unit value. This procedure is referred to as "forward pricing" to distinguish it from the procedure used to purchase stock based on a quoted price prior to the receipt of payment.

Although the number of accumulation units will stay the same for a given amount of premium paid by the policyowner, the value of the units will vary depending on the investment performance of the underlying subaccount.

Example: A client purchases a variable annuity with a $30,000 single premium and receives 3,000 units. The cost of each unit is $10 ($30,000/3,000). The client allocates 50 percent of his premium to the fixed-income subaccount and 50 percent to the large-cap subaccount. If the fixed-income subaccount grows by 6 percent ($15,000 x 1.06 = $15,900) and the large-cap account fund grows by 15 percent ($15,000 x 1.15 = $17,250), the account value is then worth $33,150 ($15,900 + $17,250 = $33,150). However, the annuity owner still has 3,000 units. Each unit has now increased in value to $11.05 ($33,150 / 3,000 = $11.05).

A hypothetical accumulation is shown in Table 5-1. In this example, the initial purchase is made at age 35 with a premium high enough to cover a $200 purchase of units each month after paying insurer expenses. The assumptions behind the Table 5-1 numbers are that the accumulation units change value once each year and that a full $200 is available each month to acquire more units. The units in this example grow at approximately 7.5 percent in most years but fluctuate more or less than that in other years as stock prices are prone to do over short intervals. In this case, there is an accumulation of $258,459.62 at the end of the 30th year (end of age 64 or beginning of age 65) consisting of 31,751.80 accumulation units.

TABLE 5-1
Variable Annuity Accumulation Units
Deferred Annuity Purchased at Age 35 at $200 per Month

Year	Age	Unit Value	New Units	Total Units	Total Value
1	35	$ 1.00	2,400.00	2,400.00	$ 2,400.00
2	36	1.08	2,232.56	4,632.56	4,980.00
3	37	1.16	2,076.80	6,709.36	7,753.50
4	38	1.24	1,931.91	8,641.26	10,735.01
5	39	1.34	1,797.12	10,438.38	13,940.14
6	40	1.07	2,242.99	12,681.37	13,569.07
7	41	1.15	2,086.50	14,767.88	16,986.75
8	42	1.24	1,940.93	16,708.81	20,660.76
9	43	1.88	1,276.60	17,985.41	33,812.56
10	44	2.12	1,132.08	19,117.48	40,529.06
15	49	3.04	788.56	23,697.73	72,124.84
20	54	3.25	738.46	27,172.57	88,310.84
25	59	5.76	416.67	30,137.70	173,590.85
30	64	8.14	294.84	31,751.80	258,459.62

Annuity Units

At the beginning of the liquidation period, the accumulation units are exchanged for annuity units. The number of annuity units that the annuitant will acquire depends on the company's assumptions as to mortality, dividend rates, and expenses, and on the market value of the assets underlying the annuity units. In essence, the number of annuity units is determined by dividing the dollar value of the accumulation units ($258,459.62 in our example) by the present value of a life annuity at the participant's attained age in an amount equal to the current value of one annuity unit (assumed to be $35 in this case). Although the number of accumulation units of a particular person increases with each premium payment and each allocation of dividends, the number of annuity units remains constant throughout the liquidation period (7,384.6 annuity units in this case). The units are revalued each year, however, reflecting the current market price of the common stock, and the mortality, investment, and expense experience for the preceding year.[1] The dollar income payable to the annuitant each month is determined by multiplying the number of annuity units by the current value of each unit. During the annuitization—or liquidation—period, the higher the market price of the stock and the greater the dividends, the greater the annuitant's dollar income will be. During the accumulation stage, however, it is to the annuitant's advantage for stock prices to be relatively low because he or she will thus be able to acquire a larger number of accumulation units for each premium payment.

Distributions. When it is time to begin the distribution phase of the variable annuity, the contract owner must decide which portion of the payment he or she wishes to receive, respectively, from the separate account and from the general account.

General Account Annuity Payout. The owner of the contract may transfer all or part of the value of the contract to the general account and elect to take one of the payout options available under the contract. Funds annuitized from the general account produce a guaranteed income that will not change from period to period.

Separate Account Annuity Payout. The contract owner may transfer all or part of the value of the contract to one or more of the subaccounts that are available in the separate account. Funds annuitized from the separate account produce an income that changes from period to period based on the performance of the subaccount in which the funds are placed.

Investment Features

Professional Management

Insurance companies usually select a number of money managers other than the insurer itself for their annuity policies. It is not unusual for a variable annuity contract to have proprietary or insurance-issuer managed subaccounts and 15 or more outside money managers. Early in the development of variable annuity contracts, all subaccounts were managed by the issuing insurance company. Many competitors, however, disparaged this proprietary management, claiming that insurance companies could not manage money as well as "professional" money managers. Because perception is often more important than reality, companies began to hire professional money managers. Initially insurers hired only highly visible money managers. This strategy of hiring a well-known money manager created favorable publicity and enhanced credibility for their variable annuity contracts; it also attracted investment capital.

In the 1990s, insurance companies were doing what most people were doing—chasing last year's performance numbers—which resulted in a high number of large capitalization growth fund managers. As insurers learned that this strategy was counterproductive to wealth retention, the public's respect for diversification returned. Insurance companies now hire and fire managers based on their performance and competency. Companies want to provide variable annuities that offer credible investments within the equity categories of large, medium, and small companies (both domestic and international) and growth, value, and blend styles of management, adding real-estate investment trusts and even hedge funds if they enhance diversification. Insurers draw bond managers from quality to high yield and from short to long duration, in addition to money market and guaranteed-interest, guaranteed-principal accounts.

Tax-Free Transfers Among Subaccounts

Some separate accounts may contain restrictions on the contract owner's ability to transfer funds. There can be limitations on the number of transfers that can be made during a particular time period or charges for making transfers from subaccount to subaccount. People's risk tolerance does change, depending on what is going on in their lives and what is going on in the markets. The ability to put money into a guaranteed-interest account can, at times, be a valuable and comforting alternative and protect some or all of the money in a variable contract from downside risk. The subaccounts have all of the upside potential and downside risk of their respective asset classes.

diversification

Diversification is essential to and possibly the single most important tool for managing risk. In effect, diversification means that the investor does not put all his or her money into one investment. Instead, he or she invests across asset categories to take advantage of the relationships among investments and to minimize risk. Diversification works because different investments tend to have highly opposite fluctuation sensitivities.

The transfer of funds within a variable deferred annuity contract will not trigger taxable income to the policyowner. The variable annuity may, however, charge a fee for transfers among subaccounts, depending on the policy. The ability to transfer funds among subaccounts enables policyowners to adjust the investments within the policy to meet their needs and suitability. They may also adopt any of the investment strategies without concerns over tracking their cost basis or triggering taxable gain and therefore taxable income. (See Chapter 7 for the income tax consequences of terminating an annuity contract with a loss.)

Most variable annuity contracts do, however, limit transfers that are part of market timing activity that the insurance company considers disruptive to the operation of its investment funds. For example, the company may limit an individual or group of contract owners if it sees repeated transfers in and out of the same investment fund within a period of five days. It will also limit the transfer of money out of the principal account to protect itself against policyowners' trying to outinvest the insurance company.

Dollar Cost Averaging

dollar cost averaging

Dollar cost averaging is the consistent investment of equal periodic payments into a diversified equity-based investment over an extended period of time. With variable deferred annuities, this concept means depositing regularly scheduled additional premiums into a flexible-premium variable deferred annuity. Another example of the dollar cost averaging concept with variable deferred annuities is making a large contribution into the general account and then regularly moving funds into the various subaccounts. Regardless of which approach is used, the point is to invest the same amount on a regularly scheduled basis. With each consistent investment, the number of shares or units purchased will vary with the share price. In some months, the investor will purchase more shares or units than in other months. The goal is to achieve a lower average cost per unit over time than the average price per unit.

Quiz Question #2 →

Dollar Cost Averaging in a Fluctuating Market		
Systematic Investment	Share Price	Number of Shares Acquired
$100	$100	1
100	50	2
100	25	4
100	50	2
100	100	1
$500	$325	10
Average cost per share $50 ($500/10) Average price per share: $65 ($325/5)		

Dollar cost averaging, rather than large single-sum investing, is a relatively conservative investment strategy, which can best be described by illustration. Table 5-2 indicates what happened when one fearful investor was persuaded to put $100 per month into a variable contract's stock account for five months, even though he was convinced that the deposit of his $100 investment was sure to trigger substantial market declines. As the table shows, this investor was right. The market had two 50 percent declines before it started to recover during the first 2 months, and as soon as the market returned to where it had been, he got out. Had he made a single deposit of the $500, it would have been an agonizing ride, with zero gain to show for it, as indicated below. However, with dollar cost averaging, the investor received a 100 percent return on his $500 investment.

TABLE 5-2
Dollar-Cost Averaging Example

Investment Strategy	Jan	Feb	March	April	May	Total Shares Purchased/ Percentage Gained
Lump-Sum Investment	$500					
Price per share	$100					$100
Shares purchased	5					5
Total value	$500	$250	$125	$250	$500	5 shares = $500 0% gain on original $500 investment

Versus

Investment Strategy	Jan	Feb	March	April	May	Total Shares Purchased/ Percentage Gained
Dollar Cost Averaging	$100	$100	$100	$100	$100	
Price per share	$100	$50	$25	$50	$100	$1,000 (10 shares at the last price per share of $100 = $1,000)
Shares purchased	1	2	4	2	1	10
Total value						100% gain on original $500 investment

Although this is a simplistic example, it shows the importance of the discipline that will help a client do what is difficult—buy low and hold for the eventual highs. The disciplined approach to investing, as well as the ability to stay invested, was extremely difficult for people in the 2000 through 2003 market. They observed that the dollar-cost-averaging strategy cannot protect against losses in a declining market. Once the investor implements a dollar-cost-averaging strategy, the only way to gain is not to sell until the market has substantially rebounded.

Most variable annuity contracts facilitate dollar cost averaging by providing a guaranteed-interest, guaranteed-principal account that usually offers an interest rate that is above current market interest rates. A lump sum of money may be put into this guaranteed-interest account and then instructions given to the insurance company to transfer money monthly from that account into client-selected subaccounts.

If this were done in a taxable account, the interest from the interest-bearing account would be taxable, and each purchase would create a cost-basis issue and possible purchase expense, which would have to be tracked until sale. At sale time, any gain or loss would be a taxable event.

The annuity contract eliminates all of this because its cost basis is whatever money the policyowner has put into it. All gain is taxable as ordinary income when withdrawn or surrendered from the annuity contract.

The cost for this feature is built into the basic cost of the annuity contract as part of the mortality and expense cost (see "Mortality and Expense Charge (M&E)" below), and in most cases, the contract owner incurs no additional expense.

Asset Allocation Services

asset allocation

Asset allocation is the process of developing a diversification strategy that allocates premium to the various asset classes to build an overall portfolio consistent with the investor's risk tolerance and long-term investment objectives. Properly used, it gives the investor an excellent opportunity to protect assets and to experience consistently favorable overall investment returns.

Most insurance companies offer asset-allocation subaccounts and asset-allocation assistance to registered representatives and their broker-dealers to help policyowners allocate the assets in their annuity policies. Allocation among the subaccounts should be accomplished in a manner that is appropriate to that client's personal investment objectives.

The basic expense of providing asset-allocation services to the registered representative is usually covered by the other fees charged in the policy, and therefore asset allocation is not a service for which either the advisor or client must pay. The registered representative who is providing the service is compensated through the normal commissions he or she is paid as a result of selling the annuity.

Automatic Rebalancing

Once an asset-allocation plan is decided and the policyowner determines the diversification among the asset classes to be appropriate, it is inevitable that the market will cause the asset-allocation percentages to change and thus necessitate rebalancing. Rebalancing is readjusting the investment portfolio back to the asset-allocation percentages that were originally chosen among subaccounts after growth in them has occurred.

Example: Suppose a policyowner allocates 60 percent of her premium to a balanced subaccount and 40 percent to the international stock subaccount. The international stock subaccount performs so well that now the ratio between the two accounts is no longer 60%/40% percent but is 70%/30%.

Automatic rebalancing would then sell off enough of the international subaccount and put the proceeds into the balanced subaccount to pull the ratio back to a 60%/40% split.

Rebalancing is selling winning asset classes and repositioning the proceeds in less favorable categories. Some investors like this strategy. Many investors find it to be counterproductive in taxable portfolios, however, because it can create current expenses and taxes. Most investors also find rebalancing difficult to do because they hate selling winners and buying losers even if they know intellectually that selling high and buying low makes sense.

automatic rebalancing

Many variable deferred annuities offer *automatic rebalancing*, which makes it easy for the investor. Once the investor decides on the appropriate strategy, all he or she has to do is identify the subaccounts to use, determine the percentages of the total to be allocated to each, and tell the insurance company at what interval to rebalance the accounts.

Charges and Expenses

One aspect of the variable deferred annuity that sets it apart from the fixed-interest deferred annuity is the fee structure. Although a fixed-interest annuity may assess a nominal yearly fee against the accumulation value, variable deferred annuities have a much more complex fee and expense structure. The detailed fee structure of the variable deferred annuity arises from its sophisticated investment structure. Charges, fees, and expenses are outlined in the variable deferred annuity prospectus.

Front-End and Back-End Loads

front-end load

The *front-end load* is deducted as a percentage from money coming into the contract. Front-end loads range from a high of 8.5 percent to a low of 2.5 percent; 5.75 percent is typical. The front-end load is often seen as a disadvantage to the client because less of the contract owner's money is put to work in the contract. Very few variable deferred annuity contracts impose a front-end load.

back-end load

The *back-end load* is also called a surrender charge or contingent deferred sales charge. This charge is assessed at the time of a withdrawal from a variable deferred annuity as a percentage of the amount withdrawn, according to a contractually defined schedule. Nearly every variable deferred annuity policy has surrender charges. These policies have surrender charge periods, surrender charge schedules, and free-corridor amounts just like fixed-interest deferred annuities.

When the variable deferred annuity is sold as an individual contract, surrender privileges are made available but on a more restricted basis than in connection with ordinary annuities. When the variable deferred annuity is used as part of a pension plan, surrender values are generally not made available.

Annual Contract Charges

annual contract
charge

Annual contract charges are designed to offset some of the insurance company's administrative costs for servicing these contracts. Charges range from $10 to $50, with an average of about $30 per year. There are a few contracts that list no annual contract charge. Most of the rest of the contracts waive this administrative charge for contracts with fund values above some minimum amount such as $10,000 or $20,000. Administrative charges, which are applied as specific dollar amounts, are not a major consideration in most contracts.

A very small number of policies, however, may impose an administrative charge as a percentage of funds in the contract. This type of charge can be more significant and costly than the flat annual fee noted above. Both financial advisors and their clients must be aware that some contracts do impose these asset-based administrative charges, and thus they should make sure that such charges do not make the total expense ratio (see "Total Expense Ratio" below) for the contract unacceptable.

Mortality and Expense Charge (M&E)

mortality and expense
charge (M&E)

Insurance expenses, often referred to as *mortality and expense charges (M&E)*, are asset-based charges against the investment subaccounts in a variable deferred annuity. The insurance company assesses these charges to cover its costs for the guarantees it provides (such as a minimum guaranteed interest rate in the general account) and for the guaranteed annuity factors for annuitization calculations. These charges also cover the guarantee that, in the event of death, the beneficiary will receive the greater of the deposits made into the contract or the account value—a protection against adverse investment results.

Typically, the M&E is the same percentage charge in all subaccounts within a variable annuity contract. In some contracts, however, M&E charges vary according to which subaccounts the policyowner has chosen. This M&E method is called layered or multiple.

Note that the M&E is not charged against the guaranteed-interest account. All charges in that account are taken from the spread between what the insurance company expects to earn on the contract owner's money and what it pays out to the contract owner. The guaranteed interest account typically specifies the net amount of interest it pays the contract owner. To the extent that funds raised by the M&E charge are not needed to provide for these minimum guarantees, they serve as a source of profit to the insurance company.

The average annual mortality and expense charge (including administrative and distribution costs) in variable deferred annuity subaccounts as tracked in Morningstar's Principia™ for VA/VL (variable annuity/variable life) subaccounts as of 2006, is 1.385. See Figure 5-2.

FIGURE 5-2
Fees and Expenses—Variable Annuities versus Mutual Funds

	2006 Average Expenses	
	Mutual Funds	Variable Annuities
Fund Expenses	1.365%	0.971%
M&E	-	1.201
Administrative	-	0.147
Distribution	-	0.037
Total	1.365%	2.356%
DIFFERENCE	0.991%	

Source: Morningstar Inc.

Higher x than mutual funds

Fund Expense

fund expense

The *fund expense* is charged at the subaccount level. It is an asset-based fee for management operations of the various subaccounts. It is the expense charged against the subaccounts for paying the fund managers and the fund's operating expenses. The fund expense may not include the brokerage costs.

As a percentage of assets under management, the fund expenses are expected to go down as a fund gets bigger and gains some economies of scale. However, this is not always the case. Fund expenses do change, and clients need to realize that an increasing expense ratio will lower their return.

The average annual fund expense in variable deferred annuity subaccounts, as tracked in Morningstar's Principia™ for VA/VL subaccounts as of 2006, is .971 percent.

A number of companies seem to be reporting fund expense ratios at zero. This does not mean that they are providing fund management for free but that they are lumping all of their asset-based charges into the mortality and expense charges. As a result, the most meaningful number for comparison purposes may be the total expense ratio.

Total Expense Ratio

total expense ratio

The *total expense ratio* combines both the M&E and the fund expenses, and it is commonly used to compare expenses inside variable deferred annuities to regular mutual funds. The average total annual expense ratio in the variable deferred annuity subaccounts as tracked in Morningstar's Principia™ for VA/L subaccounts as of 2006 is 2.356 percent.

The average annual asset-based charge in a mutual fund is 1.365 percent. Compare that to the average asset-based charge in a variable deferred annuity of 2.365 percent. The extra cost to manage assets inside, rather than outside, a variable annuity contract is about .991 percent (2.356% – 1.365% = .991%), or about $991 extra per year per $100,000 of invested assets. However, if a client is making a selection among the available variable annuity contracts, as opposed to a specific mutual fund family, a direct comparison of actual costs is a much better way to make a choice than to rely on averages.

Guaranteed Living Benefits

When applying for a variable deferred annuity, the contract owner can purchase additional benefits that will provide protection against market losses while both the contract owner and the annuitant are living. With guaranteed living benefits, which are not designed to be giveaways to contract owners, the insurance company is agreeing to relieve the policyowners of certain specified risks that the policyowners would prefer not to take. Companies impose a conservative charge for these benefits, which is designed to cover the risk and provide a margin of profit.

Each insurance company tries to design its own variation of these types of living benefits, primarily for two reasons. First, each company wants to be unique, to be separated from the pack for marketing purposes. Second, insurance companies have been trying to patent contract feature designs and have actually had some success with patents.

Guaranteed Minimum Income Benefit

guaranteed minimum income benefit

The *guaranteed minimum income benefit* increases the contract owner's investment in a variable deferred annuity by some compounded percentage amount—typically between 3 percent and 6 percent. After a period of time, such as 7 to 10 years, this increased amount may be used on any contract anniversary to change the contract to an immediate annuity using guaranteed annuity factors. Basically, by purchasing this benefit, the policyowner is making sure he or she will receive a minimum level of income, regardless of how much money was actually in the account value at the time of annuitization.

Guaranteed annuity factors for interest and mortality are conservative and typically have provided less income than the annuity factors insurance companies use to sell current immediate annuities. As a result, if the actual account value is close to but less than the guaranteed minimum income benefit, income should be calculated both ways: (1) using the account value and current annuity factors and (2) using the guaranteed minimum income benefit to determine which is more advantageous. The cost of this benefit as of 2006 was approximately 30 to 75 basis points of the policy's accumulation value deducted annually, which is 30 hundredths or 75 hundredths of one percent of the account value.

guaranteed minimum return of premium benefit

Guaranteed Minimum Return of Premium Benefit

This *guaranteed minimum return of premium benefit* guarantees that contract owners may take back their premium after a specified number of years if the investment is more than the variable deferred-annuity account value. This benefit can be costly, when it is offered, depending on its design. For example, after 10 years, a contract owner can immediately withdraw his or her premium of $50,000 even if the account value is only $43,000. This is possible even if during those 10 years, the owner has been able to pick and choose and transfer among the equity accounts. The cost of this benefit ranges from 75 to 100 basis points of the policy's accumulation value or more per year.

This expense can be reduced by extending the years that must pass prior to exercising the benefit and by allowing the insurance company to dictate how the funds must be invested for the benefit to remain in force. Another way to drive down cost is for the insurance company to repay the return of premium over some period of time as opposed to all at once.

Guaranteed Minimum Accumulation Benefit

guaranteed minimum accumulation benefit (GMAB)

The *guaranteed minimum accumulation benefit* (GMAB) guarantees the owner that his or her value will be at least equal to a certain minimum amount after a specified number of years. The GMAB is a guarantee that the value of the variable deferred annuity account can be stepped up to a certain amount on a specified date if the actual account value is lower than the guaranteed minimum accumulation amount, whether or not the contract owner annuitizes. Also, at the end of the specified holding period, if the value is higher than the guaranteed accumulation amount, the owner is entitled to walk away with the profits. Many GMABs guarantee a return of premium over a 10-year period. This guarantee eliminates the forced annuitization of the guaranteed minimum income benefit.

To minimize their own risk, some carriers' contracts require buyers to diversify risk into several subaccounts according to prescribed asset-allocation models. The cost of the GMAB is 25 to 50 basis points of the contract's accumulation value if the contract requires asset allocation to be used. If asset allocation is not required, the cost ranges from 50 to 100 basis points.

Guaranteed Minimum Withdrawal Benefit

guaranteed minimum withdrawal benefit

A *guaranteed minimum withdrawal benefit* (GMWB) guarantees the systematic withdrawal of a certain percentage (usually 5 percent to 7 percent) of premiums annually until premiums are completely recovered, regardless of market performance. This guarantee feature offers distinct tax advantages in that the portion of the guaranteed income stream that is apportioned to the principal (as opposed to income derived only from investment gains) may be withdrawn tax free. In addition, some carriers offer step-up provisions, enabling the annuity holder to participate in future investment gains.

The cost for this feature ranges from 30 to 40 basis points.

Guaranteed Lifetime Withdrawal Benefit

guaranteed lifetime withdrawal benefit

Another type of GMWB that guarantees withdrawals for life was introduced in 2004. The *guaranteed lifetime withdrawal benefit* (GLWB) guarantees that a certain percentage of the amount invested (typically 4 percent to 6 percent) can be withdrawn each year for as long as the contract holder lives, regardless of market performance. This percentage may increase depending on the person's age when withdrawals begin. For example, the insurance company might agree to pay the annuitant 5 percent at age 55, 5.5 percent at age 70, or 6 percent at age 80. New benefits, such as spousal continuation (which guarantees withdrawals for two lives), have recently been introduced.

This option is excellent for those investors who want the assurance of a guaranteed income but don't want to lose control of their money by annuitizing the contract. Therefore the annuity owner could maintain his or her asset allocations in stock subaccounts without worrying that a market crash might damage future retirement income needs.

The cost of the GLWB typically ranges from 40 to 75 basis points.

Guaranteed Death Benefits

The most basic form of death benefit in a variable deferred annuity is payment of the account value upon death. A death benefit equal to the account value will pay whatever the account value happens to be on the date it becomes payable (up or down), and it involves no insurance company minimum guarantee or subsidy.

When the death benefit in a variable deferred annuity is equal only to the account value, there is no insurance against a declining account value. This death benefit may be referred to as an accumulated value or account value death benefit. Few variable deferred annuities provide an accumulated value death benefit. There is no charge for this because it provides no real additional benefit to the contract owner.

It is important that policyowners clearly understand the death benefit provisions in the policy. Some policies pay death benefits when the owner dies; other policies pay death benefits when the annuitant dies. Furthermore, depending on who is the owner and who is the annuitant, the death benefit might not be paid, but instead the "surrender value" might be forced out as a payment to the policyowner and not the beneficiary. In addition, it is important to understand if the policy allows surrender charges to be deducted from the death proceeds.

With other types of death benefits, the contract owner can request, and pay an additional cost for, a death benefit that provides greater protection. The insurance company offers some minimum guaranteed death benefit at the death of the contract owner or at the death of the annuitant—possibly even both. Because the owner and annuitant are the same individual in most annuity contracts, many people do not concern themselves about whether the death benefit is paid out as a result of the annuitant's death or the owner's death. The minute that one party is the owner and another party is the annuitant, this distinction becomes critical. Especially if the owner has paid extra for an increased death benefit, that owner needs to understand whose death will and will not cause that extra benefit to be paid.

Guaranteed minimum death benefits that provide a death benefit equal to more than the account value come in several basic varieties:

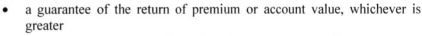

- a guarantee of the return of premium or account value, whichever is greater
- a guarantee of the return of premium plus some amount of interest
- a guarantee of the stepped-up or ratcheted death benefit
- a guarantee of a death benefit that is an extra percentage of the gain in the contract

Account Value or Premiums Paid Death Benefit

The vast majority of variable deferred annuity policies will state that at the owner's or annuitant's death, the death benefit will equal the larger of the

- contract value on the date that the required proof of death is received (by SEC regulation, contract value is determined on the date that the required proof of death is received). Note the need to submit the proof of death promptly in this type of contract to guard against market conditions that cause an erosion of value.
- sum of the net premiums less partial withdrawals

This type of guaranteed death benefit is a standard feature in most variable deferred annuities, and it is funded by the M&E charge.

> ***Example:*** A policyholder paid $24,000 in premiums into a variable annuity; upon death, the contract value is worth $52,000. With this type of death benefit in the policy, the death benefit equals the higher of the two amounts, or $52,000.

Rising Floor Death Benefit

rising floor death benefit

The *rising floor death benefit* is equal to the larger of the variable deferred-annuity account value or the premiums paid plus interest. A minimum death benefit that guarantees some amount of interest on the premium invested may be referred to as an annual compounding death benefit or a rising floor death benefit. The death benefit will be equal to the larger of the

- contract value on the date the required proof of death is received. Note the need to submit the proof of death promptly in this type of contract to guard against market conditions that cause an erosion of value.
- sum of the net premiums less partial withdrawals plus interest at a stated percentage from date of issue until the earlier of the annuitant's age 80 or date of death

Death benefits that apply compound interest to the owner's premiums have offered interest rates between 4 percent and 6 percent for premium invested in the equity subaccounts, and interest rates of 3 percent to 4 percent for premium in the quality bond, money market, and guaranteed-interest accounts. This interest rate differential encourages policyowners not only to select equity accounts but also to hold them for the long term.

The cost for this benefit is 15 to 35 basis points of the policy's annual accumulation value.

Stepped-up or Ratchet Death Benefit

stepped-up death benefit

A *stepped-up death benefit* means that the death benefit will be equal to the greater of

- the contract value at death
- total premium payments less prior withdrawals
- the contact value on specific policy anniversary dates

Stepped-up dates can occur at every anniversary of the policy up to the annuitant's age 80 or 85. Or the stepped-up dates can occur at intervals anywhere between every second to tenth policy anniversary.

Expect stepped-up death benefits to cost about 10 to 25 basis points of the policy's accumulation value per year. This is less than the rising floor death benefit and beneficial to insurance companies because policyowners must pay for the benefit even during falling markets when the benefit provides no real value.

Example:	Suppose the initial premium and death benefit for a policy is $40,000, and on the policy anniversary, the death benefit steps up to the new account value, which is $47,000. The death benefit remains at $47,000 until the next step-up trigger date in the policy even if the contract's account value declines to $35,000 at the owner's death. This feature allows the policyowner to have a higher death benefit, to lock in gains in the account value, and to allow the locked-in gains to be available to the heirs if the policyowner dies during the year.

Some policies offer a death benefit equal to the higher of a step-up provision or the rising floor compound interest. The cost of this combination benefit has increased from about 45 to about 60 basis points.

Enhanced Earnings Benefit

One of the objections to putting money into a deferred annuity has been that death benefits from deferred annuities do not receive a step-up in cost basis. (In deceased persons' estates, the beneficiaries usually receive most types of inherited assets with a cost basis equal to the value of the asset as of the date of death.) Therefore the beneficiary receives the annuity proceeds with the same cost basis as the policyowner had at death. The beneficiary is liable for income taxes on the gain over the inherited cost basis.

enhanced earnings
benefit

To deal with this objection, insurance companies created an *enhanced earnings benefit* (EEB) option that increases the death benefit from 25 percent to 40 percent of the policy gain, which would give the beneficiary enough extra to pay 25 percent to 40 percent income taxes on the gain in the policy. When available, this benefit costs around 25 to 40 basis points of the policy's accumulation value per year. The benefit is ineffective when the policy's market value provides no gain.

Example: Assume a policyowner purchases a variable annuity with a $20,000 single premium that grows to $80,000 at the time of death. The policyowner's beneficiary will receive $80,000 from the insurance company, but the beneficiary will have to pay income taxes on $60,000 in taxable income from the gain in the annuity ($80,000 – $20,000 = $60,000).

On the other hand, assume the beneficiary does not inherit an annuity but instead inherits IBM stock worth $80,000. The stock was originally purchased by the deceased for $20,000. The beneficiary inherits $80,000 in stock income tax free and with an $80,000 cost basis. The beneficiary will not have any income taxes to pay.

This difference in taxation to the beneficiary depending on what kind of asset he or she inherits led to the creation of the increased death benefit. With the additional death benefit in the EEB option, the $80,000 annuity might pay $100,000 at death. The benefit in the example above increases the death benefit by one-third of the gain. If the gain is $60,000, one-third of $60,000 is $20,000. The total death benefit therefore is increased from $80,000 to $100,000.

If the beneficiary has to pay income tax on $80,000 ($100,000 – $20,000 = $80,000) and assuming a 25 percent income tax bracket, the taxes the beneficiary owes will equal $20,000 ($80,000 x .25 = $20,000). The beneficiary receives $100,000 minus $20,000 in taxes, which means a net of $80,000 (the original value of the annuity). Therefore this benefit is the equivalent of receiving an income-tax-free inheritance.

Withdrawals Affect Death Benefits

Another aspect that policyowners and advisors need to understand about variable deferred annuities is what happens to the death benefit in the policy if the owner takes a withdrawal prior to death. Death benefits are decreased if withdrawals are taken. The issue is how much the decrease is. Generally decreases are either a dollar-for-dollar reduction or a pro rata reduction.

A dollar-for-dollar reduction of the death benefit is just that: When the policyowner withdraws $10,000 from a variable deferred annuity policy, the death benefit is reduced by $10,000.

The alternative to a dollar-for-dollar reduction is a pro rata reduction. A pro rata reduction causes a decrease in the death benefit equal to the percentage that the withdrawal is to the account value.

Example: Suppose a policy started out with a premium of $100,000, but the death benefit has now grown to $300,000 even though the policy value has tumbled back to $100,000. At this point, the policyowner chooses to withdraw $50,000. A dollar-for-dollar reduction would reduce the death benefit to $250,000 ($300,000 – $50,000 = $250,000). A pro rata reduction, which is determined by the ratio of the withdrawal over the account value ($50,000 over $100,000), would drop the death benefit by 50 percent (50% x $300,000 = $150,000) to $150,000.

Premiums paid: $100,000
Account value: $100,000
Death benefit: $300,000
Withdrawal: $ 50,000

New death benefit after withdrawal
Dollar-for-dollar reduction:
  $300,000 – $50,000 = $250,000
Pro rata reduction (based on 50% of $100,000)
  50% x $300,000 = $150,000

SELLING VARIABLE ANNUITIES

Regulation

Selling variable deferred annuities is different from selling fixed-interest deferred annuities. One difference deals with suitability. All variable products must be suitable to the client while fixed-interest annuities do not require the determination of the product's suitability to the client.

Also prospects must be given a prospectus in the sales process for variable annuities. Fixed-interest products do not have prospectuses. The regulatory environment is also different between variable and fixed annuities.

Both FINRA and the Securities and Exchange Commission (SEC) are involved in variable annuity sales regulation. But neither FINRA nor the SEC is involved in the sale of fixed annuities.

In a landmark decision, the United States Supreme Court held that an individual variable annuity contract is a security within the meaning of the Securities Act of 1933 and that any organization offering such a contract is an investment company subject to the Investment Company Act of 1940. Any company that offers individual variable annuity contracts is subject to dual supervision by the SEC and the various state insurance departments.

Persons selling variable annuities must pass FINRA's Series 6 licensing exam.

As part of its regulatory nature, the SEC developed the following list of questions for potential clients to consider before purchasing a variable annuity policy (see http://www.sec.gov/investor/pubs/varannty.htm).

Before they decide to buy a variable annuity, consider asking prospects the following questions:

- Will you use the variable annuity primarily to save for retirement or a similar long-term goal?
- Are you investing in the variable annuity through a retirement plan or IRA (which would mean that you are not receiving any additional tax-deferral benefit from the variable annuity)?
- Are you willing to take the risk that your account value may decrease if the underlying mutual fund investment options perform badly?
- Do you understand the features of the variable annuity? Do you understand all of the fees and expenses that the variable annuity charges?
- Do you intend to remain in the variable annuity long enough to avoid paying any surrender charges if you have to withdraw money?
- If a variable annuity offers a bonus credit, will the bonus outweigh any higher fees and charges that the product may charge?
- Are there features of the variable annuity, such as long-term care insurance, that you could purchase more cheaply separately?
- Have you consulted with a tax advisor and considered all the tax consequences of purchasing an annuity, including the effect of annuity payments on your tax status in retirement?
- If you are exchanging one annuity for another one, do the benefits of the exchange outweigh the costs, such as any surrender charges you will have to pay if you withdraw your money before the end of the surrender charge period for the new annuity?

FINRA's Deferred Variable Annuity Rule

On September 7, 2007, the SEC approved Rule 2821 proposed by the Financial Industry Regulatory Authority (FINRA). Rule 2821 is designed specifically to address broker-dealers' sales practices regarding purchases and exchanges of deferred variable annuities.

Rule 2821

- sets specific suitability obligations for the sale or exchange of deferred variable annuities
- sets standards for principal review and requires principals to review transactions before the customer's application is forwarded to the issuing insurance company for processing
- requires firms to develop and maintain written supervisory procedures designed to achieve compliance with the rule
- requires firms to develop and document training policies and programs to ensure compliance with the rule and the salespersons' understanding of the features of deferred variable annuities.

Rule 2821 will be discussed in greater detail in Chapter 8 of this text. The full text of Rule 2821 is available at www.finra.org/notices/07-53.

Mutual Fund versus Variable Deferred Annuity

Another difference between variable deferred annuities and fixed-interest deferred annuities lies in their competing investments. As we learned in Chapter 3, fixed-interest deferred annuities often compete against certificates of deposit. The nearest competitor to the subaccounts of a variable deferred annuity is mutual funds.

As mentioned previously, mutual funds have an average total expense ratio of 1.365 percent and have no insurance features. The average total asset charge in variable annuities is 2.356 percent. Therefore clients who wish to avoid insurance charges can do so and save an average of .991 percent by using taxable mutual funds.

However, no individual can make a personal decision based on these averages. A better process is for the client to determine which mutual fund alternative he or she wants to compare. It may be the elusive low-cost, tax-efficient fund or a mutual fund family. The best approach is to identify the actual costs in the mutual fund choice, and compare the cost difference with a variable annuity.

Product Feature Differences

Besides costs, the potential purchaser should know and understand the differences in the operation and design of variable deferred annuities versus mutual funds. Table 5-3 compares the features of a nonqualified variable deferred annuity and a nonqualified mutual fund.

TABLE 5-3 **Mutual Fund versus Variable Deferred Annuity (Nonqualified)**		
Product Feature	**Variable Deferred Annuity**	**Mutual Fund**
Guaranteed death benefit	Yes	Not available
Death benefit	Higher of account value or premium	Account value
Guaranteed lifetime income at annuitization or other payout option guarantees	Numerous	None
Transfers	Among available subaccounts without taxes and often without expenses	Within fund family are free, but each is a taxable event
Ability to purchase enhanced death benefits riders	Yes	Not available
Stepped-up cost basis at death	Not available	Yes
Ability to purchase guaranteed living benefits riders	Yes	Not available
Taxation of gains	100% tax deferred until withdrawal or death, then taxed as ordinary income	Capital gains based on increase in net asset value of fund shares when fund is sold while owner is living, but annual dividend income and distributions of capital gain income are realized by shareholders
Withdrawals	Company surrender charges during any surrender charge period or IRS penalties prior to owner's age 59 ½	Company withdrawal constraints depending on class of shares; no IRS penalties prior to age 59 ½
Excise tax on investment	A few states impose a state premium tax	None
Guaranteed minimum interest account	Available	Not available

Each product offers features that may be advantageous for the purchaser of these products. For example, the death proceeds of mutual funds receive a stepped-up or stepped-down cost basis at the owner's death that is equivalent to the fair market value of the shares at death. Thus, assuming the share value has appreciated, the increase in cost basis results in no income tax payment being immediately due when the beneficiary receives the mutual fund at the owner's death. Furthermore, less income tax will be due when the beneficiary subsequently sells those inherited mutual fund shares because of their step-up in cost basis. Also the income tax due at the time of subsequent sale will be calculated using the lower capital gains rate as long as the beneficiary maintains ownership for one year or longer.

If a mutual fund's value has declined at the time of the owner's death, a decrease in cost basis results. This lower cost basis will be the cost basis that the beneficiary of the fund assumes. Any capital gain or loss resulting from the beneficiary's future sale of the fund shares will be calculated using the fund's value at the time he or she took ownership.

On the other hand, under current tax law, the investment earnings that accrue in variable deferred annuities while the owner is alive are totally tax deferred until the funds are withdrawn or distributed or the owner/annuitant dies. At the annuity owner's death, the previously tax-deferred accumulation of gain in the cash value is then taxable as ordinary income and payable by the named beneficiary at his or her respective marginal income tax bracket. However, the beneficiary will not be taxed on the gain in the year of the annuitant's death if he or she elects, within 60 days after the annuitant's death, to apply the proceeds under a life-income or installment-payment option. These periodic payments will then be taxable to the beneficiary under the regular taxation for annuity payment rules discussed in Chapter 7.

The owner of a variable deferred annuity can also purchase the enhanced death benefits rider discussed previously in this chapter that will increase the death benefit in order to cushion the potential income taxation of death proceeds to the beneficiary of the contract.

If a variable deferred annuity experiences a loss in value at the time of the owner's death, because the death benefit is guaranteed at least to equal the premiums paid into the contract, the beneficiary will receive this amount as a death benefit payment. Thus there is no taxable loss (or gain) to him or her that results from the receipt of the proceeds. By contrast, there is no death benefit guarantee whatsoever with a mutual fund.

Some other features available in variable deferred annuities that are not found in mutual funds include

- guaranteed lifetime income options at annuitization
- the availability of a guaranteed minimum interest account

- the ability to purchase one of several guaranteed living and death benefits riders

The real downside with variable deferred annuities occurs when they are purchased or sold inappropriately or when they are subject to excessive expenses. All charges, especially those that are asset based, must be disclosed and evaluated in light of other investment alternatives. As the SEC questionnaire states, the prospective purchaser must understand the features of the policy, understand all the fees and expenses, understand the tax implications, and intend to remain in the policy long enough to avoid surrender charges.

ANALYZING THE INFORMATION AND DEVELOPING THE PLAN

In Chapter 4, we discussed information gathering—the fourth step of the selling/planning process—which results in a discovery agreement with the prospect to design a plan that will meet his or her needs. In this section, we move to the fifth step of the selling/planning process—analyzing the information—in which the financial advisor begins to develop a plan or plan alternatives to present to the prospect. In examining this step of the selling/planning process, the textbook focuses on formulating concepts and appropriate annuity products that might best enhance the prospect's current financial situation to create possible solutions to the financial problems uncovered in the fact-finding process. We will also discuss how to analyze the competition.

Plan Design Assumptions

Analysis of a prospect's information and presentation of an annuity solution is based on two assumptions: (1) using a two-interview selling/ planning process and (2) obtaining a satisfactorily completed fact finder.

Two-Interview Selling/Planning Process

This book advocates a two-interview selling/planning process in which meeting the prospect and gathering information constitute the initial interview. The interview ends with a discovery agreement and scheduling a follow-up appointment. Because the initial interview usually does not include a discussion of the prospect's desired annuity policy benefits, in-depth analysis and plan design occur after the first meeting with the prospect, giving the advisor time to develop a plan and customize a sales presentation for the closing interview.

The two-interview selling/planning process is recommended for two reasons. First, many experienced advisors have had great success with this approach and feel that a multiple-interview sale cements the advisor-prospect relationship because it demonstrates that the advisor understands the prospect's need to process the information. As one experienced financial advisor explains, "Selling annuities is usually a two-interview process because I want people to be comfortable with what they are doing." Second, a two-interview approach gives less experienced advisors time to analyze the information and seek the advice of experienced advisors, if necessary. It also allows time to customize the presentation. As less experienced advisors gain more knowledge, a one-interview approach is feasible and, depending on style and philosophy, perhaps more desirable. The key to this transition is skill in designing plans, which comes only as a result of becoming familiar with different annuity policy types and their inherent options.

Good point to do the two-interview selling process.

Relationship to the Fact Finder

An annuity plan solution for the prospect must be customized according to the information you gathered by means of either the deductive or inductive approach to identifying and establishing the prospect's financial/retirement goals.

If you used the deductive approach, you should have completed all three sections of the comprehensive Retirement Planning Fact Finder in their entirety, which consists of the personal data and retirement goals section, the quantitative section, and the retirement income sources section. With all the relevant information necessary to complete the fourth calculations section in the fact finder after the initial interview, you can then determine the annual savings the prospect requires and develop potential annuity plan recommendations according to his or her premium commitment, risk tolerance, and investment objectives.

If, on the other hand, you used the inductive (dominant need) approach, you would probably complete only the first page of the fact finder regarding personal data, the top of page 2 regarding retirement planning assumptions, and then perhaps an abbreviated cash flow statement, along with selected questions regarding risk tolerance and investment objectives. (More comprehensive risk profile analysis would always be required by your company whenever variable annuity products are proposed.) Finally only selected portions of the retirement income sources section, such as the current investments and/or the distribution options or deposits and earnings subsections, may need to be completed, depending on the prospect's dominant-need situation.

The analysis of the prospect's information involves taking the relevant information gathered from the fact finder and designing a plan that reflects the prospect's needs, preferences, and either premium or lump-sum investment commitment. Creating a solution to meet the prospect's individual needs depends heavily on the quality of the information gathered during the fact-finding process. The solution must be based on the prospect's own circumstances and preferences. Thus the importance of a thorough fact finder cannot be overemphasized.

Because fact finding affects your analysis of the prospect's situation, you can apply information in the quantitative section of the fact finder to questions that are related to the possible inclusion of annuity product features in the type of plan you recommend. For example, you can ask the prospect if he or she is concerned about reducing taxes on his or her savings. Such a concern would mean that he or she might be receptive to the concept of tax deferral. Alternatively, you could ask how the prospect feels about taking investment risks or into what risk category any additional products purchased would be included. Answers to these two questions that express a willingness to take investment risks and show that the prospect considers himself or herself to be an aggressive investor may indicate interest in a variable annuity. Understanding the prospect's preferences and priorities will dictate which features and riders to include in your recommended annuity policy options.

Designing the Plan

Your objective is to help the prospect get the best value for his or her money through an effective plan design. Plan design is a balancing act between the prospect's prioritized retirement or financial needs and his or her premium or lump-sum investment commitment. One way to approach this task is to start with the basic plan design, which is a deferred or immediate annuity, depending on whether the prospect requires tax-favored wealth accumulation or income. Next formulate choices of several possible product types according to the prospect's risk tolerance and investment objectives. Then, using the premium or investment commitment and the prospect's planning priorities, begin to adjust and fine-tune the plan to create an optimal solution that will best meet his or her financial goals within the specified premium or investment commitment.

Using the following policy classification criteria, you can then develop an annuity recommendation according to the prospect's financial goals:

- how premiums are paid—single- or flexible-premium annuity
- when annuity payments begin—deferred or immediate annuity
- how annuity funds are invested—fixed, indexed, or variable annuity

Below is a brief discussion of when each annuity product type may be applicable based on the prospect's financial circumstances.

How Premiums Are Paid

Reasons to Recommend a Single-Premium Annuity. A single-premium deferred annuity (SPDA) often makes good financial sense for a person who has received a large sum of money and would like to set it aside for a retirement nest egg. A retiree may want to invest a lump sum from a pension plan or a certificate of deposit into an SPDA. Perhaps a widow or widower who has just received the lump-sum death proceeds from a spouse's life insurance policy might be advised to invest these funds in a single-premium immediate annuity that will pay a monthly income for life. Another potential client for a single-premium deferred annuity might be a business owner who has sold all or a portion of his or her company. This can be particularly important to a business owner or self-employed person who has not been able to set up a qualified plan.

Reasons to Recommend a Flexible-Premium Annuity. A flexible-premium annuity is useful as a tool to gradually accumulate retirement benefits. The initial deposit may be as little as $25, and the contract owner can determine the schedule and amount of additional deposits. When discussing a flexible-premium annuity with a working client, point out the long-term benefits of saving a portion of each paycheck by making regular contributions to the annuity.

As you design a flexible-premium annuity policy, it is important to work within a prospect's retirement planning premium commitment as determined in the fact-finding interview. Develop some alternative policy designs that reflect the prospect's risk tolerance and investment objectives and fall within his or her premium commitment. You should limit the choices to just a few so that you do not confuse the prospect. You can always customize a policy further by using a few basic illustrations as the starting point and introducing several interest rate assumptions or policy variations within reasonable parameters. You can also enrich the selling/planning process by interjecting your personal experiences and/or making more sophisticated sales illustrations if appropriate.

When Annuity Payments Begin

Reasons to Recommend a Deferred Annuity. Most people purchase a deferred annuity because they want their money to grow tax deferred. They are attracted to deferred annuities because they provide premium flexibility and several options for the growth of funds over long periods of time. Deferred annuities can be fixed, equity-indexed, or variable, and they offer a range of annuity payout options. Later, if annuity owners choose, they can receive income from the annuity either through occasional or regularly scheduled payments.

In comprehensive retirement planning situations, the reason for buying deferred annuities is to accumulate funds for later use in retirement. This can also include situations where a retiring employee transfers funds from an employer-sponsored retirement plan into a fixed or equity-indexed deferred annuity for safety of principal and modest growth potential.

However, in dominant-needs sales situations, a prospect may have a variety of other uses for deferred annuity products. Some examples discussed in Chapter 2 include

- the retiree who buys a deferred annuity in order to reduce the interest received from other investments, such as CDs, and thus reduce his or her total income tax bill, as well as the taxation on Social Security benefits
- a prospect who has recently sold a business or who sells his or her house when retirement begins and uses the deferred annuity as a tax-favored vehicle for depositing the substantial nonqualified funds acquired
- the couple who uses a deferred annuity as part of a charitable giving strategy or as a component of a charitable remainder trust
- a grandparent who uses a deferred annuity to help fund a college education for a grandchild

Reasons to Recommend an Immediate Annuity. Immediate annuity contracts can be purchased only with a single lump-sum premium. Immediate annuities can be either fixed or variable. They also provide a range of annuity payout options, which are discussed in Chapter 6.

An immediate annuity can be useful to a senior client who has received a large sum of money and must count on these funds for income over a long period of time—for example, a senior prospect who has received a lump-sum distribution from an employer retirement plan, the proceeds from a matured CD, life insurance proceeds, or the proceeds from the sale of a business.

Immediate annuities can also be used to provide a reliable periodic stream of funds that can be applied to pay for other financial products such long-term care or life insurance. By internally directing specifically earmarked payments into these other products, a senior retired policyowner can be relieved of the worry of where the funds will come from to pay for them, as well as the responsibility of having to submit the payments by writing checks.

Fixed Immediate Annuity Distributions. Distributions from a fixed immediate annuity can give the annuitant the assurance of knowing that the income stream will remain constant for the duration of the chosen payout period. The guaranteed income stream can be used to provide a degree of investment portfolio balance in comparison to other sources of retirement income that may fluctuate. The trade-off is that these fixed-income payments will lose their purchasing power when exposed to the effects of inflation.

However, recently developed riders have become available that will increase the level annuity payments in a fixed immediate annuity by a specified percentage each year to help keep pace with the impact of inflation.

Variable Immediate Annuity Distributions. Using the separate account for annuitization offers the variable-annuity owner the opportunity for benefit amounts to increase sufficiently to keep up with inflation. If the annuitant is not comfortable with the risk and the variable aspect of the separate account, he or she can put all or a portion of the accumulated funds in the general account or choose from a variety of guaranteed living benefits riders to ensure a predictable minimum level or increasing payout income stream.

How Annuity Funds Are Invested

Reasons to Recommend a Fixed-Interest Deferred Annuity. Because of the guaranteed principal and interest, a fixed-interest deferred annuity is for conservative investors—people who want assurances about the safety of their principal and who want to know exactly what they can expect in interest on their annuity cash value. Fixed-interest deferred annuities can provide balance to an overall investment portfolio for moderate to aggressive investors. No matter what happens to stocks, bonds, gold, or mutual funds, all investors in fixed-interest deferred annuities know that at least one part of their holdings is low risk and guaranteed.

The amount of the benefit that is paid out during the distribution phase is fixed. If the annuitant chooses a life-annuity option, the amount of the check he or she receives each month will be the same without any investment decisions or risk.

The downside of the fixed-interest deferred annuity is that, over time, such an approach may fall behind the cumulative effect of inflation.

Reasons to Recommend an Equity-Indexed Annuity. You should consider recommending an equity-indexed annuity to prospects who do not want to put money into a product where there is risk of loss but who do want to take advantage of the potential gains to be made in the stock market. Seniors in their late 50s and early 60s and those who intend to work beyond retirement may find an equity-indexed annuity to be particularly well suited to their needs as they look for a place to accumulate funds over time to build their retirement nest egg. A single-premium equity-indexed annuity might be the ideal place to move funds from a CD when it matures in the hope of benefiting from future market increases without assuming the risk of losing principal.

Be sure to remind clients with equity-indexed annuities not to miss the window periods at the end of the policy terms when they can choose to continue the contract and lock it in for another term, annuitize it, or exchange it for another type of annuity. Clients coming to the end of a term who plan to retire relatively soon can usually exchange an equity-indexed annuity for either a fixed-interest or variable annuity. These two types of annuities offer greater flexibility to an individual who will retire soon because they do not have a contract term.

Reasons to Recommend a Variable Deferred Annuity. Whether or not you recommend a variable deferred annuity depends on the prospect's risk tolerance and how long the money will be invested before it must be withdrawn. People with short investment time horizons and low investment risk tolerance will generally be happier with a fixed-interest deferred annuity. If they have long time horizons and moderate risk tolerance, you might recommend an equity-indexed annuity. The advantage of both the variable deferred annuity and the equity-indexed annuity over the fixed-interest deferred annuity is that they are more likely to keep up with inflation because of their link to the financial markets.

The variable deferred annuity is for the prospect who realizes that gains and losses may occur but who wants the investment flexibility that comes from being able to move funds among subaccounts within the separate account. This flexibility allows annuity owners to change their investment focus in response to changes in the financial markets or changes in their personal situation at the different stages of their retirement. Also the use of recently available living benefits riders can provide the owner with guarantees of minimum accumulations, income, and lifetime withdrawals regardless of the performance of investment divisions within their chosen asset allocations.

Because of the separate accounts, variable annuities are considered securities under federal law. This means you must have a life insurance license and be registered with the National Association of Securities Dealers to sell variable annuities. You must also obtain state licensing powers or authorization to sell variable annuities within each jurisdiction where you transact business. Also any potential buyer of a variable annuity must be given a prospectus, and you must take steps to determine that a variable annuity is a suitable product choice for the purchaser. Suitability involves assessing a potential investor's investment objectives, time horizon, and risk tolerance.

Prospect and Client Education

Client education is a key factor in helping the owner get full benefit from annuities. Clients should understand their contracts. They should know when and how the annuity goes from the accumulation phase to the distribution phase and which distribution option best meets their needs. They should know the rules about, and possible charges for, full and partial surrenders. Potential owners of equity-indexed annuities and variable annuities particularly need to know how their contracts work and understand the investment risks.

Before buying an equity-indexed annuity, the prospect should understand the workings of the indexing method of the product—including the length of the policy terms, the participation rate, and the cap. They should be aware of the window periods at the ends of the policy terms at which they can make the decision to continue the contract for another term, annuitize it, or exchange it for another type of annuity. At the end of equity-indexed annuity terms, you may want to be on hand to guide them through these decisions.

With variable annuities, prospects should be educated about the risks involved before investing. Gains may occur, but there can also be losses. You should discuss the various subaccounts in the separate account so that prospects understand the risks and possible gains from investing in each.

Summary

There are two sides of the coin in providing the best possible solutions: Know the prospect's problems, and know how your products can work to solve those problems. On the one side, do a complete fact-finding interview, analyze the information, and communicate your observations effectively to the prospect. Know the prospect's objectives, identify the shortfalls in his or her current financial plan for reaching those objectives, and define the problems in a way that he or she can understand before making your recommendations. On the other side, strive to understand the planning applications for annuities. Acquire the knowledge necessary to put the appropriate annuity options into a plan so that the result addresses your prospect's needs.

The more you work with your annuity products, the more knowledge you will accrue about them. Sometimes you may work with annuity contracts that are so similar in design or policy features that they confuse prospects. For example, a long-term care benefit rider and terminal illness rider found in many deferred annuities may seem like the same thing to your prospect. It is your job to simplify these two riders so that the prospect can easily distinguish between them.

Finally the design of a policy and its sale to a prospect should not be considered a one-time event. The selling/planning process should be ongoing even after the sale because the client's personal situation and needs will most likely change over time. Besides, many changes could occur in the often lengthy time lapse between when the policy is sold and when an individual retires.

Analyzing the Competition

Some financial advisors prefer to shop around for the best annuity policy available. Other successful advisors report that they are not often in competitive situations with other advisors. While their experience may be due to their self-confidence or confidence in their companies and products, it is most likely due to their ability to build relationships and create confidence in prospects' minds that they are the advisors with whom to do business. They present themselves as trustworthy, knowledgeable, and having the prospects' best interests in mind.

However, because there are so many advisors and insurers offering a broad array of annuity policy features and options to the public, it is likely that you will encounter a competitive situation at some point. In case you do, the following material is designed to help you analyze and compare companies and policies.

Evaluating Insurance/Annuity Companies

There are several key areas in which you should compare the competition with your company and the products it offers.

Financial Strength. It is important for you to evaluate the financial strength and claims-paying ability of your company compared to its competitors. The real value of an annuity contract for a policyowner is the peace of mind associated with knowing that the insurer will be able to pay interest consistently, preserve principal when necessary, and pay claims should a claim be filed. Consequently prospects should buy only from insurers that (1) have strong financial reserves and are likely to be solvent far into the future, (2) have a history of stable interest rates for their policies, (3) have an excellent reputation, and (4) have a good track record for policyowner service with few or no reported complaints.

Although there is no foolproof method for assessing a company's financial strength, a useful measure is the rating given by independent rating services. Prospects are urged to obtain ratings for the companies whose policies they are considering. Also it is a good idea for you to know exactly how your company ranks and compares with others. Several companies provide independent ratings for insurance companies:

- A.M. Best Company, (908) 439-2200 or www.ambest.com
- Standard & Poor's Insurance Rating Services, (212) 438-7280 or www2.standardandpoors.com
- Moody's Investor Services Inc., (212) 553-1653 or www.moodys.com
- Duff & Phelps Inc., (212) 871-2000 or www.duffandphelps.com

- Fitch Investors Service Inc., (800) 893-4824 or www.fitchratings.com
- Weiss Research Inc., (800) 289-9222 or www.weissratings.com

Reputation. The reputation of your company is an important aspect of competition. Anything that can help you present your company in a positive light will enhance its image in the prospect's eyes. For example, if you have marketing pieces and fact sheets that champion your company's positive claims-paying experience, financial strength, corporate integrity, or proud history, include them in your sales presentation binder and use them in the initial interview. If your company runs an advertising campaign that uses a celebrity to endorse its products, this will give it credibility and implicitly boost its reputation. Everyone wants to do business with a reputable company.

Value. Many dimensions of value other than interest rates or investment returns are just as important and should also be considered. These include your level of professional expertise, the quality of the service you provide, your company's reputation and its financial strength, and the availability of desirable policy provisions and features.

Prospects normally get what they pay for, and high-interest-rate fixed-annuity policies with excessively lengthy rate guarantees marketed by shortsighted insurance carriers can lead to the following undesirable consequences:

- disappointment with the policy's subsequent current interest rates because they were intentionally set too high in the first place to attract buyers
- the need to lower the policy's interest rates because the current reserve structure cannot support the promised benefits
- low company investment performance
- problematic administrative support systems and/or poor policy service

When comparing interest rates, use extreme caution for the following reasons:

- The underlying reserve structure can be significantly different for each company. You need to understand reserve structures and be able to explain the differences to prospects.
- Marketing objectives and sales philosophies differ significantly from company to company. You must know your competitors' target markets and the interest rate compromises they make to reach those markets.
- A competitor's high interest rates today may mean rate reductions later. You need to consider the likelihood of future rate reductions

by your company and its competitors because they may be setting rates aggressively high to achieve specified market penetration objectives.

- Prospects will ask about past interest rates increases. You must know the history of interest rates for fixed-interest deferred annuity products for your company and its competitors.

Consider one last point about interest rates. Because annuity contracts can be complicated, many advisors and prospects who do not fully understand the types of policies and the differences among them will naturally be inclined to compare policies almost solely on current or bonus interest rates. Decisions based on interest rates alone can lead to wrong solutions, which is why your prospects need you to explain the differences among the annuity products that are available to them and to guide them to the best product for them.

Interest Rate Stability. There are many instances of rate reductions in fixed-interest deferred annuity contracts that have caused policies either to lapse or the policyowner to make financial sacrifices to maintain them. A series of substantial interest rate reductions can cast the advisor, the company, and the industry in a bad light.

As indicated previously, current or nonguaranteed interest rates paid by annuity carriers can vary greatly, and it is difficult to say what is the "right" interest rate. A low rate may be exploitative, but a high rate may be unrealistic, requiring a later rate reduction or series of rate reductions. Unrealistically high current interest rates could be the result of deliberate manipulation ("bait and switch" tactics) or simply the lack of adequate company investment assumptions in making interest rate decisions.

In addition, a company's investment practices will have an effect on future interest rates. On one hand, a company with liberal investment practices makes the initial interest rates offered in its annuity contract look attractive, but the trade-off may be a series of rate reductions later on. On the other hand, the initial current interest rates offered in fixed-interest deferred annuity products from a company with more conservative investment practices may seem uncompetitive at first, but the risk of future rate reductions that do not reflect the declining interest rates in the economy as a whole may be minimal.

Service. The concept of service takes two distinct forms in the competitive search for annuities: the service offered by the company and the service offered by the advisor.

- *company*—You can somewhat expedite such functions as policy administration and handling customer service requests, but they are largely out of your control. The service your company provides is part of what constitutes its reputation. A responsive service department is a great asset to tout in a competitive situation. A deficient service department can be a liability that is not easy to overcome. Company service issues are real concerns that you should be prepared to address.

- *advisor*—There is a value-added element to the personalized service you provide before, during, and after the sale. The demeanor you exhibit during the approach and fact-finding process allows you to establish your image as trustworthy and professional. You are performing an extremely valuable function by conducting the due-diligence processes described in this book. You should not underestimate the opportunity you have to distinguish yourself from the competition. You are at least as important to prospects as the company you represent because you perform valuable financial counseling. You may personally monitor processing the application, delivering the policy, and servicing in-force policies. You should also review your clients' needs periodically. This will give you a tremendous opportunity to enhance your clients' financial and emotional well-being. Take this opportunity seriously.

Differences in Policies. Due to design innovations and competition for market share, insurers offer deferred and immediate annuity policies that contain many different features. The National Association of Insurance Commissioners' (NAIC) Annuity Disclosure Model Regulation and Buyer's Guide to Fixed Deferred Annuities (discussed in Chapter 8) helps to explain fixed-interest policies, and the prospectus for variable annuities helps to explain their technical aspects. However, it is difficult, if not impossible, for prospects to comprehend subtle differences in policy features without a thorough understanding of the terminology used to describe the features. Thus the prospect is well advised to obtain all the available information to allow him or her to completely evaluate these policy differences. This is where you can provide an important value-added dimension to the buying process. Not only can you furnish additional supplementary materials, such as fact sheets and product brochures that may be relatively easy to understand, but you can also explain and illustrate the aspects of annuity products that are more complicated.

Replacement

Policyowners are sometimes faced with the question of whether they should terminate an existing annuity policy and purchase a new one. Such a replacement must be made with a careful and thorough determination that the new policy is better than the existing one. As was discussed in Chapter 3, policies should not be replaced unless doing so is in the client's best interest. Before they can make an informed decision to change insurance carriers, clients must clearly understand that new surrender charges will apply. There will be new commissions earned, and other benefits may be lost.

Despite the reasons for not replacing an existing policy, there may be valid reasons to consider a new one. For example, a new policy may be the best approach when a prospect owns a fixed-interest deferred annuity contract issued by a company with questionable internal investment practices, which has led to successive years of current interest rate reductions, seriously jeopardizing the prospect's original financial objective(s). Nevertheless, use extreme caution before proceeding with any replacement, and be sure to adhere strictly to your state's replacement disclosure requirements.

Conclusion

It takes time to master the art of designing an annuity policy recommendation to meet a prospect's needs within his or her premium or investment commitment. As you continue to read policies, study company literature, and work with prospects, you will develop a better feel for the most appropriate annuity product.

Annuity products have many features, benefits, and options that differ from company to company. A company's financial strength, reputation, price, and rate stability are important factors for a prospect to weigh when comparing policies, but the most important component is the knowledge and trustworthiness of the advisor.

Remember, when it comes to competition, the relationship you build with the prospect is the greatest differentiating factor.

CHAPTER FIVE REVIEW

Key Terms and Concepts are explained in the Glossary. Answers to the Review Questions and Self-Test Questions are found in the back of the book in the Answers to Questions section.

Key Terms and Concepts

prospectus	diversification
general account	dollar cost averaging
separate account	asset allocation
subaccounts	automatic rebalancing
accumulation units	front-end load

back-end load
annual contract charge
mortality and expense charge
(M&E)
fund expense
total expense ratio
guaranteed minimum income
benefit
guaranteed minimum return of
premium benefit

guaranteed minimum accumulation
benefit
guaranteed minimum withdrawal
benefit
guaranteed lifetime withdrawal
benefit
rising floor death benefit
stepped-up death benefit
enhanced earnings benefit

Review Questions

5-1.   Describe what a prospectus is and how it is used in the sales process.

5-2.   Describe the differences in the insurance industry regulation of fixed-interest deferred annuities and variable deferred annuities.

5-3.   Describe the differences between the variable deferred annuity's general account and separate account.

5-4.   Explain the benefits to the investor of using the dollar-cost-averaging investment strategy.

5-5.   Explain the difference between a pro rata death benefit reduction and a dollar-for-dollar death benefit reduction as a result of withdrawing funds from a variable annuity.

5-6.   Describe the difference between a front-end load and a back-end load.

5-7.   Identify the common charges and fees normally associated with a variable deferred annuity policy.

5-8.   Identify four types of death benefit guarantees available in variable deferred annuities.

5-9.   Identify the three key annuity policy classification criteria used to recommend an applicable annuity plan solution to a prospect.

5-10.   Identify the key areas to evaluate when comparing the competition with your company and the products it offers.

Self-Test Questions

Instructions: Read Chapter 5 first; then answer the following questions to test your knowledge. There are 10 questions; circle the correct answer, and then check your answers with the answer key in the back of the book.

5-1.   Variable deferred annuities are different from fixed-interest deferred annuities in which of the following ways?

(A) The annuity owner assumes the investment risk with variable policies, and the insurance company assumes the risk with fixed-interest annuities.

(B) Fees and expenses are generally higher for fixed-interest annuities than they are for variable deferred annuities.

(C) Fixed annuities offer various subaccounts for investment choices while variable deferred annuities offer only a general account.

(D) Fixed-interest annuities require that potential annuity owners receive a prospectus as part of the sales process, but variable deferred annuities do not.

5-2.   Annuities can be classified according to which of the following three criteria?

(A) how the funds are invested, when the payments begin, and the identity of the annuitant

(B) when the payments begin, the identity of the annuitant, and the identity of the contract owner

(C) when the payments begin, the identity of the contract holder, and the identity of the beneficiary

(D) how the funds are invested, when the payments begin, and how premiums are paid

5-3.   A policyowner purchases which of the following when the owner pays a premium into a variable deferred annuity subaccount?

(A) general account units

(B) accumulation units

(C) shares of stock

(D) mutual fund units

5-4.   A policyowner purchases the enhanced earnings benefit option to increase the death benefit by one-third of the policy's gain to help pay income taxes owed by the beneficiary. If the normal death benefit without the increase is $100,000 and the premium paid for the annuity is $25,000, how much will the beneficiary owe in income taxes if the beneficiary is in a 30 percent income tax bracket?

   (A) $ 25,000
   (B) $ 30,000
   (C) $ 75,000
   (D) $ 100,000

5-5.   Which of the following fees are charged against the subaccount in a variable deferred annuity to pay for the fund manager's and the fund's operating expenses?

   I.   annual contract charge
   II.   fund expense

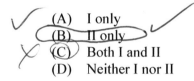

   (A)   I only
   (B)   II only
   (C)   Both I and II
   (D)   Neither I nor II

5-6.   Which of the following statements regarding variable deferred annuity subaccounts is (are) correct?

   I.   The average number of subaccounts within a variable deferred annuity policy is 44.
   II.   Subaccounts are part of the insurance company's general account assets.

   (A)   I only
   (B)   II only
   (C)   Both I and II
   (D)   Neither I nor II

5-7. Which of the following statements regarding fees and expenses within variable deferred annuity policies is (are) correct?

    I. Mortality and expense charges are assessed to cover the minimum guaranteed interest rates and guaranteed annuity factors in the policy.

    II. The majority of variable deferred annuities charge a front-end load.

    (A) I only
    (B) II only
    (C) Both I and II
    (D) Neither I nor II

5-8. All of the following services are often available to variable <u>deferred</u> annuity owners without charges or expenses EXCEPT

    (A) professional management
    (B) guaranteed minimum income benefits
    (C) automatic rebalancing
    (D) tax-free transfers among subaccounts

5-9. All of the following statements regarding the total expense ratio are correct EXCEPT

    (A) Variable deferred annuity total expense ratios are, on average, higher than those of mutual funds.
    (B) The total expense ratio is a combination of the mortality expense charge and the fund expenses.
    (C) The average variable deferred annuity total expense ratio is 2.356 percent.
    (D) The average mutual fund expense ratio is 3.01 percent.

5-10. All the following are key areas in which you should compare the competition with your company and the annuity products it offers EXCEPT

    (A) financial strength
    (B) value
    (C) reputation
    (D) price stability

NOTE

1. More precisely, the value of an annuity unit at the end of each fiscal year is obtained by dividing the current market value of the funds supporting the annuity units by the total number of annuity units expected to be paid over the future lifetimes of all participants then receiving annuity payments, in accordance with the assumptions as to mortality, investment earnings, and expense rates for the future.

Immediate Annuities; Plan Presentation Techniques

Learning Objectives

An understanding of the material in this chapter should enable you to

6-1. Explain why individuals purchase immediate annuities.

6-2. Identify the benefits that immediate annuities can provide.

6-3. Describe at least three immediate annuity payout options and how they function.

6-4. Identify several variations from the traditional immediate annuity.

6-5. Explain the difference between a variable immediate annuity and a fixed immediate annuity.

6-6. Explain why variable immediate annuities are less popular than traditional fixed immediate annuities.

6-7. Outline strategies for presenting solution alternatives to a prospect.

6-8. Identify objections to the purchase of annuity products.

6-9. Explore techniques for handling common objections and concerns.

Chapter Outline

Chapter 6 helps advisors gain an understanding of immediate annuities offered today and the various types of payout options individuals may choose. The chapter also examines annuity plan presentation techniques and how to manage prospect resistance.

INTRODUCTION TO IMMEDIATE ANNUITIES

This chapter covers the topic most people in America think of when they hear the word *annuity*—that is, a series of payments made to the annuity owner over the annuitant's lifetime. Even though we have covered in detail the three most popular types of annuities sold today—fixed, indexed, and variable deferred annuities—the type of annuity that most commonly comes to our minds is the immediate annuity.

People buy an immediate annuity for one of two main reasons: to protect against the risk of running out of income during life or to assure the receipt of a series of payments for a fixed period of time.

In the payout mode, an annuity can protect against the risk of running out of income during life by lifetime annuitization rather than periodic withdrawals. The economic risk of living too long is a growing concern because our life spans are increasing so rapidly. A generation of preretirees is becoming more concerned with the possibility that their parents may run out of money, or have a severely diminished standard of living, as a result of the dramatic increases in the cost of living during their retirement years. Many people who retired with Social Security and pension income felt much more secure the day they retired than they do now. With 20-20 hindsight, we can see that they might have been better off than they are today if they had used a portion of their money to purchase an immediate annuity. As retirees quickly learn, it is not the size of one's net worth that makes a person rich; it is the amount of ever replaceable, steady, guaranteed income that arrives every month. We must all keep in mind that one of the most devastating risks we face is outliving our income.

Individuals have a choice between fixed and variable immediate annuities. The basic contract structures of both are similar. Fixed immediate annuities generally provide level guaranteed payments. However, a variable immediate annuity provides fluctuating income payments, and this fluctuation makes its use more limited than a fixed immediate annuity. The variable immediate annuity purchaser is concerned with the long-term effects of inflation on a fixed income and is willing to accept volatility of income, both up and down, in the hope that the income stream over the long term will offset the effects of inflation. Therefore variable immediate annuities are primarily life-contingent contracts, while fixed immediate annuities have many fixed-amount and fixed-period, as well as life-contingent, applications. To distinguish between fixed and variable immediate annuities throughout this chapter, we will refer to "fixed" immediate annuities as immediate annuities and refer to variable immediate annuities as variable immediate annuities. First, we will discuss immediate annuities.

Types of Immediate Annuities

An individual can purchase an immediate annuity by giving a lump-sum amount of money to the insurance company; the company will begin to make periodic payments in accordance with the contract owner's instructions. To be classified as an immediate annuity, payments must begin within a period of time, usually ranging from one month after deposit to no longer than one year after deposit. Income is typically paid to the policyowner, but some contracts may specify that income will be paid to the annuitant.

Purchasers of immediate annuities generally have the funds originate from one of several sources. Purchasers bring their lump sums to the insurance company in exchange for a series of payments made back to the annuity owner.

A 2005 survey of annuity owners found that the typical owner of a nonqualified annuity used more than one source of funds for the purchase of his or her annuity. Overall, about half (47 percent) used money from at least one of the following one-time events to purchase an annuity contract: an inheritance (26 percent); the sale of a home, farm, or business, (14 percent); a death benefit from a life insurance policy (14 percent); a gift from a relative (13 percent); or a bonus (9 percent). Many owners also indicated that some of their annuity premiums came from regular savings (58 percent), their or their spouse's income (50 percent), or proceeds from another investment (30 percent).[1]

Another source of funds for the immediate annuity originates when the owner of either a life insurance policy or a deferred annuity policy wants to *annuitize* policy cash values. The insurance company will take the policy values and exchange them for a series of payments it will make over time for the policyowner. At present, however, it has been reported that less than one percent of annuity owners ever annuitize their policies. The other 99 percent merely ask for periodic or nonperiodic withdrawals from their deferred annuity cash values on an as-needed basis.

Non-Life-Contingent Annuities

The payment of either the fixed-period or fixed-amount immediate annuity is issued to the annuity owner in a level dollar amount for the duration of the payout period. The payout period is determined by the contract owner, who requests either the period of time during which the checks are distributed or the specific amount and interval of each check.

fixed-period annuity

Fixed Period. With a *fixed-period annuity*, the purchaser pays a premium and selects the period of time the insurance company is to make the periodic payments. The company calculates the payment amount and informs the client what that amount will be. The period chosen could be as little as 2 months or as long as desired (payments must satisfy the company's minimum payment rules—for example, no less than $20 per payment). This is not a life-contingent option. Also if the annuitant dies during the distribution period, payments continue to the annuitant's beneficiary until the end of the distribution period.

Example: Monroe negotiates with an insurance company for an immediate annuity. He requests that his checks arrive on a monthly basis for the next 10 years; he has $100,000 to invest. At the end of 10 years, the payments will terminate. Based on $100,000, prevailing interest earnings the company can afford to pay, the company's expenses, and the period of time selected, the insurance company will determine the *amount* of Monroe's periodic checks.

fixed-amount annuity

Fixed Amount. With a *fixed-amount annuity*, the purchaser pays a premium and selects the periodic payment amount the insurance company is to pay. The company informs the purchaser how long it will be able to pay the stipulated amount. Like the fixed-period option, this is not a life-contingent option, which makes it useful for distributing lump sums over time in situations when lifetime payments are not needed or when there is a shortened life expectancy for the annuitant. If the annuitant dies before the funds in the annuity have been paid, the remainder is generally paid to the annuitant's beneficiary.

Example:	Monroe could request checks of a specific amount, such as $1,000 per month, for as long as funds are available. In this case, the company will determine how long it will be able to pay $1,000 per month, based on the same factors as above. Here, the insurance company might agree to pay Monroe $1,000 per month for 12 years and 3 months.

Life-Contingent Individual Annuity

The immediate annuity is like an insurance policy that protects annuitants from the economic consequences of living too long. Just as buying any insurance creates a pool of money from which claims can be paid to those who experience losses, life-contingent annuities pay the claims of those who live exceedingly long lives.

The typical reason for the purchase of an immediate life annuity is the concern that the annuity owner's money will be exhausted before he or she dies. The solution is to purchase an annuity with payments based on the annuitant's life or on the lives of the annuitant and spouse.

life-only annuity

A life annuity, commonly called a straight life annuity or *life-only annuity*, is the least expensive type of life-contingent annuity. It provides the largest possible payment for a given deposit. It is low in cost because there is a high risk of loss of money. The risk in a life annuity is that if the annuitant dies prior to the time that an amount equal to the original deposit in the annuity has been repaid to the annuitant, the balance of the deposit is forfeited to the insurance company. This would occur even if only one check had been paid prior to death. The reason for this forfeiture is that there is no beneficiary in a straight life annuity.

Life Annuity (Straight Life/Life Only). Life-contingent annuities can be purchased by targeting either (1) an amount of income desired or (2) the amount available to invest. For example, an annuity buyer might say to the financial advisor, "How much would it cost for me to receive a $5,000 check each year for my lifetime?" Or "I have $30,000 to purchase a lifetime annuity. How much income will this provide me each year?"

For the insurance company to provide a quote, it needs to know the date of birth and sex of the annuitant or annuitants.

Example: Mary, aged 62, purchases a life-only immediate annuity with a $20,000 deposit. The life insurance company guarantees to pay her xx dollars per month for as long as Mary lives in exchange for the $20,000 deposit. Upon Mary's death, the annuity payments cease, regardless of how many payments have been made since the annuity contract was issued.

A recent immediate annuity product development is the deferred income annuity. With a deferred income annuity (sometimes called "longevity insurance"), a retiree can purchase a contract at one point in time, for example at age 65, but defer payments until a later time, for example at age 85. Those annuitants who do not live until the commencement age receive no benefits, but those who live to the required age and beyond receive income payments. Because these products have no death or living benefits, and not all contract owners will live long enough to collect income, insurance companies can maximize insurance leveraging (risk pooling) and thus maximize the income payments made to the retirees who do receive benefits.

Most buyers of immediate annuities consider that the possibility of losing all their money after receiving only one annuity check is too great a risk. They want more safety and assurance that the payout stream will continue in some fashion in the event of an early death. There are a number of payout options for continuing payments at the annuitant's death; however, each results in lower basic periodic payments. To assure some degree of safety, the following seven immediate annuity payout options are available in addition to the life-only option:

- life annuity with percent of premium death benefit
- life annuity with period certain
- life annuity with installment or cash refund
- joint and survivor life annuity
- joint and survivor life annuity with percent of premium death benefit
- joint and survivor life annuity with period certain
- joint and survivor life annuity with installment or cash refund

We will first discuss the individual annuity payout options, followed by payout options for joint and survivor life annuities.

Life-Contingent Individual Annuity with Payment Guarantees

life annuity with percent of premium death benefit

Life Annuity with Percent of Premium Death Benefit. This recently introduced life-contingent annuity pays a lifetime income and also guarantees that at the annuitant's death, a specified percentage of the initial premium payment selected at the time of purchase (i.e., 25 percent or 50 percent) will be paid to a designated beneficiary in a single sum. This is known as the *life annuity with percent of premium death benefit*. This immediate annuity alternative pays a lower income than one that does not provide a guaranteed death benefit, but it ensures a legacy for the heirs of the owner/annuitant of the contract. Furthermore, the lump sum amount payable to the annuitant's beneficiary should generally not be subject to income taxes. However, as of the printing of this book, this issue has not been addressed by the Internal Revenue Service.

Example: James, aged 65, purchases a life with 50 percent of premium death benefit immediate annuity with a $100,000 deposit. The life insurance company guarantees to pay him $559 dollars per month for as long as James lives in exchange for the $100,000 deposit. Upon James's death, the annuity payments cease; however, his beneficiary will receive a lump sum death benefit of $50,000.

life annuity with period certain

Life Annuity with Period Certain (5, 10, 15, 20, 25, and 30 Years). *Life annuity with period certain* is a life-contingent annuity in which the purchaser requests that if the annuitant's death occurs before a certain number of years have passed, payments are to continue until they reach the end of the specified period. Payments continue for life, however, if the annuitant survives longer than the specified period. Choosing this type of annuity ensures the purchaser that someone other than the insurance company, such as a named beneficiary, will benefit if the annuitant dies early.

Example: Dave, aged 71, purchases an immediate annuity with a $55,000 deposit. Dave would like to have payments continue if he dies before the end of 15 years. The insurance company offers to pay $1,000 per month for Dave's lifetime with the guarantee that if Dave dies before the end of 15 years, the $1,000 per month payment will be made to his beneficiary, his daughter, Hope, until the end of the 15th year. If Dave lives longer than 15 years, payments will continue for as long as he lives. If Dave dies beyond year 15, all payments cease.

Life Annuity With Installment or Cash Refund. This life-contingent annuity assures the purchaser that if the annuitant dies prior to payout of a total dollar amount that is equivalent to the contract's initial deposit, installment payments will continue until a full refund of the deposit has been paid. This is known as *life annuity with installment refund*. If cash refund is the option selected, the payment is likely to be a lump sum equal to the discounted present value of the beneficiary's remaining payments. This is known as *life annuity with cash refund*.

Example: Susan, aged 80, purchases an immediate annuity for her life with a cash refund option. Her initial deposit of $75,000 will provide her with $1,000 per month for life. If Susan dies before the total of her payments equals $75,000, then Susan's named beneficiary, her cousin Natalie, will receive the difference between $75,000 and the amount Susan received prior to her death. For example, if Susan dies 15 months after the policy is issued, Natalie will receive $60,000 ($75,000 − $15,000 = $60,000) discounted to a present value as a lump-sum death benefit. However, if installment refund is chosen by the annuity owner, then Natalie will receive $1,000 per month for 60 months. If she dies after $75,000 in payments are received by her, then all payments will cease.

Period-certain, refund-certain, and life with percent of premium death benefit guarantees are added to life-only immediate annuities as insurance against dying too soon. Table 6-1 shows the approximate cost of the guarantees (as a percentage of the total cost) for a life-only annuity. The cost ranges from about 3 percent more for a 10-year minimum, to 7 percent more for a refund guarantee, to 16 percent more for a 20-year guarantee, and to 24 percent more for a life with 50 percent of premium death benefit. This annuity purchaser in the year 2007 is effectively buying insurance that costs $4,641 ($149,506 − $144,865 = $4,641) to ensure that payments continue for at least 10 years by purchasing life with 10 years certain over the life-only option. Additionally the insurance guarantee costs $22,625 ($167,490 − $144,865 = $22,625) to ensure that payments continue for 20 years.

TABLE 6-1
Lump-Sum Costs for Immediate Annuities

Type of Annuity Male Age 65	Year 2007 Cost to Purchase $1,000 per Month
Life only	$144,865
Life with 10 years certain	$149,506 (3% higher than life only)
Life with refund certain	$155,703 (7% higher than life only)
Life with 50 percent of premium death benefit	$180,149 (24% higher than life only)
Life with 20 years certain	$167,490 (16% higher than life only)

The table illustrates the correlation of increased immediate annuity costs to provide them and their beneficiaries with guaranteed payout options and underscores the importance of purchasers to carefully examine illustrated quotes when purchasing immediate annuities so that they can make informed decisions based on their individual annuity income needs.

Annuity payout rates will generally change with each insurance company as often as every month. Therefore it is always critical to obtain the most current immediate annuity payout rates from the insurance company.

Moreover, it is important to remember that the costs to purchase an immediate annuity quoted in the following pages are not reliable for quoting purposes to individuals. These rates are given only as examples of the relative cost of an immediate annuity that stops payments immediately at the annuitant's death compared to the costs for contracts that provide some minimum payments if the annuitant dies early.

Joint and Survivor Life Annuities

joint and survivor life annuity

Joint and Survivor Life Annuity. A *joint and survivor life annuity* pays income for the lives of two individuals. After the death of the first annuitant, the insurance company continues to make full payments until the death of the second annuitant. Variations of this form of payout can provide for higher payments while both annuitants are living with reduced income payments of, for example, 75 percent, 66 percent, or 50 percent to the survivor. Some insurance companies offer joint life annuities for more than two lives.

Example: Adam and Kendra are each aged 70 and have $100,000 to purchase an immediate annuity for both of their lifetimes. The insurance company will pay $1,000 per month for both of their lifetimes. When the first of the two of them passes away, the payments will continue until the death of the second person. Upon the second death, payments will cease and no death benefit will be available to any named beneficiary. This is called joint life with 100 percent to the survivor, meaning that the second annuitant receives 100 percent of the payment after the first death.

If Adam and Kendra desire, they can have payments decrease at the first death to either 75 percent or $750, 66.6 percent or $667, or 50 percent or $500. If they choose to have a decreasing payment for the survivor, then the total cost up front will be less than $100,000 because the insurance company will not have to pay the full $1,000 for the length of two lives but instead can pay a reduced amount. Alternatively, the same $100,000 premium can purchase a somewhat higher payment during both lives, with a decreased amount payable at the first death.

Joint and Survivor Life Annuity with Percent of Premium Death Benefit. This life-contingent annuity pays a lifetime income and also guarantees that at the surviving annuitant's death, a specified percentage of the initial premium payment selected at the time of purchase (that is, 25 percent or 50 percent) will be paid to a designated beneficiary in a single sum. This is known as the *joint and survivor life annuity with percent of premium death benefit*. This immediate annuity alternative pays a lower income than one that does not provide a guaranteed death benefit, but it ensures a legacy for the heirs of the owners/annuitants of the contract. Furthermore, the lump-sum amount payable to their beneficiary will generally not be subject to income taxes.

joint and survivor life annuity with percent of premium death benefit

Example: James, aged 65, and Joan, aged 62, purchase a life with 50 percent of premium death benefit immediate annuity with a $100,000 deposit. The life insurance company guarantees to pay them $498 dollars per month jointly for as long as either of them lives in exchange for the $100,000 deposit. Upon the last surviving annuitant's death, the annuity payments cease; however, their beneficiary will receive a lump sum death benefit of $50,000.

joint and survivor life annuity with period certain

Joint and Survivor Life Annuity with Period Certain. The *joint and survivor life annuity with period certain* protects against the early termination of payments if both of the annuitants die early. The insurance company is instructed to continue payments until the death of the last to die, with a guaranteed minimum payout period, generally 5, 10, 15, 20, 25, or 30 years.

Example: Consider in the above example that Adam and Kendra wish to have payments made for both of their lives at $1,000, but they also would like to have payments continue to their children if they should die before the end of 20 years. They name both of their children as beneficiaries. If Adam dies in 5 years, payments will continue to Kendra at $1,000 per month for as long as Kendra lives. If Kendra dies 6 years later, a total of 11 years of payments will have been made. Therefore the insurance company will pay the two children as beneficiaries $500 each (two beneficiaries at $500 each = $1,000 for 9 years). On the other hand, if Kendra dies 17 years later, a total of 22 years of payments will have been made. In that case, no further payments will be made to their children as beneficiaries.

joint and survivor life annuity with installment or cash refund

Joint and Survivor Life Annuity with Installment or Cash Refund. The *joint and survivor life annuity with installment or cash refund* protects against the early termination of payments due to the death of both or all annuitants. Under the installment refund option, the insurance company is instructed to refund the remaining balance of the deposit by continuing payments to the named beneficiary after the death of all annuitants until the full deposit is returned. If the cash refund option is selected, the lump-sum payout will be the discounted present value of the remaining payments.

Example: Adam and Kendra have $100,000 to purchase joint life incomes, but instead of a 20-year payment guarantee, they elect a cash refund. If Adam and Kendra die after 7 years of payments at $1,000 per month, the total payments equal $84,000 (7 x 12 x $1,000). Therefore the discounted present value of the remaining $16,000 is refunded in a lump-sum payment to their named beneficiaries upon the second death.

A joint and survivor life annuity is designed to provide payments over the lives of two or more people. Level payments continue beyond the death of the first person until the death of the second person. Typically this type of annuity option is used by married couples to ensure that the income stream will not terminate at the death of the first spouse, leaving the second spouse without any income.

We have already discussed the alternatives under the joint and survivorship annuity option. We learned that if both annuitants need greater joint income while both are living, and less income is acceptable to the survivor after the first annuitant's death, the contract can be tailored to fill that need. During the lives of both annuitants, the income will be one amount, but after the death of the first annuitant, that income can be reduced to 75 percent, 66.6 percent, or 50 percent of the original payment. Such an election reduces the overall cost.

For instance, according to Table 6-2, to assure $1,000 level payments for both lives in 2007, the cost is $176,991. Providing only $500 per month to the survivor reduces the cost to $146,902, a savings of $30,089.

TABLE 6-2
Lump-Sum Costs for Joint Life Annuities

Type of Annuity (Male Aged 65/Female Aged 62)	Year 2007 Cost to Purchase $1,000 per Month
Joint and survivor life	$176,991
Joint and survivor refund	$180,909 (102% of the cost of life only)
Joint life with 50 percent of premium death benefit	$200,454 (113% of the cost of life only)
Joint and survivor 10-year certain	$180,171 (102% of the cost of life only)
Joint and survivor 20-year certain	$207,480 (103% of the cost of life only)
Joint and 75% to the survivor	$162,831 (92% of the cost of life only)
Joint and 66% to the survivor	$157,521 (89% of the cost of life only)
Joint and 50% to the survivor	$146,902 (83% of the cost of life only)

The above examples illustrate one of the two approaches a potential annuity buyer uses to determine how much the annuity will cost. What will it cost to provide $1,000 per month? The other approach a client might take is to ask the financial advisor what a given dollar amount of investment will purchase on a periodic basis. For example, a client may ask, "How much income will $100,000 provide for me at my age?" Table 6-3 shows the amount of annual income $100,000 will provide for a male aged 65 with various life guarantee options. It also shows the annual income for a couple (male aged 65, female aged 62) for the same $100,000 investment.

Table 6-3 illustrates the amount of income available from a given investment in an immediate annuity for the year 2007. For example, a 65-year-old male in the year 2007 could have purchased $7,296 of annual annuity income, life with refund certain, with $100,000. This is $252 less in annual income, a decrease of about 3.5 percent from the $7,548 life income option. In contrast, the life with 50 percent of premium death benefit option involves $2,856 less income or about a 38 percent decrease from the life income-only option.

Likewise the annual annuity income for a couple (male aged 65, female aged 62) decreases from the basic joint and survivor with 100 percent payable to the survivor option depending on the guarantee of a refund, death benefit, or period certain chosen, or increases based on reduced income percentages chosen for the survivor.

TABLE 6-3
Fixed Immediate Annuity Income With $100,000 Lump Sum

Male, Aged 65	Annual Annuity Income Year 2007
Life income	$7,548
Life income with refund certain	7,296
Life income with 50 percent of premium death benefit	4,692
Life income with 10 years certain	7,344
Life income with 20 years certain	6,984
Male Aged 65; Female Aged 62	**Year 2007**
Joint and survivor with 100% to the survivor	$6,780
Joint and survivor with refund certain	6,680
Joint life with 50 percent of premium death benefit	3,840
Joint and survivor with 10 years certain	6,766
Joint and survivor with 20 years certain	6,520
Joint and survivor with 75% to the survivor	7,397
Joint and survivor with 66% to the survivor	7,648
Joint and survivor with 50% to the survivor	8,137

Immediate Annuity Costs

The cost of an immediate annuity depends primarily on the prevailing level of interest rates at the time it is purchased and the age(s) and sex(es) of the annuitant(s).

The insurance company invests the purchaser's deposit to guarantee the payments promised by the contract. The company expects to pay out the deposit and the interest earned on the deposit over the annuitant's lifetime.

Within the insurance company's total "life only" annuity business, certain annuitants will die before their deposit is expended, which, in actuarial terms, will make up for annuitants who live beyond their life expectancy. Those annuity funds assure annuitants who live an exceedingly long time that their income will last as long as they do. The insurance company spreads its risk by having a large book of business and many annuitants. In the actuarial pricing model that insurance companies use to price their immediate annuities, the forfeitures of those who die early are available in the large pool for payments to those who live a very long time. The company also factors into the formula costs associated with issuing the contract and an allowance for profit.

The state in which the purchaser lives can also influence what he or she must pay for an annuity. Each state may have different rules regarding what annuities can be offered to its residents and the costs of those annuities. Purchasers may find that the annuity they want is not available in their state of residence or that it costs more or less than it does in another state.

For instance, some states levy a tax on the purchase price of immediate annuity contracts, as shown in Table 6-4. Many states repealed their application of the premium tax to annuities. Today only a few states tax annuity premiums. An advisor should check with each of the insurance companies with which he or she writes annuity contracts to determine if the insurance company passes along the premium taxes to the annuity owner or if the company absorbs them. Depending on how the company handles the costs of premium taxes, the consumer may find much more competitive annuities at one insurance company than another.

Annuity Variations

This chapter has discussed the various types of immediate annuities available to individuals through traditional life insurance companies. Several variations from the traditional immediate annuity exist. The following section will explore two variations of immediate annuities.

TABLE 6-4
State Premium Taxes (Percentage of Cost) on the Purchase of an Immediate Annuity

State	Nonqualified Annuity	Qualified Immediate Annuity
California	2.35	.50
Maine	2.00	0
Nevada	3.50	0
South Dakota	1.25	0
West Virginia	1.00	1.00
Wyoming	1.00	0

Structured Settlements

A structured settlement, as discussed in Chapter 2, is a form of immediate annuity commonly ordered by a court through a jury award or court settlement. Structured settlements normally do not follow the same pattern of annuity options as traditional immediate annuities such as life only or a fixed period. They are usually a series of payments that escalate at predetermined intervals and last for a set number of years. For example, a structured settlement might be ordered to pay $10,000 per year for an individual from ages 23 to 29, then $13,500 from ages 30 to 36, then $17,450 from ages 37 to 46, and then stop.

Structured settlements are offered through only a few companies in the United States. The market is narrow, and any financial advisor who comes in contact with a structured settlement situation should seek specialized companies for current quotes.

Substandard Annuities

Substandard annuities are a special type of immediate annuity in which the insurance company requires the annuitant to undergo medical underwriting. The underwriting process is similar to the process used for applying for life insurance. Through the underwriting process, the annuitants show the insurance company that their life expectancy is less than normal. Evidence of ill health that is likely to reduce life expectancy may increase the amount of income provided in medically underwritten annuities. The substandard annuity pays higher income because the insurance company will not be making the payments for as long as normally expected. Not all insurance companies offer medically underwritten, or substandard, annuities. The financial advisor should check to determine which companies offer substandard annuities.

Dealing with Inflation

The purchaser's risk with an immediate annuity is the never increasing, constant amount of the check that the annuity owner will receive for the duration of the annuity period. If inflation increases at 5 percent per year, the dollars received from an annuity, although fixed in amount, will purchase 5 percent less each year. This decrease in purchasing power will mean a reduction in the standard of living.

Assuming 5 percent inflation, a check that purchased $1,000 worth of goods in 1997 will purchase an equivalent of only $340.56 worth of goods 21 years later in 2018. The annuitant's standard of living will have been cut to one-third of what it was in 1997. To deal with this risk and avoid the volatility of variable annuities, cost-of-living adjustment riders are available in some fixed immediate annuities that can provide, at the contract owner's option, a 1 percent to a 6 percent cost-of-living adjustment (COLA) in the monthly (and annualized) annuity payments. Innovations in annuity products are constantly being made to offset the impact of inflation on an annuitant's standard of living. It would be wise for advisors to be familiar with the latest innovations in annuities in order to tailor a contract to a specific annuitant's needs.

For a comparable lump-sum investment of $100,000 by the annuity owner, the insurance company prices this COLA feature by reducing the payments that would be available from a corresponding level-payout annuity so that the income not paid early in the contract years can be used to increase the income in later years. For example, the above $100,000 deposit purchases $700 per month on a 20-year fixed-period annuity. A comparable annuity providing income that would increase by 3 percent per year would have an initial payment of about $550 per month. See Table 6-5 comparing a $100,000 lump sum for a male aged 55.

Insurance companies have recently begun to offer other creative methods for annuitants to take advantage of changes in the economy to increase their otherwise fixed payouts from immediate annuities. One such "income enhancement option" works in conjunction with a benchmark interest rate index such as the 10-year Constant Maturity Treasury (CMT) Index. For example, if after the fifth policy anniversary the index increases by 2 percent, then future annuity payments would automatically increase one time to reflect the interest-rate environment. But if the index decreases, the fixed annuity payout amount would remain unchanged at its original level amount.

In another attempt to offer payment flexibility to immediate annuity owners, some companies have offered annuitants a one-time opportunity to increase or decrease their future income payments within certain specified contractually permitted limits, at some future date, such as beyond the third policy anniversary. This option must be selected and indicated at the inception of the contract. This allows for the owner to adjust the immediate annuity payout amount according to his or her potential changing future income needs.

TABLE 6-5 Level Payments: Cost of Living Comparison		
100,000 Lump-Sum Male Age 55	Level Payments	Payments with 3% COLA
Year 1	$700	$550
Year 2	$700	$567
Year 3	$700	$584
Year 4	$700	$602
Year 5	$700	$620
Year 6	$700	$639
Year 7	$700	$658
Year 8	$700	$678
Year 9	$700	$698
Year 10	$700	$719
Year 11	$700	$741
Year 12	$700	$763
Year 13	$700	$786
Year 14	$700	$810
Year 15	$700	$834

Postannuitization Liquidity

annuitization

Annuitization may be defined as contracting for a series of payments from a deferred annuity or from life insurance cash values. There are risks to the annuity owner with annuitizing. First, as we have discussed, the annuity owner carries the risk that the annuitant will die too early or that he or she will select the wrong guarantee and not receive back from the insurance company what could have been received under another payout arrangement.

The second risk is that once the insurance company has issued the annuity, if the annuity owner suddenly needs to have the money, there is no turning back. Immediate annuities do not have account balances that the owner can access. There are usually no surrender or withdrawal provisions. The annuity owner has purchased a right to receive a stipulated income at future intervals.

Example: The purchaser deposits $65,000 for an immediate annuity that pays $1,000 per month for life. The owner now owns the right to receive $1,000 per month for life. The owner does not own an account with a $65,000 balance.

However, some companies have recently begun to market immediate annuities that do offer limited access to lump-sum cash withdrawals under certain contingencies and with various restrictions. For example, one liquidity option offered by at least one company is for the annuitant to take a one-time lump-sum withdrawal of up to 30 percent of the discounted value of the remaining payments expected to be received based on life expectancy at the policyowner's issue age. This is accompanied by a downward adjustment in the amount of future periodic annuity payments within the contract. Another liquidity option allows for the annuitant to receive the next 6 monthly annuity payments in advance on an accelerated basis and skip the next six regularly scheduled monthly payments. These contracts, however, are the exception and not the rule regarding immediate annuities. The majority of contracts do not contain lump-sum liquidity provisions once annuitization has begun.

This customary lack of access to the principal deposit is the downside of purchasing an immediate annuity. This is one of the obstacles that prospective buyers must understand in order to feel comfortable about purchasing an immediate annuity.

The annuity owner's alternative to annuitizing the policy is to keep the deferred annuity intact but to take partial surrenders or withdrawals as needed from the annuity policy. Taking partial withdrawals leaves the principal balance available to the policyowner, but it does not guarantee he or she will not run out of money.

Competition

A common approach when selling deferred annuities is to check which insurance company is paying the highest guaranteed interest rate for a given period of time. Unfortunately, this same approach is actually a mistake if used to determine the most competitive immediate annuity rates. When determining the most competitive immediate annuity policies, the financial advisor must focus not on what interest rate the insurance company used in the actuarial formula to ascertain the guaranteed payout rates but on the actual dollar amount of income.

The advisor and the potential purchaser need to look at two issues when shopping for immediate annuity rates: The first issue is the strength and financial stability of the insurance company that is guaranteeing the payments. Because the annuity purchaser is buying a contractual right to receive these payments guaranteed by the insurance company, the contract will not be worth much if the insurance company is financially unstable and cannot stand behind a lifetime of guaranteed payments.

Second, the purchaser must compare the dollar amount of the payments among companies. If the purchaser is aged 65 and has $45,000 to purchase an immediate annuity for life with 10 years certain, the most competitive quote is determined by which stable insurance company offers the highest payment. It will not help the advisor or potential purchaser to know what the interest rate is inside the actuarial formula that calculated the actual payment. Mortality costs and expenses are other factors used to determine the payment. Because these costs could be relatively higher or lower than another company's, it is useless to learn what the interest factor is when the other factors in the formula remain unknown and therefore can skew the payment. See Table 6-6 for a comparison of immediate annuity quotes and how the highest interest rate does not accurately reflect the competitiveness of the annuity.

TABLE 6-6 Comparison: $100,000 Immediate Annuity Female Aged 72, Monthly Payments			
	Company A	Company B	Company C
Interest rate	6.7%	7.0%	6.0%
Expenses	6.1%	5.0%	3.7%
Monthly income	$988.72	$1,004.12	$1,010.99

When comparing immediate annuity quotes, the advisor must make sure to have equivalent quotes from the competing insurance companies. The quotes must be examined to ascertain whether the date of birth, sex of annuitant, payment guarantee, and amount of dollars deposited are the same for each quote. Each quote must also accurately state whether the funds are qualified or nonqualified, the time of the first payment, and the state in which the contract will be written.

Variable Immediate Annuities

variable immediate annuity

A *variable immediate annuity* is one in which the periodic payments received from the contract vary with the investment experience of the underlying investment vehicle. The variable immediate annuity was developed to answer the problem of a fixed-payment immediate annuity's purchasing power being eroded by inflation. The variable annuity is designed to adjust its payments to reflect the current purchasing power and offset the eroding effects of inflation on annuity income. The variable immediate annuity can accomplish this objective but not without risk. The risk to the annuity owner is that the payments can decrease as well as increase.

With fixed immediate annuities, the insurance company accepts the mortality risk, the expense risk, and the interest rate risk. The contract owner accepts the liquidity and the purchasing power risks. With the variable annuity, the contract owner trades guarantees and unwavering income for variable payments. The mortality and expense risks stay with the insurance company.

Assumed Investment Return (AIR)

In the process of implementing a variable immediate annuity, the annuity owner selects from among the various subaccounts offered in the contract to create a diversified portfolio and a suitable asset allocation. In most cases, this asset allocation can be changed among the subaccounts offered within the contract. However, exchanging one contract for another will not be possible after annuitization has begun. The annuity owner may also select automatic rebalancing within most variable immediate annuity contracts. The proceeds to be immediately annuitized buy units of the selected subaccounts on the date of purchase; future changes in value of the selected subaccounts will determine the amount of the future annuity payments.

**assumed investment
return (AIR)**

The amount of the two initial monthly annuity checks will be determined by the insurance-company-offered and contract-owner-accepted *assumed investment return (AIR)*. Once the assumed base rate of investment return is applied to the money, with the other assumptions of expenses and mortality—life expectancy in this case—the amount of the initial two checks is determined. If the contract owner is given a choice of AIRs, such as 3 percent, 5 percent, and 7 percent, the two initial checks will be calculated using the chosen AIR. However, after the two initial checks, the underlying investment accounts have to exceed the AIR to increase the amount of future checks. If the subaccount performance is below the chosen AIR, future checks will decrease. Accepting a low AIR increases the chances of having higher future checks whereas accepting a high AIR increases the chances of receiving lower future checks.

It is also important for advisors and purchasers to understand that the AIR is a net number. It is not the final number, however. Underlying fund expenses need to be added to it. The underlying investment in the contract must gross 7 percent to net 5 percent. Because the underlying investment accounts must exceed the AIR, a low AIR increases the chance of having higher payments to the contract owner. Therefore if a purchaser wants to increase the probability of achieving positive income in the future, selecting the lowest AIR available would be wise.

Level Annuity Payments

Some variable immediate annuity contracts provide payment streams that can be adjusted at periodic intervals of up to 12 months rather than on a monthly basis in order to provide the annuitant with an element of certainty. This allows the annuitant to plan on a given level of payments for the period in question. When the periodic adjustments are made, however, they are likely to be more substantial than if the adjustments had been calculated more frequently.[2]

Payment Stabilization Guarantees

Other variable immediate annuity contracts offer payments supported by *floors*. These floors guarantee that subsequent payments will never be less than a given percentage of the original payment (for example, 85 percent or 100 percent) regardless of the performance of the underlying portfolio. Some provisions limit the investment choices underlying the annuity, providing the insurance company with the opportunity to hedge its guarantee with derivative instruments. These floors provide contract owners with a safety net that may make them more comfortable with having their annuity payments subject to the variability of stock market performance. If a contract owner chooses this feature, however, payment amounts will be lower than if no floor were elected.[3]

Cost and Market Considerations

The prospectus for a variable immediate annuity itemizes expenses, so cost identification and quantification should not be a problem. Typically individuals considering a variable immediate annuity purchase compare initial income with that provided by a comparable fixed immediate annuity. Because of internal expense charges, the amount of annuity income a variable immediate annuity provides will be less than the income offered by a fixed immediate annuity with comparable guarantees.

Currently, the market for variable immediate annuities is small, but it is expected to increase as the baby boomers deal with retirement. Trying to live for several decades on money from a 401(k) plan can be stressful and difficult. It is likely that those with extreme longevity in their families will opt to have some portion of their income guaranteed for life while still being able to withstand inflation. The baby boomers have watched their parents live a lot longer than they expected and have seen their parents' pensions, which seemed sufficient when they retired, become insufficient to maintain their standard of living. That lesson will not be lost. It will cause more and more people to purchase variable immediate annuities to provide a portion of their retirement income.

PRESENTING THE PLAN

After you have analyzed the prospect's information and developed an appropriate plan, the next step is to conduct a closing interview in which you present the possible solutions to the prospect and obtain the prospect's agreement to proceed toward implementing the plan. In this section we will focus on step six of the selling/planning process: presenting the plan.

Presenting Solutions

In presenting the solution, the financial advisor shares a plan with the prospect that is designed to meet his or her objectives. The advisor presents in summary form the facts and personal attitudes the prospect previously expressed to see if there is any reason why he or she would not want to find a solution and, upon finding a reasonable solution, not want to take action. A successful presentation enables the prospect to see how the advisor's recommendations clearly support his or her objectives. It motivates but does not manipulate or strong-arm the prospect to buy. As you present solutions, keep in mind that the prospect must make the final decision about policy options because he or she is buying the policy, not you.

Delivering a presentation that will motivate a prospect requires thorough preparation and careful execution. Preparation begins with a vision of what a good presentation should cover. From this vision, you can develop an outline to ensure that you cover critical points. With the outline as your guide, you will be able to gather the necessary sales materials and organize your presentation. Now you are ready to make your presentation to the prospect.

The Mind Rehearsal

Before you meet with the prospect to conclude the sale, visualize what will happen in your presentation. How will the prospect answer your questions? How will you reply if the prospect asks a difficult question or voices an objection that makes you hesitate? What papers will you need? How will you handle all the forms? Where will you sit when making the presentation? What will the expression on the prospect's face be when he or she signs the application?

This is a "mind rehearsal" for the sales interview. Sit quietly and let your imagination take over the process of making the sale. When you can see the sale in progress and visualize the prospect saying yes, then you have the necessary confidence and are prepared to meet. Visualization prepares you for the close.

Elements of the Presentation

Although the specifics of an effective presentation will vary from advisor to advisor, there are two main components to every presentation within a two-interview annuity selling/planning process. The first component is to re-establish the prospect's need for action; the second is to present annuity plan options.

Reestablish the Reestablish   the   Need. In a two-interview selling/planning process, some time will elapse between the first and second interviews. Therefore it is important to re-establish the prospect's interest in and need for enhanced retirement income by summarizing the relevant points from the first interview. The best way to rekindle the prospect's interest is to review the gap between his or her desired retirement income and the projected retirement income without the proposed annuity plan. Essentially this should involve nothing more than reviewing the key points of the fact-finding interview, including how the prospect felt about them. You want the prospect not only to recognize the retirement income gap again but <u>also to feel it</u>. Here is one method for accomplishing this goal.

Review the Facts and Planning Assumptions. What assumptions were incorporated into planning? Has anything changed in the prospect's mind since the fact-finding interview? Would the prospect like to change any of the assumptions? In addition, review the qualitative retirement planning goals and objectives from the fact-finding interview.

List the Prospect's Objectives. Review and confirm the prospect's objectives, concerns, and priorities. Essentially you are summarizing the prospect's answers to the following questions:

- What priorities does the prospect have for his or her lifestyle in retirement?
- Does the prospect expect to maintain his or her preretirement standard of living in retirement?
- Does the prospect plan to travel, relocate, or remain involved in community and family activities?
- Has the prospect taken steps to protect against all other types of financial risks?
- Is the prospect concerned with reducing the taxes on his or her savings?
- Is the prospect concerned about outliving or depleting the assets accumulated in his or her life's savings?
- What is the prospect's premium or investment commitment?

- Is the prospect willing to consider purchasing additional financial products to help reach his or her retirement goals?

It is extremely important to match annuity policy type and benefits with a prospect's financial objectives and priorities. These will vary for each prospect, depending on his or her age and circumstances. In many cases, the sales presentation will be built around a "hot button" or primary concern of the prospect. For example, an older prospect may be most concerned with asset preservation and having enough money to last through his or her retirement. He or she may also desire to pass money on to the next generation or to provide for charitable bequests. In addition, independence is often a key objective of older prospects. Thus a lifetime income and not burdening their children are often prospects' hot buttons.

Relatively young prospects typically look ahead, plan their retirement, and seek wealth accumulation devices. However, younger prospects often have other demands on their financial resources such as paying down mortgages, paying for their children's educations, and perhaps even paying for their parents' long-term care. These prospects often need help with a whole host of financial problems. Consequently an important selling point for young prospects is that investing in an annuity over many years starting at a fairly young age can be much less expensive than waiting to begin investing many years in the future because of the cumulative effect of compounding interest. Furthermore, buying a variable deferred annuity policy at a younger age also helps to protect against market volatility. If young purchasers encounter declines in cash values due to fluctuations in the net asset values of the separate accounts within their contracts, then because of their longer investment time horizons, they have more time to recover from such setbacks. This fact alone should be a strong motivating force for buying annuities at a young age.

Outline the Expected Cost of Retirement. While re-establishing the prospect's need for retirement income, you should also refresh his or her understanding of just how expensive funding retirement can be, especially with the effect inflation has on purchasing power.

Summarize the Prospect's Current Retirement Plans or Investments. This is a review of what may happen if the prospect does not take action regarding retirement funding or buying an annuity to accomplish a desired investment objective. Recap the information from the fact-finding interview. Give the prospect your professional assessment of the current plan's ability to achieve his or her stated objectives with respect to

- *Social Security benefits*—Review the prospect's projected annual Social Security benefit amount at retirement. Demonstrate how this income is only a partial solution to the retirement funding problem. Also reprise any discussion of doubts that the prospect may have expressed regarding the probability of future reductions in Social Security benefits.
- *total other additional income*—Project the funds within the current plan, including the prospect's indexed income and fixed income that he or she has committed to using for retirement.

Then, in conjunction with these total income sources and the retirement planning assumptions from the fact-finder relating to age at retirement, years during retirement, interest rate, and inflation rate, show how you used this information in the retirement income calculation worksheet to determine the accumulation need and annual required savings.

Presenting Annuity Solutions. Once you have re-established the prospect's need for additional savings, you are ready to present possible solutions to the prospect. Here are some suggested steps.

Summarize your Observations. Summarize your observations about the current plan's inability to accomplish the prospect's objectives. These observations point out gaps you found in the current plan, demonstrating just how important it is that the prospect implement the recommendations you are about to make if he or she wants to achieve his or her stated objectives to meet retirement income needs.

Make Your Recommendations. Outline your recommendations, including both annuity and nonannuity solutions. If you are working with affluent prospects, write your recommendations in a proposal that you give them. You should have a recommendation for each observation.

In the interview, present your recommendations, beginning with the nonannuity solutions that are the easiest to implement. For example, if you see the prospect does not have a living will, you can recommend that he or she see an attorney and have one drafted. Starting with a product recommendation might make the prospect cynical, raising his or her fears that you are interested only in making a sale.

During your presentation, you want to focus the discussion on the plan alternatives you are recommending. You want the prospect to pick the alternative that suits his or her needs, investment objectives, and budget. Discussion creates a sense of involvement on the part of the prospect and reinforces in his or her mind the selected alternative's ability to meet the objectives.

In the final analysis, the annuity solution to retirement income funding must be appropriate for the prospect and consistent with his or her risk tolerance and investment objectives if a sale is to be made. By purchasing an annuity policy, the financial and psychological burdens of the problem of the prospect's retirement funding can be at least temporarily resolved.

Outline the Implementation Plan. The implementation plan gives you a way to review your recommendations while giving the prospect the action steps necessary to complete them. It should identify who is responsible for accomplishing each step and establish deadlines for the implementation.

Preparing for the Presentation

The key to an effective presentation is preparation. Take the time to prepare a standardized presentation using your sales presentation binder. The amount of time needed to prepare will decrease as you gain more experience, but initially you will want to create a detailed presentation outline for each closing interview. Here are some suggestions of ways to prepare for this interview:

- Analyze your prospect. What were his or her attitudes toward retirement income funding? Does he or she appear to recognize the risk of underfunding? What are the prospect's probable motives for buying? What are the barriers?
- Create a summary of the fact-finding interview that you can use as an outline when you re-establish the retirement income need. Use the outline suggested in the previous section as a start.
- Check your suggested annuity plan alternatives. How do they reflect the prospect's risk tolerance, investment objectives, and budget? What are the pros and cons to each alternative? Which do you feel is the best alternative and why?
- Collect any company-approved sales material you will use in the presentation. If you have a series of such items, put them in order in your sales presentation binder.
- Create policy illustrations for all of your recommendations ahead of time. Check the prospect information (name, age, and so forth) for accuracy.
- Put together any written proposals you will use with your presentation.
- Confirm the appointment time and location with the prospect.

The better prepared you are, the more you can concentrate on the prospect and handle any objections or concerns. Furthermore, you will present a professional image to the prospect if everything you need is right there.

Presentation Techniques and Tips

There are many complicated aspects to annuities: product types, interest rate or investment divisions, and feature and benefit choices. Moreover, you must be able to help the prospect understand them. No matter how well you have prepared, or how good your recommendations, presenting these recommendations is still the critical element. There are a few things you can do to enhance the effectiveness of your presentation.

Presentation Checklist

Review the following items in preparing to deliver your solution presentation:

- What are the prospect's financial objectives, goals, and needs that you will help him or her solve?
- Who is your prospect, and what decision makers will be present?
- What are the buying motives of the prospect and/or the decision makers?
- What is the prospect's current situation?
- What is the prospect's desired situation?
- What are the specific buying conditions such as budget (premium commitment), other investments, desired policy features and riders, start date for immediate annuities, investment objectives, and so on?
- Does the prospect agree with your assessment of the problem?
- Have you developed your solution and statements to support it? (This may involve a few alternative plans.)
- Did you review the specific factual and feeling-finding information you collected?
- Have you anticipated any objections or concerns the prospect may have and prepared responses?
- Have you rehearsed your presentation and answers to objections or any other anticipated verbal exchanges?

Focus on Relevant Features and Benefits. One mistake financial advisors make is to think that the purpose of the presentation is to educate the prospect about the technical, legal, tax, and product aspects of an annuity.

feature

benefit

While an advisor should discuss these aspects, the discussion should be in light of the features and corresponding benefits that are relevant to the prospect and the basis for the recommendations.

A product *feature* is a characteristic of the product itself—what it is and what it does. A feature is a fact about the product. On the other hand, a *benefit* is what the prospect gets as a result of the feature. It is what the product does for the prospect and usually why he or she wants it. Features produce benefits. For example, you buy a drill because you need a hole.

When you explain a feature of an annuity policy, stress the benefits that the prospect will receive. Prospects respond to benefits. How a feature provides a benefit is not the point. Focus your presentation on the benefits— what a feature will do for a prospect is what he or she cares about. Concentrate on the benefits that matter most to your prospect—those you uncovered in the fact-finding process. For example, if the prospect values financial independence, show how the annuity will give him or her control over when, where, and how he or she will retire. If not paying income taxes on Social Security retirement benefits is important, demonstrate how a deferred annuity will accomplish this without sacrificing wealth accumulation.

When presenting a recommendation, you want to explain what it is, how it solves a retirement income or financial problem, and what it does for the prospect. The benefit aspect is very important. Is it worth buying? Is it the best option? Will it save money? How well will it work for the prospect? These and other similar questions must be addressed and answered if the prospect is to accept your solution. Thus you must clearly communicate the benefits for the prospect.

Keep the Prospect Involved. It is important to have prospects' involvement in the sales process for several reasons:

- It helps prospects feel responsible for solving their own problems.
- It helps you know whether you are on target with your presentation.
- It builds agreement one step at a time.
- It helps clarify any misunderstanding by either party.
- It helps lead to a logical and successful close—a conclusion to buy.
- It provides opportunities to deal with objections before asking prospects to buy.

The simplest and most effective way to keep the prospect involved is to ask questions throughout the presentation. Use questions to help the prospect express his or her feelings and to confirm that he or she understands what you are saying. For example, after explaining the settlement options in a deferred annuity contract to the prospect, you can ask, "What would these settlement options mean to you or your beneficiary?" This will reveal not only if the prospect understands the concept of a lifetime benefit but also how he or she feels about it.

Insist on All Decision Makers Being Present. All relevant parties who affect the decision to buy the annuity should be in attendance. Both spouses should be present at the interviews, but the advisor should encourage the prospects to have other family members who will be participating in the purchase decision to be there as well. Experienced advisors know they need to have all decision makers present for a positive outcome. In fact, often the other family members, especially the adult children, are the unseen decision makers in the purchase of an annuity product.

Presenting Solutions

Here is one advisor's advice for presenting solutions to prospects:

- Summarize the discovery agreement, including a self-assessment of the prospect's current situation, desired changes, and retirement or financial goals.
- Summarize the benefits and possible shortcomings of each alternative annuity solution.
- Ask checking questions (trial closes) to confirm the prospect's position such as "How does that sound to you?" or "Could this help your situation?"
- Make your presentation and reinforce how the solution addresses the problem. Present alternatives if the prospect requests comparisons.
- Ask a summarizing question such as " Has everything been addressed?" or "Do you have any further questions about this?"

If all issues are resolved, ask the prospect to buy.

Be Alert for Buying Signals. Sometimes advisors find that they have talked themselves out of a sale. The prospect was ready to buy, but the advisor kept on explaining details that confused and bored the prospect. To

buying signals

avoid this situation, monitor the prospect for *buying signals*. Many people who show a desire to fulfill their unmet needs are ready to buy long before they ever say so. From the prospect's comments, you should be able to distinguish some fairly obvious verbal and nonverbal signals that indicate acceptance or rejection. The following are some examples.

Verbal signals

- "It would feel good knowing I had this kind of product."
- "I see what you mean."
- "Can we include that benefit you described earlier?"
- "What you're saying makes a lot of sense to me."
- "I appreciate the thoroughness of your presentation."
- "How do I get this started?"

nonverbal signals

Nonverbal signals

- leaning forward
- listening attentively
- making good eye contact
- nodding, showing appreciation
- smiling

Paying attention to the verbal and nonverbal clues will alert you that you should attempt to close the sale. Simply acknowledge the signal, whether verbal or nonverbal, and proceed with your close. For example, if the prospect says, "When would the interest rate become effective?" you could reply, "It starts as soon as I have collected the first premium. We can get started with an application right now if you would like." Or if you and the prospect have good eye contact, you could say, "It looks like you might be ready to proceed with an application. Do you have any questions before we do that?"

Obtaining the Prospect's Agreement to Proceed

A successful presentation ends with obtaining the prospect's agreement to proceed to step seven of the selling/planning process—implementing the plan. Asking the prospect to buy your product, the last part of step six, must be successfully completed to continue moving through the selling/planning process.

Summary of Presentation Steps

- **Warm up**—Begin by recapping the need for retirement income. Discuss the prospect's financial situation and personal retirement plans.

- **Discuss the need for action**—The prospect must agree that there is a real need to take action to close the potential retirement income funding gap and that the costs could be staggering.

- **Consider what current sources will not pay**—Review the six potential current retirement income funding sources. Show how they may leave the prospect without enough money to cover the income needed in retirement.

- **Find the premium**—Discuss a budget amount that can be a premium or investment commitment. Discuss types of annuity plans according to the prospect's risk tolerance and investment objectives. Discuss how any shortfall can be alleviated and the problem at least partially solved.

- **Present the solution**—Develop an annuity product solution to provide at least part of the desired retirement income and to coincide with the prospect's premium commitment and investment objectives.

- **Close the sale**—Assume consent. Complete the application and ask the prospect to pay the initial premium.

Closing the Sale

You should not be pushy or manipulative during this portion of the selling/planning process. You may, however, need to be firm and assertive with the prospect. How you conduct yourself will depend somewhat on the prospect's behavior and social style as discussed in Chapter 3. Closing will also depend on how well the selling/planning process has gone to this point. For example, if you have anticipated and pre-empted all the prospect's objections, your close may be as simple as "How do you spell your middle name?"

When purchasing an annuity policy, a prospect must choose an advisor that he or she feels is trustworthy. Establishing trust begins with your showing genuine concern for the prospect's well-being and a professional knowledge of financial and retirement planning issues. You can build on this foundation by using an educational and consultative approach with the prospect. He or she will want to make an informed decision and be treated with respect. Your job is to provide objective information and assist the prospect in making a decision that meets his or her needs in a noncombative way. As a reliable and dependable advisor, you can develop this all-important trust over a period of time.

If the sale has progressed through the process as outlined in this book, then there is no place or need for manipulation or pressure tactics to close the sale. If the need for additional retirement funding has been established, the alternatives discussed, the solution designed and presented clearly, and a trusting relationship established, then the sale should result. If not, determine where you went wrong. With a few changes, it is possible that you can still make the sale.

Client-focused planning does not mean that you allow a prospect's natural inclination to do nothing go unchallenged. Closing an annuity sale is like selling any other insurance or financial product. Sometimes you have to be blunt with the prospect to get your point across. This does not mean you should be rude or pushy but sincerely concerned. If action is necessary to ensure a more comfortable living in retirement, you need to warn the prospect about the consequences of inaction. You have to tactfully convey a sense of urgency to the prospect that now is the time to act.

Fear of Closing. Advisors often fail to ask prospects to buy because they feel they are imposing on them, they feel they have not explained the solution adequately, or they fear rejection. There is some natural emotional tension between advisors and prospects at this point because it is the moment of truth—the time to make a commitment to a product, a company, and a relationship.

To move past this fear, remember that asking for the business is a natural step in the selling/planning process. The prospect expects you to ask him or her to buy a financial product. The prospect knows as well as you that the reason you have been spending time together is to obtain information so you can design a plan for him or her. You have earned the right to ask for the business because you thoroughly understand the prospect's situation and are recommending a solution to help him or her address an important need.

Summary

If you have developed an annuity plan solution based on the prospect's need(s) uncovered from the fact finder and have presented it according to the strategy outlined above, you should expect the prospect's agreement to implement the plan. Implementing the plan involves overcoming any objections and/or addressing concerns you may receive from the prospect. Implementing the plan will be discussed in the next chapter. Handling objections is discussed below.

OBJECTIONS: MANAGING RESISTANCE

Objections to the sale of annuities are abundant. However, experience shows that many of the objections that prospects express tend to disguise the real reasons they fail to buy annuity products. The real reasons most people do not buy (assuming they can afford to) are that they do not believe they need to buy an annuity today, and they do not necessarily have confidence that the product will deliver on the promised benefits in the future. In fact, most of the objections discussed below are variations of these two common themes. Just as the impetus to buy an annuity is sparked by emotion, so is the resistance to buying it.

If the fact-finding process has allowed you to ask the right questions and the prospect has answered them candidly, most, if not all, of the prospect's concerns should have already been addressed. Nonetheless, a prospect may not feel comfortable or understand the process or the problems well enough to have disclosed all of his or her concerns, which may emerge at the closing interview.

Objections are liable to surface at any time during the selling process, not just at the close of the sale. Therefore you need to have a general strategy in place to deal with prospects' concerns, as well as specific responses to handle their objections whenever they arise.

Handling Concerns and Objections

The first step in handling an objection is to listen to the prospect. No one likes to be interrupted or feel that he or she is not being taken seriously. Listening to what the prospect has to say will help you understand the objection. Therefore encourage the prospect to explain how he or she feels about the issue.

Give yourself an opportunity to confirm your understanding of the prospect's objection by restating or rephrasing it. This gives you a chance to learn more about the exact nature of the objection, and it also puts you in a better position to handle it.

The sales presentation should build momentum until the prospect reaches the inescapable conclusion that he or she needs the product and should buy it immediately. Each step in the process supports the one that follows. By the time the prospect begins to raise concerns and objections, you should know enough about his or her personal and financial situation, and his or her attitudes and feelings, that you can address them directly, honestly, and convincingly.

A well-prepared sales presentation can reduce the number of objections encountered by anticipating and preparing for them before they are raised. For example, if you satisfactorily obtain a dollar or investment commitment from the prospect early in the interview process, this will prevent the "no money" objection from surfacing later. You can also reduce the number of objections by

- developing rapport and trust (combats the "no confidence" objection)
- getting an agreement at each step in the presentation (reduces the "no need" objection)
- focusing on the benefits of your recommendations (forestalls the "no hurry" objection)

These four general categories of objections will be discussed later in this chapter.

Although you can reduce the number of objections, you will always encounter them. Do not take them personally. It is natural for a prospect to have objections to purchasing financial products such as annuities. This is a natural reaction to the idea of spending money. People hate to spend money needlessly and waste it on something they do not need or something they perceive to be of little immediate value. Therefore prospects may raise objections to purchasing annuities because they may have difficulty in understanding policy features. Overcoming objections takes practice and experience, so it is important not to get discouraged if at first you are not successful.

The Problem-Solving Approach. In general, you should take a problem-solving approach to objections, focusing on three things:

- building trust and rapport with prospects
- dealing with the needs involved, not the personalities
- instilling a sense of urgency to act now

You can build trust and rapport by demonstrating, with your professionalism and forthrightness, that you care about answering the prospect's concerns with real answers. Be empathetic—put yourself in the prospect's shoes. Reassure prospects that by keeping their objectives in mind and reviewing the various alternatives available, they can move toward their goals—or as far along as possible. Working together can help to resolve the issues that are concerning them.

You can deal with needs rather than personalities by looking at the issues instead of winning debate points, getting the upper hand, or having the last word. When prospects raise difficult objections, their real concern may be a lack of money or improper timing. Avoid arguing with prospects. Pointing out to prospects that their objections are not valid is sales suicide. You may win the argument, but you will surely end up losing the sale. In other words, you should not become so focused on overcoming their objections that you forget they have a real need.

Finally remember that your prospects are making an important decision. Comments, concerns, and questions are a natural and expected part of the decision-making process. In answering their objections and even in dealing with their excuses, you give your prospects perspectives and information that will help them understand the need for retirement income planning, how your annuity product meets the need, and the urgency of acting now to put the plan into force.

As you talk with your prospect, use trial closes such as "Other than affordability, is this the product you think will best suit your needs?" Use questions to determine the prospect's agreement at each stage of your presentation:

- Does this make sense to you?
- Do you see how this benefits your family?
- Is this what you had in mind?
- Do you want to include this in your plan?
- Do you have any questions?

Because overcoming objections takes practice and experience, it is important not to get discouraged if at first you are not successful. There are many techniques at your disposal to help you. The "acknowledge, clarify, and resolve" and the "feel, felt, found" methods are two effective examples that are discussed below.

Techniques for Dealing with Prospect Resistance

Acknowledge, Clarify, and Resolve

There are a few commonly used methods for dealing with objections. One is a three-step technique for responding to prospect resistance. It simply acknowledges a concern and then clarifies and resolves it.

Acknowledge a Concern. Using this technique, you validate the prospect's thoughts and feelings by acknowledging his or her concern. If you do not acknowledge the concern but instead take it head on and try to wrestle it down, all you will succeed in doing is putting more distance between the prospect and you.

Responses such as "I understand how you feel" or "I can appreciate that" show your prospects that you are listening to them and care about what they say.

Clarify. Clarifying a vague or negative response from a prospect is often necessary before it can be effectively resolved. Any statement that is too global, vague, or overreaching needs to be clarified and explored. Clarification can take many forms such as "Could you please explain that?" or "I don't understand what you mean; can you give me an example?"

Resolve. Once a prospect's concern is acknowledged and clarified, you can resolve the concern by making appropriate recommendations. This may involve educating the prospect on some point by clarifying and repeating what has already been covered.

Feel, Felt, Found

Another popular three-step technique used to deal with objections is to use the words *feel*, *felt*, and *found* in three successive sentences as demonstrated below:

- "I understand how you *feel.*"
- "Many of my prospects have *felt* the same way."
- "Until they *found* that . . . " (Briefly state a benefit explaining how the plan was a good solution for the specific situation. For example, ". . . after meeting with me that accumulating money on a tax-deferred basis was more advantageous for them.")

Notice that this technique uses the acknowledgment step of handling objections mentioned above. Empathetic acknowledgment puts the prospect at ease since his or her feeling was common to others until the others found that the solution provided them with a desirable benefit. This neutralizes the situation and gives you an opportunity to remain poised as you address the prospect's specific concern or objection by explaining the benefit that is being provided.

Common Objections to Purchasing Annuities

Objections to purchasing annuity products fall into one of four general categories:

- no need
- no money
- no hurry
- no confidence

We will discuss nine common objections within those four categories. Then we will explain the tactics for dealing with each of these objections.

No Need

The Cost of Funding Retirement Is Not That Expensive. A favorite objection prospects use is to question why they should buy a deferred annuity when the cost of retirement funding is not that expensive. Use of general statistics (such as the figures cited in Chapter 3) of average incomes of retirees based on certain age brackets can be useful to counteract this argument. However, many prospects may simply be ignorant of the real costs involved in funding their specific retirement goals, or they may greatly underestimate them because, until now, they may have had no reason to think about or explore retirement funding.

The potential cost to those with middle-class incomes and lifestyles may be much more than anticipated because of the increasing annual costs during retirement that are caused by inflation. Prospects have often viewed the targeted annual retirement income goal as static when, in fact, it will steadily increase with even a modest inflation assumption. For instance, recall that the first-year retirement goal was $37,080 in the example in Chapter 4 that demonstrated the use of the retirement calculation worksheet. However, this cost indexed at a 3 percent inflation rate over 20 years of retirement will increase dramatically to $65,020, as Table 6-7 shows.

TABLE 6-7 Effect of 3% Inflation over 20 Years on $37,080			
Retirement Year	**Inflation-Indexed Income**	**Retirement Year**	**Inflation-Indexed Income**
1	$37,080	11	$49,832
2	$38,192	12	$51,327
3	$39,338	13	$52,867
4	$40,518	14	$54,453
5	$41,734	15	$56,087
6	$42,986	16	$57,769
7	$44,275	17	$59,503
8	$45,604	18	$61,288
9	$46,972	19	$63,126
10	$48,381	20	$65,020

The erosive effect that inflation has on a retiree's purchasing power is often overlooked. Prospects have one chance to prepare financially for retirement. If their planning is based on false assumptions regarding their need for income, the fear associated with the postretirement mentality syndrome (discussed previously) can create circumstances in which they may

- be forced to delay retiring
- continue working in some capacity to make up the gap
- compromise their lifestyle during retirement

None of these are desirable options when realistic planning can preclude the necessity of having to ruin what should be the retiree's golden years.

Therefore you may want to ask the prospect, "Does it make sense to work hard all your life to set aside money for retirement, only to see it all disappear because you underestimated the cost?" Then use an example like the one in Table 6-9 that applies to the prospect's specific retirement income goal.

Social Security Will Take Care of Most of It. This objection presents an opportunity for you to educate the prospect about the relationship between Social Security and retirement funding and to build your credibility in the process. Do not let the prospect be lulled into complacency by thinking that Social Security will take care of his or her retirement needs. As tables 3-5 and 3-6 show, Social Security, on average, does represent about 37 percent of retirees' income; however, the actual percentage decreases as total income increases.

After you have determined the percentage of retirement income that Social Security is projected to provide, using the prospect's Social Security benefit statement and specific retirement income goal from the fact finder, ask your prospect just what percentage of that projected benefit he or she believes the government will actually pay by the time he or she reaches retirement. Given the solvency problems of Social Security and the dwindling ratio of current workers to retirees, there is some probability that the full retirement age will be pushed further back and/or that benefit payments will be reduced sometime in the future.

You should also remind prospects that the primary responsibility for funding retirement rests with them. Assets accumulated within financial vehicles, such as immediate annuities that are part of a comprehensive retirement funding strategy, will pay guaranteed benefits regardless of the amount of money they receive from Social Security. Prospects' assets, accumulated predictably within fixed-interest deferred annuities, can be spent enjoying life during retirement or can be preserved for heirs, at the prospect's option and according to individual needs. Therefore overreliance on Social Security can be avoided.

Finally make the point that investment returns within the variable deferred and indexed annuity policy types are potentially enhanced over a long period of time when a person owns them. This can generate results that may outpace inflation, further building accumulations needed for funding retirement.

No Money

I Can't Afford It Right Now. As mentioned previously, as long as you have obtained a dollar or investment commitment from the prospect in the fact-finding interview and taken steps to qualify the prospect using the personal retirement planning review form, the "no money" objection should not occur. In other words, it should be apparent to you that the prospect has the money and has satisfied this key criterion of being a qualified prospect.

As discussed in Chapter 3 in the section on prospects who do not qualify, if a large monetary commitment is a problem, one useful tactic is to pivot to another less expensive financial product, or simply offer to keep in touch with the prospect. If the prospect's financial situation improves, he or she might consider doing business with you at some time in the future.

What may sometimes happen, however, is that the prospect is unwilling to allocate the money for an annuity product within a plan for retirement even though the prospect can afford to do so. Such resistance to buying a financial product of any kind is usually evidence of a more abstract hidden objection that falls into the "no confidence" objection category. In this case, the "I can't afford it right now" objection may be a smokescreen for lack of confidence in you, your company, or the annuity product itself. The truth is that you may never know which one it is. If this type of nonspecific objection occurs, and pivoting does not work for you, a graceful exit with the offer to stay in touch may be the best strategy.

However, always try to salvage something positive from the expenditure of your time. By all means, just because this prospect is ostensibly financially unable or unwilling to purchase an annuity product at this time, ask for referred leads to friends or relatives who may be receptive to talking with you.

No Hurry

Let Me Think About It. This is the classic unspecific objection that is probably hiding the real reason(s) for not continuing the buying process. This objection usually conceals something that the prospect does not want to tell you or simply cannot articulate. The earlier in the sales process that you uncover this objection, the less frustrating it will be for you because you cannot combat buyer ambiguity.

You can ask the prospect why he or she wants to think about it or what specifically he or she wants to think about, but this can be adversarial, and the answer may not reveal the real reason for hesitation. Overcoming their preconceptions about personal retirement funding objectives or dealing with the possibility of becoming financially uncomfortable can emotionally overwhelm some prospects. You need to be sensitive to their emotions and to their prerogative to take no action now. Unless you can elicit the real objection, the best way to deal with this situation is to offer to stay in touch with the prospect, put the paperwork in your tickler file, and move on to other prospects.

It's Too Early to Plan. This objection is most often encountered from those prospects in the under-age-45 group. These prospects have the most time before they retire so that the miracle of compound interest can perform surprisingly well for them. However, they tend to be apathetic about retirement planning or are far too preoccupied with career building to realize the risks involved in delaying the initiation of a retirement plan.

There are several risks in waiting to purchase financial products that fund retirement. These risks include the possibilities that prospects may not be able to achieve their desired retirement accumulation objectives and that the required contribution will get higher each year if they delay taking action today. To counter the "it's too early to plan" objection, you could offer responses such as the following:

- "Will you be able to accumulate the sufficient retirement funds by the time you need them? Even if you could, it's likely to cost you far more than it would today, all else being equal."
- "I suggest we compare the costs of buying today and waiting until tomorrow. Typically you can accumulate much more in a deferred annuity for less at your current age than if you wait just a few more years."

Also consider using the example at the end of this section titled "The Power of Compounding Interest." It can serve as an eye-opening motivator for younger prospects to take action now.

I Would Like to Shop Around a Little More. When the prospect raises this objection, it is important to do the following:

- Acknowledge the objection and do not pressure him or her into making a decision.

- Emphasize what factors he or she should consider in shopping, such as price versus value, personalized service, company strength, and policy benefits.
- If it is feasible, ask if he or she would allow you to help make annuity policy comparisons.

This is a competitive market where several quotes from different companies offering annuities should be presented. Find out if there are any companies in which the prospect is particularly interested. There may be competition, which is often the case in this market. Not offering alternative plans and companies leaves you vulnerable to this objection.

Bear in mind, however, that this is a relationship-based sale. Therefore shopping may simply involve the comparison of several different annuity policy options available from the single insurer you represent. Ask the prospect if providing this type of policy comparison would satisfy his or her desire to shop around.

No Confidence

I'd Like to Talk to (My Kids, Attorney, Physician, CPA). Early in the sales process you should try to find out who else will be involved in the purchasing decision and seek their participation in the selling/ planning process. You may be surprised to find that advisory professionals or even family members are supportive of the concept of responsibly planning ahead for retirement using a tax-deferred annuity product. Furthermore, for prospects in the age-65-and-older group who are already retired, immediate annuities will protect the owner's assets while deferred annuities will allow him or her to control the amount of income taxes paid on Social Security retirement benefits and unearned taxable income from CDs and savings accounts. Both products can enhance the sense of financial independence and reduce the fear of depleting the prospect's life's savings.

My Principal Is Not Insured. It is true that the principal in either fixed-interest deferred annuities or the general interest account in deferred variable annuities is not insured by the FDIC. Nevertheless, the insurance industry goes to great lengths to guarantee the safety of principal within these contracts. However, you should point out the following facts.

There are several key safety benefits that are unique to annuity investments. All insurance companies in the country are required by the National Association of Insurance Commissioners to maintain reserves. A qualified legal reserve life insurance company is required to meet its contractual obligations to policyholders. Legal reserve refers to the strict financial requirements that an insurance company must meet to protect the money paid in by all policyholders. State insurance laws also require that a life insurance company must maintain certain minimum levels of capital and surplus, which provide additional policyholder protection.

Also fixed immediate annuity income options are guaranteed. If an investor is going to use an annuity for retirement and wants it to provide payments for life, the company is obligated to make these payments— without exception. The same applies to payments for a fixed period or fixed amount or to payments continuing to survivors such as a spouse. The company guarantees to make payments as specified by the owner's instructions in the contract.

A response to get prospects to reconsider their feelings regarding this type of "no confidence" objection might be as simple as "Do you really believe that the bank is the only place where you can safely accumulate money?"

I Don't Have Free Access to My Money. This is a common objection that you must deal with honestly and effectively. In virtually all three types of tax-deferred annuities, there are company surrender charges that are scheduled according to the three basic contract types. Usually they apply to partial withdrawals and full surrenders and exist in the early years of the contract on a declining scale basis.

First, it is important to explain the reason for the surrender charges, which is to discourage deferred annuity policyowners from constantly switching companies for 25 extra basis points of annual interest. This frequent replacement hurts the profitability of all insurance companies because they do not have time to recoup the up-front acquisition costs such as reserve requirements and commission payments involved in selling the annuity product.

What is also important to point out to the prospect is that there is almost always about a 10 percent window of liquidity on the cash value that is not subject to these charges. Furthermore, there are much more generous windows of liquidity (50 percent or more) on the cash value contained in some popular benefit riders that allow penalty-free access to cash in the event of the annuitant's entering a long-term care facility, becoming terminally ill, or, in some contracts, even becoming unemployed.

You should expect that investors are somewhat familiar with early surrender charges because they have existed in CDs for many years. Certificates of deposit impose penalties for early withdrawals before their respective interest-paying periods (such as six months, one year, or two years) expire. Therefore you may want to ask the prospect, "Which would you prefer, 10 percent liquidity for 365 days a year (for the next 7 years only) or 100 percent liquidity for 7 days a year with your bank CD?"

The advantage of fixed-interest deferred annuities by comparison is that the current interest rates payable are usually higher than one-year CDs, as illustrated in Chapter 3. However, you should also point out that part of the trade-off for the advantages of tax deferral is that the IRS imposes a 10 percent penalty on withdrawals made from these contracts before age 59 ½.

Summary

For a two-interview selling/planning process, the gap in time between the initial and closing interviews means that the presentation will need to re-establish the need for retirement income enhancement and the motivation to buy financial products, such as annuities, to help achieve it. In addition, you will want to present a product solution that reflects the prospect's needs, priorities, and budget. Using the simple concept of features and benefits, you can effectively demonstrate how an annuity can meet the prospect's needs.

If the selling process has progressed properly, implementing the solution means nothing more than a transition to taking an application. Of course, objections can and do arise, and when they do, you should be prepared to handle them in light of the prospect's circumstances and motivations. Closing the sale need not be manipulative or heavy-handed, but it should not allow prospects to escape from being told the truth about what would happen if they fail to act.

The Power of Compounding Interest

Starting Early Can Provide Young Savers With Financial Advantages at Retirement

Retirement planning is far from the first thing on the minds of many young people today. Yet consider how a small amount of money put into an accumulation plan early in life can have a long-term impact on a person's financial security if it is left to grow until retirement. By encouraging young adults to start thinking now about the power of tax-deferred accumulation vehicles, you may establish a more financially secure client base that saves on a consistent basis as they grow older.

The following example shows how investing in an annuity at an early age may help an individual accumulate more money for retirement than someone who begins investing later.

Example:	Let's compare the results of identical twin siblings, Early and Late Saver. At age 23, Early Saver graduates from college and enters the work force

earning $30,000. Early invests $3,000 in a deferred annuity for only 10 years (ages 23 to 32), and then stops making payments into it.

Sibling Late Saver, who waits until age 33 when earning $60,000 a year, decides to start putting $3,000 a year into a deferred annuity. Late contributes $3,000 each year for 32 years (ages 33 to 64).

Compare the results when both reach age 65. Assuming both annuities earn a consistent annual rate of 7 percent interest, Early's retirement savings will grow to $386,529, while Late's savings will accumulate to only $353,800. Because Early began saving in life 10 years before Late, Early will accumulate $32,729 more by contributing $3,000 for only 10 years and letting it grow than Late will accumulate by contributing $3,000 for 32 years.

Even though Early's total contributions were only $30,000 ($3,000 per year for 10 years) compared to Late's total payments of $96,000 ($3,000 per year for 32 years), Early has a larger retirement nest egg. The key to Early's larger savings is the power of compounding interest over a longer period of time. Early began 10 years before Late so Early's contributions had up to 42 years to compound. Therefore it pays to encourage your clients to start planning for retirement as early as possible in order for them to enjoy greater financial rewards later in life.

The financial obligations in a young person's life, such as education, a down payment for a house, and child care, can move retirement savings to the bottom of the list of priorities. However, as Table 6-8 shows, setting money aside early in life can really pay off in the long run. Successfully conveying to younger individuals the benefits of starting to save early by contributing now whatever amount they can to their future may help them achieve financial security when they retire.

TABLE 6-8
Comparison of Contributions to an Annuity for 10 Years From Ages 23 to 32 to Contributions for 32 Years From Ages 33 to 64

End of Year	Age	Early Saver Deposits	Total Accumulation	Late Saver Deposits	Total Accumulation
–	23	$3,000	–		
1	24	$3,000	$ 3,210		
2	25	$3,000	6,645		
3	26	$3,000	10,320		
4	27	$3,000	14,252		
5	28	$3,000	18,460		
6	29	$3,000	22,962		
7	30	$3,000	27,779		
8	31	$3,000	32,934		
9	32	$3,000	38,449		
10	33		44,351	$3,000	
11	34		47,455	3,000	$ 3,210
12	35		50,777	3,000	6,645
13	36		54,332	3,000	10,320
14	37		58,135	3,000	14,252
15	38		62,204	3,000	18,460
16	39		66,559	3,000	22,962
17	40		71,218	3,000	27,779
18	41		76,203	3,000	32,934
19	42		81,537	3,000	38,449
20	43		87,245	3,000	44,351
21	44		93,352	3,000	50,665
22	45		99,886	3,000	57,422
23	46		106,879	3,000	64,651
24	47		114,360	3,000	72,387
25	48		122,365	3,000	80,664
26	49		130,931	3,000	89,521
27	50		140,096	3,000	98,997
28	51		149,903	3,000	109,137
29	52		160,396	3,000	119,986
30	53		171,624	3,000	131,596
31	54		183,637	3,000	144,017
32	55		196,492	3,000	157,308
33	56		210,246	3,000	171,530
34	57		224,964	3,000	186,747
35	58		240,711	3,000	203,029
36	59		257,561	3,000	220,451
37	60		275,590	3,000	239,093
38	61		294,881	3,000	259,040
39	62		315,523	3,000	280,382
40	63		337,610	3,000	303,219
41	64		361,242	3,000	327,654
42	65		386,520		353,800

CASE HISTORY

Using an Annuity to Fund the Purchase of Long-Term Care Insurance

Mary is 75 years old. She has $20,400 of interest earnings per year coming from $340,000 in certificates of deposit that generate 6 percent interest. She also has $10,000 in annual Social Security income. Although she is doing all right on her income of $30,400 per year, there is no room for inflation or for paying $2,000 for minimal long-term care insurance. This amount of long-term care premium would reduce her current standard of living. She and her son are worried about her running out of money if she ends up needing nursing home care. Her son is ready to pay $5,000 per year for a top-quality long-term care insurance policy, but Mary really wants to avoid having her son pay for her insurance.

The solution to Mary's problem could be an immediate annuity, which could be structured to solve Mary's needs in a couple of different ways.

Mary could invest $220,000 in an immediate annuity that would provide $20,400 in annual income. This would increase her income from $30,400 per year to $37,600 as follows:

Social Security	$10,000
$120,000 in CDs at 6 percent	$ 7,200
Immediate annuity	$20,400
Total	$37,600

Mary's income will increase by $7,200 ($37,600 − $30,400 = $7,200) per year, an increase of almost 24 percent. This means that Mary will not have to reduce her standard of living because of the purchase of a long-term care insurance policy. She can, using her own resources, increase her standard of living and be assured that her total income, in or out of a nursing home, will be enough to cover her expenses.

Alternatively, she could put all $340,000 into an annuity and have a life income, including her Social Security, of $45,000 per year, a 48 percent increase in income.

Social Security	$10,000
Immediate annuity	35,000
Total	$45,000

Mary's mother lived to age 95, so Mary feels she could live even longer. Mary's son says that a guaranteed income of $45,000 per year could change his mother from a woman who is worried about outliving her money to a woman who is enjoying life every step of the way. Her son is relieved because he is more concerned about his mother running out of money than he is about inheriting her investments.

Mary's son encourages her to choose the first option so his mother still has access to the principal in the remaining certificates of deposit for emergencies if needed. They both feel secure with her decision.

CHAPTER SIX REVIEW

Key Terms and Concepts are explained in the Glossary. Answers to the Review Questions and Self-Test Questions are found in the back of the book in the Answers to Questions section.

Key Terms and Concepts

fixed-period annuity
fixed-amount annuity
life-only annuity
life annuity with percent of
    premium death benefit
life annuity with period certain
life annuity with installment refund
life annuity with cash refund
joint and survivor life annuity
joint and survivor life annuity with
    percent of premium death benefit

joint and survivor life annuity with
    period certain
joint and survivor life annuity with
    installment or cash refund
annuitization
variable immediate annuity
assumed investment return (AIR)
feature
benefit
buying signals
nonverbal signals

Review Questions

6-1. Describe the difference between fixed-amount and fixed-period annuities.

6-2. Identify the risk to the annuity owner of purchasing a life-only annuity payout.

6-3. Explain how a life annuity with a 10-year period certain guarantee functions if the annuitant dies within 7 years after issue.

6-4. Identify which risk a variable annuity purchaser assumes from the insurance company.

6-5. Describe at least two joint and survivor life annuity payout options for a married couple, and explain how they work.

6-6. Describe the two important considerations when comparing competitive immediate annuity quotations.

6-7. Explain the difference between a policy feature and a policy benefit.

6-8.   Explain why it is important to have the prospect's participation and involvement in the selling/planning process.

6-9.   Give some examples of nonverbal buying signals.

6-10. Identify three things to put in focus when taking a problem-solving approach to handling a prospect's objections.

6-11. Describe two three-step techniques for responding to prospect resistance.

6-12. Identify the four general categories of objections to purchasing annuity products.

Self-Test Questions

Instructions: Read Chapter 6 first; then answer the following questions to test your knowledge. There are 10 questions; circle the correct answer, and then check your answers with the answer key in the back of the book.

6-1.   Which immediate annuity payout option for a given age will produce the highest payment?

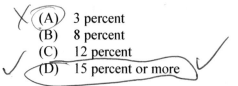

   (A)   life only
   (B)   life with 10 years period certain
   (C)   life with 5 years period certain
   (D)   joint and 100 percent survivor

6-2.   The decision to purchase a life annuity with 20 years certain instead of a life-only annuity can increase the cost by how much?

   (A)   3 percent
   (B)   8 percent
   (C)   12 percent
   (D)   15 percent or more

6-3.   If a fixed-period immediate annuity pays $1,000 per month income but the purchaser opts for a cost-of-living adjustment (COLA), for the same single premium the payment would normally start at what amount?

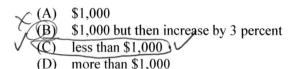

   (A) $1,000
   (B) $1,000 but then increase by 3 percent
   (C)   less than $1,000
   (D)   more than $1,000

6-4. If a low assumed investment return (AIR) is chosen with a variable immediate annuity, what happens to future payments?

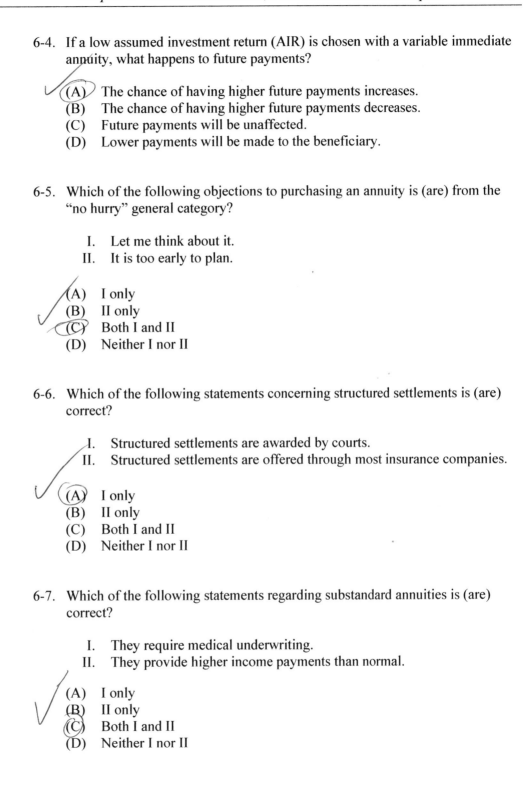

   (A)   The chance of having higher future payments increases.
   (B)   The chance of having higher future payments decreases.
   (C)   Future payments will be unaffected.
   (D)   Lower payments will be made to the beneficiary.

6-5. Which of the following objections to purchasing an annuity is (are) from the "no hurry" general category?

   I.   Let me think about it.
   II.   It is too early to plan.

   (A)   I only
   (B)   II only
   (C)   Both I and II
   (D)   Neither I nor II

6-6. Which of the following statements concerning structured settlements is (are) correct?

   I.   Structured settlements are awarded by courts.
   II.   Structured settlements are offered through most insurance companies.

   (A)   I only
   (B)   II only
   (C)   Both I and II
   (D)   Neither I nor II

6-7. Which of the following statements regarding substandard annuities is (are) correct?

   I.   They require medical underwriting.
   II.   They provide higher income payments than normal.

   (A)   I only
   (B)   II only
   (C)   Both I and II
   (D)   Neither I nor II

6-8.   Suggested steps for presenting possible annuity product solutions to a prospect include all of the following EXCEPT

(A)   Outline the implementation plan.
(B)   Summarize your observations.
(C)   Make your recommendations.
(D)   Obtain a dollar commitment.

6-9.   All of the following attributes of a fixed immediate annuity are positive in the eyes of the owner EXCEPT

(A)   several payout options from which to choose
(B)   guaranteed payments
(C)   the security of receiving steady income
(D)   increasing payout amounts

6-10. All of the following are alternatives to annuitization EXCEPT

(A)   penalty-free withdrawals
(B)   withdrawals
(C)   partial surrenders
(D)   savings bonds

NOTES

1. 2007 Annuity Fact Book, 6th ed., p. 95, ©2007 NAVA®. Inc.
2. Ibid. p. 43.
3. Ibid. p. 44.

Taxation, Plan Implementation, and Servicing Annuity Products

---

Learning Objectives

An understanding of the material in this chapter should enable you to

---

7-1. Explain the income tax differences between qualified and nonqualified annuities.

7-2. Explain the requirements of ownership and annuitant designations to complete an IRC Sec. 1035 exchange for a nonqualified annuity.

7-3. Explain the time limit to roll over one qualified annuity to another.

7-4. Identify the payout options a beneficiary has if the payout is due to the death of the annuitant or the death of the owner.

7-5. Describe what is involved in implementing the annuity plan and processing an application.

7-6. Explain how to conduct an effective policy delivery.

7-7. Describe methods to service the annuity plan.

7-8. Explain the relationship of annuities to other financial planning need

---

Chapter Outline

This chapter examines legal issues regarding annuities, including ownership and beneficiary designations. It also addresses the income, estate, and gift tax implications of annuities. In addition, the chapter discusses IRC Sec. 1035 exchanges for nonqualified annuities, as well as rollovers and transfers for qualified annuities. Finally, the chapter explores the implementation, servicing, and relationship of annuity products to other aspects of financial planning.

NONQUALIFIED ANNUITIES

Ownership and Beneficiary Issues

The policyowner is the person or entity that applies for and purchases the annuity and whose Social Security number or tax identification number is shown on the policy. It is possible in many annuity policies to name two owners as joint owners. However, this means that all owners will have to agree on any changes to the policy, or the insurance company will have to refuse the change.

It is usually possible to change owners and beneficiaries during the lifetime of an annuity policy (although there may be adverse tax consequences with a change of owner), but it is not possible to change annuitants.

Once a potential client has determined that an annuity is a suitable investment, the next step in the sales process is to determine who should own the annuity. Should the prospect own the annuity? Or would it be more advantageous if someone else were the policyowner? It might sound like a fairly simple decision, and it is—if the owner and the annuitant are the same. The following discussion addresses questions about unique ownership situations.

Revocable Living Trusts

The majority of annuity purchasers are elderly, and some have even gone through the estate planning process. A popular estate planning tool is the revocable living trust (RLT). The prospective purchaser might ask the financial advisor if the annuity under consideration should be owned inside the prospect's RLT.

The answer is that it depends on the situation. Normally revocable living trusts are probate avoidance techniques. Because annuities already avoid the probate process, putting their ownership in an RLT offers no additional benefit. The answer may be different if the annuity owner wants someone to step in and manage his or her assets if the owner becomes disabled or incapacitated, in which case an RLT can be a powerful tool for elderly clients. If this is why the annuity owner has a revocable living trust, it may be appropriate to name the trustee as the owner and beneficiary of the annuity.

Example: If Louis Trustworthy, aged 89, becomes unable to manage his assets and he is the current trustee of his own RLT, the successor trustee can step in and manage Louis's assets and therefore manage and control the annuity. However, if the trust does not own the annuity but it is owned directly by the incapacitated man, there is nothing that can be done to manage the annuity, short of legal intervention by the family.

Whether or not the policyowner is the trustee of the revocable living trust, often the beneficiary can still be the RLT. For example, Louis might name himself as the owner and annuitant of his newly purchased annuity but list the trustee of his revocable living trust as beneficiary: Nancy Trustworthy, Trustee, or its Successor in Interest, of the Revocable Living

Trust of Louis Trustworthy, dated October 1, 2003.

Nonnatural Persons as Owners

nonnatural person

If an individual owns a deferred annuity, that person enjoys the benefit of income tax deferral from the gains in the annuity account value. However, if a *nonnatural person* owns an annuity, the benefit of tax deferral is lost. The owner must pay income tax each year on the growth in the annuity. Therefore the owner does not enjoy tax deferral. This tax rule applies to premiums paid after February 28, 1986, regardless of the issue date of the annuity.

The next question to address is "What is a nonnatural person?" Corporations are nonnatural persons, as are family limited partnerships. Therefore if this type of entity owns a deferred annuity, it loses the tax-deferred status, and it must pay income tax each year on the gain.

A deferred annuity held by a trust, corporation, or other entity as an agent for a natural person is not subject to the loss of tax deferral (IRC Sec. 72(u)(1)). In other words, if a trust owns the deferred annuity as an agent for an individual person, the annuity cash value will still grow on a tax-deferred basis. A trust that owns a deferred annuity that is to be distributed to the trust's beneficiary who is a natural person will not lose the benefit of tax deferral.

If a charity owns a deferred annuity, the charity is still considered a nonnatural person. The interest earnings will be taxed yearly to the charity. Furthermore, a charitable remainder trust that owns a deferred annuity will not be considered a natural person and hence will lose its tax deferral. However, because charities and charitable remainder trusts are tax-exempt entities, it is of no consequence to the charity to be subject to taxable income each year.

Goodman Rule

If the policyowner is not the annuitant and has named a beneficiary other than himself or herself, the owner may be surprised to discover that the death benefits are considered a gift and may require filing a gift tax return. This tax problem can arise when an annuity is issued with three different individuals as owner, annuitant, and beneficiary.

The court in *Goodman v. Commissioner* (156 F.2d 218 (2nd Cir. 1946)) held that the owner is deemed to have made a taxable gift to the beneficiary for the amount of the death benefit. The logic behind this holds that because the owner could have named anybody in the world as the beneficiary, it must be a gift from the owner to the beneficiary. Note:

This happens only when three different individuals hold the position of owner, annuitant, and beneficiary.

Example:

If a husband owns a $100,000 deferred annuity policy on his wife's life and he names his son as the beneficiary, when the wife dies, the death benefit is payable to the son.

- owner—husband
- annuitant—wife
- beneficiary—son

The father, as owner, is deemed to have made a $100,000 gift to the son. Upon the wife's death, the husband will have to declare a taxable gift to his son of $100,000. Depending on the amount of gift tax exemption the father has in the year of his wife's death, this may or may not cause an out-of-pocket gift tax to be paid by the father. With small estates or small annuity policies, this might not be a big issue. But with larger estates, annuities, or life insurance policies, this can turn into a significant tax situation that can be avoided with proper planning.

Income Taxation of Nonqualified Annuities

The general rules for taxation of annuities are found in Internal Revenue Code Sec. 72, which is reproduced in its entirety in Appendix B.

Premiums and Cash Value Growth

Premiums paid to nonqualified deferred annuities are not tax deductible by the policyowner. However, the growth in the annuity value each year is tax deferred to the owner. This means that as the cash value increases each year, the owner does not have to include the increase in his or her taxable income. The earnings are not tax free, simply tax deferred until some later date.

Example:

If Rex, a policyholder, pays a one-time single premium of $20,000 to purchase a deferred annuity, the $20,000 premium is not a tax-deductible amount for Rex. After the first policy anniversary, if the annuity has grown to $22,000, the $2,000 ($22,000 − $20,000 = $2,000) of growth is not subject to income tax but instead will grow on a tax-deferred basis.

A special rule exists for variable deferred annuities to receive tax deferral on the cash-value growth. This rule requires the underlying investments of the segregated asset accounts to be "adequately diversified" according to IRS regulations.

Multiple Annuity Contracts

If a policyowner purchases more than one deferred annuity in a calendar year, the deferred annuities must be treated as though they were one annuity policy for purposes of determining the amount of any distribution includible in income. This rule applies only if the policies are issued by the same insurance company and after October 21, 1988. The purpose of this rule is to preclude the serial purchase of deferred annuities as a means for making abusive tax-free withdrawals from only one of these contracts. This rule is commonly referred to as the "aggregation rule."

cost basis

Example: Jim purchases Policy A in January 2004 with a $16,000 single premium and Policy B in July 2004 with an $11,000 single premium from the same insurance company. Therefore Jim's combined total *cost basis* is $27,000. Jim will have to aggregate the two deferred annuities purchased in the same calendar year. Therefore the deferred annuities purchased in January and July 2004 (A and B) will be aggregated for income tax purposes.

A few years later, Policy A has $4,000 of gain and Policy B has $9,000 of gain, for a total of $13,000. Each policy has grown to $20,000. Jim wants to take a $10,000 withdrawal. He would like to take all $10,000 from Policy A because he thinks he will have to receive only $4,000 of taxable income since $6,000 will be a tax-free return of his premium. But the two policies must be aggregated for tax purposes. Together the two policies have a total gain of $13,000. Therefore the first $13,000 withdrawn, regardless of which policy the money is withdrawn from, will be taxable income to Jim.

Because not all insurance companies have the administrative capacity to properly report the taxation of aggregated deferred annuities, it is the financial advisor's obligation to be sure the company with which he or she is working is capable of administering aggregated deferred annuities properly.

Borrowing Against an Annuity

Most nonqualified annuities do not offer the option of taking a loan against the annuity cash value. This is probably due to the fact that amounts borrowed from a deferred annuity are considered taxable income to the owner to the extent that the cash value in the contract immediately before the loan is taken exceeds the investment in the contract.[1] This rule also applies to deferred annuities used as a pledge or as part of an assignment, and it pertains to deferred annuities issued after August 13, 1982.

Example:	A policyowner has a deferred annuity worth $225,000 and his cost basis is $100,000. Therefore the policy has $125,000 of gain. If he uses the annuity as collateral for a $50,000 loan at the local bank, the policyowner must recognize $50,000 as ordinary income. This is true even if the owner does not technically withdraw any funds from the deferred annuity. Furthermore, the 10 percent IRS penalty tax will apply if the owner is under age 59 ½.

Sale of an Existing Annuity Contract

If a deferred annuity policy is sold by the owner, any gain in the policy is taxed to the seller of the annuity. The gain is ordinary income. If a deferred annuity is sold for $30,000 and the owner has paid $10,000 in premiums, the seller of the annuity must pay ordinary income taxes on $20,000 ($30,000 − $10,000 = $20,000).

If the seller of an annuity sells the policy at a loss, the loss can be claimed as a deduction against taxable income if the annuity was part of the taxpayer's business or trade or entered into for profit, as stated in IRC Sec. 165.

Over the years, various rulings have concluded that the purchase of an annuity, even if it is a personal annuity, is properly characterized as a transaction entered into for profit.[2] If this is true, then an annuity owner who surrenders an annuity and receives less in return than his basis in the annuity should be able to take an income tax deduction for the difference between the basis in the annuity and the amount received. (Generally the basis in an annuity is equal to the premiums paid, but any amount received income tax free during the time the annuity was held must be subtracted from this amount to arrive at the true basis figure.)

Given that a loss on the surrender may be deducted, the next question to be considered is whether the loss should be considered a capital loss or an ordinary loss. Generally it is thought that the loss on the surrender of an annuity is an ordinary loss.[3] If the loss is considered to be an ordinary loss, the next question is whether it is deductible as a miscellaneous deduction subject to the two-percent-of-income floor. The answer to this question does not seem to have been addressed by the Internal Revenue Service in any actual ruling. There is one piece of information from the Internal Revenue Service that does given an indication of its viewpoint on this question. In IRS Publication 575[4] the service indicates that a loss under a commercial variable annuity is deductible as a miscellaneous itemized deduction subject to the two-percent floor.[5]

So whether the loss is subject to the two-percent floor or whether it can be deducted simply as an ordinary loss has not been settled definitively.[6] The more conservative approach would be to consider the loss deductible subject to the two-percent floor while the more aggressive view would be to view that the loss is deductible as an ordinary loss.

Incidentally if a taxpayer sustains a loss upon the surrender of a refund annuity contract, he or she may claim a deduction for the loss regardless of whether or not it was purchased in connection with a trade or business or as a personal investment.

Annuitization and Exclusion Ratios

Once an annuity owner decides to use an annuity to provide a guaranteed income stream, the insurance company will give the owner the guaranteed dollar amount of the payments. In addition, the insurance company will provide the owner with an *exclusion ratio*. The exclusion ratio is the percentage of each payment that is receivable on

exclusion ratio

an income-tax-free basis. The remaining amount of each payment is subject to ordinary income taxes.

The purpose of the exclusion ratio is to allow the policyowner to receive back over time the amount of premium dollars he or she paid in. The premium is returned in the form of payments without being subject to income tax. The exclusion ratio is determined by dividing the total **expected return** investment in the annuity by the *expected return*. In other words, it is roughly equivalent to the premiums paid divided by the amount of income the annuitant should receive back over the specific period of time.

$$\frac{\text{Total investment}}{\text{Expected return}} = \text{Exclusion ratio}$$

Fixed-Period, Fixed-Amount, and Straight Life Annuities

With fixed-period or fixed-payment annuities, the expected return is the sum of the guaranteed payments. With life expectancy annuities, it is the number of years until the annuitant reaches his or life expectancy multiplied by the annual payment.

Life expectancies are found in IRS Annuity Tables, contained in IRS Publication 939, which is available on the Internet at www.irs.gov. Single life expectancy tables are listed in Tables I and V. Joint and survivor life expectancies are listed in Tables II, IIA, VI, and VIA. Sex-distinct life expectancies are listed in Tables I through IV. These tables apply if investments in the annuities were made before June 30, 1986. Unisex life expectancies are listed in Tables V through VIII. Unisex tables are applicable to investments made after June 30, 1986.

Example: Sharon buys an immediate annuity from an insurance company. Her total investment is $119, 714.16. She will receive $12,000 per year paid in monthly installments of $1,000 for the rest of her life. Sharon is aged 72, and her life expectancy is 14.6 years from Table V. The exclusion ratio for her payment is 68.3 percent. This means that 68.3 percent, or $683.00, of each $1,000 monthly payment is income tax free to Sharon.

$$\frac{\$119,714.16}{\$12,000 \times 14.6} = \frac{\$119,714.16}{\$175,200} = 68.3\%$$

$$\$12,000 \times .683 = \$8,196$$

The balance, $3,804 ($12,000 − $8,196 = $3,804), will be taxed to her as ordinary income. The insurance company gives Sharon the income tax information (IRS Form 1099) at the end of each year so she can account for the income on her annual tax return.

The exclusion ratio will remain constant each year until Sharon reaches her life expectancy. At that point she has recovered her investment in the contract. Once she reaches her life expectancy, the full $1,000 monthly payment will be taxable to her as ordinary income, and the exclusion ratio will no longer be applicable. This rule applies to annuities purchased after December 31, 1986.

TABLE 7-1
Ordinary Life Annuities—One Life—Expected Return Multiple (IRS TABLE V)

Age	Multiple (Years)
70	16.0
71	15.3
72	**14.6**
73	13.9
74	13.2
75	12.5

Policies issued before January 1, 1987, do not lose the exclusion ratio once the annuitant reaches life expectancy. Therefore those annuitants can receive partially tax-free income for their entire lives.

Life Annuity With Refund or Period Certain Guarantee

The computation above is for a straight life annuity (without refund or period-certain guarantee). The exclusion ratio for a single life refund or period-certain guarantee is determined in the same way, but the investment in the contract must first be adjusted by subtracting the actuarial value of the refund or period-certain guarantee.

Thus the formula for calculating the exclusion ratio for a life annuity with a refund or period certain guarantee would appear as

$$\frac{\text{Total investment} \; - \; \text{Value of refund or period-certain}}{\text{Expected return}} = \text{Exclusion ratio}$$

The actuarial value of the refund or period-certain guarantee which is computed using IRS annuity tables is not shown because these numbers are typically provided in the software of computer-generated sales illustrations.

However, we will illustrate exclusion ratio for the purchase of an installment refund annuity only to describe how the steps in the computation are applied. The steps in the computation that applies to a period-certain annuity are very similar.

Once the investment in the contract has been adjusted by subtracting the value of the refund (or period-certain guarantee), an exclusion ratio is determined in the same way as for a straight life annuity. That is, expected return is computed; then the adjusted investment in the contract is divided by the expected return.

Example:	Continuing the refund annuity example for Sharon, above:

Investment in the contract (adjusted for a refund guarantee amount of $17,957 in this case) is ($119,714 – $17,957)	$101,757
One year's guaranteed annuity payments, which are lower than in the straight life annuity (12 x $900)	$10,800
Life expectancy from Table V for a post-1986 annuity for a 72-year-old	14.6 years
Expected return (14.6 x $10,800)	$157,680
Exclusion ratio ($101,757 ÷ $157,680)	64.6%
Amount excludible from income each year (annualized) (64.6% of 10,800)*	$6,976.80
Amount includible in gross income ($10,800 – $6,976.80)	$3,823.20

*Since the annuity starting date is after December 31, 1986, the total amount excludible is limited to the investment in the contract; after that has been recovered, the remaining amounts received are includible in income. However, if the annuity has a refund or guaranteed feature, the value of the refund or guarantee feature is not subtracted when calculating the unrecovered investment (IRC Sec. 72(b)(4)). Therefore the annuity exclusion ratio would apply to each of Sharon's payments for this refund annuity contract until her tax-free payments exceed a total of $119,714.

Variable Immediate Annuities

Variable immediate annuities (discussed in detail later in this chapter) do not necessarily have an expected return because the dollar amount of the income benefit is unknown. Therefore for variable immediate annuities, the calculation is a little different. Because the expected return under a variable annuity is unknown, it is considered to be the investment in the contract. A fixed portion of each annuity payment is excludible from gross income as a tax-free recovery of the annuity purchaser's investment. The amount of tax-free payments is determined by simply dividing the investment in the contract (adjusted for any period-certain or refund guarantee) by the number of years over which it is anticipated the annuity will be paid.

$$\frac{\text{Total investment (adjusted if necessary)}}{\text{Number of years payments will be made}} = \text{Tax-free portion of each payment}$$

If payments are to be made for a fixed number of years without regard to life expectancy, the divisor is the fixed number of years. If payments are to be made for a single life, the divisor is the appropriate life expectancy multiple as determined by IRS Table I for pre-January 1, 1987, premiums or Table V for premiums paid into the policy after December 31, 1986. If payments are to be made for a joint and survivor basis, the divisor is the appropriate life expectancy multiple as determined by IRS Table II for pre-January 1, 1987, premiums or Table VI for premiums paid into the policy after December 31, 1986.

To illustrate, assume that a male aged 65 elects an immediate variable life annuity, and his investment in the deferred variable annuity is $100,000, made after January 1, 1987. His annual variable annuity payments are initially $8,000. IRS Table V indicates his life expectancy is 20 years. One hundred thousand dollars divided by 20 years is $5,000, which is the portion of each payment that is excluded from income. During each of the first 20 years, $5,000 of the annual payments are excluded from income, and the balance will be included in income. Whether the variable annual payments increase to $10,000 or decrease to $6,000 for any given year, the tax-free portion remains at $5,000 per year. After 20 years, assuming the man is still alive, the cost basis of $100,000 will have been returned to him tax free, and any future annual payments to him would be fully taxable.

The financial advisor should have a working knowledge of how the exclusion ratio is derived in order to communicate it to clients. However, the financial advisor does not usually calculate this ratio for the policyowner. It is normally provided by the insurance company's home office or from its computerized illustration system.

IRC Sec. 1035 Exchanges

The IRS provides tax relief to the purchasers of life insurance, endowment policies, or nonqualified deferred annuities if the purchaser wants to move funds from one insurance company to another. The tax code allows this transaction, a *Sec. 1035 exchange*, to occur without making it a taxable event.

Sec. 1035 exchange

The tax-free exchange rules under IRC Sec. 1035 state that a life insurance policy can be exchanged for a life insurance policy, an annuity can be exchanged for an annuity policy, and a life insurance policy can be exchanged for an annuity policy. It does not matter what type of annuity is under consideration. It can be variable, fixed, equity indexed, and so on. The same is true for life insurance. (Sec. 1035 is reprinted in full in Appendix B.)

Internal Revenue Code
Sec. 1035 Exchanges

- **Life insurance:**
  Can be exchanged for life insurance, endowment policies, or annuities

- **Endowment policies or annuities:**
  Can be exchanged for endowment policies, or annuities

- **Annuities:**
  Can be exchanged for annuities

A deferred annuity policy, however, cannot be transferred on a tax-free exchange into a life insurance policy. This is partly because the IRS does not want a taxpayer to exchange a taxable asset—such as an annuity—for a potentially tax-free asset—such as life insurance. It does, however, allow the taxpayer to move from a potentially tax-free asset to a taxable asset.

(Note: The tax-free exchange rules under IRC Sec. 1035, as revised under the Pension Protection Act of 2006, state that beginning January 1, 2010, a life insurance policy can be exchanged for a life insurance, endowment, annuity, or qualified LTCI policy; an endowment policy can be exchanged for another endowment policy, an annuity, or a qualified LTCI; an annuity can be exchanged for an annuity policy or a qualified LTCI; and a qualified LTCI can be exchanged for another qualified LTCI.)

These rules apply to nonqualified annuities. Qualified annuities are addressed in the next section.

A tax-free exchange is important because it allows the policyowner to exchange one deferred annuity for another without having to recognize any taxable gain in the annuity policy upon transfer. Instead, the policyowner is allowed to carry the cost basis from the old annuity into the new annuity and defer recognition of gain.

Example:	A policyowner has a deferred annuity worth $100,000 and a cost basis of $25,000. If the owner decides to purchase a new deferred annuity, he can transfer the cash value of $100,000 into a new deferred annuity policy, and that new policy will have the cost basis of $25,000 from the old policy.

To have a valid 1035 exchange, the owner of the deferred annuity must be the same on the old and the new policy. In addition, the annuitant must also be the same person on the old and the new policy. The beneficiary designation, however, does not have to be the same on both policies.

A unique IRC 1035 exchange transaction involves the exchange of a life insurance policy into an immediate annuity. Normally individuals exchange deferred annuities for deferred annuities and life insurance for life insurance, but in this instance, a policyowner can move from life insurance to an immediate annuity. The benefit of this transaction is to allow the cost basis in the immediate annuity to be carried over from the cost basis of the life insurance policy.

Note that if a deferred annuity issued before August 14, 1982, is 1035 exchanged into a new deferred annuity, the new annuity should retain the FIFO (first in, first out) taxation of withdrawals. It is important that the financial advisor who is working with the policyowner verify the old policy's cost basis so that the favorable taxation can continue without disruption.

It is generally a valid exchange to take multiple deferred annuities and exchange them into one single deferred annuity. When moving in the other direction—that is, moving from one policy to multiple policies— the issue has been somewhat more complex. The IRS has addressed similar fact situations involving IRC Sec. 1035 exchanges in the following private letter rulings. Although private letter rulings cannot be relied upon by other taxpayers, they can provide insight into how the IRS views certain issues and transactions:

- A single-premium deferred annuity was validly 1035 exchanged for two deferred annuity policies when all three annuities were issued by the same insurance company (PLR199644016).
- One deferred annuity was validly exchanged for two deferred annuities issued by either the same or different insurers (PLR199937042).

Furthermore, the IRS provided a revenue ruling with the following 1035 exchange scenario and declared it a valid tax-free exchange: An assignment of a deferred annuity for consolidation into a pre-existing deferred annuity via an IRC Sec. 1035 tax-free exchange was valid even though the two annuities were issued by different issuers (Rev. Rul 2002-75, 2002-45 IRB 812). The new cost basis in the pre-existing deferred annuity is the total cost basis from both annuities.

partial Sec. 1035 exchange

Partial Sec. 1035 Exchanges. For an IRC Sec. 1035 exchange to be valid, the old policy must be given up entirely and generally a brand new policy purchased with the values of the old policy. In a recent case, however, the Tax Court (see *Conway v. Commissioner*, 111 TC 350 (1998)) held that a partial surrender of an existing deferred annuity can be 1035 exchanged into a new deferred annuity policy. In a *partial Sec. 1035 exchange*, the cash values must be directly transferred from one insurer to the other, and the cost basis is prorated between the old and new policies.

Although the rules under Section 1035 now cover a broader array of annuity exchanges, funds in nonqualified annuities are not freely movable. The IRS is reviewing whether multiple deferred annuities resulting from partial exchanges are taxed as if there was only one policy under the aggregation rules. In the meantime, the IRS does not provide guidance on the transfer of a portion of the funds in one nonqualified annuity to a second existing annuity. Thus it is not certain that such a transaction is covered under Sections 1035, and therefore this type of transaction may not receive tax-free treatment.

Withdrawals, Surrenders, and Penalty Taxes

Nonqualified deferred annuities purchased after August 13, 1982, are taxed on a last in, first out basis (LIFO). Withdrawals are taxed first to the extent that there is any gain in the annuity. This is referred to as the "interest first" rule. The purpose of the "interest first" rule applicable to investments in contracts after August 13, 1982, is to limit the tax advantages of deferred annuity contracts to long-term investment goals, such as retirement income security, and to prevent the use of tax-deferred inside build-up as a method of sheltering income on freely withdrawable short-term investments. Once all the gain has been withdrawn, any further withdrawal is not taxable income to the annuity owner but is considered a tax-free withdrawal of the cost basis.

Example:	Bill has a nonqualified deferred annuity policy worth $80,000. His cost basis is $25,000. Bill is aged 52 and decides to surrender the entire annuity. His gain upon surrender is $55,000 ($80,000 – $25,000 = $55,000). If he surrenders the policy, he will be subject to ordinary income taxes on $55,000. If Bill does not surrender the entire policy but instead withdraws just $30,000, the first $30,000 is all taxable income. Not until he withdraws all $55,000 will he start to receive income-tax-free withdrawals.

Withdrawals from policies issued before August 14, 1982, are taxed differently from the LIFO method. This rule applies only to contributions made prior to August 14, 1982, and the accompanying growth on those contributions. Withdrawals are first considered a return of premium, and second as interest earnings—the first dollars in are the first dollars out (FIFO). The first dollars withdrawn from the policy are tax free to the extent that they are considered a return of the policyowner's premiums. Once all the premium dollars have been withdrawn tax free, any remaining amounts withdrawn are taxed to the policyowner as ordinary income. This is called the "cost recovery rule."

Example:	Let's assume Bill's policy in the previous example was issued before August 14, 1982. Bill wants to withdraw $40,000. Of that $40,000, the first $25,000 of this withdrawal is considered a tax-free return of Bill's original premium. He'll receive the first $25,000 free of any taxes. The remaining $15,000 is fully taxable to Bill as ordinary income in the year of withdrawal.

If the deferred annuity has income from *both* pre-August 14, 1982, and post-August 13, 1982, premiums, the taxation of withdrawals is more complex. Withdrawals are first considered a tax-free return of pre-August 14, 1982, premiums; then interest income on pre-August 14, 1982, premiums; then interest income on post-August 13, 1982, premiums; and finally a tax-free return of post-August 13, 1982, premiums.

> • **Interest first rule (LIFO taxation):** Withdrawals are taxed first to the extent that there is any gain in the annuity. Once all the gain has been withdrawn, any further withdrawal is not taxable income to the annuity owner.
>
> • **Cost recovery rule (FIFO taxation):** The first dollars withdrawn are tax free to the extent they are a return of the policyowner's premiums. Once all premium dollars have been withdrawn, the remaining amounts withdrawn are taxed as ordinary income.

pre-59 1/2 IRS penalty tax

Penalty Tax. The general rule of thumb with nonqualified deferred annuities is that distributions taken from these accounts prior to the policyowner's age 59 ½ will cause the taxable amount of the withdrawal to be subject to a 10 percent penalty tax levied by the IRS. The policyowner, not the insurance company, pays the *pre-59 ½ IRS penalty tax* It is paid to the IRS with the taxpayer's IRS Form 1040 by April 15, the usual tax filing deadline.

In the first example, with a $30,000 taxable withdrawal from a deferred annuity issued after August 13, 1982, if Bill is under age 59 ½, the entire $30,000 withdrawal will be subject to the 10 percent IRS penalty tax.

In the second example, with a deferred annuity issued before August 14, 1982, Bill will receive the first $25,000 of the $40,000 withdrawal free of income tax and IRS penalties if Bill is under age 59 ½. The remaining $15,000 of the $40,000 is taxable income. However, the $15,000 of taxable earnings on pre-August 14, 1982, premiums falls under one of the IRC Sec. 72(q) exceptions to the 10 penalty tax (see the following page). Thus it would *not* be subject to the 10 percent penalty.

When surrender charges reduce the net amount of the withdrawal, the net amount is used to calculate any income tax liability and IRS penalty taxes to the extent that there is gain in the policy.

Example: If a policyowner takes a $3,000 withdrawal from a policy with a 6 percent surrender charge, the company will deduct $180 ($3,000 x .06 = $180). Therefore $2,820 is income taxable and the client is in a 25 percent income tax bracket, so the tax liability is $705 ($2,850 x .25 = $705). If the client is under age 59 ½, a 10 percent penalty tax of $282 will apply ($2,820 x .10 = $282). The total amount the client will net after all taxes and surrender charges is $1,833, calculated as follows:

$3,000 withdrawals
− 180 surrender charge
− 705 income taxes
− 282 penalty taxes
$1,833

The following are the major exceptions to the 10 percent penalty tax that exist under IRC Sec. 72(q) for distributions taken from a nonqualified deferred annuity. (Note the exceptions for nonqualified funds are different from the exceptions for qualified funds—see pages 7-28 and 7-29.) Several additional minor exceptions exist, as shown in the full text of IRC Sec. 72 in Appendix B. The exceptions for nonqualified funds are as follows:

- payments made if the taxpayer is aged 59 ½ or older
- any payment made on or after the death of the participant (or the primary annuitant if the holder is a nonnatural person). This means that beneficiaries of deceased persons under the age of 59 ½ are not subject to the penalty tax if they receive the death benefit in a lump sum.
- a payment attributable to the taxpayer's becoming disabled
- any payment allocated to premiums paid before August 14, 1982, including earnings on pre-August 1982 premiums
- any payments under a qualified funding asset (that is, any annuity policy issued by a licensed insurance company that is purchased as a result of a liability to make periodic payments for damages, by suit or agreement, or on account of personal physical injury or sickness)
- any payment made under an immediate annuity (one that is purchased with the starting date no later than one year from issue). If the taxpayer purchases an immediate annuity, it is not subject to the 10 percent penalty tax.

substantially equal periodic payments (SEPP)

- any payment that is part of a series of *substantially equal periodic payments (SEPP)* made for the life or life expectancy of the taxpayer or the joint lives or joint life expectancies of the taxpayer and the taxpayer's designated beneficiary. The IRS has approved three methods to determine substantially equal periodic payments: (1) the life expectancy method (required minimum distribution), (2) the fixed amortization method, and (3) the fixed annuitization method. However, the distribution schedule cannot be altered for the later of 5 years or the taxpayer's reaching age 59 ½ without the taxpayer's having to pay back penalty taxes plus interest.

The three most common exceptions are payments made after age 59 ½, as death benefits, and under immediate annuities. The last exception cited above using substantially equal periodic payments is often discussed but, in reality, seldom activated.

Advisors can be curious about how the age 59 ½ or older exception works: What if the policyowner turns age 59 1/2 in December and wants to take a withdrawal in October—2 months prior to age 59 ½? Is the withdrawal in October penalty free as long as the policyowner is age 59 ½ in the same year as the withdrawal? Or does the policyowner need to wait until December to make a penalty-free withdrawal? The answer is that the policyowner must be age 59 ½ as of the date of the withdrawal. Age 59 ½ occurs exactly 6 months to the date past the policyowner's 59th birthday. The policyowner should wait until December.

Death Benefits

Deferred annuity death benefits are not income tax free to the beneficiary like the proceeds of a typical life insurance policy. The gain in the deferred annuity policy is taxed to the beneficiary as ordinary income. Unless the beneficiary is a valid charitable organization, the taxable gain in the policy cannot be avoided.

This can be a troublesome feature of deferred annuity policies—that the income tax liability for gain does not disappear via a step-up in cost basis. The tax liability just moves from owner to beneficiary at death.

Variable deferred annuities, not fixed annuities, issued prior to October 29, 1979, do enjoy a step-up in cost basis at death to the current value of the annuity, as long as no further contributions are made after October 29, 1979, and the annuitant dies prior to the annuity starting date. If these variable policies are exchanged for new policies, the step-up in basis is lost.

Death of Annuitant

The surviving beneficiary may or may not be the one who will receive any death benefits payable under the annuity policy in the event of the death of the annuitant, the policyowner, or both, depending on the provisions of the individual annuity policy. Furthermore, the owner should maintain current primary and secondary beneficiaries at all times.

The best advice is twofold: The financial advisor and the policyowner should (1) read through the policy provisions and understand how the policy operates, how it pays death benefits, and what the default provisions state, and (2) walk through each scenario of what happens if the owner dies first, the annuitant dies first, and so on.

Options for Nonspouse Beneficiaries. When a beneficiary is notified by the insurance company of the death of the annuitant and that proceeds are eligible for payment to the beneficiary, the beneficiary might inquire as to what his or her options are. For example, the typical option is taking the proceeds as a lump-sum death benefit. But what other options are available to a nonspouse beneficiary?

If the annuitant dies and the annuitant and the owner are not the same person, the death terminates the policy for income tax purposes. In this case, the beneficiary has only 60 days to make an important choice. If the beneficiary elects within 60 days after the annuitant's death to apply the death benefit under a life-income or installment option, the beneficiary will not be taxed on the gain in the year of the annuitant's death. Rather, the beneficiary will be taxed under the immediate annuity rules. The exclusion ratio will be based on the cost basis in the policy at the annuitant's death and the beneficiary's expected payments over time.

If the beneficiary does not elect an option within 60 days of the annuitant's death, the beneficiary will not be able to defer the built-up gain in the death proceeds. The beneficiary will be subject to tax on the entire gain even if he or she later chooses a settlement option.

Some companies interpret this part of the law to mean that the 60-day period begins at the point when all requirements needed to pay the death claim have been met, which could be more than 60 days after the death.

Options for Spouse Beneficiaries. The annuitant's spouse has more options available at the annuitant's death than the nonspouse beneficiary. In addition to the options available to a nonspouse beneficiary, if death occurs prior to the time that annuitization payments have begun and the spouse is the beneficiary, the spouse can become the policyowner and continue the annuity as the new policyowner and annuitant.

Death of Owner

Options for Nonspouse Beneficiaries. It is not the insurance company or the policyowner who decides what happens to an annuity policy at the *owner's* death. These provisions are dictated by IRC Sec. 72(s), which states that a policy issued after January 18, 1985, will not be treated as an annuity unless it provides the following:

- If any holder of such a policy dies on or after the annuity starting date and before the entire interest in such contract has been distributed, the remaining portion of the interest will be distributed at least as rapidly as under the method of distribution being used as of the date of death. (The IRS uses the term "holder" and, although it does not specifically define the term, it seems to mean whoever is holding the income tax liability, no matter what other title that holder might have.)
- If any holder of such a policy dies before the annuity starting date, the entire interest in the policy will be distributed within 5 years after the death of holder.
- If any portion of the holder's interest is payable to, or for the benefit of, a designated beneficiary, such portions will be distributed in accordance with regulations over the life of the designated beneficiary or over a period not extending beyond the life expectancy of such beneficiary. Distributions are to begin no later than one year after the death or such later date as the Secretary of the Treasury may, by regulations, prescribe.
- If the holder of the annuity policy is not an individual, the primary annuitant will be treated as the holder of the policy for distribution purposes.

 In a nutshell, if the owner dies, (1) the entire policy value must be distributed within 5 years of the owner's death or (2) a life annuity option must be taken. If a policy issued before January 18, 1985, is exchanged for a new policy, the new policy must be subject to these distribution rules.

Options for Spouse Beneficiaries. If a surviving spouse is the beneficiary, successor owner, joint owner, or annuitant, the surviving spouse may step into the shoes of the owner and become the owner and annuitant of the policy. The spouse, as with the death of the annuitant, may also receive the proceeds in a lump sum or choose any of the settlement options available under the policy.

TABLE 7-2
Nonqualified Annuity Distributions at Death
(During Accumulation Phase)

Death of	Successor Owner or Beneficiary	Income Tax Status
Owner (who is not annuitant) or Owner/annuitant	Spouse: must receive the entire interest in the policy	Spouse becomes owner and deferral may continue without restriction. A lump sum may be taken.
Owner (who is not annuitant) or Owner/annuitant	Nonspouse: must receive the entire interest in the policy	Contract value must be entirely distributed within 5 years of death or must begin to be distributed within one year of death in the form of a life annuity or life expectancy annuity. A lump sum may be taken.
Annuitant (who is not owner)	Spouse beneficiary	Spouse may continue as new owner and annuitant of the policy and continue deferral without restriction or may choose lump sum or a settlement option.
Annuitant (who is not owner)	Nonspouse beneficiary	Beneficiary must pay income taxes due in the year of the annuitant's death unless the beneficiary elects (within 60 days of the annuitant's death) to take a life-income or installment payout. Beneficiary may take a lump-sum benefit.

Joint Owners. If the policy has joint owners, and the policy was issued after April 22, 1987, the above rules apply at the death of the first of the joint owners. In a jointly owned policy, at the death of either owner, the surviving owner becomes the person who must take receipt of the entire interest in the policy. This person, in effect, replaces any named policy beneficiary because this person is the one who must take the annuity distribution.

Note that having a joint owner does *not* prevent the forced distribution of the entire interest in the policy at the first owner's death. Also note that the required forced distribution is the policy value, which is not necessarily the same amount as a death benefit. Depending on the policy, the amount payable at the death of the owner may be reduced by surrender charges if they are still applicable at the time of the death.

Gift and Estate Taxation of Nonqualified Annuities

Gift Taxation

Policies Issued after April 22, 1987. If a policyowner gives a policy as a gift to another person and the policy was issued after April 22, 1987, the policyowner will have to pay ordinary income taxes on the gain in the annuity. The donor of the policy pays the tax on the gain that existed at the time the gift was made. Even though a person gives an annuity to someone else, he or she is still liable for the taxes. The donor cannot give away the gain. The donor no longer owns the policy but is still liable to pay the taxes on the built-in gain without having the annuity to use as a resource.

The recipient of the gifted annuity (the donee) will assume the annuity with a cost basis equal to (1) the donor's cost basis plus (2) the amount of gain on which the donor was required to pay taxes.

In essence, the recipient will have a cost basis equal to the annuity's cash value.

Example:	Luci gives her deferred annuity policy to her brother Jim. Luci's cost basis in the annuity is $40,000. It has now grown to $100,000. When Luci gives the policy to Jim, she is liable for the income taxes on $60,000 of gain ($100,000 − $40,000 = $60,000). Jim's $40,000 cost basis is carried over from Luci; he also is allowed to add the amount on which Luci paid taxes to his cost basis. By adding the additional $60,000 to the original $40,000 cost basis, Jim's total cost basis is now $100,000.

Policies Issued before April 23, 1987. When policies issued before April 23, 1987, are gifted, the owner (donor) does not recognize taxable gain in the policy until the person who is given the policy (the donee) surrenders it. However, any gain in the policy over the policy's value as of the date of the gift will be taxed to the person who received the policy.

Example:	Kim purchased a policy in 1985 for $30,000. It is now worth $160,000. Kim gives the deferred annuity policy to her brother, Kevin, to help him start a business. Kim will not have to recognize the gain in the policy until the year Kevin

surrenders the policy. The gain is $130,000 ($160,000 − $30,000 = $130,000). If Kevin later surrenders the policy when its value is $200,000, Kevin is responsible for paying tax on the gain from the point he became the new owner. Therefore Kevin will be responsible for the income taxes on $40,000 ($200,000 − $160,000 = $40,000).

Had Kim purchased the policy in 1995, Kim would have to recognize $130,000 ($160,000 − $30,000 = $130,000) as ordinary income in the year she gave the policy to Kevin.

Gifts to a Spouse. A policyowner may give a policy to his or her spouse without having to pay income tax on the gain in the policy. Gifts of policies to spouses are generally also exempt from gift taxes due to the unlimited gift tax marital deduction.

Furthermore, gifts to spouses that are considered "incident to a divorce" are also exempt from gift taxes. This normally occurs in the context of a divorce settlement where one spouse owns the annuity and pursuant to the divorce decree, the owner must give the annuity to the nonowner spouse. This type of transaction will not subject either spouse to gift taxes even when the transaction occurs after the two are no longer legally married, as long as it was incident to their divorce.

Gifts to Charities or Charitable Trusts. Gifts to charities or charitable trusts are not generally subject to gift tax. Therefore if an annuity owner chooses to give a deferred annuity to a charitable organization, neither the annuity owner nor the charitable organization will be subject to gift taxes. However, income taxes will still apply to the built-in gain. This can catch a generous donor off guard if he or she gives away an annuity and later finds out that income tax is due on an asset the donor just gave away.

Gifts of Immediate Annuity Income. If a person owns an immediate annuity and requests the insurance company to make the annuity payments to someone else, the owner is still liable for the ongoing income tax on the continual annuity income. The owner cannot give away the tax burden to the recipient of the money.

Estate Taxation

Deferred Annuities. With deferred annuities, the general rule under IRC Sec. 2039 (see Appendix B) is that the death benefit paid upon the death of the owner will be included in the deceased owner's estate. For example, if the death benefit is $86,000 and paid to a beneficiary, the deceased's estate will have to include the $86,000 annuity as an asset subject to federal estate taxes.

Because the death proceeds of the annuity are paid to a named beneficiary, however, the annuity itself will bypass the probate process. This means that the annuity is not subject to the claims of the deceased's creditors. In some states, however, although the annuity is not part of the probate process, the value of the annuity may be included in the probate inventory for purposes of determining attorney fees.

If the owner and the annuitant are two different people and the annuitant dies, the value of the annuity is not included in the annuitant's estate because he or she is not the owner.

Example:	Craig owns a $75,000 deferred annuity with his sister Elizabeth as the annuitant. If Craig dies, $75,000 will be included in Craig's estate for estate tax purposes. On the other hand, if Elizabeth dies, the value of the deferred annuity will not be included in her estate because she has no ownership or rights to the annuity. She is merely the measuring life.

Immediate Annuities. Immediate annuities are included in the estate of the deceased annuitant if that annuitant is also the owner. The same is true if the owner dies and the owner is not the annuitant. However, if the annuitant dies and the annuitant is not the owner, nothing is includible in the annuitant's estate because the annuitant had no ownership rights.

The value of the annuity depends on which type of immediate annuity was payable. A life-only immediate annuity will have zero value because no more annuity payments are payable at the annuitant's death.

An immediate annuity with a period certain that has not run its course will have its remaining value included in the insured/owner's estate. This value includible in the estate is the present value of the remaining payments.

Example: Sam purchased a life annuity with 10 years certain and died 6 years after he purchased the policy. Sam's estate will show the present value of the last 4 years of immediate annuity payments as an asset for federal estate tax calculations.

If the immediate annuity is a joint life annuity and either one of the joint owners dies, the annuity will be included in the estate of the first joint owner who dies. The value of the annuity is included in proportion to the premium actually paid by the deceased owner. If the deceased joint owner paid nothing toward the premium cost, the value of the annuity will be zero in the estate. If the two joint owners each paid 50 percent of the premium, the value of the annuity in the estate will be 50 percent of the value of the remaining payments.

If the two joint owners are husband and wife, the value in the first spouse's estate can be reduced by the unlimited marital deduction and therefore can be transferred to the surviving spouse without tax.

Charitable Beneficiaries. If the beneficiary is a qualified charitable organization, the death benefit payable to the charity is not subject to estate tax. Technically the death benefit amount is included in the estate tax return, but then it is 100 percent deductible as a charitable deduction against the state. Therefore the end result is that the annuity is not subject to estate tax.

QUALIFIED ANNUITIES

This section discusses tax-qualified annuities. Qualified annuities are funded with pretax dollars. They can be in the form of IRAs, SEP IRAs, tax-sheltered annuities (TSAs), SIMPLE IRAs, 401(k) plans, and pension and profit-sharing plans. Although Roth IRAs are funded with after-tax dollars, they are subject to many of the same rules as IRAs. The purpose of this section is to introduce the financial advisor to the general terms and rules governing annuities funded with qualified funds.

Ownership and Beneficiary Issues

IRAs, TSAs, and Roth IRAs are owned by the individual participant. None of these types of funds can have joint ownership. Therefore if a husband owns an IRA, it must be owned in the husband's name alone. It cannot be owned jointly by the husband and the wife. When financial advisors review their client's list of assets in the estate or financial planning process, the issue of ownership often arises. If the client is unsure of the ownership designation, it is always the best practice to verify ownership information with the qualified plan or IRA custodian.

Some qualified plans require that the participant's spouse must be named as the beneficiary of the plan. If the spouse will not be named as beneficiary, the spouse must first sign a waiver of his or her right to be named as beneficiary. This rule does not apply to IRAs.

Income Taxation of Qualified Annuities

Premiums and Cash Value Growth

Unlike nonqualified annuities, the premiums or contributions made to qualified policies are normally made on a pretax basis. This means in most instances the taxpayer may be able to deduct the premiums against his or her taxable income for the year.

The cash values continue to grow on a tax-deferred basis, exactly like a nonqualified annuity. The difference, however, is that the funds in qualified policies do not need to be invested in an annuity contract to receive tax deferral. Instead, they can be invested is almost any other type of investment—for example, mutual funds or stocks—and still enjoy the benefit of tax deferral.

Loans

A typical feature found in qualified plans is the participant's ability to borrow against the plan. Therefore certain annuities within qualified plans will have loan features. These loans follow the general rules for loans in qualified plans and do not carry the adverse income taxation rules applicable to nonqualified annuities.

Rollovers and Transfers

Qualified annuities do not follow the IRC Sec. 1035 exchange rules. Instead, qualified annuities have their own set of rules with respect to transferring qualified funds from one account to another.

rollover

There are two ways a person can make an IRA *rollover*. The first is to receive the money from the retirement account and deposit it into the new account. This is risky and can lead to tax penalties.

60-Day Rule. A participant has 60 days in which to take a qualified plan or IRA distribution and place those funds into a rollover IRA account. Rollovers can be done once a year. The IRS has not usually been flexible with taxpayers who have gone past the 60-day period.

If a person chooses to take the money and redeposit it, the law requires his or her employer to withhold 20 percent of the distribution for federal income taxes. This means that out of a $100,000 distribution, the person will receive only $80,000 ($100,000 minus the $20,000 sent to the IRS). To complete the rollover, he or she must come up with an additional $20,000. If the deposit is only $80,000, the $20,000 will be considered a taxable distribution. If the person is under age 59 ½, the undeposited amount will be subject to the 10 percent penalty tax for early distributions.

The IRS may waive the 60-day requirement when the failure to waive it would be against good conscience, including disaster, casualty, or other events beyond the control of the participant. The IRS will consider all appropriate facts and circumstances such as errors by the IRA custodian; delays due to death, disability, incarceration, hospitalization, postal error, or restrictions placed by a foreign country; the amount of time elapsed; and the use of the amount distributed.

The way to avoid this problem is to use the second rollover technique—the direct rollover or trustee-to-trustee transfer.

transfer

Trustee-to-Trustee Transfer. The IRA holder can move funds from one IRA to another an unlimited number of times during a year without being in violation of the 60-day rule as long as the transfer is completed on a "trustee-to-trustee" basis. This means that one financial institution must directly transfer the funds to the new financial institution without the funds ever going into the participant's hands. In a direct rollover or trustee-to-trustee transfer, no withholding is required.

Withdrawals, Distributions, and Penalty Taxes

Any withdrawal made from a qualified annuity is generally 100 percent taxable as ordinary income to the taxpayer. An IRS 10 percent penalty tax under IRC Sec. 72(t) applies to withdrawals and distributions made by an individual prior to age 59 ½. However, the major exceptions to this rule listed below are somewhat different from the exceptions for nonqualified annuities:

- distributions made on or after the participant is aged 59 ½
- distributions made to a beneficiary or the individual's estate on or after the death of the individual
- distributions attributable to the individual's disability
- distributions made to an employee after separation from service during or after the year of his or her attainment of age 55 (does not apply to IRAs)
- distributions made on account of a levy under Sec. 6331 on the qualified retirement plan
- distributions made for medical care but only to the extent allowable as a medical expense deduction for amounts paid during the taxable year for medical care
- distributions made under a qualified domestic relations order (QDRO). This does *not* apply to IRAs.
- distributions made by unemployed individuals for the payment of health insurance premiums. This applies to IRAs only.
- distributions made to pay qualified higher education expenses during the taxable year for the taxpayer, the taxpayer's spouse, and the child or grandchild of the taxpayer or the taxpayer's spouse. This applies to IRAs only.
- distributions that are qualified first-time home-buyer distributions. This applies to IRAs only.
- distributions that are part of a series of substantially equal periodic payments made for the life or life expectancy of the individual or the joint lives or joint life expectancy of the individual and his/her designated beneficiary. Three methods are available to determine substantially equal periodic payments: (1) life expectancy method (required minimum distribution), (2) fixed amortization method, and (3) fixed annuitization method.

These distributions are known as 72(t) or SEPP distributions. It is important to note that these distributions are not an annuitization but instead are a stream of withdrawals. These rules must be followed carefully. The participant must keep this special distribution in force for the longer of 5 years or until age 59 ½. If not, the IRS will retroactively charge the 10 percent penalty tax plus interest.

Distributions from Roth IRAs are taxed under a different set of rules. Contributions are withdrawn tax free. Distributions of earnings from Roth IRAs can be income tax free if the participant holds the Roth IRA for at least 5 years and is

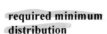

- age 59 ½
- the beneficiary of the participant's Roth IRA
- disabled
- a first-time home buyer

required minimum distribution

Required Minimum Distribution Rules

When qualified plan holders reach age 70 ½ or retirement age, if later, the tax code provides that the participant must begin to take distributions from the account, or an *age 70 ½ IRS penalty tax* is imposed. For IRA holders, only age 70 ½ is used.

age 70 ½ IRS penalty tax

The first distribution must be taken by April 1 following the year in which the participant turns age 70 ½ or retires, if applicable. This date is technically referred to as the *required beginning date*.

required beginning date

The second distribution must be taken by December 31 of the year following the year the IRA holder turns age 70 ½. Each distribution thereafter must be taken by December 31.

Roth IRAs have no minimum distribution rules during the lifetime of the participant. However, these rules do apply upon the participant's death. Therefore if a Roth IRA owner dies, the minimum distribution rules that apply to traditional IRAs apply to Roth IRAs as though the Roth IRA owner died before his or her required beginning date. (See the detailed discussion under the heading "Death Benefits" below.)

If the participant waits until April 1 of the year following the year in which he or she turns age 70 ½ to take his or her first distribution, because the second distribution is also due that same year, in many cases the participant will take the first two minimum distributions in the same calendar year. To avoid a double distribution in one year, the participant can take the first distribution in the calendar he or she turns 70 ½ and not wait until April 1 of the following year.

Example:	Chuck turned age 70 in December 2008, and 70 ½ in June 2009. Therefore Chuck's first required distribution is due on April 1, 2010. Chuck's second distribution is due by December 31, 2010. If Chuck does not want the burden of paying income taxes on two distributions in 2010, Chuck can take his first distribution by December 31, 2009, and the second distribution by December 31, 2010.

The dollar amount of the distribution is determined by the RMD Uniform Lifetime Table, as shown in Table 7-3. This table applies to all participants except those whose spouses are named as sole beneficiary and are more than 10 years younger than the participant. In this case, the Joint and Last Survivor Table is used to determine the minimum distribution. (See Appendix C, Table II, for excerpts from this table, along with instructions on how to use it.)

TABLE 7-3
RMD Uniform Lifetime Table—Distribution Period

Age	Distribution Period	Age	Distribution Period
70	27.4	93	9.6
71	26.5	94	9.1
72	25.6	95	8.6
73	24.7	96	8.1
74	23.8	97	7.6
75	22.9	98	7.1
76	22.0	99	6.7
77	21.2	100	6.3
78	20.3	101	5.9
79	19.5	102	5.5
80	18.7	103	5.2
81	17.9	104	4.9
82	17.1	105	4.5
83	16.3	106	4.2
84	15.5	107	3.9
85	14.8	108	3.7
86	14.1	109	3.4
87	13.4	110	3.1
88	12.7	111	2.9
89	12.0	112	2.6
90	11.4	113	2.4
91	10.8	114	2.1
92	10.2	115+	1.9

To illustrate, Chuck has an account balance of $148,727.20 as of December 31, 2008. The distribution period factor is 27.4 years, according to the RMD Uniform Lifetime Table. His required minimum distribution is $5,428, calculated as follows:

$$\frac{\$148,727.20}{27.4} = \$5,428$$

The penalty tax for a participant who does not take the required minimum distribution is 50 percent of the amount that should have been distributed but was not. In the above example, if Chuck's required minimum distribution is $5,428 and is due by April 1, 2010, and Chuck does not take the distribution until later in 2010, Chuck must pay a penalty tax of 50 percent of $5,428, or $2,714.

If a person owns more than one IRA, special rules apply. If a taxpayer owns more than one IRA account, the taxpayer may take his or her total required distribution from any one of the IRAs. The taxpayer does not have to take the proportionate amount out of each IRA policy; the policies may instead be aggregated. Amounts taken as an IRA owner may not be aggregated with amounts taken as a beneficiary for purposes **minimum distribution** of meeting the *minimum distribution requirements*. Similarly **requirements** distributions form Roth IRAs and 403(b) contracts or annuities may not be aggregated with traditional IRA distributions to meet the minimum distribution requirements for either the IRA or the 403(b) contract; the taxpayer must take out exactly the required minimum distribution separately from each annuity. However, owners of multiple 403(b) accounts may aggregate required distributions from one contract in the same manner as that allowed with multiple IRAs.

Death Benefits

The death benefits from qualified annuities are 100 percent taxable to the beneficiary. Because there is generally no cost basis in the policy, the death benefits are fully taxable.

The beneficiary's options available at death depend on whether the participant died before or after the required beginning date. The required beginning date is normally April 1 following the year the participant turns age 70 ½. If the participant dies prior to this date, the beneficiary has the following two choices for calendar years beginning January 1, 2003:

- The entire interest must be distributed by the end of the calendar year in which the fifth anniversary of the participant's death falls.
- The benefit can be payable over the life or life expectancy of the designated beneficiary, and benefits must begin within one year

of death. (See Appendix C, Table III, for the Single Life Expectancy Table for beneficiaries.)

A spouse beneficiary can roll over the account into his or her own name, or he or she must begin to receive payments by the later of
*   the end of the year (December 31) after the year in which the participant died
*   the end of the year (December 31) in which the deceased would have turned age 70 ½

If the participant dies after the required beginning date, the beneficiary has these two choices:

*   The remaining account balance must be distributed at least as rapidly as under the method in effect as of the death of the participant.
*   It can be distributed over the longer of the beneficiary's life expectancy or the remaining life expectancy of the deceased (just prior to death).

designated beneficiary   If no *designated beneficiary* is named (that is, a beneficiary that is a natural person), then the amount must be distributed over the deceased's remaining life expectancy. Naming a charity or the estate as a beneficiary is the equivalent of having no designated beneficiary. In these cases, the longest time frame the charity or estate can stretch out the death benefit is over the remaining life expectancy of the deceased. In practical terms, for the charity at least, the lump-sum option is almost always taken.

The participant's spouse has the option to continue the annuity as the new owner and annuitant at the participant's death. Or the spouse may choose a lump-sum or settlement option.

Beginning for distributions in 2007, a nonspouse designated beneficiary of a qualified plan, a tax sheltered annuity, or an eligible IRC Section 457 governmental plan may make a direct rollover of the proceeds into an inherited IRA. The rollover must be made by means of a trustee-to-trustee transfer. The transfer will be treated as an eligible rollover distribution.

The inherited IRA created under this provision is subject to the same required minimum distributions as for any IRA payable to a designated beneficiary.

TABLE 7-4
Required Minimum Distribution Rules

Beneficiary	Death Before Required Beginning Date*	Death After Required Beginning Date*
Spouse who does not roll over account into own name	Can defer distributions until deceased participant would have been age 70 ½	Life expectancy of surviving spouse used
Spousal rollover	Available	Available
Nonspouse named as beneficiary who does not roll over account into inherited IRA	Life expectancy of the beneficiary (must begin within one year of IRA owner's death)	Life expectancy of beneficiary used
Nonspouse named as beneficiary wishing to roll over funds to an inherited IRA	Available	Available
Charity	5-year rule; full distribution by end of fifth year after year of death	Remaining life expectancy of deceased used
Estate	5-year rule; full distribution by the end of fifth year after year of death	Remaining life expectancy of deceased used

* These are the slowest distributions allowed. However, lump sums and faster distributions are permitted.

Gift and Estate Taxation of Qualified Annuities

Qualified annuities cannot be gifted, sold, transferred, or assigned to any other person or entity. These annuities can be owned only by the participant. To make a gift, the participant would have to cash in the annuity, take the proceeds subject to income taxes, and give a gift of cash to the other party.

The full value of the account is includible in the participant's estate upon death. The participant may, however, name a charity as beneficiary and, as such, the estate will receive a charitable deduction for the full value of the annuity, thus eliminating both estate and income taxes due on the death benefit.

IMPLEMENTING AND SERVICING THE PLAN

Implementing the Plan

Completing the Annuity Application

The advisor is responsible for completing the application, obtaining all the required information, including signatures, and providing all disclosure information to the applicant. The application, with the advisor's and applicant's signatures, becomes part of the policy, which is a legal contract. By signing the application, the advisor and applicant represent that all the information in the application is true.

When completing the application, the advisor should focus on the following objectives:

- obtaining all the information requested, leaving no questions unanswered. Unanswered and/or incomplete questions slow down the application processing considerably.
- completing the application in the applicant's presence
- accurately recording all information as provided by the applicant
- obtaining necessary signatures
- completing a suitability form for variable annuities
- providing the applicant with all receipts, disclosure documentation, and the appropriate annuity buyer's guide according to the laws of the state and the requirements of the insurer

Reviewing the Application. Check the application for completeness and accuracy. Ask a staff member or other person neutral to the case to review it. A fresh set of eyes may discover missing information or errors in the application. Process the application and follow up on any additional requirements promptly.

Most states prohibit advisors from making any changes on an application once the applicant has signed it. If an error is discovered, arrangements must be made to return the application to the applicant for any needed changes. Never use correction fluid; errors must be crossed out and initialed by the applicant, or a new application must be taken. Changing or adding information by anyone other than the applicant is a misdemeanor in most states. Any information the advisor wishes to provide the company can be entered in the advisor's statement.

Proper Disclosure

Annuity Disclosure. To assist consumers in determining whether a fixed annuity is appropriate for them, the National Association of Insurance Commissioners (NAIC) has developed a model regulation for annuities that it offered for adoption by the states in 1999 called "Annuity Disclosure Model Regulation, Section 5B(3)." The purpose of this regulation (which is discussed further in chapter 8) is to provide standards for the disclosure of certain minimum information about all fixed annuity contracts containing nonguaranteed values to protect consumers and foster consumer education. The regulation specifies the minimum information that must be disclosed and the method for disclosing it in connection with the sale of annuity contracts. The goal of this regulation is to ensure that purchasers of annuity contracts understand certain basic features of annuity contracts.

The decision to buy an annuity product is very important and one that is not right for everyone. The regulation states, "An applicant for an annuity contract shall be given both a disclosure document (and the appropriate NAIC Buyer's Guide to Fixed Deferred Annuities) at the time of application in a face-to-face meeting or, in the case of a sale conducted by means of direct solicitation through the telephone, mails, the Internet, or other mass communication media, within two (2) business days after the application is received by the insurer." Accordingly the model regulation recommends that the following types of information should be disclosed in the document:

- the guaranteed, nonguaranteed, and determinable elements of the contract and an explanation of how those elements operate
- an explanation of the initial interest rate, the duration of the rate, and a statement that the rates may change and are not guaranteed
- information about periodic income options both on a guaranteed and nonguaranteed basis
- any reductions in the amount of the contract value that will result from withdrawals or surrenders
- an explanation of how the contract owner may gain access to contract values
- information about the death benefit, if any, and how it will be calculated
- a summary of the federal tax status of the contract and any penalties imposed on withdrawals
- an explanation of how any riders affect the contract

Not all states have fully adopted the model regulation. Some insurance companies offer a disclosure document even if the particular state does not require it. This will help limit client disappointment by using this disclosure. It is another tool in the sales process to help explain the features and benefits of the particular annuity under consideration. In fact, the required disclosures can serve as an excellent checklist for prospects and advisors. These points could be used as the agenda in a meeting where a client wishes to explore his or her annuity options.

Communicating the Annuity Application Process to the Applicant

Once the annuity application is complete and the first premium or single premium is collected, it is important to inform the applicant what to expect over the next several weeks. The applicant may have many questions and uncertainties about the annuity purchased and the process of obtaining it. By being forthright and communicating clearly what to expect, the advisor builds trust and solidifies the advisor-client relationship through professional behavior. This can prevent unexpected surprises that may upset the applicant and cause a change of mind about the purchase of the annuity product. You want the applicant to feel good about the decision to buy the annuity by reassuring him or her that the buy decision was the right one.

Communicating the application processing is an excellent opportunity for you to reinforce the relationship you are developing with the applicant. The advisor should review and explain the processing time frame to the applicant. Explain when you expect to receive the annuity policy, and note that you will deliver it in person at that time. Assure the client that if any unforeseen administrative delays occur in producing the contract, you will contact him or her immediately. Also explain that you will call to schedule the delivery interview when you receive the policy and have checked it for accuracy.

Advisor Follow-up of the Annuity Application Process

Ongoing Communication With the Applicant. Keep the applicant informed of the annuity application's progress from submission to the insurance company until a formal policy is produced for delivery. This increases trust and builds the relationship. Always be positive when communicating with the prospect. Complaining about or criticizing any department in your company only creates doubt about you and your company's ability to deliver on promises. If there are delays in the process, explain the situation simply and honestly. By staying in touch, you demonstrate your commitment to service and your personal interest in the prospect.

Creating a Client File. Keep a file with complete and accurate records, including copies of forms, correspondence, fact finders, phone contacts, review sessions, and a summary of what was discussed or done in any conversations or follow-up activities. The file should also include copies of sales literature and illustrations showing the amount of coverage, the plan, and the premium. You should also send a thank-you note in a timely manner.

Company Requirements. Insurers adopt their own requirements relating to the annuity application and delivery process. Delivery receipts, disclosure notices, privacy disclosures, and other forms may have to be distributed and signatures obtained. Be sure you are familiar with the application processing and delivery requirements of your company.

Summary

Although completing the annuity application may seem to be an afterthought in the selling/planning process, it is the first step in implementing the plan. It needs to be done properly so that it can be processed promptly and smoothly. Also your adherence to state, FINRA, and company compliance procedures will help to sufficiently inform the client, legally protect you, and expedite the issuance of the annuity contract.

Delivering the Annuity Policy

Now that you have received the issued annuity policy, it is time to visit your new client and perform some very important functions that will help you build your practice. This step in the sales process must not be taken lightly, for it offers an occasion to strengthen the sale and the advisor-client relationship and to build future sales opportunities.

Preparing for the Delivery

A small amount of time spent preparing for the policy delivery enables the advisor to reinforce his or her commitment to the client. This also greatly enhances the advisor's professional image in the client's eyes. When delivering the annuity policy, the advisor should take the necessary time to educate the client about the policy. This can help avoid embarrassing and potentially costly misunderstandings regarding future claims.

Therefore when you receive the policy, carefully check it over for accuracy to be sure that no mistakes have been made. Mistakes can happen, and they should be caught before you deliver the policy. Mistakes, however, are not the only reason why a policy may be issued that is different from what was requested in the application. The issuing company may have made changes to policy benefits because of availability or eligibility. You should understand any changes that have been made to the contract by the company so that you can fully explain them to your client.

Prepare the policy for delivery by including with it any approved brochure, sales literature, or other material that supports you, your company, or the client's decision to buy this annuity product. Presenting this information and the policy in a handsome yet inexpensive policy wallet can enhance the value and image of the policy—and you. Most companies require that the policy be delivered to the insured within 30 to 60 days of the advisor's receipt of the policy.

Conducting the Delivery Interview

The delivery interview has several objectives.

Reinforce the Buying Decision. It is common for buyers to feel that they made a mistake in a purchase or that there are other product options that may represent better planning solutions for them. This is known as buyer's remorse. It is critical that you answer any questions your client may have and reinforce his or her decision to buy the annuity policy. If you do not and the client has concerns, there is a danger that the client will lapse the policy, exercise the policy's free-look provision, or succumb to the competition's attempts to replace it.

Review the Policy. The advisor is required by law in most states to fully explain the policy. This is in the advisor's best interest because most people have very little knowledge of insurance products and appreciate a clear explanation of the policy.

Build the Advisor-Client Relationship. Continued contact helps to build trust. You want the client to see you as his or her financial advisor, a relationship that is based on feelings of respect and trust. Commit yourself to serving and servicing your clients.

Obtain Required Forms. In today's environment of disclosure and sensitivity to compliance, there are a number of forms that you either need to complete, have the client sign, or both. In addition, a delivery receipt and, in most states, an outline of coverage must be delivered to the policyowner. Failure to comply with these requirements can lead to the policy's not being put in force and the client's not being properly protected. It is critical to deliver all required documents and obtain completed forms with signatures at the time of delivery.

Develop Other Sales Opportunities. There may be other sales opportunities that were uncovered in the fact-finding process that you can now revisit. The client may have an interest in and need for other insurance products, investments, or estate planning that you can provide. You should also ask for referrals. If you have done a professional job, you have earned the right to ask the client if you can speak to people whom he or she knows who may benefit from your products and services.

Servicing the Plan

Maintaining Records

Many companies today have file inspection and maintenance requirements as a routine part of the compliance process. In all cases, follow your company's procedures, which may require that you keep records of such things as the following:

- fact-finding forms
- written notes describing basic events and discussions with the client
- contact log with dates and topics discussed
- copies of quotes or illustrations
- copies of applications and related materials
- copies of correspondence with the client

Generally no original documents or blank signed documents should be in a file. Original documents should have been submitted to the company, and blank signed documents are strictly forbidden.

Periodic Reviews

The periodic review covers many objectives of the advisor-client relationship. Relationship building is fostered by regular contact, which should lead to policy persistency, cross-selling, networking, and referral opportunities. Proper servicing is based on timely reviews and contacts, and prompt responses to client requests. Any changes within the contract, such as asset allocation changes in variable annuities or even beneficiary changes, should be done with your assistance. Any changes made to the annuity policy should be made to conform to changes in the client's situation. Although the traditional review period is annually, a mutually agreed-upon interval should be established based on the client's circumstances and needs.

Keeping in touch by various methods is an important part of this process. Newsletters, birthday or anniversary phone calls, and periodic mailings about topics of interest continue to put you in front of the client, build prestige, and foster the advisor-client relationship.

Retaining clients can have a huge effect on your bottom line. Here are some tips for conserving your existing clients:

- *Relate one-to-one.* All business is personal, and no relationship is static.
- *Reinforce relationships.* Seize every opportunity to learn about your client's needs, dreams, and realities. Communicate and reinforce the reason your client chose you. People do business with people, not companies.
- *Exceed expectations.* Meeting clients' expectations is the price of admission into today's market. Strive to exceed expectations to create client commitment and loyalty. Expect to lose business if you deliver only what the client needs because he or she probably has many avenues to get it. Instead, discover and deliver what the client wants. If you do not add value, you are no longer necessary.
- *Be an expert listener.* Demonstrate your knowledge and gain client loyalty by asking the right questions and listening closely to the answers.
- *Differentiate yourself.* Do not compete on interest rates but rather on the value of your expertise and products. Differentiate your services in clients' minds by providing choice, research, responsiveness, and superior knowledge. Most clients do not buy on interest rates or return on investment alone. Your job is to offer the best overall value, not the lowest price. Educate clients about the value of your annuity products and service.
- *Establish strategic alliances.* Look to all of your clients and even competitors for joint opportunities that will add value to your clients. Introduce your clients to your other clients who can build value in their situations.
- *Become referable.* To get referrals, you need to be referable. This means you must offer more than a product. You have to offer a process and, even better, a memorable experience. *You have to earn the trust of your clients.*

Expediting the Claims Process

At some point, the beneficiary or beneficiaries of annuities in force at the death of the owner/annuitant will file claims under their annuity policies. The policy outlines the procedures that they must follow to collect on a death claim. Failure to follow the procedures may jeopardize the prompt receipt of benefit payments. Therefore you can play an important role in expediting the claim process that is a part of the ongoing service you will provide.

Notification of Loss

The beneficiary or his or her representative must initially notify the insurer that a death claim is being made. Policies often specify that this be done promptly or as soon as is reasonably possible. In most cases, the notification will be by telephone. However, all insurers will also want a written claim form to be submitted subsequently.

Some insurers initially do little other than send the claim forms to the beneficiary/claimant with instructions to have them completed and returned to the insurer. Many insurers, however, are very proactive and work with the beneficiary/claimant to see that all necessary paperwork is properly completed. If the deceased is your client or even if you have been assigned to assist in processing the death claim of an orphan policyholder, be sure that you do it in person. You will need to be sensitive to the loss of the beneficiary's loved one and to exercise decorum in handling the claims process. This is a service opportunity that can lead to goodwill between you and the deceased family and can result in subsequent sales opportunities or referred leads.

Proof of Loss

The insurer will require a written proof of loss. The proof of loss required is a claimant's statement that the beneficiary must complete (with your assistance) and sign and a death certificate, which is easily obtained from the county coroner's office.

Payment of Benefits

Benefits are payable as soon as the insurance company receives the required proof of loss. The beneficiary is entitled to the benefit payment in either a lump sum or in accordance with one of the settlement options in the annuity contract. This represents an opportunity to advise the beneficiary about the tax ramifications of the various payment options, as well as the possible reinvestment consequences. Providing financial advice within the context of a death claim is one important aspect of the selling/planning process that is seldom done but that requires adequate fact finding and careful deliberation.

Summary of the Selling/Planning and Application Process

1. **Initial interview**—The advisor explains the general need to plan for retirement and the financing alternatives for funding it. He or she gathers information about the prospect's goals, priorities, and financial and human resources.
2. **Analysis of the information**—The advisor, using facts gathered in the interview, designs a plan that fits the client's needs and budget. This plan may include annuity products.
3. **Second interview**—A second appointment is usually required during which the advisor makes his or her recommendations.
4. **Application and required forms**—The application must be completed accurately and in its entirety. Other forms such as a privacy notice, suitability, and replacement disclosures must be delivered. The advisor must provide the insurer with a statement about the applicant. The advisor (in most states) must furnish the applicant with an annuity disclosure statement for fixed annuities and an annuity buyer's guide prior to accepting a signed application. A 1035 exchange does not require a cash deposit with the application.
5. **Premium deposit and receipt**—When a premium deposit is made with the application, a receipt must be given to any prospect.
6. **Explanation of the application process**—Advisors can alleviate any concerns or misunderstandings that applicants may have in the initial stage of policy issuance by explaining the process that takes place from the submission of the application until the policy is produced.
7. **Application submission to the insurer**—After reviewing the application for accuracy, the advisor is legally obligated to forward the application and premium deposit (if one was paid) to the home office without delay.
8. **Policy issue**—If the applicant is financially suitable, the policy is issued and sent to the advisor for personal delivery to the new client.
9. **Policy delivery**—The advisor must schedule a delivery appointment, during which the entire annuity policy is explained. All required delivery receipts and disclosure forms must be signed by the advisor and client and returned to the insurer.
10. **Policy service**—The advisor should schedule regular communications with the client to maintain and build the professional relationship. He or she should perform annual or other periodic reviews to see that retirement funding objectives reflect the current and possibly changing needs of the client. The advisor should assist and monitor any processing of beneficiary or asset allocation changes within the annuity.

Summary

The delivery and service aspects of the selling/planning process are where the advisor proves his or her worth to the client. These two functions provide the advisor with many opportunities to develop the advisor-client relationship and to cultivate future sales opportunities. If the functions are performed properly, the advisor earns the right to be referred to the client's personal friends and acquaintances as well as business contacts.

ANNUITIES AND FINANCIAL PLANNING

Relationship of Annuities to Comprehensive Financial Needs

Comprehensive financial planning involves examining a prospect's overall financial affairs, not just his or her potential need for annuities. As part of the fact-finding process, you need to ask the prospect questions about his or her overall financial and personal situation as it exists now and into the future, considering goals and likely outcomes. Depending on the extent to which the prospect has already planned for current and future financial needs, you may find opportunities to educate the prospect beyond the need for annuities. This could lead to cross-selling opportunities and building a stronger advisor-client relationship. The following overview of related financial planning topics includes concepts referred to in the retirement planning fact-finder in chapter 4 that you will want to learn more about if you hope to be successful in the broader financial services market.

To participate in the broader market, you must be properly licensed to advise about and/or sell products other than fixed-interest or indexed annuity products. However, you need to be careful not to go beyond the bounds of your authority because some of the planning requirements of this broader market need the counsel and drafting expertise of an attorney. This advice should be put in proper perspective; it is not meant to discourage you from being an active financial advisor to your clients. Also it is important for you to keep in mind that other financial services professionals are now aware of annuity products. In some cases, they may even be advising about and/or selling them. Be prepared to work with these other professionals as part of a financial planning team if the opportunity or need arises.

Role of Annuities in Estate Planning

There is more to estate planning than simply saving transfer taxes although that sometimes appears to be the primary or only focus. The goal of estate planning is to fulfill the wishes of the individual regarding the disposition of property during life and ultimately the disposition of his or her property at death.

Because of the enormous potential costs of funding retirement, a person's assets may be severely depleted or his or her retirement lifestyle compromised if not planned for appropriately. Immediate annuities and estate concerns are inextricably intertwined as both are concerned with the preservation of assets. Deferred annuities enhance the value of financial assets within a person's estate through the deferral of taxation on wealth accumulation prior to and subsequent to retirement, and through the reduction of income taxation on Social Security retirement benefits.

Asset Protection

One feature of annuities that is often overlooked is that they can be used to protect the owner's assets from creditors, depending on the type of annuity chosen and applicable state law. This protection is unique to life insurance products, and it cannot be provided by stocks, bonds, mutual funds, or any other investment.

In most states, the person who invests money in an annuity is usually assured that those funds within the contract are protected from creditors. This protection may not exist in all situations. Be sure to check with your company before mentioning this feature; be sure to check also with your client's attorney.

Estate Inclusion

One aspect of an individual's ownership of either deferred or immediate annuity products is their inclusion in the estate of the owner. This leads to the inevitable estate taxation of these products based on the value (or commuted value) at the time of death that must be paid for from the deceased owner's estate, leaving less money for his or her heirs. You need to have a working knowledge of the consequences of estate taxation on the value of either nonqualified or qualified annuity products because they may affect other areas of your client's financial planning. It is important to apprise your clients that although they may use annuities as part of an overall wealth accumulation strategy to fund their financial needs during retirement, the value of these annuities may contribute to the shrinkage of your clients' estates after death because of the estate taxes that annuities generate. This is another factor that points to the need for clients periodically to examine their life insurance coverage to ensure that it provides the liquidity to pay their estate tax liability and to take maximum advantage of other estate planning tools that can help in the management and distribution of wealth before and after death.

Estate Planning Concepts and Documents

The following material briefly looks at some of the more important basic estate planning concepts and documents that might come into play in a discussion of retirement planning and/or other uses for annuities. Your job as a financial advisor is to make your clients aware of these concepts and documents and how they may affect the clients' lives. Because you cannot practice law (unless you are a licensed attorney), you are prohibited from giving specific legal advice or drafting documents. Nonetheless you can make your clients aware of the need to periodically review their estate plans and the corresponding documents. These should be reviewed every 3 to 5 years, or whenever important changes occur that would affect their contents and purpose.

Will. A will is a legal document that specifies how an individual wishes his or her property to be distributed upon death. Wills are governed by state law, which determines their validity. State law also determines what happens if a person dies without having a valid will. In these cases, property is distributed under state intestacy laws, which apportion the property according to family relationships. State intestacy laws typically do not reflect the way an individual would want his or her property distributed at death.

A will names an executor who is responsible for administering the estate under the jurisdiction of the probate (or surrogate) court in the county where the deceased was residing at the time of death. Normally it is recommended that either a bank or an individual who is both trustworthy and younger than the testator be named as the executor. A well-drafted will can serve to reduce or even eliminate family squabbles and disagreements over the deceased's assets.

Deferred Annuities Can Reduce Estate Costs

Probate avoidance is an important concept. If assets are in deferred annuities, they escape not only probate, but in many states they also escape the estate attorney's administration fee on those nonprobated assets. This helps conserve the estate for the deceased's heirs.

EXAMPLE: In one state, the first $100,000 of estate assets is subject to a 5 percent attorney's fee, with a sliding scale that reduces as the total size of the estate gets larger. Thus, an estate of $500,000 could easily cost $12,000 to $14,000 in estate administration fees alone.

Power of Attorney. A power of attorney is a document that is legally signed by one person authorizing another person to act on behalf of the signer. These documents are sometimes used, for example, at house closings when one spouse cannot be present. Another example is when a parent creates a power of attorney to give an adult child access to a bank account.

general power of attorney

A *general power of attorney* grants specific and limited powers. Sometimes it has an expiration date, but often it does not. A general power of attorney instantly becomes invalid when the signer becomes mentally or physically incapacitated. In many instances, this is the key time when the power to deal with property is needed.

durable power of attorney

Durable Power of Attorney. A *durable power of attorney* grants authority to a designated person to act on behalf of the signer and continues in effect after his or her incapacity. A durable power of attorney facilitates quick action and avoids unnecessary court intervention.

springing durable power of attorney

Springing Durable Power of Attorney. A variation of the durable power of attorney is the *springing durable power of attorney.* The springing durable power of attorney is almost the opposite of the general power of attorney. It remains dormant until disability or incapacity occurs.

living will

Living Will. A *living will* is a legal document that describes the types of medical treatment your senior client wishes to receive and also specifies the types of medical treatment he or she does not wish to receive. The purpose of a living will is to let others know of your senior client's medical wishes if he or she is terminally ill or in a vegetative state and unable to communicate.

health care power of attorney

Health Care Power of Attorney. A *health care power of attorney* is usually a companion document to a well-drafted living will. Although a living will makes your senior client's medical treatment wishes known, it does not guarantee that these wishes will be followed. Someone still has to make necessary medical decisions regarding whether or not to continue treatment. This is often a difficult and emotional decision; close relatives are reluctant to let their loved one die. A health care power of attorney is a signed and witnessed legal document that designates the person your senior client wants to make important medical decisions about his or her care. Given the difficult nature of a decision that often amounts to termination of treatment and death, serious thought needs to be given to naming this individual.

trust

Trusts. A *trust* is a legal vehicle with four key components: a corpus, a grantor, a trustee, and a beneficiary (or beneficiaries). The property transferred into a trust is called the corpus. The person who transfers the property into the trust is called the grantor. The person or persons for whom the trust assets are to be used is the beneficiary or beneficiaries.

The trustee both holds and manages the corpus for the benefit of the beneficiary or beneficiaries, according to a trust agreement. The trust agreement is a contract between the grantor and trustee, who is the legal owner of the trust corpus (that is, the cash or property in the trust). The trust agreement contains the provisions that act as the instructions to the trustee from the grantor regarding what can and cannot be done with the trust property.

A-B trust

A-B Tax Plan Trusts—The *A-B trust* has estate tax savings as one of its primary objectives. Its focus is preservation of the exemption equivalent available to the first spouse to die. This is accomplished by placing assets outside the full control of the surviving spouse. At the death of the grantor, the deceased's property is divided into two parts. Part A goes to the surviving spouse. This portion of the property will qualify for the marital deduction, and there will be no estate tax due on this portion at the first death. Part B is a credit equivalent/exclusion bypass trust (CEBT). Often the spouse is permitted a life income from these assets but has no control over the eventual disposition of the B trust property. Assets in the B trust do not form part of the surviving spouse's estate and thus are not subject to estate taxation at the second death.

The nonmarital B trust can also be used to provide the surviving spouse with additional income and even limited amounts of principal to meet retirement living expenses without causing the trust corpus to be included in the surviving spouse's estate. However, the real purpose of the B trust is to preserve the full estate tax credit for the grantor spouse.

The choice of one framework over another depends on the senior's financial status, family situation, and personal preferences. Although the use of an A-B trust plan can save taxes, a senior client and his or her family may reject the idea of any limits being placed on the survivor's access to property.

Role of Annuities in Income Tax Planning

There are many tax issues that are of real concern to annuity owners, especially seniors who are the primary market segment that purchases them. Knowledge of these issues will help you to enhance your value to this market segment. Although you should not be preparing to give tax advice (unless you are qualified and your contract or practice permits it), you may nonetheless have an opportunity to inform older prospects and clients that they can benefit from such advice and that you can help them obtain it.

Here are several tax areas with which you may want to be familiar:

- gains from the sale of a principal residence
- capital gain rules on the sale of capital assets (stocks, bonds, and mutual funds)
- the income tax treatment of death benefits paid to beneficiaries from within deferred annuities
- the last-in-first-out (LIFO) tax treatment of withdrawals from deferred annuities
- the IRS penalties for early withdrawals (before age 59 ½) from qualified plans, IRAs, and nonqualified annuities
- tax advantages and distribution rules for IRAs, pensions, and other qualified retirement plans
- the income and estate tax ramifications to an estate for income in respect of a decedent that is caused by the transfer of funds from within qualified plans to heirs of the deceased planholder
- rules on the taxation of Social Security retirement benefits
- tax deferral on the accumulation of cash values within deferred annuities
- tax-favored treatment of benefits paid from immediate annuities or deferred annuity settlement options under the annuity exclusion ratio rule

Using an Annuity to Reduce Taxation of Social Security Benefits

Generally Social Security benefits are received tax free for federal income tax purposes, but they can be taxed for seniors with high income. The amount of a senior client's Social Security benefits that is taxable depends on whether the person is receiving income from sources in addition to Social Security. To find out if any of your client's benefits are taxable, begin by totaling the following items:

- the individual's adjusted gross income
- half the client's Social Security benefits
- tax-exempt interest such as interest on municipal bonds
- exclusions such as tax-free foreign earned income and foreign housing

Compare the total to the applicable threshold to calculate the portion of Social Security benefits that will be taxed. The thresholds for determining the potential taxation of Social Security retirement benefits are shown in Table 7-5.

TABLE 7-5		
Thresholds for Taxation of Social Security Retirement Benefits		
Single Filer	**Amount Taxable**	**Married Filing Jointly**
$25,000	Taxation of up to 50% of Social Security benefits	$32,000
$34,000	Taxation of up to 85% of Social Security benefits	$44,000

One way that seniors may reduce their taxes is to roll over some investments that are producing taxable income into a tax-deferred annuity product. The cash accumulation inside a tax-deferred annuity does not count toward the provisional income used in determining the potential taxation of Social Security retirement benefits. Also deferred annuity products can help to reduce the overall amount of current income that these seniors pay.

Example: Retiree Mr. Johnson is over age 65, collecting Social Security retirement benefits, and married filing a joint federal income tax return. He and his wife take a standard deduction of $11,400 and personal exemptions that total $6,100. Mr. Johnson is currently earning $10,000 in taxable interest income that he really does not need. What if he transfers those funds that generate this current income into a tax-deferred annuity? The exposure of his Social Security benefits to income taxation—as well as his total tax liability—is significantly reduced.

As shown in Table 7-6, the transfer of funds from taxable vehicles that generate $10,000 in currently taxable interest into tax-deferred funds yields a total federal income tax savings of $2,625 (or 26.25 percent) even though Mr. Johnson is in only a 15 percent tax bracket. This consists of $1,500 in direct income tax savings and an additional $1,125 in indirect income tax savings that result from the reduction in the amount of taxable Social Security benefits.

Details of the calculations of taxable Social Security benefits under Mr. Johnson's "current" and "what-if" scenarios are shown in Table 7-7.

TABLE 7-6
What-if Tax Calculation Program Prepared for Retiree Mr. Johnson
Summary Based on Tax Return for Recent Tax Year

	Current	What if	Difference
8a. Taxable interest	$10,000.00	$ 0.00	$10,000.00
9. Dividend income	5,000.00	5,000.00	0.00
16a. Total pensions and annuities	30,000.00	30,000.00	0.00
20a. Total Social Security benefits	15,000.00	15,000.00	0.00
Total income from all sources	**$60,000.00**	**$50,000.00**	**$10,000.00**
Federal income tax	**(5,338.00)**	**(2,713.00)**	**(2,625.00)**
Net income after federal tax	**$54,662.00**	**$47,287.00**	**$ 7,375.00**
Federal tax bracket	15.0%	15.0%	
Total Social Security benefits	$15,000.00	$15,000.00	$ 0.00
Taxable Social Security benefits	12,750.00	5,250.00	7,500.00
Federal tax paid on Social Security	1,913.00	788.00	1,125.00

Although decisions about retirement should not be based solely on their tax impact, income tax ramifications should be considered. When planning, it is necessary to examine all the alternatives. The best choice may be the one that minimizes seniors' taxes.

Role of Annuities in Long-Term Care Planning

The tremendous financial and personal risk exposure that long-term care (LTC) poses must be a serious consideration in every retirement plan. A retirement plan that does not address this issue would have to be considered incomplete. To fail to take into account circumstances that could leave a person and his or her family impoverished would be a breach of your professional duties. It is insufficient to plan for financial security in retirement by focusing solely on income and investments. A secure retirement depends not only on accumulating sufficient assets but also on protecting those assets from the potentially devastating effects of long-term care.

Somewhere in your discussions with prospects and clients you should mention the topic of long-term care. One appropriate time to do this is after you have agreed on a funding strategy for the retirement plan. The following demonstrates one way to introduce long-term care into the

Good Transition into LTC

retirement plan discussion: "We have taken great care in planning your retirement. As with any plan, we should talk about possible obstacles that may interfere with the plan and what we can do to be prepared for them. One such obstacle is the need for long-term care."

TABLE 7-7
Calculating Your Taxable Social Security Amount

Retiree Mr. Johnson	Current	What if
1. Social Security Benefit amount	$15,000	$15,000
2. Adjusted gross income (excluding Social Security)	45,000	35,000
3. Tax-exempt interest (and other excluded income)	0	0
4. Half of Social Security benefits (from line 1)	7,500	7,500
5. Add lines 2, 3, and 4 to get provisional income	52,500	42,500
6. Threshold amounts: $32,000 (married); $25,000 (single)	32,000	32,000
7. Subtract line 6 from line 5	20,500	10,500
8. 50% of line 7	10,250	5,250
9. Smaller of lines 4 and 8	7,500	5,250
10. Enter $6,000 (married); $4,500 (single)	6,000	6,000
11. Smaller of lines 9 and 10	6,000	5,250
12. 85% of (line 5 minus $44,000 if married) 85% of (line 5 minus $34,000 if single)	7,225	0
13. Sum of lines 11 and 12	13,225	5,250
14. 85% of Social Security benefits (line 1)	12,750	12,750
15. Lesser of lines 13 or 14 = taxable benefits	12,750	5,250

Another logical time to initiate this discussion is when you are calculating monthly expenses. As you address the issue of health insurance, you will need to discuss the various possibilities. You can point out what Medicare, Medicaid, Medicare supplemental insurance, and major medical insurance cover and what they do not cover. You can then ask how the prospect plans to cover the cost of long-term care and what financial alternatives he or she may have. Paying for long-term care can quickly deplete a person's retirement nest egg and adversely affect retirement income. The average person does not know much about long-term care or how it is financed. Many people incorrectly believe that government programs or private health insurance will cover the costs. Dealing with both the costs and emotional decisions involved in long-term care is a major step toward facing a potentially overwhelming situation. You need to help your clients eliminate the uncertainty of who will pay for this care.

The central issue in the sale of long-term care insurance (LTCI) is one of educating the prospect about its need. Once the prospect understands the need for it, he or she is much more likely to do something about it. It appears that people who buy LTCI understand its need and accept responsibility for taking care of the need. Those who have not bought LTCI or have no plans to buy it appear to lack an understanding of its value and the role it plays in retirement planning. Therefore take time to explore the prospect's potential need for buying long-term care insurance.

Medicaid Planning

Medicaid planning involves methods used by elder-law attorneys to qualify their clients for Medicaid benefits. Such planning can assist those with modest assets, pre-existing medical conditions, or the inability to pay for long-term care insurance. Simply put, Medicaid planning is turning countable assets into inaccessible assets by giving them away or transferring them into a trust.

It was once a common practice for people to divest themselves of all assets to qualify for Medicaid payments of their LTC expenses. Attorneys specializing in elder law have often used plans to transfer assets to achieve Medicaid eligibility. Legally the client no longer has those assets. Because of the look-back rules, estate-recovery rules, and other legislation enacted over the last decade, however, it has become more difficult for those who desire to transfer assets to effectively do this. Now, since the enactment of the Deficit Reduction Act (DRA) on February 8, 2006, states can "look back" to find transfers of assets for 60 months prior to the date the individual is institutionalized or, if later, the date he or she applies for Medicaid.

Ethical Questions Concerning Medicaid Planning. There is no current risk of prosecution for giving your prospects and clients advice about Medicaid planning. However, the use of Medicaid planning to become eligible for the payment of LTC costs creates moral, ethical, and malpractice risks for attorneys and other financial advisors. The Medicaid eligibility requirements, asset transfer, and income rules are fairly complex, vary from state to state, and are constantly changing. Even experienced attorneys can become confused by state and federal policies regarding Medicaid.

Furthermore, an advisor needs to ask this question: Ethically is it proper for middle-class people to use health-care benefits intended for poor people? The problems that may result from doing this are poorer care for nursing-home residents, a reduction in benefits available to those who truly need them, a financial strain on nursing homes that receive a reduced Medicaid reimbursement payment, and taxpayers having to pay for nursing-home costs for the middle class rather than the needy.

The need for long-term care insurance can result in joint selling opportunities that involve the sale of an immediate annuity in conjunction with long-term care insurance. An example of this concept was demonstrated in the case history, "Using an Annuity to Fund the

Purchase of Long-Term Care Insurance," in chapter 6. Two additional ideas are seen in the box on the next page.

Role of Annuities in Life Planning

Life planning is viewed as a new and innovative model in retirement and financial planning. Life planning adds a "holistic" element to the process of financial planning by considering the nonfinancial needs of retirement. This model seeks to develop a balanced and meaningful retirement experience by attending to multiple areas of life, including finances, work, leisure, relationships, physical health, mental health, housing, and personal growth. Life planning emphasizes the identification of personal lifestyle goals based on the individual's values and priorities. It focuses on personal goals and then assigns a financial cost to satisfying those goals and wants. Its emphasis is away from product and toward process, from economic values to human values, linking financial assets with the values in our lives.

Relevance in Planning

Because of the holistic nature of this model, life planning helps individuals to place financial planning activities in a context that is personally meaningful and therefore more motivating. As a result, financial planning activities are directed toward achieving personal and specific goals rather than the more nebulous target of "building wealth and security for the future."

Financial planning starts where life planning leaves off—you do not start with the financial plan and then work the life plan into it. Life planning is a dynamic educational process that allows people to visualize their personal goals and then model the financial consequences of those choices.

Retirement Affected by Nonfinancial Issues

A person's retirement experience is affected by such factors as role transitions, relationship changes, time management issues, and a sense of meaning and purpose. These factors can have a profound effect on a retiree's quality of life in retirement. Management consultants McClung and Wass write, "Workplace demands leave many employees little time or energy to develop outside interests or activities." They recommend that retirement planning programming include a "life management" module that focuses on issues such as health, nutrition, outside interests, volunteering, stress, and attitudes. "The goal is to encourage a healthy and active lifestyle, both on the job and in retirement," they advise.

Using Annuities to Fund Long-Term Care Insurance (LTCI)

Fixed annuities only: Because most of one advisor's LTCI clients are in their sixties and seventies—and at this age, they usually should scale back some percentage of their asset allocation from variable products into more fixed products—he suggests a deferred annuity to fund their LTCI.

First, the advisor determines the premium the couple needs for LTCI, which in this case is $3,500. Then the advisor divides the premium by .05, which is the conservative interest rate that can be earned on the capital needed to deposit into the deferred annuity. Therefore $70,000 is needed to fund the LTCI, which is put into a deferred annuity:

$$\$3,500 \div .05 = \$70,000$$

Thus the couple never dips into the principal, and the interest from the annuity funds the LTCI. In this example, a couple is using the average cost of a nursing home for one person for one year ($70,000) to fund LTCI forever for both of them. Also the principal of $70,000 then goes to the heirs at the couple's death rather than being consumed many times over if used personally to fund long-term care facility costs directly.

Objection: "The withdrawals are taxable." This is true, but this method is a whole lot less expensive than paying for LTC out of pocket. It also helps to prevent asset depletion and the need to go on Medicaid where clients lose control of their LTC options.

Approach talk: "Mr. and Mrs. Prospect, the LTCI will cost $70,000. What do you think?" They will be shocked. You can explain, "Oh no, you don't spend $70,000; you just put $70,000 in this account, and the yield will pay the LTCI premiums. In this way, you do not have to alter your lifestyle or make financial sacrifices to pay for LTCI or LTC. In essence, the interest from the annuity is doing guard dog duty to protect your entire estate."

The client enjoys great peace of mind. The advisor, in this case, uses a product with a 10-year guaranteed fixed interest rate so that the premiums will be there every year. The couple can forget about it for at least 10 years.

An alternative: "If $70,000 is too much, you could use a life-income immediate annuity to fund the LTCI with a lot less than $70,000—maybe only $45,000, depending on age. Or maybe a joint life with 50 percent survivor benefit is a possibility so that if one spouse dies, only half the income from the annuity is needed for LTCI. This may cost only $30,000. There are solutions right on down the line, depending on affordability."

A second alternative: Using a medically underwritten (substandard) immediate annuity is an ethical answer to the unethical practice of using an immediate annuity payable to the community spouse to hide a lump sum. A medically underwritten immediate annuity is recommended by some advisors so that the sick spouse can qualify for Medicaid. If a person is sick and needs long-term care in a facility, this annuity product will base payments on a rated-up age with the assumption that life expectancy is greatly reduced and thus the payments the annuitant receives are much higher. Such an approach to LTC funding is both legal and ethical.

An important goal of life planning is to develop proactive strategies for successfully making the role changes that are inherent in the retirement transition. Annuities can serve as one important ingredient in a comprehensive retirement plan that helps to empower retirees to feel more financially independent and free to explore activities that enhance their quality of life. Individuals who believe they have the power to shape their own lives are more likely to actively seek out new activities and roles after retirement. Life planning also helps preretirees to increase their sense of control over the direction their lives are taking. Moreover, it bolsters confidence in their ability to respond to change, to overcome challenges, and to take advantage of opportunities—key elements of successful transitions in every stage of life.

Conclusion

As annuities become more visible and commonly used in the American financial planning landscape, they will naturally become a more integral part of the retirement, estate, long-term care, and income tax planning process. Clearly, because of the flexibility of plan options and the multiple uses these products serve, you cannot ignore annuities when doing serious financial planning for your clients. As you become increasingly aware of the importance of annuities in financial planning, you can integrate their use more fully into your practice.

CASE HISTORY

The Split-Annuity Concept in Action

Wendy is a 65-year-old retired widow. She has two children and four grandchildren. She has $100,000 she would like to invest to supplement the retirement income she receives from Social Security and her pension plan for at least the next 10 years. She is in the 28 percent tax bracket and wants to keep taxes generated from the earnings on her $100,000 to a bare minimum, if possible. Wendy is curious about annuities, but she is conservative with her money and does not want to expose her savings to the risk of loss.

A friend tells her to consider a fixed-interest deferred annuity that she can use to withdraw only the current interest, now 5 percent, to provide some income. However, the entire $5,000 amount will be subject to income tax, so Wendy will net only $3,600 after taxes.

Wendy also hears about immediate life annuities. She is disenchanted by this alternative, however, because she would like the entire $100,000 to go to her heirs at her death rather than having it depleted in some type of immediate annuity, leaving only a residual amount behind.

Her financial advisor suggests that she explore an alternative he refers to as the split-annuity concept. He says that this alternative can provide her with a dependable source of income that will be taxed only minimally each year. Wendy's principal will be preserved, and the total death benefit to her heirs will remain virtually intact for the next 10 years.

The hypothetical example below shows what could happen if Wendy apportions her $100,000 as follows:

- $39,284 deposited into a 10-year fixed-period annuity
- $60,716 deposited into a fixed-interest deferred annuity

The fixed-period annuity generates $414.94 per month in income. Of this amount, over 94 percent of it, or $390.43, is net of current income taxation, assuming a 28 percent tax bracket.* Over the next 10 years, the fixed-period portion generates $49,792 of total income.

Simultaneously the fixed-interest deferred annuity premium of $60,716 compounds tax deferred over the next 10 years, growing to $100,000, assuming no withdrawals.** This is the same amount Wendy originally invested in both the fixed-period and the fixed-interest deferred annuity. In essence, she will receive a steady income stream for 10 years while preserving her original premium (assuming the interest rates shown below).

* This example assumes a monthly income for the fixed-period annuity with a payout of 10 years using a 5 percent crediting rate.

**Based on an assumed interest rate of 5 percent, credited for all 10 years. This interest rate is not guaranteed.

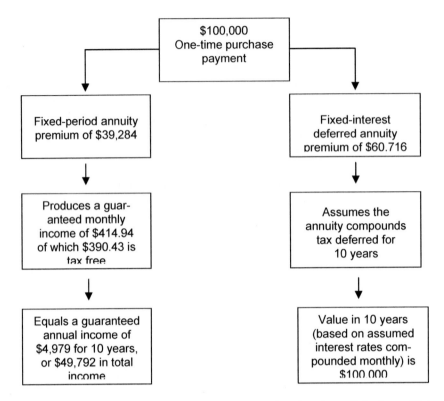

Now Wendy can feel secure knowing that her beneficiaries will be protected if she dies unexpectedly. Her deferred annuity policy's beneficiaries will receive the full cash value from her fixed-interest deferred annuity contract while her fixed-period annuity policy's beneficiaries will continue to receive any remaining income payments for the balance of the 10-year period after her death. These benefits will be paid directly to her beneficiaries, thus avoiding the costs and delays of probate. If Wendy is alive at the end of the 10-year payout period, she has the option of purchasing a split annuity again so that similar income and tax benefits she enjoyed for the first 10 years can be renewed.

CHAPTER SEVEN REVIEW

Key Terms and Concepts are explained in the Glossary. Answers to the Review Questions and Self-Test Questions are found in the back of the book in the Answers to Questions section.

Key Terms and Concepts

nonnatural person
cost basis

exclusion ratio
expected return

Sec. 1035 exchange
partial Sec. 1035 exchange
pre-59 ½ IRS penalty tax
substantially equal periodic
  payments (SEPPs)
rollover
transfer
required minimum distribution
age 70 ½ IRS penalty tax
required beginning date

minimum distribution
  requirements
designated beneficiary
general power of attorney
durable power of attorney
springing durable power of attorney
living will
health care power of attorney
trust
A-B trust

Review Questions

7-1.   Explain the gift tax problem when a different person is named as owner, annuitant, and beneficiary of the same nonqualified annuity.

7-2.   Explain why borrowing funds from a nonqualified annuity can have income tax consequences to the policyowner.

7-3.   Explain the tax benefits of an IRC Sec. 1035 exchange.

7-4.   Identify the exceptions to the 10 percent IRS penalty tax for withdrawals from nonqualified annuities prior to age 59 ½.

7-5.   Explain how a qualified annuity owner can move funds from one account to another without incurring income taxes on the amount of the funds transferred.

7-6.   Define when a qualified plan or IRA participant reaches his or her required beginning date.

7-7.   Explain the required minimum distribution rules that apply when an IRA participant reaches age 70 ½.

7-8.   Identify what options a surviving spouse has as beneficiary of a qualified annuity owned by the deceased spouse.

7-9.   List the steps the advisor must take to complete the application for an annuity policy.

7-10. Identify the objectives of the delivery interview.

7-11. Briefly describe the important aspects for servicing existing clients.

7-12. Briefly explain why the possibility of needing annuities has to be considered in
       a.   long-term care planning
       b.   estate planning

Self-Test Questions

Instructions: Read Chapter 7 first; then answer the following questions to test your knowledge. There are 10 questions; circle the correct answer, and then check your answers with the answer key in the back of the book.

7-1. If a client purchases an immediate annuity with a 10-year fixed period and each annual payment equals $10,000, which of the following statements is correct?

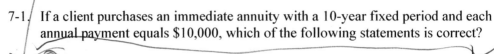

(A)   A portion of each $10,000 will be considered taxable income to the client.

(B)   At the end of 10 years, the remaining value will be payable to the client's named beneficiary.

(C)   The exclusion ratio is $1,000 per year.

(D)   The client will be subject to a 10 percent penalty tax if he or she is under age 59 ½.

7-2. Monroe has a deferred annuity worth $110,000. He paid $25,000 into the annuity 10 years ago. Monroe would like to borrow $40,000 from his bank to start a new business venture. Which of the following statements regarding a loan from this deferred annuity is correct?

(A)   Monroe cannot use his annuity as collateral for a loan.

(B)   Monroe will have to pay income tax on $40,000 if he uses his annuity as collateral for a loan.

(C)   Monroe will have to pay income tax only on the amount of the loan that is greater than his cost basis ($40,000 – $25,000 = $15,000) if he borrows $40,000.

(D)   Monroe can borrow up to $110,000 without any tax consequences.

7-3. If a client gives his nonqualified deferred annuity worth $47,000 (he purchased it 2 years ago with a $40,000 single premium) to his church for its annual fund-raising campaign, which of the following statements is correct?

(A)   The church will pay any income tax on the $7,000 gain in the annuity.

(B)   The client will pay income taxes on $7,000 of gain in the annuity.

(C)   Neither the client nor the church will have to pay income tax on the $7,000 gain in the annuity.

(D)   The annuity cannot be given to the church because the church does not have a person as a measuring life.

7-4. A legal document signed by one person authorizing another person to act on behalf of the signer if he or she becomes incapacitated is a

    (A)   durable power of attorney
    (B)   revocable living trust
    (C)   A-B trust
    (D)   will

7-5. Which of the following statements regarding the sale of a personally owned nonqualified deferred annuity is (are) correct?

    I.   Any gain in the policy is taxed to the seller of the annuity as ordinary income.
    II. If the owner sells the policy at a loss, the loss can be claimed as a deduction against taxable income.

    (A)   I only
    (B)   II only
    (C)   Both I and II
    (D)   Neither I nor II

7-6. If Joe owns an annuity with his wife, Cindy, as the annuitant and their son Rocky as the beneficiary, what happens at Cindy's death?

    I.   Rocky is the beneficiary and recipient of the proceeds.
    II. Joe has made a gift to Rocky in the amount of the death benefit.

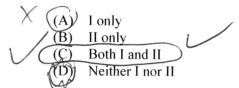

    (A)   I only
    (B)   II only
    (C)   Both I and II
    (D)   Neither I nor II

7-7. Johnny is aged 52 and purchases a nonqualified annuity. Which of the following statements regarding distributions and withdrawals from the annuity is (are) correct?

   I.   Johnny is subject to tax on the withdrawals of interest made before age 59 ½.
   II. Johnny must take minimum distributions at age 70 ½.

   (A) I only
   (B) II only
   (C) I and II both
   (D) Neither I nor II

7-8. A trust is a legal vehicle with all of the following key components EXCEPT a

   (A) trustee
   (B) prospect
   (C) corpus
   (D) beneficiary

7-9. All of the following statements regarding annuity death proceeds are correct EXCEPT

   (A) When the owner of an annuity dies, the insurance company must distribute the annuity within 5 years or a life expectancy settlement option must be elected.
   (B) The beneficiary is generally subject to income tax on the gain in the annuity when it is payable in the form of a death benefit.
   (C) When an annuitant dies, the beneficiary has 60 days to elect a settlement option and defer any tax due.
   (D) A policy with joint owners will trigger the distribution rules at the death of the second joint owner.

7-10. All of the following statements regarding the gifting of an annuity made before April 22, 1987, are correct EXCEPT

(A) The recipient/donee of the gifted annuity will assume the annuity with a cost basis equal to the donor's cost basis plus the amount of gain on which the donor was required to pay taxes.

(B) Even though a person gives an annuity away to someone else, that donor is still liable for the taxes.

(C) If a policyowner gifts a policy to another person, the policyowner/donor will have to pay ordinary income taxes on the gain in the annuity at the time the gift was made.

(D) When an annuity policy is gifted, the owner/donor does not recognize taxable gain in the policy until the recipient/donee surrenders it.

NOTES

[1]. IRC Sec. 72(e).

[2]. Rev. Rul. 61-201, 1961-2 CB 46; Cohan v. Comm, 39 F2d 540 (2nd Cir. 1903), aff'g 11 BTA 743.

[3]. Ibid.

[4]. IRS Publication 575 (Pension and Annuity Income), 2004 ed., p. 19.

[5]. Ibid.

[6]. Norse N. Blazzard and Judith A. Hasenauer, "When Exchanging, Surrendering, or Selling a Variable Annuity May Be Called For," *National Underwriter, Life and Health/Financial Services Edition*, September 6, 2004, pp. 19, 22.

8

Regulation of Annuities

Learning Objectives

An understanding of the material in this chapter should enable you to

---

8-1. Explain the differences in state and federal regulation of annuities.

8-2. Identify the roles of the SEC and FINRA regarding the sale of variable annuity policies.

8-3. Explain the purpose of the variable annuity prospectus.

8-4. Explain the purpose of state guaranty funds.

8-5. Explain how annuities in some instances can be protected from creditors of the policyowner.

8-6. Identify the components of professionalism in expanding your practice.

8-7. Identify strategies for working effectively with other professional advisors.

Chapter Outline

This chapter examines the regulation of annuity contracts at the federal and state level, covering both fixed annuities and variable annuities, which are subject to intense regulation from the Securities and Exchange Commission (SEC) and the Financial Industry Regulatory Authority (FINRA). In addition, the chapter addresses market conduct, suitability, and creditor protection issues

STATE REGULATION

state insurance department

Traditionally insurance companies and insurance policies have been regulated primarily at the state, not the federal, level. Each of the states has established its own department of insurance to regulate the insurance activities conducted within the particular state. In addition to the *state insurance department*, the legislative bodies of each state set policy for the regulation of insurance. Each state legislature passes laws to guide the insurance company's activities and products.

The state regulation of insurance companies has several key functions:

- insurance company licensing
- producer licensing
- product regulation
- market conduct
- financial regulation
- consumer services

solvency

State insurance departments regulate the financial aspects of insurance companies. Therefore states must be concerned with financial *solvency* of their insurers. They want assurance that the insurance companies have enough money invested to cover their policyholders. Making sure their insurance companies stay solvent to pay claims is of primary importance to state regulators.

market conduct

Regulation also occurs on the basis of *market conduct*. Insurance departments supervise the sales and marketing practices of both insurance companies and advisors. The goal is to make sure consumers are treated fairly. In fact, each state insurance department's number one priority is the protection of its insurance consumers.

In order for an insurance company to have the ability to sell annuities in a particular state, the insurance company offering the annuity must first be licensed by the state department of insurance. The insurance company must apply for a license and meet the specific requirements by the particular state.

The insurance company is required to file all the products it sells with the state insurance department. Some states require a mere informational filing, depending on the type of product. Other states require that the insurance company receive an official stamp of approval by the insurance department before the insurer can offer its products for sale.

Next, the particular advisor who is selling the annuity must also be licensed in the particular state. Normally the state requires that the advisor be licensed in the state where the application is written. This may or may not be the state of residence for the policyowner. Advisors may be licensed in more than one state to sell insurance products. Generally an advisor will carry a resident license in his or her home state and then may have additional nonresident licenses in other states.

The advisor must also obtain an appointment from one or more companies. This appointment is what allows the insurance agent to sell a particular insurance company's products. During the appointment process, the insurance company will verify the existence of the advisor's insurance license and will most likely perform both financial and criminal background checks. If an advisor sells for several insurance companies, he or she will have several appointments.

Your Financial Services Practice: Unauthorized Entities

Regulation of insurance products and services varies from state to state. In Florida, for example, regulations prohibit doing business with an unauthorized insurance entity. An unauthorized entity is an insurance company that has not gained approval to place insurance in the jurisdiction where it or a producer wants to sell insurance. These carriers are unlicensed and prohibited from doing business in that state. In most cases where these carriers have operated, they have characterized themselves as one of several types that are exempt from state regulation. It is the financial advisor's responsibility to exercise due diligence to make sure the carriers for whom they are selling are approved by the department of insurance in that state.

Minimum Interest Rates Lowered for Fixed-Interest Deferred Annuities

As stated in chapter 3, recently state legislatures have lowered the minimum guaranteed interest rate for newly issued fixed-interest deferred annuities. Before now, 3 percent had been the standard minimum interest rate guarantee. The reason for the legislative rate decrease is the low interest rate environment in which insurance companies conducted business during the early years of this centuiry. Most insurance companies cannot maintain a 3 percent guarantee for such a prolonged decreased interest rate period. To address these market conditions, legislators allowed a decrease in the guaranteed minimum interest rate so that companies could compete in the insurance market and still maintain some level of profitability.

Some annuity contracts now offer a guaranteed minimum rate as low as 1.5 percent. Other companies have adopted the practice of determining the guaranteed rate referenced to an index. Generally states that have adopted the index method for minimum guaranteed interest rates for fixed-interest deferred annuities provide that the guaranteed rate will always be more than 1 percent but less than 3 percent.

Free-Look Period

Most states require insurance companies to offer purchasers a free-look period, during which purchasers can examine the annuity contract to make sure it matches what they assumed they bought. This is necessary because annuity contracts are intended to be a product the buyer holds for a long time. Therefore the importance of having the correct terms, conditions, fees, and charges is critical.

Furthermore, the policy is developed entirely by the insurance company with no opportunity for the consumer to haggle over specific terms in the policy. It's a take-it-or-leave-it proposition to the consumer. Once a contract is in force, the contract owner will be subject to penalties if he or she wants to exit the contract early.

If, during the free-look period, the purchaser decides not to accept the contract, he or she can return it for a full refund. The refund is made directly to the applicant. In most states, the free-look period is 10 days from the date the policy is delivered to the client. Some states require a free-look period to last a full 30 days.

If the applicant decides not to keep the annuity, he or she does not have to prove a specific reason why he or she is returning the policy. The policy can be returned for any reason whether or not the insurance company thinks the client's reasoning is correct or valid.

From time to time a policyowner may wish to return a policy that was purchased via an IRC Sec. 1035 exchange. Although this does not occur frequently, the company whose policy was exchanged does not have to accept the return of the policy. If the insurance company will not accept the money back, the policyowner will have to accept the proceeds. The proceeds will be then taxed to the policyowner as though he or she surrendered the original policy. To the extent that the policy has taxable gain, the owner will have to pay ordinary income taxes on the gain. Furthermore, penalty taxes may apply if the owner is under age 59 ½. (See chapter 7 for more information on taxes and penalties.)

Example: Samantha has an annuity (Policy A) with Company A and purchases a new annuity (Policy B) with Company B using Policy A's cash values through an IRC Sec. 1035 exchange. Upon delivery of Policy B, Samantha decides she does not want the policy because it does not have a 10 percent penalty-free withdrawal in year one. Samantha returns the policy within the policy's free-look period.

Insurance Company B receives the policy back from Samantha and cancels the entire transaction. Because the policy came to Company B via a Sec. 1035 exchange, Company B then contacts Company A and returns the funds to it to re-establish Policy A. In most cases, Company A will not reject the proceeds and will reinstate Policy A.

But this may not always be the case. Company A can refuse to accept the proceeds. If this occurs, the funds will instead be returned to the policyowner. If Policy A had a cost basis of $10,000 and a current value of $30,000, the policyowner will have to accept $30,000 and will have to pay ordinary income tax on $20,000 ($30,000 − $10,000 = $20,000). If Samantha is under age 59 ½, this could further complicate the issue by subjecting her to a 10 percent penalty tax on $20,000 of gain.

Annuity Replacements

Most states adhere to the National Association of Insurance Commissioners (NAIC) model replacement regulation. This model regulation describes the disclosures required when an annuity policy is replaced by another policy.

What is a replacement? Generally a replacement is considered to occur anytime a policy is lapsed, forfeited, or surrendered in connection with the purchase of a new annuity. The model act applies to Sec. 1035 exchanges and pure replacements that are not processed under the Sec. 1035 exchange rules.

Most annuity applications ask the advisor to declare whether or not the purchase of the annuity is a replacement of another annuity. If the advisor answers "yes," states that have adopted this model act require the insurance company to provide a special notice to the annuity purchaser.

Furthermore, the model act requires the insurance company to notify the company whose policy is being replaced. Notification must include the name of the insured and the particular policy being replaced. This notice is required within a few days from when the insurance company receives the annuity application. In addition, the free-look period is usually longer for replaced annuities than it is for nonreplaced annuities.

State Guaranty Associations

state guaranty association

Insurance companies operating in each state are required to be members of the *state guaranty association*. States have this guaranty fund to cover losses of consumers' funds if insurance companies become insolvent. Unlike the FDIC, the federal government does not fund or operate guaranty funds for insurance products.

All insurance companies doing business in the respective state participate in the guaranty association and provide funding through state premium taxes. Funding is also provided by assessments against financially stable insurance companies. Funding is proportional to the percentage of premium that the company collects in the state relative to the other insurers in the state. These assessments fund the liabilities to policyowners of failing insurance companies.

Even though guaranty associations exist in each state to protect policyowners, the insurance departments prohibit advisors from discussing the guaranty fund as part of their sales presentations. In fact, using the existence of the guaranty association as any type of inducement to encourage a person to buy a policy is strictly prohibited.

The Life and Health Insurance Association Model Act, Section 19 D, 1999, recommended the following Guaranty Association disclaimer to the states:

> The State Life and Health Insurance Guaranty Association provides coverage of claims under some types of policies if the insurer becomes impaired or insolvent. COVERAGE MAY NOT BE AVAILABLE FOR YOUR POLICY. Even if coverage is provided, there are significant limits and exclusions. Coverage is always conditioned on residence in this state. Other conditions may also preclude coverage.
>
> The Life and Health Insurance Guaranty Association or the insurance department will respond to any questions you may have

which are not answered in this document. Your insurer and agent are prohibited by law from using the existence of the association or its coverage to sell you an insurance policy.

You should not rely on availability of coverage under the Life and Health Insurance Guaranty Association when selecting an insurer.

Almost all 50 states have enacted specific legislation preventing an advisor from using the existence of the guaranty fund as an incentive to a potential buyer. As an example, Indiana Statute 27-8-8-18 states, "A person, including an insurer, insurance producer, employee, agent, or affiliate of an insurer, shall not make, publish, disseminate, circulate, or place before the public or cause, directly or indirectly, to be made, published, disseminated, circulated, or placed before the public, in any newspaper, magazine, or other publication, or in the form of a notice, circular, pamphlet, letter, or poster, or over any radio station or television station, or in any other way, an advertisement, an announcement, or a statement, written or oral, that uses the existence of the association for the purpose of the sale of, solicitation of, or inducement to purchase any form of insurance covered by this chapter. This section does not apply to the association or any other entity that does not sell or solicit insurance."

If, during a sales presentation, a prospect asks the advisor about the existence of or coverage under the state guaranty fund, the advisor should answer the question if he or she knows the answer. Then the advisor should refer the prospect to the state guaranty association for more information. So that the client understands the advisor's obligations, the advisor should let the prospect know that the advisor cannot use the existence of the fund in the presentation of the annuity.

Guaranty associations cover only the cash values accumulated by fixed annuity policyowners. Variable annuity policyowners are covered only to the extent that the owner invested in the variable annuity's fixed account. Any money invested in the variable annuity's separate accounts is not affected by the insurance company's financial problems. This is because the monies in the separate account are not attachable by the insurance company's creditors. Therefore the money invested in separate accounts should not be affected by the company's financial difficulties. As such, the full dollar amount of monies in the separate account will always be available to policyowners, and no guaranty fund is needed.

FEDERAL REGULATION

State insurance departments generally regulate fixed deferred annuities, immediate annuities, and equity-indexed annuities. Variable annuities, on the other hand, are subject not only to state insurance department regulation but also to intensive regulation by the federal securities industry.

Fixed annuities, however, are not subject to securities regulations. Although fixed annuities are technically considered a security, they are not regulated as such. In fact, fixed annuities are exempt from securities regulation. With fixed annuities, the risk of investment loss is on the insurer. With variable annuities, the risk of investment loss is on the shoulders of the annuity owner. The shifting of the risk of loss from the insurer to the policyowner is the reason variable annuities are not exempt from securities regulation.

Securities and Exchange Commission (SEC)

security

The *Securities and Exchange Commission (SEC)* analyzes how an insurance company markets an annuity to determine whether it should be regulated as a *security*. A fixed annuity that is marketed like an investment will catch the SEC's eye. In this regard, equity-indexed annuities have come closer to the line in terms of marketing an annuity like it is a security. Indeed, some insurance companies have voluntarily chosen to register their equity-indexed annuities with the SEC although the vast majority of insurers have not.

Securities and Exchange Commission

The SEC is the overseer and regulator of U.S. securities markets. It protects investors and helps to maintain the operation of the securities markets. The SEC monitors the stock exchange, broker-dealers, investment advisors, mutual fund companies, and public utility holding companies. Its concern is the accurate disclosure of information to investors.

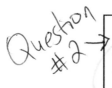

SEC Mission Statement
The primary mission of the U.S. Securities and Exchange Commission is to protect investors and maintain fair, orderly and efficient markets, and facilitate capital formation.

Because the securities market is complex compared to other investments that come with guarantees like bank deposits and CDs, the SEC requires a certain level of consumer disclosure by companies that offer the securities. The SEC's basic premise is that all investors, large and small, should have access to fundamental facts about an investment before they buy it.

Federal securities laws are administered by the SEC. The SEC has the ability to enforce its authority. In fact, the SEC brings civil enforcements against those who break the securities laws. Common violations include insider trading, accounting fraud, and providing false or misleading information about securities or the companies that issue them.

The SEC regulates the prospectus, the people selling the variable annuity, and the variable annuity market. Insurance companies that offer variable annuities must register their products with the SEC by filing a special form. The SEC will review and comment on the insurer's filing. The insurer cannot begin to sell the variable annuity until the registration has been filed and usually not until the review by the SEC is completed.

The SEC regulates the contents inside the variable annuity prospectus, as well as when it must be distributed. It mandates that each potential policyowner must receive a prospectus for each of the funds in the annuity. The prospectus must include the following:

- variable annuity fees (the most important disclosure)
- description of the separate account
- description of the annuity contract
- description of how the separate account is organized
- description of the underlying fund accounts
- description of the benefits and policyowner rights in the policy
- risks of investing in a variable policy
- tax consequences of investing in a variable policy

Furthermore, the prospectus must be written in simple and understandable terms. The delivery of marketing materials for variable annuities is prohibited without the accompanying prospectus.

In addition to the SEC rules governing variable annuities, the Financial Industry Regulatory Authority (FINRA) rules govern variable annuity advertisements. Any marketing materials for variable annuities must be filed with FINRA. Marketing materials cannot be misleading. In addition, sales material must clearly describe the product as a variable annuity, must not overly emphasize any guarantees, and must clearly state that variable annuities are not short-term investments.

Federal law also requires how quickly the insurer must process variable annuity applications. The insurer has two business days to apply the premium to the policy once a completed application is received. If the application is not complete, this rule does not apply. Instead, the insurer must contact the proposed policyowner within five days and return the premium. The proposed owner can agree to allow the insurer to keep the premium until the application is complete and all proper forms have been received by the insurance company.

On the other side of this equation, federal law also requires that the insurer must pay withdrawals or surrender proceeds to the policyowner within seven days of the request.

Some attempts have been made to have state securities regulators obtain jurisdiction over variable annuities. The result would make financial professionals who sell variable annuities acquire a state securities license in addition to the licenses they already must obtain—that is, a state insurance license, state variable products license, and FINRA Series 6 or Series 7 license to sell variable products. Furthermore, this would give state securities commissioners oversight of and jurisdiction over the marketing and sales of variable annuities.

Many in the insurance industry oppose these attempts because the professional advisor who sells variable annuities is already under the jurisdiction of FINRA and the state insurance department. They feel the additional layer of scrutiny by the state securities commissioner is unnecessary.

Financial Industry Regulatory Authority (FINRA)

Financial Industry Regulatory Authority (FINRA)

The *Financial Industry Regulatory Authority (FINRA)* is the largest non-governmental regulator for all securities firms doing business in the United States. All told, FINRA oversees nearly 5,100 brokerage firms, about 173,000 branch offices, and more than 676,000 registered securities representatives. FINRA accomplishes its oversight of the securities industry by registering, educating, and testing member firms and their staffs, as well as by creating and enforcing rules.

The National Association of Securities Dealers was a self-regulatory organization created in 1938 that was previously responsible for regulating the securities industry in the United States.

Created in July 2007 through the consolidation of the NASD and the member regulation, enforcement, and arbitration functions of the New York Stock Exchange, FINRA is dedicated to investor protection and market integrity through effective and efficient regulation and complementary compliance and technology-based services.

broker-dealer

Insurance companies offering variable annuities are considered broker-dealers. A *broker-dealer* is a person who "engages in the business of effecting transactions in securities for the account of others or who is engaged in the business of buying and selling securities for his or her own account."

FINRA self-regulates broker-dealers subject to SEC oversight. Broker-dealers must become FINRA members. FINRA provides rules for sellers of variable annuities, including suitability requirements, which are discussed later in this chapter.

A registered representative sells products of the broker-dealer. To become a registered representative, an individual must be affiliated with a broker-dealer, submit an application to FINRA, and pass the appropriate

FINRA series examination. The Series 6 is the Investment Company/ Variable Contracts Representative examination that enables registered representatives to sell variable annuity products and, in some states, mutual funds as well. The Series 7 is the General Securities Representative examination that also empowers the registered representative to sell stocks and bonds. Many states also require a state securities exam called Series 63. The Series 63 exam is the Uniform Securities Agent State Law examination, which is required by most states in conjunction with either the Series 6 or Series 7 exam in order to sell the respective securities products permitted with these registrations.

FINRA requires broker-dealers to supervise their registered representatives who sell variable annuities. Therefore the insurance company must direct and supervise all persons engaged directly or indirectly in the offer and sale of variable annuities.

FINRA regulates the broker-dealers' business practices. Requirements of broker-dealers include the following:

- FINRA members must not share commissions earned with nonmembers.
- FINRA members must promptly report customer complaints.
- FINRA members must comply with annuity advertising rules.
- Recommendations to customers must comply with FINRA suitability rules.
- The broker-dealer must supervise all people who are associated with the broker-dealer, including providing adequate training, supervision of sales practices, and review of all transactions by a registered principal.
- The broker-dealer must annually review its business to detect and prevent violations of laws.
- Each person must be assigned to a supervisory person.
- Each person must attend an annual meeting on compliance, including training and review.

FINRA Rules of Conduct

The FINRA rulebook currently consists of both NASD Rules and certain NYSE Rules that FINRA has incorporated (Incorporated NYSE Rules). Firms that were members only of NASD as of July 30, 2007, remain subject only to NASD Rules, provided they do not become NYSE members in which case they would be subject to both NASD Rules and the Incorporated NYSE Rules as "Dual Members." Dual Members also must comply with NASD Rules. Similarly a firm that becomes a new member of FINRA only (and not a member of NYSE) will be subject only to NASD Rules.

In interpreting the rule sets, FINRA will continue to apply the same interpretive materials that NASD and NYSE applied prior to the July 2007 consolidation. For example, FINRA will consider existing NASD interpretive letters and Notices to Members in applying NASD Rules.

FINRA sets forth its expectations for the ethical treatment of customers in its NASD Rules of Conduct. These rules spell out two fundamental steps, which the registered representative must follow to deal fairly with clients:

- The registered representative must understand the client's current financial status.
- He or she must understand the client's financial goals.

Only with these two pieces of information is it possible to offer appropriate advice to a client.

For example, an older client who has accumulated a relatively modest retirement nest egg and seeks some income along with preservation of capital would be an unlikely candidate for a financial product that stresses high-risk, emerging-growth funds.

Changing client circumstances are also part of the fair dealings equation. For example, in midlife, successful clients have accumulated more assets and may be able to tolerate greater risk in order to seek higher return. On the other hand, clients near the end of their working careers may find that the high-risk strategies which enabled them to achieve earlier financial success no longer fit their needs.

Rules of Conduct—An Application to Financial Advisors

The essence of the NASD Rules of Conduct is not really all that different from needs selling. Those who sell annuities, whether variable or fixed, by uncovering client needs and goals are already substantially following the NASD guidelines. Financial advisors who conduct periodic reviews of their clients' insurance and investment products are taking into account changing client circumstances, needs, and goals.

The various financial products available today can be characterized by different levels of risk and potential return, elements that have long been considered in the promotion and sale of securities. Ethics, backed increasingly by corresponding regulatory principles, requires financial advisors to consider these factors when recommending the purchase of an annuity product.

The result is that the spirit of the NASD Rules of Conduct will continue to influence the sale of annuities. Financial advisors can expect a continued emphasis on disclosure, both about the products they sell and the methods they use in the sale of those products. In addition, financial advisors should expect that both regulators and the courts will focus on whether or not a particular product is appropriate in light of the client's financial condition, risk tolerance, and goals.

Mandatory Continuing Education Program

FINRA, in conjunction with other self-regulatory organizations and the Securities Industry/Regulatory Council on Continuing Education, administers a two-part mandatory Continuing Education Program. The program consists of a Regulatory Element and a Firm Element. The Regulatory Element requires all registered persons to take computer-based training in industry rules and regulations on the second anniversary of their initial securities registration and every three years thereafter. The Firm Element requires broker-dealers to keep their "covered persons"—employees who deal with customers, and their supervisors—up to date on job- and product-related subjects by way of an annual firm-developed and administered training program.

The Regulatory Element is designed to focus on compliance, ethics, business conduct, sales-practice standards, and other regulatory concerns. Its content is derived from rules and regulations as well as standards and practices widely accepted within the industry.

The Firm Element requires an organization annually to develop its own training plan for covered registered persons. The goal of the Firm Element is to ensure that these persons are trained regularly in the investments or services in which they deal and to keep them current on matters relating to their particular areas of responsibility. Among the subjects firms should consider for inclusion in Firm Element training are new rules and regulations, such as supervisory control amendments, business continuity plans, and any new products or services the firm plans to offer.

National Association of Insurance Commissioners

National Association of Insurance Commissioners (NAIC)

The *National Association of Insurance Commissioners (NAIC)* serves as the forum for creating uniform insurance laws and regulations among the states. Comprised of the state insurance commissioners from all 50 states, the District of Columbia, and four U.S. territories, it has helped coordinate regulation among the states since 1871. NAIC commissioners discuss issues of common concern and align their oversight of the insurance industry.

The NAIC has been responsible for passing many model laws. Once the NAIC passes a model law, each state has complete autonomy as to whether or not the state will adopt the law in its own legislature. The state may choose to adopt the law exactly as written by the NAIC, to change parts of the law and therefore pass a unique version of it, or not to adopt any portion of the model law. The NAIC has no binding authority on the individual states. Indeed, the NAIC functions merely as an advisory board.

To facilitate the goal of fair treatment of consumers, the NAIC implemented a Consumer Protection and Antifraud Division. Its mission is to assist state insurance regulators in their efforts to protect consumers, address fraudulent activities, and supervise insurance market-related activities in a responsive, efficient, and cost-effective manner, consistent with the wishes of the NAIC members.

The Consumer Protection and Antifraud Division achieves its mission in the following ways:

- coordinating the NAIC's activities to attain fair and equitable treatment for insurance consumers
- facilitating the continual improvement of the underwriting and market practices of insurers and producers
- assisting the continual improvement of the market conduct examination process, including the facilitation of market conduct examinations and interstate communication
- serving as the primary liaison for consumers to provide input on insurance regulation
- aiding the coordination of antifraud activities among the states and with federal authorities when appropriate

---

NAIC Mission Statement

The mission of the NAIC is to assist state insurance regulators, individually and collectively, in serving the public interest and achieving the following fundamental insurance regulatory goals in a responsive, efficient, and cost-effective manner, consistent with the wishes of its members:

- Protect the public interest
- Promote the competition markets
- Facilitate the fair and equitable treatment of insurance consumers
- Promote the reliability, solvency, and financial solidity of insurance institutions
- Support and improve state regulation of insurance

SUITABILITY AND DISCLOSURE

Criticism of Annuities

Annuities compete for the client's attention and money in an environment of expanding investment opportunities and changing personal needs. A nonqualified annuity is just one financial tool available to help clients accomplish their financial goals. The annuity is constructed, and enabled by the tax code, to accomplish specific financial security goals for the client. These goals are long-term accumulation and long-term distribution of retirement funds.

Financial services professionals, who facilitate the investment of clients' money into various financial products and services, know that it is the client's long-term satisfaction that will drive the financial advisor's business success. Products that meet client needs and expectations will unite the client to the advisor and attract further business from the client's family and friends.

When clients become disappointed with their financial products and services, it means they, their family, and their friends will look elsewhere for future help. Disappointment can occur because the client did not comprehend what he or she was buying. It can occur because the client did not understand how the annuity would be funded. It can occur because annuities are perceived as too complex and so the person did not read the policy or disclosure. Disappointment can occur because the client does not understand how to obtain cash surrenders from the annuity and becomes alarmed at the thought of surrender charges being imposed. Disappointment can occur in many ways after the annuity sale is complete.

In general, disappointment in annuities focuses on two major areas:

Question #6 →

1. the specific financial advisor who sold the annuity
2. the annuity product itself

Disappointment with annuities has resulted in criticism of financial advisors and annuity products.

Criticisms of Financial Advisors

Salespeople. There are unethical salespeople, but they are in the minority. Most salespeople are ethical and always put the client first.

Sales Tactics. The industry has paid a heavy price both in image and money for its excesses, especially in terms of overly high commissions and lack of suitability.

Product Criticisms

High Commissions. Some companies deliberately construct their contracts with relatively high commissions to encourage sales.

"Bait and Switch" on Interest Rates. Some companies pay high interest rates on bonus annuities in the first year but follow in later years with low and uncompetitive interest rates, while surrender charges continue.

Lack of Liquidity. Illiquidity, caused by surrender charges, income taxes, and penalty taxes, highlights the fact that annuities, if used for retirement accumulation, are not designed to be liquid prior to retirement.

No Step-up in Cost Basis at Death. Beneficiaries have to pay income tax on the taxable gain from the annuity death benefits.

Gimmicky Options. Clients need to learn what options are available, understand those options, and see how they apply to their current situation. Educated clients are willing to buy and pay for options that are appropriate.

Mind-Numbing Complexity. Annuities are not as easy to understand as other financial product purchases.

To begin to overcome the criticisms of the market, the financial advisor must make sure the client understands the annuity he or she is purchasing. Furthermore, the financial advisor must determine if the annuity product is suitable and appropriate for the client, taking into account the client's age, liquidity needs, other assets, tax situation, and other relevant factors. The client must have full disclosure of all the provisions of the annuity contract and must understand what it is he or she is buying, including the limitations of the policy. To aid in this regard and to answer the concerns about the annuity industry, the SEC, FINRA, and the NAIC have developed several model rules and regulations to address the suitability of annuity sales.

FINRA's Deferred Variable Annuity Transactions Rule

The Financial Industry Regulatory Authority (FINRA) published guidance to firms on a new rule that was approved by the SEC in September 2007 covering transactions in deferred variable annuities. FINRA Regulatory Notice 07-53, published in November 2007, outlines the provisions of Rule 2821, which for the most part became effective on May 5, 2008. (Paragraph (C) of FINRA Rule 2821, which addresses principal review and approval procedures, was delayed from going into effect until August 4, 2008.)

FINRA developed Rule 2821 to enhance broker-dealers' compliance and supervisory systems and to provide more comprehensive and targeted protection to investors who buy or exchange deferred variable annuities.

Rule 2821, also called the Variable Annuity Rule, imposes requirements in the following four main areas:

suitability

- Suitability
- Principal Review Standards
- Written supervisory procedures

- Training program implementation

Registered   Representative   Requirements   for   Recommended Transactions. When recommending a deferred annuity transaction, a registered representative must

- make a reasonable effort to obtain and consider various types of customer-specific information, including age, income, financial situation and needs, investment experience and objectives, intended use of the deferred variable annuity, investment time horizon, existing assets, liquidity needs, liquid net worth, risk tolerance, and tax status
- have a reasonable basis to believe the customer has been informed of the material features of a deferred variable annuity, such as a surrender charge, potential tax penalty, various fees and costs, and market risk
- have a reasonable basis to believe that the customer would benefit from certain features of deferred variable annuities, such as tax-deferred growth, annuitization or death or living benefits
- make a customer suitability determination as to the investment in the deferred variable annuity, the investments in the underlying sub-accounts at the time of purchase or exchange, and all riders and other product enhancements and features contained in the annuity contract
- have a reasonable basis to believe that a deferred annuity exchange transaction is suitable for the particular customer, considering, among other factors, whether the customer would incur a surrender charge, be subject to a new surrender period, lose existing benefits, be subject to increased fees or charges, and has had another exchange within the preceding 36 months.

Principal Review and Approval Obligations for All Transactions. The new rule requires a registered principal to review and determine whether to approve the customer's application for a deferred variable annuity before transmitting the application to the issuing insurance company but no later than seven business days after the customer signs the application. A principal must treat all transactions as if they have been recommended for purposes of review and can approve the transaction only if it is suitable based on the factors that a registered representative must consider when making a recommendation. However, the principal *may* authorize the processing of the transaction even if he or she does not approve it based on suitability if, but only if, the following two determinations are made: (1) the transaction was not recommended, and (2) the customer, after being told why the principal found it to be unsuitable, still wants to proceed with the purchase or exchange.

Firm Supervisory Procedures. Rule 2821 requires broker-dealers to establish and maintain written supervisory procedures reasonably designed to achieve compliance with the rule's standards. That includes requirements that the broker-dealer implement surveillance procedures to determine whether any brokers have rates of effecting variable annuity exchanges that might evidence misconduct, and have policies and procedures in place to address inappropriate exchanges.

Firm Training Program. The new rule requires firms to create training programs for registered representatives who sell deferred variable annuities and for registered principals who review deferred variable annuity transactions.

The full text of Rule 2821 is available at www.finra.org/notices/07-53.

Senior Protection in Annuity Transactions Model Regulation

Until 2003, determining the suitability of a product offered to the consumer had not been a requirement in the sale of fixed annuities. Suitability, however, has been an element in variable annuity sales in which registered representatives are required to complete an investor profile form that asks a prospective client questions about risk tolerance, time horizon, and investment objectives when applying for a policy. In 2003, the NAIC adopted a model regulation to deal with the increasing criticisms against the insurance industry for inappropriate sales of annuity products to senior citizens. This model regulation provides protection for senior citizens against abusive annuity sales. The key points of the model regulation are as follows:

- The regulation helps protect senior citizens either at the point of purchase or upon the surrender of an annuity.
- It ensures that the insurance needs of seniors are appropriately addressed.
- It establishes standards and procedures for both insurance companies and financial advisors.
- The regulation applies to both variable and fixed annuities.
- It requires that financial advisors obtain financial information from prospective clients and determine whether or not the annuity products are suitable for those clients.
- It directs that the advisor must have reasonable grounds for believing the annuity product is appropriate for the senior.

- It provides that insurance companies set standards for compliance, guidelines, education, and monitoring devices.

Purpose

Senior Protection in Annuity Transactions Model Regulation

The *Senior Protection in Annuity Transactions Model Regulation* sets standards and procedures for recommendations of annuity products to senior citizens. The purpose is to make sure that seniors' insurance needs and financial objectives are appropriately addressed at the time the financial advisor makes the recommendation to purchase the annuity. The model regulation includes these definitions:

- An annuity is defined as any fixed or variable annuity that is individually solicited, whether classified as an individual or group annuity.
- Recommendation is defined as the advice provided by an insurance producer to an individual senior consumer that results in a purchase or exchange of an annuity product based on that advice.
- A senior consumer is defined as any person aged 65 or older.

Scope

The model regulation applies to any recommendation the financial advisor makes to purchase or exchange an annuity, resulting in the purchase or exchange of an annuity product. Compliance with FINRA Conduct Rules regarding suitability will satisfy the requirements for variable annuities. However, this does not limit the insurance commissioner's ability to enforce the provision of the new regulation.

There are several exemptions from the suitability requirement, including the following:

- direct response annuity solicitations
- employee pension or welfare plans covered by ERISA
- 401(a), 401(k), 403(b), 408(k), or 408(p) plans if established or maintained by an employer
- government or church plans under IRC Sec. 414
- IRC Sec. 457 plans
- nonqualified deferred-compensation arrangements
- structured settlement annuities
- prepaid funeral contracts

Duties of Insurer and Producers

In making a recommendation, the advisor must have reasonable grounds to believe that the recommendation is suitable on the basis of facts the senior consumer disclosed about his or her investments and other insurance products and about his or her financial situation and needs.

Prior to completing a transaction, the advisor must make a reasonable effort to obtain information concerning the client's

- financial status
- tax status
- investment objectives
- other information used or considered reasonable in making recommendations

The recommendation must be reasonable under all circumstances actually known to the advisor at the time of the recommendation. The advisor does not have an obligation to a senior consumer concerning any recommendation if that consumer

- refuses to provide relevant information requested
- fails to provide accurate or complete information
- decides to enter into a transaction not based on the advisor's recommendation

Insurers have to establish and maintain a system to supervise advisors' recommendations reasonably designed to achieve compliance, including

- written procedures
- periodic reviews of its records aimed at detecting and preventing violations of the regulation
- other processes as necessary

Insurance companies are not required to

- review all producer-solicited transactions
- include recommendations to senior consumers for insurance products that are not that insurer's annuities

Record Keeping

Records of the information collected from the consumer or other information collected and used in making recommendations must be kept.

The length of time for keeping these records is up to each individual state, but the expectation is that it will be for at least five years after the annuity ceases to exist or for five years after the date of any other such transaction based on the recommendation.

Annuity Disclosure Model Regulation

The National Association of Insurance Commissioners created a model regulation for fixed deferred annuities that it offered for adoption by the states in 1999 called the Annuity Disclosure Model Regulation.

annuity disclosure

Purpose

The purpose of this *annuity disclosure* regulation is to provide standards for the disclosure of certain minimum information about annuity contracts to protect consumers and foster consumer education. The regulation specifies the minimum information which must be disclosed and the method for disclosing it in connection with the sale of annuity contracts. The goal of this regulation is to ensure that purchasers of annuity contacts understand certain basic features of annuity contracts.

Applicability and Scope

This regulation applies to all group and individual annuity contracts except

- registered or nonregistered variable annuities or other registered products
- immediate or deferred annuities that contain no nonguaranteed elements
- annuities used to fund
  - employee pension or welfare plans covered by ERISA
  - 401(a), 401(k), or 403(b) plans if established or maintained by an employer
  - government or church plans under IRC Sec. 414
  - IRC Sec. 457 plans
  - nonqualified deferred-compensation arrangements
  - structured settlement annuities
  - charitable gift annuities
  - funding agreements made by an insurer that are not based on mortality or morbidity contingencies

Standards for the Disclosure Document

When the application for an annuity contract is taken in a face-to-face meeting, at or before the time of application, the applicant must be given both the disclosure document described in Sec. 5C (described below) and the prescribed NAIC fixed annuities buyers' guide containing an appendix section addressing equity-indexed annuities.

When the application for an annuity contract is taken by means other than in a face-to-face meeting, at or before the time of application, the applicant must be sent both the disclosure document and the NAIC fixed annuities buyers guide no later than two business days after the completed application is received by the insurer.

Sec. 5C. At a minimum, the following information must be included in the disclosure document required to be provided under this regulation:

- the generic name of the contract, the company product name, if different, and form number, and the fact that it is an annuity
- the insurer's name and address

The model regulation recommends that the following types of information be disclosed in the document:

a description of the contract and its benefits, emphasizing its long-term nature, including examples where appropriate:

- the guaranteed, nonguaranteed, and determinable elements of the contract, and an explanation of how those elements operate
- an explanation of the initial interest rate and the duration of the rate, and a statement that the rates may change and are not guaranteed
- information about periodic income options both on a guaranteed and nonguaranteed basis
- any reductions in the amount of the contract value that will result from withdrawals or surrenders
- an explanation of how the contract owner may gain access to contract values
- information about the death benefit, if any, and how it will be calculated
- a summary of the federal tax status of the contract and any penalties imposed on withdrawals
- an explanation of how any riders affect the contract

In addition, the regulation requires the following disclosures to be included:

- a listing of specific dollar amounts or percentage charges and fees with an explanation of how they apply
- information about the current guaranteed rate for new policies that contains a clear notice that the rate is subject to change

Report to Contract Owners

For annuities in the payout period with changes in nonguaranteed elements and for the accumulation period of a deferred annuity, the insurer must provide each contract owner with a report, at least annually, on the status of the contract that contains at least the following information:

- the beginning and end date of the current period
- the accumulation and cash surrender value, if any, at the end of the previous report period and at the end of the current report period
- the total amounts, if any, that have been credited, charged to the contract value, or paid during the current report period
- the amount of outstanding loans, if any, as of the end of the current report period

Not all states have fully adopted this model regulation. Some insurance companies offer a disclosure document even if the particular state does not require it. Using this disclosure will help to limit client disappointment. It is another tool in the selling/planning process to explain the features and benefits of the particular annuity under consideration. In fact, the required disclosures can serve as an excellent checklist for prospects and advisors. The advisor can use these points as the agenda in a meeting in which a client wishes to explore his or her annuity options.

CREDITOR PROTECTION

Typically the assets that people own are subject to the claims of their creditors. If a person files for bankruptcy, the assets are pooled together and distributed among the person's creditors to help cover the debt to the creditors. Not all assets are part of the creditor pool. Assets like the individual's home are usually protected. The government does not want its citizens losing everything they own in bankruptcy. This is why each state generally has a list of assets protected from creditors' reach. Even annuities can appear on the list of protected assets. Not all states afford annuities this protection, but some do.

creditor protection   *Creditor protection* can be especially important to professional practitioners, people who serve on boards of directors, and individuals who can be sued for their own accidental acts or for the acts of any other family members or animals in their households.

Some people might wonder if the protection from creditors is a protection offered by the insurance company and, even further, if this is a benefit for which the insurance company can charge. The answer is no. Annuities' protection from creditors is a matter that each state legislature addresses; whether or not the annuity has protection is part of the particular state's laws. Because laws are subject to frequent changes, the protection afforded to annuities can be added or removed by the state at any time.

The first issue to address is which particular state law is applicable. Generally the state of residence of the person seeking protection from his or her creditors is the relevant state law.

Next, determine whether or not the particular annuity policy is non-qualified or qualified. This distinction is critical for creditor protection because a different set of rules applies to funds that are IRAs and qualified plans than applies to nonqualified annuities.

Nonqualified annuity exemptions from the claims of creditors are generally less favorable than those afforded to qualified retirement plans. However, the laws vary considerably on a state-by-state basis. In fact, consider the following laws for five different states, and note how widely they vary from one another:

- state 1—There is no exemption at all from creditors for annuities owned by the debtor.
- state 2—Only $250 per month in annuity income payments is exempt from creditors. This means that the debtor must give up all but $250 in immediate-annuity income payments. Deferred annuities are not protected at all.
- state 3—Only annuities that are necessary for the support of the debtor's dependents are exempt from creditors. This usually means that a judge will have to determine what is "necessary," and any amounts over that will be given over to the creditors.
- state 4—Only annuity contracts inside IRAs are exempt from creditors. If the debtor owns nonqualified annuities, they are not protected and must be given over to the debtor's creditors.
- state 5—Annuities are completely exempt from creditors. This is the most liberal protection for annuities. No matter what type of annuity the debtor owns (qualified or nonqualified) or how large the annuity is in terms of cash value, all annuities are exempt from a creditor's reach.

Because the issue of creditor protection is controlled by state law, each policyowner must seek legal counsel in his or her state to determine the level of creditor protection for annuity holdings. The financial advisor should not give advice to clients regarding creditor protection of annuities and should refer clients to legal counsel.

Federal Law—Government as Creditor

It is noteworthy to mention that despite varying levels of protection from creditors extended to policyowners in most states, the federal government has the superseding right to collect unpaid policyowner income taxes from life insurance policies. The government can also collect from disability payments, joint tax returns, community property—and annuity contracts.

YOUR PROFESSIONAL PRACTICE

Your Role as a Professional Financial Advisor

Your dual role in the financial planning process can be that of motivator and coordinator. First, through your work in identifying, approaching, and qualifying prospects, and then by motivating them to take appropriate action, you play a crucial role in the financial services arena. You are the only member of the financial planning team that solicits business from new prospects, gathers information, analyzes it, develops suitable product recommendations, and then assists clients in implmenting solutions. Finally, you service clients' financial plans and make periodic recommendations as needed.

Coordinating the labors of other financial planning professionals can be a daunting task, which is one reason that many clients delay doing the retirement and estate planning they need. The tasks involved in planning for the security of their finances and the proper disposition of their assets can seem overwhelming to many people. Confusion about where to begin the complex process of wealth management contributes to their tendency to procrastinate. Therefore financial advisors often have to orchestrate a team effort to assist our prospects and clients to achieve their financial goals.

Professionalism

To work successfully with other professionals, you must be a professional. You must have the technical knowledge necessary to provide meaningful support and accurate advice to your prospects and clients. As a competent financial advisor, you must be knowledgeable about the legal and tax ramifications of the recommendations you make. You must also be able to outline the positive and negative implications of the various annuity plan options available so that your prospects and clients can make informed purchasing decisions. You therefore must have a thorough understanding of your products, the problems that face your prospects and clients, and how your products can be used to provide solutions.

Professionals must also adhere to a code of ethics. You should endorse and follow the code of ethics of your chosen professional organizations. The American College, The National Association of Insurance and Financial Advisors (NAIFA), and the Million Dollar Round Table, as well as other financial services organizations, all provide professional codes of ethics.

Client Focus. To be a professional, you need to be client centered. This means you have to put your clients' interests before your own. In financial, estate, and retirement planning, your job goes beyond simply making a single product sale. Your professional responsibility is to help your prospects and clients identify and implement all the steps that will help them accomplish their financial planning goals.

Legal Requirements. Professionalism also requires you to meet the legal and ethical standards of the insurance and financial services industries. You must, for example, be licensed to discuss the products you sell in all jurisdictions in which you work. Unless you are a licensed attorney, it is illegal for you to give legal advice. It is also illegal for you to give tax advice when acting in the role of financial advisor. While you can discuss legal and tax considerations in general terms, you cannot provide specific legal or tax advice; nor can you draft legal documents.

Protecting Yourself. In spite of all your professionalism, mistakes and misunderstandings do happen. Therefore you need to protect yourself. Your exposure to the risk of lawsuits, like any other liability, can and should be insured with errors and omissions insurance.

Proper documentation helps you to protect yourself. As you start making a complete assessment of your prospect's needs, consider all of his or her needs, not only the ones that may represent a sale for you. Make your recommendations in writing, and keep copies that are signed or initialed by your prospect in the appropriate files. Likewise keep copies of all correspondence and records of all conversations.

Working With Other Professional Advisors

Acting in your capacity as a professional financial advisor will certainly require contact with other professional advisors. Consequently you will inevitably need to put your clients in touch with various members of a network of professional advisors that you will develop throughout your career. You must also learn effective techniques to work with your client's existing advisor(s). For example, in basic estate planning, a qualified attorney should be involved in preparing a will, a trust, a durable power of attorney, and an advance medical directive. As a person's estate becomes more complicated with the acquisition of more assets and various forms of property, other advisors, including accountants, trust officers, and securities brokers, may also be needed.

Creating Relationships. Most advisors who have been in the financial services business for any length of time have at least one story of an accountant or attorney who squelched a big sale. This experience, which is common to many of you, can leave a bad impression regarding the effect that other professionals can have on your recommendations.

If a prospect already has a relationship with a professional advisor, it is unrealistic to expect the prospect to make a decision without first consulting that advisor. These advisors are important to the planning process, so try to involve them in your planning as it becomes apparent that they will influence the prospect's decision. Your relationship with the prospect's advisors should not be adversarial; instead, it should be a cooperative relationship with all of you having the same objective—the best plan for your prospect.

Other Advisors. One of the first things you should find out as you develop your relationship with a prospect is to whom he or she turns for advice. You should determine this early in your first fact-finding interview, as discussed in chapters 3 and 4. Find out if the advisors help in a professional or personal capacity. Also try to ascertain the strength of the relationship with each advisor so that you can determine how influential the advisor will be in the final decision about purchasing annuity products.

The attitude of outside advisors, whether they are professional or personal, can make or break your proposal. Try to involve these advisors in the sales process from the beginning. Make sure they understand your proposal and buy into it before you attempt to close the sale. Try to make them advocates for what you are proposing instead of adversaries.

Confidentiality. As a professional, you have an obligation to keep the prospect and client information you collect confidential. Accordingly you should not expect other professionals to share information or discuss your prospect's financial planning matters with you without the prospect's permission. When you begin to work with new prospects, share with them your potential need to discuss their situation with their other advisors.

If there is an outside advisor with whom you find it necessary to make contact, you should never do so without first getting the prospect's permission. Otherwise, you may find the advisor very unreceptive to your call. Like you, attorneys and accountants have a responsibility to keep confidential the information they have about a client.

Getting Permission. The best way to get permission to approach the prospect's other advisors is to have your prospect contact them, alert them that you are working together, and authorize them to provide the information you need. If possible, it is best to have this authorization in writing so the other advisors have a copy for their files. You can give the prospect a letter or form to use.

If any of the other advisors are family members, invite them to attend your next meeting with the prospect. This will avoid many misunderstandings about what is being discussed and will demonstrate your willingness to work amicably with them through the planning process.

Following Up. When you know that letters to the advisors have been sent, follow up with a phone call. You will want to introduce yourself, refer to the prospect's letter, and then briefly explain the area of planning you are doing for the prospect. If you agree that it is appropriate to meet in person, ask for an appointment.

To be effective, you will need to prepare carefully for a meeting with the prospect's other advisors. You want your discussion with them to be concise, so be prepared to explain what you are proposing and what information you seek, if any. If the other advisors include an elder-law attorney, for example, you may suggest that some planning documents, such as an updated will and a durable power of attorney, be drafted or considered. You can also educate the other advisor on the terms of the annuity policy you are recommending. Remember, this may be an opportunity to develop an ongoing and mutually beneficial professional relationship. It does not hurt to encourage teamwork on behalf of the prospect. Be sure to let the other advisor know that both you and the prospect value his or her input.

Keeping It Positive. If the other advisors oppose your ideas or have a preferred approach, it is best to know this early in the process. Sometimes the first sale must be made to the advisors. Ask about their objections and tell them that you need their input to tailor the annuity plan to the prospect's needs. Try to get the advisors' opinions on how to approach retirement income planning. Listen closely and always try to find common ground.

If the other advisors disagree with each other, consider the validity of their opinions, explore additional options, and try to build a consensus. This is a useful strategy whether the advisors are the prospect's accountant and attorney or the prospect's son and daughter.

Under no circumstances should you make negative comments about other advisors to your prospect. In addition to being unprofessional, it can confuse the prospect about the merit of the proposed options, which may, in turn, lead to his or her taking no action at all. Instead, acknowledge different points of view and explain why you think yours is the best one. You can address the concerns or objections of the other advisors without attacking their credibility or expertise.

Concluding Thoughts

To educate your prospects, you must be continuously educating yourself. Not only do you have to learn the basic concepts involved in financial planning, but you must also keep studying to learn advanced concepts. You have to be prepared to address the exceptions and complications that are often part of the responsible planning process, as well as the routine situations that you most frequently encounter. You must stay abreast of product innovations, legislative trends, and tax rulings that can affect your ability to provide the highest level of service. By doing so, you will become a competent member of your prospects' and clients' financial planning teams.

Now that you have finished reading the last chapter of *Essentials of Annuities,* it is time to assimilate all the sales skills techniques, product essentials, and planning foundations into your marketing activities. As you develop your business and focus on your future, remember that one day *you* too will retire. It is never too early to start preparing for it. Ideally you will use what you have learned from reading this book to determine the role that annuities will play in your own retirement plan.

CHAPTER EIGHT REVIEW

Key Terms and Concepts are explained in the Glossary. Answers to the Review Questions and Self-Test Questions are found in the back of the book in the Answers to Questions section.

Key Terms and Concepts

state insurance department
solvency
market conduct
state guaranty association
Securities and Exchange
    Commission (SEC)
security
Financial Industry Regulatory
    Authority (FINRA)

broker-dealer
National Association of Insurance
    Commissioners (NAIC)
suitability
Senior Protection in Annuity
    Transactions Model Regulation
annuity disclosure
creditor protection

Review Questions

8-1. Explain why state insurance departments are concerned with the solvency of their insurers.

8-2. Describe the role of the state insurance department in licensing advisors.

8-3. Explain why recent legislation has allowed insurers to lower the guaranteed minimum interest rates in fixed-interest annuity policies.

8-4. Explain why an advisor is prohibited from using the existence of a state guaranty fund to encourage an annuity sale to a consumer.

8-5. Describe the NAIC's role in the insurance industry.

8-6. Describe how FINRA and the SEC differ in their regulation of the variable annuity market.

8-7. Explain what additional licensing or education requirements an advisor needs to sell variable annuities if he or she is already licensed to sell fixed annuities.

8-8. Explain what a financial advisor should do if a client asks if his or her annuity is protected from creditors.

Self-Test Questions

Instructions: Read chapter eight first; then answer the following questions to test your knowledge. There are 10 questions; circle the correct answer, and then check your answers with the answer key in the back of the book.

8-1. Which of the following FINRA registration exams must be completed successfully to sell variable annuities but is not required for selling individual stocks and bonds?

    (A)   Series 6
    (B)   Series 7
    (C)   Series 63
    (D)   Series 24

8-2. The fixed-annuity market is actively regulated by which of the following entities?

    (A)   SEC
    (B)   FINRA
    (C)   ACLU
    (D)   state insurance departments

8-3. A variable annuity prospectus serves which of the following functions?

    (A)   It provides the free-look period option.
    (B)   It provides protection against policyowner creditors.
    (C)   It discloses fees and charges to the policyowner.
    (D)   It discloses the financial suitability of the policyowner.

8-4. Which of the following best describes the role of the SEC?

    (A)   to protect investors and maintain fair, orderly, and efficient markets
    (B)   to regulate the sale of variable annuities
    (C)   to provide oversight to FINRA
    (D)   to provide model legislation for all states

8-5. Which of the following annuity sales are not exempt from the Senior Protection in Annuity Transactions Model Regulation?

    (A)   IRC Sec. 457 plans
    (B)   nonqualified deferred-compensation arrangements
    (C)   variable annuities
    (D)   structured settlement annuities

8-6. Which of the following statements regarding the Senior Protection in Annuity Transactions Model Regulation is (are) correct?

    I.   It applies to variable annuities.
    II.   It applies to fixed annuities.

    (A)   I only
    (B)   II only
    (C)   Both I and II
    (D)   Neither I nor II

8-7. Which of the following criticisms have been aimed at the annuity marketplace?

    I.   Insurance advisor commissions are overly high.
    II. Annuities are not designed to be liquid.

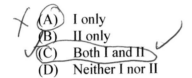

    (A)   I only
    (B)   II only
    (C)   Both I and II
    (D)   Neither I nor II

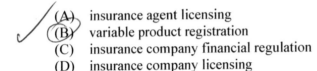

8-8. All of the following are roles of state insurance departments EXCEPT

    (A)   insurance agent licensing
    (B)   variable product registration
    (C)   insurance company financial regulation
    (D)   insurance company licensing

8-9. When working with other professional advisors, you should do all of the following EXCEPT

    (A)   involve the prospect's other advisors in the sales process from the beginning
    (B)   keep information you collect about the prospect confidential unless he or she authorizes you to share it with other advisors
    (C)   have the prospect contact his or her other advisors to let them know that you may get in touch with them
    (D)   attack the credibility or expertise of the prospect's other advisors who disagree with you

8-10. All of the following must be disclosed under the Model Annuity Disclosure Act EXCEPT

    (A)   the guaranteed elements of the annuity policy
    (B)   the duration of the initial interest rate guarantee
    (C)   how the insurance company will invest the premiums
    (D)   how any riders affect the policy

Appendix A

Retirement Planning Fact Finder

Retirement Planning Fact Finder
Personal Data and Retirement Goals

Personal Data

Your Name _____   Your Spouse's Name _____

Social Security Number_____   Social Security Number _____

Date of Birth _____   Date of Birth _____

Home Address
Street _____

City _____   State _____ Zip _____

Home Phone _____   Your Business Phone _____

Your Cell Phone _____   Spouse's Cell Phone _____

Your Fax _____   Spouse's Fax _____

Your E-mail _____   Spouse's E-mail _____

Children

Name	Address	Age
_____	_____	_____
_____	_____	_____
_____	_____	_____

What are the names, addresses, and phone numbers of your professional and personal advisors?

Advisor	Name	Address	Phone
Attorney			
Insurance Advisor			
Securities Broker			
Accountant			
Banker / Trust Officer / Others			

Have you had any of the following documents prepared? If so, by whom and when?

Document	Prepared by	Date
Will	Yes / No _____	_____
Living Will	Yes / No _____	_____
Durable Power of Attorney	Yes / No _____	_____
Health Care Power of Attorney	Yes / No _____	_____
Revocable Living Trust	Yes / No _____	_____
Irrevocable Trust	Yes / No _____	_____
Financial Plan	Yes / No _____	_____
Estate Plan	Yes / No _____	_____

What other services have any of your professional advisors performed for you?

_____

1

Retirement Goals—Assumptions

1) Is your spouse to be included in this plan?   Yes   No

   *At what age do you (and your spouse) plan to retire?
   (When did you retire?)   You _____   Spouse _____

   How many years of retirement do you wish to plan for?   You _____   Spouse _____

2) Average inflation rate estimated over the span of this plan   _____%

3) Average compound interest rate assigned to all savings prior to retirement (optional)   _____%

4) Average compound interest rate assigned to all savings during retirement   _____%

5) Estimated average tax rate on taxable earnings prior to retirement   _____%

6) Estimated average tax rate on taxable earnings during retirement   _____%

Retirement Goals—Qualitative

*Where do you plan to live when you retire?

_____

What does retirement mean to you personally?

_____

*Do you expect to maintain your preretirement standard of living in retirement?   Yes   No

What types of recreational activities do your retirement plans involve?

_____

Will any of your children be involved in your retirement planning financial decisions?   Yes   No

*Indicates questions that are also found on the Personal Retirement Planning Review form.

QUANTITATIVE DATA

Financial Position Statement

Assets			Liabilities and Net Worth	
Cash, Near-Cash Equivalents	**Current Value**			**Current Value**
Checking accounts/cash			Charge accounts/credit cards	
Savings accounts			Family/personal/auto loans	
Money market funds			Margin/bank/life insurance loans	
Treasury bills			Income taxes (federal, state, local)	
Short-term CDs			Property taxes	
Savings bonds			Investment liabilities	
Other (specify)			Mortgage(s)	
Subtotal			Lease(s)	
Other Financial Assets			Child support	
Stock			Alimony	
Bonds, taxable			Other (specify)	
Bonds, tax exempt			Other (specify)	
Mutual funds			Other (specify)	
Other securities			**Total Liabilities**	$
Investment real estate				
Long-term CDs			**Net Worth (Total Assets Minus Total Liabilities)**	
Vested retirement benefits				$
Annuities (cash values)				
Life insurance cash values				
IRAs (Roth/traditional)				
Limited partnership units				
Interest(s) in trust(s)				
Value of business interest				
Other (specify)				
Other (specify)				
Other (specify)				
Subtotal				
Personal Assets				
Personal residence				
Seasonal residence				
Automobiles, other vehicles				
Household furnishings				
Boats				
Jewelry/furs				
Collections (art, coins, etc.)				
Other (specify)				
Subtotal				
Total Assets	$		**Total Liabilities Plus Net Worth**	$

3

Cash Flow Statement	
Annual Income	**Amount**
Wages, salary, bonus, etc.: Client	
Wages, salary, bonus, etc.: Spouse	
Business (self-employment) income	
Real estate rental	
Dividends—investments	
Dividends—close corporation stock	
Interest on bonds, taxable	
Interest on bonds, tax exempt	
Interest on savings accounts, CDs	
Interest on loans, notes, etc.	
Trust income	
Life insurance settlement options	
Annuities	
Child support/alimony	
Other sources (specify)	
Total Annual Income	$
Housing (mortgage/rent)	
Utilities and telephone	
Food, groceries, etc.	
Clothing and cleaning	
Federal income and Social Security taxes	
State and local income taxes	
Property taxes	
Transportation (auto/commuting)	
Medical/dental/drugs/health insurance	
Debt repayment	
House upkeep/repairs/maintenance	
Life, property, and liability insurance	
Child support/alimony	
Total Fixed Expenses	
Vacations/travel/etc.	
Recreation/entertainment	
Contributions/gifts	
Household furnishings	
Education fund	
Savings/investments	
Other (specify)	
Total Discretionary Expenses	
Total Annual Expenses	$
Net Cash Flow (Total Annual Income Minus Total Annual Expenses)	$

Using today's before-tax dollars, what percentage of total income is required during retirement?   _____%

(Multiply total income by percentage above)
Annual retirement income goal when you retire $_____

*Are you satisfied with the amount of money you currently have accumulated thus far?   Yes   No

*Are you currently saving and investing enough to reach your retirement goals?   Yes   No

*Do you feel you need to increase your savings?   Yes   No

(If yes) *By how much are you willing to increase your savings on a monthly basis? $_____

If you made additional investments or purchased additional financial products, what would your future objectives be in doing so?

_____

*Are you concerned with reducing the taxes on your savings?   Yes   No

How do you feel about taking investment risks?

_____

Do you consider yourself a successful investor?   Yes   No

Why or why not?

_____

Do you have any funds on hand now that you might want to invest?   Yes   No

If yes, how much? $_____

Into what risk category(ies) would any additional financial products you purchase be included?

    High risk (aggressive)   _____%

    Moderate risk   _____%

    Balanced risk (some aggressive, some conservative)   _____%

    Conservative (little or no risk)   _____%

Do you worry about outliving or depleting the assets you've accumulated in your life's savings?   Yes   No

How much cash or pure liquid assets do you feel you should have available to you at all times? $_____

Have you purchased insurance coverage to protect against all other types of financial risks?   Yes   No

What kinds of insurance products do you own?

_____

*Are you willing to consider purchasing additional financial products to help you reach your retirement goals?   Yes   No

Indicates questions that are also found on the Personal Retirement Planning Review form.

5

Retirement Income Sources

SUMMARY—INFLATION-INDEXED INCOME

Before and after retirement commences:

**Category 1: Total Social Security Benefits in Today's Dollars
(from page 7)**   **(line 1-1)** $_____

After retirement income commences:

Total annual pension and taxable funded income
payments—indexed (from page 7)   (line 1-2) $_____

Total annual retirement income from current
investments—indexed (from page 8)   (line 1-3) $_____

Total projected income from all deposits and
earnings—indexed (from page 9)   (line 1-4) $_____

Total income from all distribution options—indexed
(from page 10)   (line 1-5) $_____

Net amount of additional funds/expenses per year—
indexed (from page 11)   (line 1-6) $_____

**Category 2: Other Inflation-Indexed Income
(Sum of lines 1-2 through 1-6)**   **SOURCE 1** $_____

SUMMARY—FIXED INCOME

Total annual pension and taxable funded income
payments—fixed (from page 7)   SOURCE 2 $_____

Total annual retirement income from current
investments—fixed (from page 8)   SOURCE 3 $_____

Total projected income from all deposits and
earnings—fixed (from page 9)   SOURCE 4 $_____

Total income from all distribution options—fixed
(from page 10)   SOURCE 5 $_____

Net amount of additional funds/expenses per year—
fixed (from page 11)   SOURCE 6 $_____

Total Fixed Income   **(Total of SOURCES 2 + 3 + 4 + 5 + 6)** $_____

*To convert total fixed income into its inflation-adjusted equivalent income, divide total
fixed income by the average inflation rate factor during retirement.*

Total fixed income	÷	*Average inflation rate factor during retirement*	=	*Inflation-adjusted fixed income*
$_____	÷	_____	=	$_____

Category 3: Total Inflation-Adjusted Fixed Income
                    (SOURCES 2 through 6 Adjusted for Inflation) $_____

1. **SOCIAL SECURITY BENEFITS**
   1) Age you plan to start Social Security benefits   _____

   2) Estimated Social Security annual benefit $_____

   3) Age your spouse will start Social Security benefits   _____

   4) Spouse's estimated Social Security annual benefit $_____

   Total Social Security Benefits in Today's Dollars (line 1-1) $_____

2. **PENSION AND OTHER FUNDED INCOME PAYMENTS**
   (Employer-funded pension, deferred compensation, taxable trust income, etc.)

   1) Source _____

   2) Annual projected future retirement income from this source $_____

   3) Your age when these payments will start   _____

   4) Number of years benefits will be paid (use 0 if through lifetime) _____

   5) Check one: ____ Indexed starting now
                          ____ Indexed starting with first payment

   Additional pension or taxable funded income

   1) Source _____

   2) Annual projected future retirement income from this source $_____

   3) Your age when these payments will start   _____

   4) Number of years benefits will be paid (use 0 if through lifetime) _____

   5) Check one: ____ Indexed starting now
                          ____ Indexed starting with first payment

   (Please use additional sheets to list other income payment streams.)

Total Annual Pension and Funded Income Payments—Indexed (line 1-2) $_____

                                    —Fixed SOURCE 2 $_____

7

3. CURRENT INVESTMENTS

Tax categories: taxable (T), tax free (TF), deductible tax deferred (TD), nondeductible tax deferred (ND), and Roth IRA (R)

Tax Category	Asset Class (Stocks, Bonds, Mutual Funds, CDs, Savings, etc.)	Current Value	Rate of Return	Future Value	Amount for Use in Retirement
_____	_____	$_____	_____ %	$_____	$_____
_____	_____	$_____	_____ %	$_____	$_____
_____	_____	$_____	_____ %	$_____	$_____
_____	_____	$_____	_____ %	$_____	$_____
_____	_____	$_____	_____ %	$_____	$_____
_____	_____	$_____	_____ %	$_____	$_____
_____	_____	$_____	_____ %	$_____	$_____
_____	_____	$_____	_____ %	$_____	$_____

Total Lump Sum of Capital From Investments for Use in Retirement $_____ +

+ This total may include tax-free income that will need to be converted to taxable equivalent amounts. See the bottom of page 11 for an example of how to convert tax-free income into taxable equivalent income.

How to Calculate the Fixed Income From Investments. Multiply the result from line above by the percentage of compound interest before taxes that this lump sum is expected to earn (i.e., if $100,000 earns 8%, then $100,000 x .08 = $8,000 annual fixed retirement income).

How to Calculate the Inflation-Indexed Income From Investments. Divide the sum above by the appropriate factor from table 4 (i.e., $100,000 ÷ by 13.23 = $7,558 of real income for 20 years at 8% interest and 3% inflation).

Total Annual Retirement Income from Investments—Indexed (line 1-3) $_____

—Fixed (SOURCE 3) $_____

4. **DEPOSITS and EARNINGS**
    The following five sections ask for annual savings and investments in the future. Targeted rates of return are assumed to be the average rates of return found in questions 3 or 4 of the Personal Data and Retirement Goals Section on page 2 of this form unless otherwise specified.

    Taxable Investments (e.g., stocks, bonds, mutual funds, money market, savings)
    1) Amount you plan to invest yearly in taxable assets   _____
    2) Percentage increase in these deposits each year   _____%
    3) Targeted annual rate of return prior to retirement   _____%
    4) Total projected lump-sum accumulation at retirement $_____

    Projected Income at Retirement $_____+

    Tax-Free Investments (e.g., municipal bonds, tax-free mutual funds)
    1) Amount you plan to invest yearly in tax-free assets   _____
    2) Percentage increase in these deposits each year   _____%
    3) Targeted annual rate of return prior to retirement   _____%
    4) Total projected lump-sum accumulation at retirement $_____

    Projected Income at Retirement $_____+

    Deductible Tax-Deferred Investments (e.g., traditional IRAs; 401(k), 403(b), and profit-sharing plans; Keoghs; SEPs)
    1) Annual tax-deferred contribution now planned   _____
    2) Percentage increase in tax-deferred deposits each year   _____%
    3) Targeted annual rate of return prior to retirement   _____%
    4) Total projected lump-sum accumulation at retirement $_____

    Projected Income at Retirement $_____

    Nondeductible Tax-Deferred Investments (after-tax dollars in annuities accumulating tax-deferred earnings)
    1) Total after-tax premium payments you will make each year   _____
    2) Percentage increase in these premiums each year   _____%
    3) Targeted annual rate of return prior to retirement   _____%
    4) Total projected lump-sum accumulation at retirement $_____

    Projected Income at Retirement $_____+

    Roth IRA
    1) Amount you plan to invest yearly in tax-free assets   _____
    2) Percentage increase in premiums each year if IRS allows   _____%
    3) Targeted annual rate of return prior to retirement   _____%
    4) Total projected lump-sum accumulation at retirement $_____

    Projected Income at Retirement $_____+

    + These totals may include tax-free income that will need to be converted to taxable equivalent amounts. See the bottom of page 11 for an example of how to convert tax-free income into taxable equivalent income.

    Total Projected Income from All Deposits and Earnings—Indexed (line 1-4) $_____

                                   —Fixed (SOURCE 4) $_____

9

5. DISTRIBUTION OPTIONS

Alternatives on default selections for distributing portfolio funds when required during retirement

Calculation of Minimum Distributions

Client _____Single-life calculation   _____ Joint-and-last-survivor calculation   _____ Other

Spouse _____Single-life calculation   _____ Joint-and-last-survivor calculation   _____ Other

Annuity Payout Option for Deductible Tax-Deferred Assets

a)   Annual distributions in the amount of $_____

b)   Distributions will begin at your age   _____

c)   Distributions will continue for ? years (Enter 0 for lifetime or until funds are depleted)   _____

Annuity Payout Option for Nondeductible Tax-Deferred Assets

a)   Annual distributions in the amount of $_____ +

b)   Distributions will begin at your age   _____

c)   Distributions will continue for ? years (Enter 0 for lifetime or until funds are depleted)   _____

Insurance Products (private pensions, single-premium annuities)

Retirement benefits from insurance products should be listed here. Data entered should be taken only from an illustration prepared by the vendor of the insurance product.

Type of Product	Description	Cost Basis*	Start Age	Years**	Index	Annual Benefit
Life / annuity	_____	$_____	_____	_____	____%	$____ +
Life / annuity	_____	$_____	_____	_____	____%	$____ +
Life / annuity	_____	$_____	_____	_____	____%	$____ +
Life / annuity	_____	$_____	_____	_____	____%	$____ +

Total Income from Insurance Products $_____ +

  * Enter 0 if these benefits are tax-free draws from a life insurance policy.

** 0 years = lifetime

Total Income from All Distribution Options	**—Indexed (line 1-5)**	$_____
	—Fixed (SOURCE 5)	$_____

+ These totals may include tax-free income that will need to be converted to taxable equivalent amounts. See the bottom of page 11 for an explanation of how to convert tax-free income into taxable equivalent income.

6.   INCOME AND EXPENSES IN ADDITION TO LIVING REQUIREMENTS

ADDITIONAL FUNDS EXPECTED (e.g., sale of house or business, inheritance, wages, rent, royalties, etc.)

Description	Tax Category	Start Age	Years	Amount per Year
_____	_____	_____	_____	$_____
_____	_____	_____	_____	$_____
_____	_____	_____	_____	$_____

ROTH IRA CONVERSIONS

Description	Tax Category	Start Age	Conversion Amount	Pay Taxes From Roth Savings	Net After Taxes	Tax-Free Amount per Year
_____	Roth IRA	_____	$_____	_____	$_____	$_____ +
_____	Roth IRA	_____	$_____	_____	$_____	$_____ +

+ These totals may include tax-free income that will need to be converted to taxable equivalent
amounts. See the bottom of page 11 for an explanation of how to convert tax-free income into taxable
equivalent income.

Total Additional Funds Expected per Year $_____

ADDITIONAL MAJOR EXPENSES (e.g., college education, major purchase, medical expenses, world cruise, etc.)

Description	Tax Category	Start Age	Years	Amount per Year
_____	_____	_____	_____	$_____
_____	_____	_____	_____	$_____
_____	_____	_____	_____	$_____

Total Major Expenses per Year in Retirement   – $_____

Net Additional Funds/Expenses per Year   —Indexed (line 1-6)   (+ or –) $_____

                                     —Fixed (SOURCE 6)   (+ or –) $_____

Converting Annual Tax-Free Income Into Its Taxable Equivalent Income Amount:

*1. Obtain gross annual tax-free income from each respective income source—i.e., $1,000.
Determine the taxable equivalent factor for tax-free income by applying the following formula:
Tax-free income divided by (1 minus average tax rate %) = Taxable equivalent income factor:
$1,000/(1 – .15) = $1,000/.85 = 1.1765 (rounded to 1.18)*

*2. Multiply tax-free income from step 1 by the factor derived from formula above to obtain taxable
equivalent income: $1,000 x 1.18 = $1,180*

11

Calculations and Interest Tables

Retirement Income Calculation Worksheet

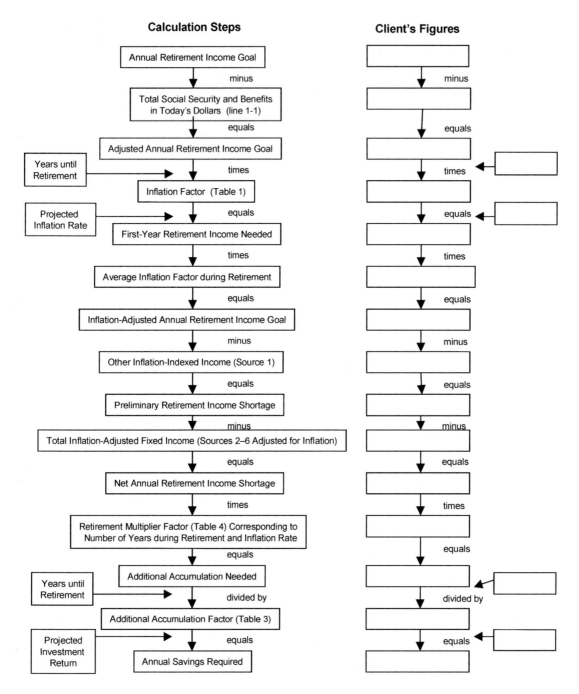

Calculation Steps

Annual Retirement Income Goal

↓ minus

Total Social Security and Benefits in Today's Dollars (line 1-1)

↓ equals

Adjusted Annual Retirement Income Goal

Years until Retirement → ↓ times

Inflation Factor (Table 1)

Projected Inflation Rate → ↓ equals

First-Year Retirement Income Needed

↓ times

Average Inflation Factor during Retirement

↓ equals

Inflation-Adjusted Annual Retirement Income Goal

↓ minus

Other Inflation-Indexed Income (Source 1)

↓ equals

Preliminary Retirement Income Shortage

↓ minus

Total Inflation-Adjusted Fixed Income (Sources 2–6 Adjusted for Inflation)

↓ equals

Net Annual Retirement Income Shortage

↓ times

Retirement Multiplier Factor (Table 4) Corresponding to Number of Years during Retirement and Inflation Rate

↓ equals

Years until Retirement → Additional Accumulation Needed

↓ divided by

Additional Accumulation Factor (Table 3)

Projected Investment Return → ↓ equals

Annual Savings Required

Client's Figures

12

FACT FINDER TABLE 1
Inflation Factors (Compound Interest Factors for a Single Sum)
Where i = Inflation Rate and n = Number of Years until Retirement

i =	1%	2%	3%	4%	5%	6%	7%	8%	9%	10%
n =1	1.0100	1.0200	1.0300	1.0400	1.0500	1.0600	1.0700	1.0800	1.0900	1.1000
2	1.0201	1.0404	1.0609	1.0816	1.1025	1.1236	1.1449	1.1664	1.1881	1.2100
3	1.0303	1.0612	1.0927	1.1249	1.1576	1.1910	1.2250	1.2597	1.2950	1.3310
4	1.0406	1.0824	1.1255	1.1699	1.2155	1.2625	1.3108	1.3605	1.4116	1.4641
5	1.0510	1.1041	1.1593	1.2167	1.2763	1.3382	1.4026	1.4693	1.5386	1.6105
6	1.0615	1.1262	1.1941	1.2653	1.3401	1.4185	1.5007	1.5869	1.6771	1.7716
7	1.0721	1.1487	1.2299	1.3159	1.4071	1.5036	1.6058	1.7138	1.8280	1.9487
8	1.0829	1.1717	1.2668	1.3686	1.4775	1.5938	1.7182	1.8509	1.9926	2.1436
9	1.0937	1.1951	1.3048	1.4233	1.5513	1.6895	1.8385	1.9990	2.1719	2.3579
10	1.1046	1.2190	1.3439	1.4802	1.6289	1.7908	1.9672	2.1589	2.3674	2.5937
11	1.1157	1.2434	1.3842	1.5395	1.7103	1.8983	2.1049	2.3316	2.5804	2.8531
12	1.1268	1.2682	1.4258	1.6010	1.7959	2.0122	2.2522	2.5182	2.8127	3.1384
13	1.1381	1.2936	1.4685	1.6651	1.8856	2.1329	2.4098	2.7196	3.0658	3.4523
14	1.1495	1.3195	1.5126	1.7317	1.9799	2.2609	2.5785	2.9372	3.3417	3.7975
15	1.1610	1.3459	1.5580	1.8009	2.0789	2.3966	2.7590	3.1722	3.6425	4.1772
16	1.1726	1.3728	1.6047	1.8730	2.1829	2.5404	2.9522	3.4259	3.9703	4.5950
17	1.1843	1.4002	1.6528	1.9479	2.2920	2.6928	3.1588	3.7000	4.3276	5.0545
18	1.1961	1.4282	1.7024	2.0258	2.4066	2.8543	3.3799	3.9960	4.7171	5.5599
19	1.2081	1.4568	1.7535	2.1068	2.5270	3.0256	3.6165	4.3157	5.1417	6.1159
20	1.2202	1.4859	1.8061	2.1911	2.6533	3.2071	3.8697	4.6610	5.6044	6.7275
21	1.2324	1.5156	1.8603	2.2787	2.7860	3.3995	4.1406	5.0339	6.1088	7.4003
22	1.2447	1.5459	1.9161	2.3699	2.9253	3.6035	4.4304	5.4366	6.6586	8.1403
23	1.2572	1.5768	1.9736	2.4647	3.0715	3.8179	4.7405	5.8715	7.2579	8.9543
24	1.2697	1.6084	2.0328	2.5633	3.2251	4.0489	5.0724	6.3412	7.9111	9.8497
25	1.2824	1.6406	2.0938	2.6658	3.3864	4.2918	5.4275	6.8485	8.6231	10.8347

* Table values can be interpolated for partial years and/or inflation and investment return rates that are not represented in the tables.

FACT FINDER TABLE 2
Consumer Price Index
Average Inflation Rates; Most Recent Time Periods

3 years	1.9%
5 years	2.3%
10 years	2.4%
15 years	2.9%
20 years	3.1%

Prospect's Inflation Rate Assumption _____ %

13

FACT FINDER TABLE 3
Annual Accumulation Factors: One Dollar per Year in Advance
Where R= Compound Interest Rate of Return and n= Number of Years until Retirement

R =	2%	3%	4%	5%	6%	7%	8%	9%	10%	11%	12%
Year											
n=1	1.020	1.030	1.040	1.050	1.060	1.070	1.080	1.090	1.100	1.110	1.120
2	2.060	2.091	2.122	2.153	2.184	2.215	2.246	2.278	2.310	2.342	2.374
3	3.122	3.184	3.246	3.310	3.375	3.440	3.506	3.573	3.641	3.710	3.779
4	4.204	4.309	4.416	4.526	4.637	4.751	4.867	4.985	5.105	5.228	5.353
5	5.308	5.468	5.633	5.802	5.975	6.153	6.336	6.523	6.716	6.913	7.115
6	6.434	6.662	6.898	7.142	7.394	7.654	7.923	8.200	8.487	8.783	9.089
7	7.583	7.892	8.214	8.549	8.897	9.260	9.637	10.028	10.436	10.859	11.300
8	8.755	9.159	9.583	10.027	10.491	10.978	11.488	12.021	12.579	13.164	13.776
9	9.950	10.464	11.006	11.578	12.181	12.816	13.487	14.193	14.937	15.722	16.549
10	11.169	11.808	12.486	13.207	13.972	14.784	15.645	16.560	17.531	18.561	19.655
11	12.412	13.192	14.026	14.917	15.870	16.888	17.977	19.141	20.384	21.713	23.133
12	13.680	14.618	15.627	16.713	17.882	19.141	20.495	21.953	23.523	25.212	27.029
13	14.974	16.086	17.292	18.599	20.015	21.550	23.215	25.019	26.975	29.095	31.393
14	16.293	17.599	19.024	20.579	22.276	24.129	26.152	28.361	30.772	33.405	36.280
15	17.639	19.157	20.825	22.657	24.673	26.888	29.324	32.003	34.950	38.190	41.753
16	19.012	20.762	22.698	24.840	27.213	29.840	32.750	35.974	39.545	43.501	47.884
17	20.412	22.414	24.645	27.132	29.906	32.999	36.450	40.301	44.599	49.396	54.750
18	21.841	24.117	26.671	29.539	32.760	36.379	40.446	45.018	50.159	55.939	62.440
19	23.297	25.870	28.778	32.066	35.786	39.995	44.762	50.160	56.275	63.203	71.052
20	24.783	27.676	30.969	34.719	38.993	43.865	49.423	55.765	63.002	71.265	80.699
21	26.299	29.537	33.248	37.505	42.392	48.006	54.457	61.873	70.403	80.214	91.503
22	27.845	31.453	35.618	40.430	45.996	52.436	59.893	68.532	78.543	90.148	103.603
23	29.422	33.426	38.083	43.502	49.816	57.177	65.765	75.790	87.497	101.174	117.155
24	31.030	35.459	40.646	46.727	53.865	62.249	72.106	83.701	97.347	113.413	132.334
25	32.671	37.553	43.312	50.113	58.156	67.676	78.954	92.324	108.182	126.999	149.334

* Table values can be interpolated for partial years and/or inflation and investment return rates that are not represented in the tables.

FACT FINDER TABLE 4
Retirement Income Multiplier/Divisor Factors
Compound Interest Rates

		Retirement Time Period—25 Years			
		4%	**6%**	**8%**	**10%**
I	**5%**	28.11	22.36	18.20	15.12
	4%	25	20.08	16.49	13.82
	3%	22.32	18.10	15	12.68
	2%	20	16.37	13.69	11.67
	1%	17.99	14.87	12.54	10.78
N		Retirement Time Period—20 Years			
		4%	**6%**	**8%**	**10%**
F	**5%**	21.94	18.31	15.51	13.32
	4%	20	16.79	14.31	12.36
L	**3%**	18.27	15.44	13.23	11.50
A	**2%**	16.74	14.22	12.26	10.71
	1%	15.36	13.13	11.39	10.01
T		Retirement Time Period—15 Years			
		4%	**6%**	**8%**	**10%**
I	**5%**	16.05	14.05	12.41	11.05
	4%	15	13.17	11.67	10.43
O	**3%**	13.99	12.36	10.99	9.85
	2%	13.14	11.62	10.36	9.32
N	**1%**	12.32	10.93	9.78	8.83
		Retirement Time Period—10 Years			
		4%	**6%**	**8%**	**10%**
R	**5%**	10.44	9.59	8.84	8.18
	4%	10	9.19	8.49	7.87
A	**3%**	9.58	8.82	8.15	7.57
	2%	9.18	8.46	7.84	7.29
T	**1%**	8.80	8.12	7.53	7.02
E		Retirement Time Period—5 Years			
		4%	**6%**	**8%**	**10%**
S	**5%**	5.10	4.91	4.73	4.57
	4%	5	4.81	4.64	4.48
	3%	4.90	4.72	4.56	4.40
	2%	4.81	4.64	4.47	4.32
	1%	4.72	4.55	4.39	4.25

15

§ 72 Annuities; certain proceeds of endowment and life insurance contracts

(a) General rule for annuities

Except as otherwise provided in this chapter, gross income includes any amount received as an annuity (whether for a period certain or during one or more lives) under an annuity, endowment, or life insurance contract.

(b) Exclusion ratio

(1) In general

Gross income does not include that part of any amount received as an annuity under an annuity, endowment, or life insurance contract, which bears the same ratio to such amount as the investment in the contract (as of the annuity starting date) bears to the expected return under the contract (as of such date).

(2) Exclusion limited to investment

The portion of any amount received as an annuity, which is excluded from gross income under paragraph (1), shall not exceed the unrecovered investment in the contract immediately before the receipt of such amount.

(3) Deduction where annuity payments cease before entire investment recovered

(A) In general. If

(i) after the annuity starting date, payments as an annuity under the contract cease by reason of the death of an annuitant, and

(ii) as of the date of such cessation, there is unrecovered investment in the contract, the amount of such unrecovered investment (in excess of any amount specified in subsection (e)(5) which was not included in gross income) shall be allowed as a deduction to the annuitant for his or her last taxable year.

(B) Payments to other persons. In the case of any contract which provides for payments meeting the requirements of subparagraphs (B) and (C) of subsection (c)(2), the deduction under subparagraph (A) shall be allowed to the person entitled to such payments for the taxable year in which such payments are received.

(C)   Net operating loss deductions provided. For purposes of section 172, a deduction allowed under this paragraph shall be treated as if it were attributable to a trade or business of the taxpayer.

(4) Unrecovered investment

For purposes of this subsection, the unrecovered investment in the contract as of any date is

(A)   the investment in the contract (determined without regard to subsection (c)(2)) as of the annuity starting date, reduced by

(B)   the aggregate amount received under the contract on or after such annuity starting date and before the date as of which the determination is being made, to the extent such amount was excludible from gross income under this subtitle.

(c)   Definitions

(1) Investment in the contract

For purposes of subsection (b), the investment in the contract as of the annuity starting date is

(A)   the aggregate amount of premiums or other consideration paid for the contract, minus

(B)   the aggregate amount received under the contract before such date, to the extent that such amount was excludible from gross income under this subtitle or prior income tax laws.

(2) Adjustment in investment where there is refund feature

If

(A)   the expected return under the contract depends in whole or in part on the life expectancy of one or more individuals

(B)   the contract provides for payments to be made to a beneficiary (or to the estate of an annuitant) on or after the death of the annuitant or annuitants

(C)   such payments are in the nature of a refund of the consideration paid

then the value (computed without discount for interest) of such payments on the annuity starting date shall be subtracted from the amount determined under paragraph (1). Such value shall be computed in accordance with actuarial tables prescribed by the Secretary. For purposes of this paragraph and of subsection (e)(2)(A), the term "refund of the consideration paid" includes amounts payable after the death of an annuitant by reason of a provision in the contract for a life annuity with minimum period of payments certain but (if part of the consideration was contributed by an employer) does not include that part of any payment to a beneficiary (or to the estate of the annuitant) which is not attributable to the consideration paid by the employee for the contract as determined under paragraph (1)(A).

(3) Expected return

For purposes of subsection (b), the expected return under the contract shall be determined as follows:

(A)   Life expectancy. If the expected return under the contract, for the period on and after the annuity starting date, depends in whole or in part on the life expectancy of one or more individuals, the expected return shall be computed with reference to actuarial tables prescribed by the Secretary.

(B)   Installment payments. If subparagraph (A) does not apply, the expected return is the aggregate of the amounts receivable under the contract as an annuity.

(4) Annuity starting date

For purposes of this section, the annuity starting date in the case of any contract is the first day of the first period for which an amount is received as an annuity under the contract except that if such date was before January 1, 1954, then the annuity starting date is January 1, 1954.

(d)   Special rules for qualified employer retirement plans

(1) Simplified method of taxing annuity payments

(A)   In general. In the case of any amount received as an annuity under a qualified employer retirement plan

(i) subsection (b) shall not apply

(ii) the investment in the contract shall be recovered as provided in this paragraph

(B)   Method of recovering investment in contract

(i) In general. Gross income shall not include so much of any monthly annuity payment under a qualified employer retirement plan as does not exceed the amount obtained by dividing

    (I)   the investment in the contract (as of the annuity starting date) by

    (II)   the number of anticipated payments determined under the table contained in clause (iii) (or, in the case of a contract to which subsection (c)(3)(B) applies, the number of monthly annuity payments under such contract).

(ii) Certain rules made applicable. Rules similar to the rules of paragraphs (2) and (3) of subsection (b) shall apply for purposes of this paragraph.

(iii) Number of anticipated payments. If the annuity is payable over the life of a single individual, the number of anticipated payments shall be determined as follows:

If the age of the annuitant on the annuity starting date is	The number of anticipated payments is
Not more than 55	360
More than 55 but not more than 60	310
More than 60 but not more than 65	260
More than 65 but not more than 70	210
More than 70	160

(iv) Number of anticipated payments where more than one life. If the annuity is payable over the lives of more than 1 individual, the number of anticipated payments shall be determined as follows:

(v)

If the combined ages of annuitants are	The number is
Not more than 110	410
More than 110 but not more than 120	360
More than 120 but not more than 130	310
More than 130 but not more than 140	260
More than 140	210.

(C)   Adjustment for refund feature not applicable. For purposes of this paragraph, investment in the contract shall be determined under subsection (c)(1) without regard to subsection (c)(2).

(D)   Special rule where lump sum paid in connection with commencement of annuity payments. If, in connection with the commencement of annuity payments under any qualified employer retirement plan, the taxpayer receives a lump sum payment,

     (i)   such payment shall be taxable under subsection (e) as if received before the annuity starting date

     (ii)   the investment in the contract for purposes of this paragraph shall be determined as if such payment had been so received

(E)   Exception. This paragraph shall not apply in any case where the primary annuitant has attained age 75 on the annuity starting date unless there are fewer than 5 years of guaranteed payments under the annuity.

(F)   Adjustment where annuity payments not on monthly basis. In any case where the annuity payments are not made on a monthly basis, appropriate adjustments in the application of this paragraph shall be made to take into account the period on the basis of which such payments are made.

(G)   Qualified employer retirement plan. For purposes of this paragraph, the term "qualified employer retirement plan" means any plan or contract described in paragraph (1), (2), or (3) of section 4974(c).

(2) Treatment of employee contributions under defined contribution plans
For purposes of this section, employee contributions (and any income allocable thereto) under a defined contribution plan may be treated as a separate contract.

(e)   Amounts not received as annuities

(1) Application of subsection

(A)   In general. This subsection shall apply to any amount which

     (i)   is received under an annuity, endowment, or life insurance contract

     (ii)   is not received as an annuity if no provision of this subtitle (other than this subsection) applies with respect to such amount

(B) Dividends. For purposes of this section, any amount received which is in the nature of a dividend or similar distribution shall be treated as an amount not received as an annuity.

(2) General rule
Any amount to which this subsection applies

(A) if received on or after the annuity starting date, shall be included in gross income

(B) if received before the annuity starting date

   (i) shall be included in gross income to the extent allocable to income on the contract

   (ii) shall not be included in gross income to the extent allocable to the investment in the contract.

(3) Allocation of amounts to income and investment
For purposes of paragraph (2)(B)

(A) Allocation to income. Any amount to which this subsection applies shall be treated as allocable to income on the contract to the extent that such amount does not exceed the excess (if any) of

   (i) the cash value of the contract (determined without regard to any surrender charge) immediately before the amount is received, over

   (ii) the investment in the contract at such time.

(B) Allocation to investment. Any amount to which this subsection applies shall be treated as allocable to investment in the contract to the extent that such amount is not allocated to income under subparagraph (A).

(4) Special rules for application of paragraph (2)(B)
For purposes of paragraph (2)(B)

(A) Loans treated as distributions. If, during any taxable year, an individual

   (i) receives (directly or indirectly) any amount as a loan under any contract to which this subsection applies

      (ii)   assigns or pledges (or agrees to assign or pledge) any portion of the value of any such contract

such amount or portion shall be treated as received under the contract as an amount not received as an annuity. The preceding sentence shall not apply for purposes of determining investment in the contract except that the investment in the contract shall be increased by any amount included in gross income by reason of the amount treated as received under the preceding sentence.

(B)   Treatment of policyholder dividends. Any amount described in paragraph (1)(B) shall not be included in gross income under paragraph (2)(B)(i) to the extent such amount is retained by the insurer as a premium or other consideration paid for the contract.

(C)   Treatment of transfers without adequate consideration.

      (i)   In general. If an individual who holds an annuity contract transfers it without full and adequate consideration, such individual shall be treated as receiving an amount equal to the excess of

          (I)   the cash surrender value of such contract at the time of transfer, over
          (II)   the investment in such contract at such time

under the contract as an amount not received as an annuity.

      (ii)   Exception for certain transfers between spouses or former spouses. Clause (i) shall not apply to any transfer to which section 1041(a) (relating to transfers of property between spouses or incident to divorce) applies.

      (iii)   Adjustment to investment in contract of transferee. If under clause (i) an amount is included in the gross income of the transferor of an annuity contract, the investment in the contract of the transferee in such contract shall be increased by the amount so included.

(5) Retention of existing rules in certain cases

(A)   In general. In any case to which this paragraph applies

      (i)   paragraphs (2)(B) and (4)(A) shall not apply, and

(ii)   if paragraph (2)(A) does not apply,

the amount shall be included in gross income but only to the extent it exceeds the investment in the contract.

(B)   Existing contracts. This paragraph shall apply to contracts entered into before August 14, 1982. Any amount allocable to investment in the contract after August 13, 1982, shall be treated as from a contract entered into after such date.

(C)   Certain life insurance and endowment contracts. Except as provided in paragraph (10) and except to the extent prescribed by the Secretary by regulations, this paragraph shall apply to any amount not received as an annuity, which is received under a life insurance or endowment contract.

(D)   Contracts under qualified plans. Except as provided in paragraph (8), this paragraph shall apply to any amount received

       (i)   from a trust described in section 401(a) which is exempt from tax under section 501(a)

       (ii)   from a contract

             (I)   purchased by a trust described in clause (i)

             (II)   purchased as part of a plan described in section 403(a)

             (III)   described in section 403(b)

             (IV)   provided for employees of a life insurance company under a plan described in section 818(a)(3)

       (iii)   from an individual retirement account or an individual retirement annuity

Any dividend described in section 404(k) which is received by a participant or beneficiary shall, for purposes of this subparagraph, be treated as paid under a separate contract to which clause (ii)(I) applies.

(E)   Full refunds, surrenders, redemptions, and maturities. This paragraph shall apply to

(i)   any amount received, whether in a single sum or otherwise, under a contract in full discharge of the obligation under the contract which is in the nature of a refund of the consideration paid for the contract

(ii)   any amount received under a contract on its complete surrender, redemption, or maturity

In the case of any amount to which the preceding sentence applies, the rule of paragraph (2)(A) shall not apply.

(6) Investment in the contract
For purposes of this subsection , the investment in the contract as of any date is

(A)   the aggregate amount of premiums or other consideration paid for the contract before such date, minus

(B)   the aggregate amount received under the contract before such date, to the extent that such amount was excludable from gross income under this subtitle or prior income tax laws.

(7) Repealed

(8) Extension of paragraph (2)(B) to qualified plans

(A)   In general. Notwithstanding any other provision of this subsection, in the case of any amount received before the annuity starting date from a trust or contract described in paragraph (5)(D), paragraph (2)(B) shall apply to such amounts.

(B)   Allocation of amount received. For purposes of paragraph (2)(B), the amount allocated to the investment in the contract shall be the portion of the amount described in subparagraph (A) which bears the same ratio to such amount as the investment in the contract bears to the account balance. The determination under the preceding sentence shall be made as of the time of the distribution or at such other time as the Secretary may prescribe.

(C)   Treatment of forfeitable rights. If an employee does not have a nonforfeitable right to any amount under any trust or contract to which subparagraph (A) applies, such amount shall not be treated as part of the account balance.

(D)   Investment in the contract before 1987. In the case of a plan which on May 5, 1986, permitted withdrawal of any employee contributions before separation from service, subparagraph (A) shall apply only to the extent that amounts received before the annuity starting date (when increased by amounts previously received under the contract after December 31, 1986) exceed the investment in the contract as of December 31, 1986.

(9) Extension of paragraph (2)(B) to qualified tuition programs and Coverdell education savings accounts

Notwithstanding any other provision of this subsection , paragraph (2)(B) shall apply to amounts received under a qualified tuition program (as defined in section 529(b)) or under a Coverdell education savings account (as defined in section 530(b)). The rule of paragraph (8)(B) shall apply for purposes of this paragraph.

(10) Treatment of modified endowment contracts

(A) In general. Notwithstanding paragraph (5)(C), in the case of any modified endowment contract (as defined in section 7702A)

    (i) paragraphs (2)(B) and (4)(A) shall apply

    (ii) in applying paragraph (4)(A) , "any person" shall be substituted for "an individual."

(B) Treatment of certain burial contracts. Notwithstanding subparagraph (A), paragraph (4)(A) shall not apply to any assignment (or pledge) of a modified endowment contract if such assignment (or pledge) is solely to cover the payment of expenses referred to in section 7702(e)(2)(C)(iii) and if the maximum death benefit under such contract does not exceed $25,000.

(11) Antiabuse rules

(A) In general. For purposes of determining the amount includible in gross income under this subsection

    (i) all modified endowment contracts issued by the same company to the same policyholder during any calendar year shall be treated as 1 modified endowment contract

    (ii) all annuity contracts issued by the same company to the same policyholder during any calendar year shall be treated as one annuity contract

The preceding sentence shall not apply to any contract described in paragraph (5)(D).

(B)   Regulatory authority. The Secretary may by regulations prescribe such additional rules as may be necessary or appropriate to prevent avoidance of the purposes of this subsection through serial purchases of contracts or otherwise.

(f)   Special rules for computing employees' contributions

In computing, for purposes of subsection (c)(1)(A), the aggregate amount of premiums or other consideration paid for the contract, and for purposes of subsection (e)(6), the aggregate premiums or other consideration paid, amounts contributed by the employer shall be included but only to the extent that

(1)   such amounts were includible in the gross income of the employee under this subtitle or prior income tax laws

(2)   if such amounts had been paid directly to the employee at the time they were contributed, they would not have been includible in the gross income of the employee under the law applicable at the time of such contribution

Paragraph (2) shall not apply to amounts which were contributed by the employer after December 31, 1962, and which would not have been includible in the gross income of the employee by reason of the application of section 911 if such amounts had been paid directly to the employee at the time of contribution. The preceding sentence shall not apply to amounts which were contributed by the employer as determined under regulations prescribed by the Secretary to provide pension or annuity credits to the extent such credits are attributable to services performed before January 1, 1963, and are provided pursuant to pension or annuity plan provisions in existence on March 12, 1962, and on that date applicable to such services, or to the extent such credits are attributable to services performed as a foreign missionary (within the meaning of section 403(b)(2)(D)(iii) as in effect before the enactment of the Economic Growth and Tax Relief Reconciliation Act of 2001.

(g)   Rules for transferee where transfer was for value

Where any contract (or any interest therein) is transferred (by assignment or otherwise) for a valuable consideration to the extent that the contract (or interest therein) does not, in the hands of the transferee, have a basis, which is determined by reference to the basis in the hands of the transferor, then

(1)   for purposes of this section , only the actual value of such consideration plus the amount of the premiums and other consideration paid by the transferee after the transfer shall be taken into account in computing the aggregate amount of the premiums or other consideration paid for the contract

(2)   for purposes of subsection (c)(1)(B), there shall be taken into account only the aggregate amount received under the contract by the transferee before the annuity starting date, to the extent that such amount was excludible from gross income under this subtitle or prior income tax laws

(3)   the annuity starting date is January 1, 1954, or the first day of the first period for which the transferee received an amount under the contract as an annuity, whichever is the later.

For purposes of this subsection, the term "transferee" includes a beneficiary of, or the estate of, the transferee.

(h)   **Option to receive annuity in lieu of lump sum**
If

(1)   a contract provides for payment of a lump sum in full discharge of an obligation under the contract, subject to an option to receive an annuity in lieu of such lump sum

(2)   the option is exercised within 60 days after the day on which such lump sum first became payable

(3)   part or all of such lump sum would (but for this subsection) be includible in gross income by reason of subsection (e)(1)

then, for purposes of this subtitle, no part of such lump sum shall be considered as includible in gross income at the time such lump sum first became payable.

(j)   **Interest**
Notwithstanding any other provision of this section, if any amount is held under an agreement to pay interest thereon, the interest payments shall be included in gross income.

(k)   **Repealed**

(l)   **Face-amount certificates**
For purposes of this section, the term "endowment contract" includes a face-amount certificate, as defined in section 2(a)(15) of the Investment Company Act of 1940 (15 U.S.C., Sec. 80a-2), issued after December 31, 1954.

(m)   **Special rules applicable to employee annuities and distributions under employee plans**

(1) Repealed

(2) Computation of consideration paid by the employee
In computing

(A) the aggregate amount of premiums or other consideration paid for the contract for purposes of subsection (c)(1)(A) (relating to the investment in the contract)

(B) the aggregate premiums or other consideration paid for purposes of subsection (e)(6) (relating to certain amounts not received as an annuity)

any amount allowed as a deduction with respect to the contract under section 404 which was paid while the employee was an employee within the meaning of section 401(c)(1) shall be treated as consideration contributed by the employer, and there shall not be taken into account any portion of the premiums or other consideration for the contract paid while the employee was an owner-employee which is properly allocable (as determined under regulations prescribed by the Secretary) to the cost of life, accident, health, or other insurance.

(3) Life insurance contracts

(A) This paragraph shall apply to any life insurance contract

   (i) purchased as a part of a plan described in section 403(a)

   (ii) purchased by a trust described in section 401(a) which is exempt from tax under section 501(a) if the proceeds of such contract are payable directly or indirectly to a participant in such trust or to a beneficiary of such participant

(B) Any contribution to a plan described in subparagraph (A)(i) or a trust described in subparagraph (A)(ii) which is allowed as a deduction under section 404, and any income of a trust described in subparagraph (A)(ii) which is determined in accordance with regulations prescribed by the Secretary to have been applied to purchase the life insurance protection under a contract described in subparagraph (A), is includible in the gross income of the participant for the taxable year when so applied.

(C) In the case of the death of an individual insured under a contract described in subparagraph (A), an amount equal to the cash surrender value of the contract immediately before the death of the insured shall be treated as a payment under such plan or a distribution by such trust, and the excess of the amount payable by reason of the death of the insured over such cash surrender value shall not be includible in gross income under this section and shall be treated as provided in section 101.

(4)   Repealed

(5)   Penalties applicable to certain amounts received by 5-percent owners

(A)   This paragraph applies to amounts which are received from a qualified trust described in section 401(a) or under a plan described in section 403(a) at any time by an individual who is, or has been, a 5-percent owner, or by a successor of such an individual, but only to the extent such amounts are determined, under regulations prescribed by the Secretary, to exceed the benefits provided for such individual under the plan formula.

(B)   If a person receives an amount to which this paragraph applies, his or her tax under this chapter for the taxable year in which such amount is received shall be increased by an amount equal to 10 percent of the portion of the amount so received, which is includible in his or her gross income for such taxable year.

(C)   For purposes of this paragraph, the term *5-percent owner* means any individual who, at any time during the 5 plan years preceding the plan year ending in the taxable year in which the amount is received is a 5-percent owner (as defined in section 416(i)(1)(B)).

(6)   Owner-employee defined
For purposes of this subsection, the term *owner-employee* has the meaning assigned to it by section 401(c)(3) and includes an individual for whose benefit an individual retirement account or annuity described in section 408(a) or (b) is maintained. For purposes of the preceding sentence, the term *owner-employee* shall include an employee within the meaning of section 401(c)(1).

(7)   Meaning of disabled
For purposes of this section, an individual shall be considered to be disabled if he or she is unable to engage in any substantial gainful activity by reason of any medically determinable physical or mental impairment which can be expected to result in death or to be of long-continued and indefinite duration. An individual shall not be considered to be disabled unless he or she furnishes proof of the existence thereof in such form and manner as the Secretary may require.

(8) **Repealed**

(9) **Repealed**

(10) **Determination of investment in the contract in the case of qualified domestic relations orders**
Under regulations prescribed by the Secretary, in the case of a distribution or payment made to an alternate payee who is the spouse or former spouse of the participant pursuant to a qualified domestic relations order (as defined in section 414(p)), the investment in the contract as of the date prescribed in such regulations shall be allocated on a pro rata basis between the present value of such distribution or payment and the present value of all other benefits payable with respect to the participant to whom such order relates.

(n) **Annuities under retired serviceman's family protection plan or survivor benefit plan**
Subsection (b) shall not apply in the case of amounts received after December 31, 1965, as an annuity under chapter 73 of title 10 of the United States Code, but all such amounts shall be excluded from gross income until there has been so excluded (under section 122(b)(1) or this section, including amounts excluded before January 1, 1966) an amount equal to the consideration for the contract (as defined by section 122(b)(2)), plus any amount treated pursuant to section 101(b)(2)(D) (as in effect on the day before the date of the enactment of the Small Business Job Protection Act of 1996) as additional consideration paid by the employee. Thereafter all amounts so received shall be included in gross income.

(o) **Special rules for distributions from qualified plans to which employee made deductible contributions**

(1) **Treatment of contributions**
For purposes of this section and sections 402 and 403, notwithstanding section 414(h), any deductible employee contribution made to a qualified employer plan or government plan shall be treated as an amount contributed by the employer which is not includible in the gross income of the employee.

(2) **Repealed**

(3) **Amounts constructively received**

(A) In general. For purposes of this subsection, rules similar to the rules provided by subsection (p) (other than the exception contained in paragraph (2) thereof) shall apply.

(B) Purchase of life insurance. To the extent any amount of accumulated deductible employee contributions of an employee are applied to the purchase of life insurance contracts, such amount shall be treated as distributed to the employee in the year so applied.

(4) Special rule for treatment of rollover amounts

For purposes of sections 402(c), 403(a)(4), 403(b)(8), 408(d)(3), and 457(e)(16), the Secretary shall prescribe regulations providing for such allocations of amounts attributable to accumulated deductible employee contributions and for such other rules as may be necessary to insure that such accumulated deductible employee contributions do not become eligible for additional tax benefits (or freed from limitations) through the use of rollovers.

(5) Definitions and special rules

For purposes of this subsection

(A) Deductible employee contributions. The term *deductible employee contributions* means any qualified voluntary employee contribution (as defined in section 219(e)(2)) made after December 31, 1981, in a taxable year beginning after such date and made for a taxable year beginning before January 1, 1987, and allowable as a deduction under section 219(a) for such taxable year.

(B) Accumulated deductible employee contributions. The term *accumulated deductible employee contributions* means the deductible employee contributions

(i) increased by the amount of income and gain allocable to such contributions

(ii) reduced by the sum of the amount of loss and expense allocable to such contributions and the amounts distributed with respect to the employee which are attributable to such contributions (or income or gain allocable to such contributions)

(C) Qualified employer plan. The term *qualified employer plan* has the meaning given to such term by subsection (p)(3)(A)(i).

(D) Government plan. The term *government plan* has the meaning given such term by subsection (p)(3)(B).

(6)   Ordering rules

Unless the plan specifies otherwise, any distribution from such plan shall not be treated as being made from the accumulated deductible employee contributions until all other amounts to the credit of the employee have been distributed.

(p)   Loans treated as distributions

For purposes of this section

(1)   Treatment as distributions

(A)   Loans. If during any taxable year a participant or beneficiary receives (directly or indirectly) any amount as a loan from a qualified employer plan, such amount shall be treated as having been received by such individual as a distribution under such plan.

(B)   Assignments or pledges. If during any taxable year a participant or beneficiary assigns (or agrees to assign) or pledges (or agrees to pledge) any portion of his interest in a qualified employer plan, such portion shall be treated as having been received by such individual as a loan from such plan.

(2)   Exception for certain loans

(A)   General rule. Paragraph (1) shall not apply to any loan to the extent that such loan (when added to the outstanding balance of all other loans from such plan whether made on, before, or after August 13, 1982) does not exceed the lesser of

(i) $50,000, reduced by the excess (if any) of

(I)   the highest outstanding balance of loans from the plan during the one-year period ending on the day before the date on which such loan was made, over

(II)   the outstanding balance of loans from the plan on the date on which such loan was made, or

(iii)   the greater of (I) one-half of the present value of the nonforfeitable accrued benefit of the employee under the plan, or (II) $10,000.

For purposes of clause (ii), the present value of the nonforfeitable accrued benefit shall be determined without regard to any accumulated deductible employee contributions (as defined in subsection (o)(5)(B)).

(B)   Requirement that loan be repayable within 5 years.

    (i)   In general. Subparagraph (A) shall not apply to any loan unless such loan, by its terms, is required to be repaid within 5 years.

    (ii)   Exception for home loans. Clause (i) shall not apply to any loan used to acquire any dwelling unit which within a reasonable time is to be used (determined at the time the loan is made) as the principal residence of the participant.

(C)   Requirement of level amortization. Except as provided in regulations, this paragraph shall not apply to any loan unless substantially level amortization of such loan (with payments not less frequently than quarterly) is required over the term of the loan.

(D)   Related employers and related plans. For purposes of this paragraph

    (i)   the rules of subsections (b), (c), and (m) of section 414 shall apply

    (ii)   all plans of an employer (determined after the application of such subsections) shall be treated as one plan

(3)   Denial of interest deductions in certain cases

(A)   In general. No deduction otherwise allowable under this chapter shall be allowed under this chapter for any interest paid or accrued on any loan to which paragraph (1) does not apply by reason of paragraph (2) during the period described in subparagraph (B).

(B)   Period to which subparagraph (A) applies. For purposes of subparagraph (A), the period described in this subparagraph is the period

    (i)   on or after the 1st day on which the individual to whom the loan is made is a key employee (as defined in section 416(i)), or

    (ii)   such loan is secured by amounts attributable to elective deferrals described in subparagraph (A) or (C) of section 402(g)(3).

(4)   Qualified employer plan, etc
For purposes of this subsection

(A)   Qualified employer plan

(i)   In general. The term *qualified employer plan* means

(I)   a plan described in section 401(a) which includes a trust exempt from tax under section 501(a)

(II)   an annuity plan described in section 403(a)

(III)   a plan under which amounts are contributed by an individual's employer for an annuity contract described in section 403(b)

(ii)   Special rule. The term *qualified employer plan* shall include any plan which was (or was determined to be) a qualified employer plan or a government plan.

(B)   Government plan. The term *government plan* means any plan, whether or not qualified, established, and maintained for its employees by the United States, by a state or political subdivision thereof, or by an agency or instrumentality of any of the foregoing.

(5)   Special rules for loans, etc., from certain contracts
For purposes of this subsection, any amount received as a loan under a contract purchased under a qualified employer plan (and any assignment or pledge with respect to such a contract) shall be treated as a loan under such employer plan.

(q)   10-percent penalty for premature distributions from annuity contracts

(1)   Imposition of penalty
If any taxpayer receives any amount under an annuity contract, the taxpayer's tax under this chapter for the taxable year in which such amount is received shall be increased by an amount equal to 10 percent of the portion of such amount which is includible in gross income.

(2)   Subsection not to apply to certain distributions
Paragraph (1) shall not apply to any distribution
(A)   made on or after the date on which the taxpayer attains age 59 ½

(B)   made on or after the death of the holder (or, where the holder is not an individual, the death of the primary annuitant (as defined in subsection (s)(6)(B))

(C)   attributable to the taxpayer's becoming disabled within the meaning of subsection (m)(7)

(D)   which is a part of a series of substantially equal periodic payments (not less frequently than annually) made for the life (or life expectancy) of the taxpayer or the joint lives (or joint life expectancies) of such taxpayer and his designated beneficiary

(E)   from a plan, contract, account, trust, or annuity described in subsection (e)(5)(D)

(F)   allocable to investment in the contract before August 14, 1982

(G)   under a qualified funding asset (within the meaning of section 130(d) but without regard to whether there is a qualified assignment)

(H)   to which subsection (t) applies (without regard to paragraph (2) thereof)

(I)   under an immediate annuity contract (within the meaning of section 72(u)(4))

(J)   which is purchased by an employer upon the termination of a plan described in section 401(a) or 403(a) and which is held by the employer until such time as the employee separates from service

(3)   Change in substantially equal payments
If

(A)   paragraph (1) does not apply to a distribution by reason of paragraph (2)(D)

(B)   the series of payments under such paragraph are subsequently modified (other than by reason of death or disability)

(i)   before the close of the 5-year period beginning on the date of the first payment and after the taxpayer attains age 59 ½

(ii)   before the taxpayer attains age 59 ½

the taxpayer's tax for the 1st taxable year in which such modification occurs shall be increased by an amount, determined under regulations, equal to the tax which (but for paragraph (2)(D)) would have been imposed, plus interest for the deferral period (within the meaning of subsection (t)(4)(B)).

(r)   Certain railroad retirement benefits treated as received under employer plans

(1)   In general
Notwithstanding any other provision of law, any benefit provided under the Railroad Retirement Act of 1974 (other than a tier 1 railroad retirement benefit) shall be treated for purposes of this title as a benefit provided under an employer plan which meets the requirements of section 401(a).

(2)   Tier 2 taxes treated as contributions

(A)   In general. For purposes of paragraph (1)

(i)   the tier 2 portion of the tax imposed by section 3201 (relating to tax on employees) shall be treated as an employee contribution

(ii)   the tier 2 portion of the tax imposed by section 3211 (relating to tax on employee representatives) shall be treated as an employee contribution

(iii)   the tier 2 portion of the tax imposed by section 3221 (relating to tax on employers) shall be treated as an employer contribution.

(B)   Tier 2 portion. For purposes of subparagraph (A)

(i)   After 1984. With respect to compensation paid after 1984, the tier 2 portion shall be the taxes imposed by sections 3201(b), 3211(b), and 3221(b).

(ii)   After September 30, 1981, and before 1985. With respect to compensation paid before 1985 for services rendered after September 30, 1981, the tier 2 portion shall be

(I)   so much of the tax imposed by section 3201 as is determined at the 2 percent rate

(II)   so much of the taxes imposed by sections 3211 and 3221 as is determined at the 11.75 percent rate

With respect to compensation paid for services rendered after December 31, 1983, and before 1985, subclause (I) shall be applied by substituting "2.75 percent" for "2 percent," and subclause (II) shall be applied by substituting "12.75 percent" for "11.75 percent."

(iii)   Before October 1, 1981. With respect to compensation paid for services rendered during any period before October 1, 1981, the tier 2 portion shall be the excess (if any) of

(I)   the tax imposed for such period by section 3201, 3211, or 3221, as the case may be (other than any tax imposed with respect to man-hours), over

(II)   the tax which would have been imposed by such section for such period had the rates of the comparable taxes imposed by chapter 21 for such period applied under such section.

(C)   Contributions not allocable to supplemental annuity or windfall benefits. For purposes of paragraph (1), no amount treated as an employee contribution under this paragraph shall be allocated to

(i)   any supplemental annuity paid under section 2(b) of the Railroad Retirement Act of 1974
(ii)   any benefit paid under section 3(h), 4(e), or 4(h) of such Act

(3)   Tier 1 railroad retirement benefit
For purposes of paragraph (1), the term *tier 1 railroad retirement benefit* has the meaning given such term by section 86(d)(4).

(s)   Required distributions where holder dies before entire interest is distributed

(1)   In general
A contract shall not be treated as an annuity contract for purposes of this title unless it provides that
(A)   if any holder of such contract dies on or after the annuity starting date and before the entire interest in such contract has been distributed, the remaining portion of such interest will be distributed at least as rapidly as under the method of distributions being used as of the date of his or her death.

(B)   if any holder of such contract dies before the annuity starting date, the entire interest in such contract will be distributed within 5 years after the death of such holder.

(2)   Exception for certain amounts payable over life of beneficiary
If

(A)   any portion of the holder's interest is payable to (or for the benefit of) a designated beneficiary

(B)   such portion will be distributed (in accordance with regulations) over the life of such designated beneficiary (or over a period not extending beyond the life expectancy of such beneficiary)

(C)   such distributions begin not later than 1 year after the date of the holder's death or such later date as the Secretary may by regulations prescribe

then for purposes of paragraph (1), the portion referred to in subparagraph (A) shall be treated as distributed on the day on which such distributions begin.

(3)   Special rule where surviving spouse is beneficiary
If the designated beneficiary referred to in paragraph (2)(A) is the surviving spouse of the holder of the contract, paragraphs (1) and (2) shall be applied by treating such spouse as the holder of such contract.

(4)   Designated beneficiary
For purposes of this subsection, the term *designated beneficiary* means any individual designated a beneficiary by the holder of the contract.

(5)   Exception for certain annuity contracts.
This subsection shall not apply to any annuity contract

(A)   which is provided

(i)   under a plan described in section 401(a) which includes a trust exempt from tax under section 501

(ii)   under a plan described in section 403(a)

(B)   which is described in section 403(b)

(C)   which is an individual retirement annuity or provided under an individual retirement account or annuity

(D)   which is a qualified funding asset (as defined in section 130(d) but without regard to whether there is a qualified assignment)

(6) Special rule where holder is corporation or other non-individual

(A) In general. For purposes of this subsection, if the holder of the contract is not an individual, the primary annuitant shall be treated as the holder of the contract.

(B) Primary annuitant. For purposes of subparagraph (A), the term *primary annuitant* means the individual, the events in the life of whom are of primary importance in affecting the timing or amount of the payout under the contract.

(7) Treatment of changes in primary annuitant where holder of contract is not an individual

For purposes of this subsection, in the case of a holder of an annuity contract which is not an individual, if there is a change in a primary annuitant (as defined in paragraph (6)(B)), such change shall be treated as the death of the holder.

(t) 10-percent additional tax on early distributions from qualified retirement plans

(1) Imposition of additional tax

If any taxpayer receives any amount from a qualified retirement plan (as defined in section 4974(c)), the taxpayer's tax under this chapter for the taxable year in which such amount is received shall be increased by an amount equal to 10 percent of the portion of such amount which is includible in gross income.

(2) Subsection not to apply to certain distributions

Except as provided in paragraphs (3) and (4), paragraph (1) shall not apply to any of the following distributions:

(A) In general. Distributions which are

  (i) made on or after the date on which the employee attains age 59 ½

  (ii) made to a beneficiary (or to the estate of the employee) on or after the death of the employee

  (iii) attributable to the employee's being disabled within the meaning of subsection (m)(7)

  (iv) part of a series of substantially equal periodic payments (not less frequently than annually) made for the life (or life expectancy) of the employee or the joint lives (or joint life expectancies) of such employee and his or her designated beneficiary

(v) made to an employee after separation from service after attainment of age 55

(vi) dividends paid with respect to stock of a corporation which are described in section 404(k)

(vii) made on account of a levy under section 6331 on the qualified retirement plan.

(B) Medical expenses. Distributions made to the employee (other than distributions described in subparagraph (A), (C), or (D)) to the extent such distributions do not exceed the amount allowable as a deduction under section 213 to the employee for amounts paid during the taxable year for medical care (determined without regard to whether the employee itemizes deductions for such taxable year).

(C) Payments to alternate payees pursuant to qualified domestic relations orders. Any distribution to an alternate payee pursuant to a qualified domestic relations order (within the meaning of section 414(p)(1)).

(D) Distributions to unemployed individuals for health insurance premiums.

(i) In general. Distributions from an individual retirement plan to an individual after separation from employment

(I) if such individual has received unemployment compensation for 12 consecutive weeks under any federal or state unemployment compensation law by reason of such separation

(II) if such distributions are made during any taxable year during which such unemployment compensation is paid or the succeeding taxable year

(III) to the extent such distributions do not exceed the amount paid during the taxable year for insurance described in section 213(d)(1)(D) with respect to the individual and the individual's spouse and dependents (as defined in section 152)

(ii) Distributions after re-employment. Clause (i) shall not apply to any distribution made after the individual has been employed for at least 60 days after the separation from employment to which clause (i) applies.

(iii) Self-employed individuals. To the extent provided in regulations, a self-employed individual shall be treated as meeting the requirements of clause (i)(I) if, under federal or state law, the individual would have received unemployment compensation but for the fact the individual was self-employed.

(E) Distributions from individual retirement plans for higher education expenses. Distributions to an individual from an individual retirement plan to the extent such distributions do not exceed the qualified higher education expenses (as defined in paragraph (7)) of the taxpayer for the taxable year. Distributions shall not be taken into account under the preceding sentence if such distributions are described in subparagraph (A), (C), or (D) or to the extent paragraph (1) does not apply to such distributions by reason of subparagraph (B).

(F) Distributions from certain plans for first-home purchases. Distributions to an individual from an individual retirement plan which are qualified first-time homebuyer distributions (as defined in paragraph (8)). Distributions shall not be taken into account under the preceding sentence if such distributions are described in subparagraph (A), (C), (D), or (E) or to the extent paragraph (1) does not apply to such distributions by reason of subparagraph (B).

(3)　Limitations

(A) Certain exceptions not to apply to individual retirement plans. Subparagraphs (A)(v) and (C) of paragraph (2) shall not apply to distributions from an individual retirement plan.

(B) Periodic payments under qualified plans must begin after separation. Paragraph (2)(A)(iv) shall not apply to any amount paid from a trust described in section 401(a) which is exempt from tax under section 501(a) or from a contract described in section 72(e)(5)(D)(ii) unless the series of payments begins after the employee separates from service.

(4)   Change in substantially equal payments

    (A)   In general. If

        (i)   paragraph (1) does not apply to a distribution by reason of paragraph (2)(A)(iv)

        (ii)   the series of payments under such paragraph are subsequently modified (other than by reason of death or disability)

            (I)   before the close of the 5-year period beginning with the date of the first payment and after the employee attains age 59 ½

            (II)   before the employee attains age 59 ½

        the taxpayer's tax for the first taxable year in which such modification occurs shall be increased by an amount, determined under regulations, equal to the tax which (but for paragraph (2)(A)(iv)) would have been imposed, plus interest for the deferral period.

    (B)   Deferral period. For purposes of this paragraph, the term *deferral period* means the period beginning with the taxable year in which (without regard to paragraph (2)(A)(iv)) the distribution would have been includible in gross income and ending with the taxable year in which the modification described in subparagraph (A) occurs.

(5)   Employee
For purposes of this subsection , the term *employee* includes any participant, and in the case of an individual retirement plan, the individual for whose benefit such plan was established.

(6)   Special rules for SIMPLE retirement accounts
In the case of any amount received from a SIMPLE retirement account (within the meaning of section 408(p)) during the 2-year period beginning on the date such individual first participated in any qualified salary reduction arrangement maintained by the individual's employer under section 408(p)(2), paragraph (1) shall be applied by substituting "25 percent" for "10 percent."

(7)   Qualified higher education expenses
For purposes of paragraph (2)(E)

(A) In general. The term *qualified higher education expenses* means qualified higher education expenses (as defined in section 529(e)(3)) for education furnished to

   (i)   the taxpayer

   (ii)   the taxpayer's spouse

   (iii) any child (as defined in section 151(c)(3)) or grandchild of the taxpayer or the taxpayer's spouse

at an eligible educational institution (as defined in section 529(e)(5)).

(B) Coordination with other benefits. The amount of qualified higher education expenses for any taxable year shall be reduced as provided in section 25A(g)(2).

(8) Qualified first-time homebuyer distributions
For purposes of paragraph (2)(F)

(A) In general. The term *qualified first-time homebuyer distribution* means any payment or distribution received by an individual to the extent such payment or distribution is used by the individual before the close of the 120th day after the day on which such payment or distribution is received to pay qualified acquisition costs with respect to a principal residence of a first-time homebuyer who is such individual, the spouse of such individual, or any child, grandchild, or ancestor of such individual or the individual's spouse.

(B) Lifetime dollar limitation. The aggregate amount of payments or distributions received by an individual which may be treated as qualified first-time homebuyer distributions for any taxable year shall not exceed the excess (if any) of

   (i) $10,000, over

   (ii)   the aggregate amounts treated as qualified first-time homebuyer distributions with respect to such individual for all prior taxable years.

(C) Qualified acquisition costs. For purposes of this paragraph, the term *qualified acquisition costs* means the costs of acquiring, constructing, or reconstructing a residence. Such term includes any usual or reasonable settlement, financing, or other closing costs.

(D) First-time homebuyer; other definitions. For purposes of this paragraph

(i) First-time homebuyer. The term *first-time homebuyer* means any individual if

(I) such individual (and if married, such individual's spouse) had no present ownership interest in a principal residence during the two-year period ending on the date of acquisition of the principal residence to which this paragraph applies

(II) subsection (h) or (k) of section 1034 (as in effect on the day before the date of the enactment of this paragraph) did not suspend the running of any period of time specified in section 1034 (as so in effect) with respect to such individual on the day before the date the distribution is applied pursuant to subparagraph (A)

(ii) Principal residence. The term *principal residence* has the same meaning as when used in section 121.

(iii) Date of acquisition. The term *date of acquisition* means the date

(I) on which a binding contract to acquire the principal residence to which subparagraph (A) applies is entered into

(II) on which construction or reconstruction of such a principal residence is commenced

(E) Special rule where delay in acquisition. If any distribution from any individual retirement plan fails to meet the requirements of subparagraph (A) solely by reason of a delay or cancellation of the purchase or construction of the residence, the amount of the distribution may be contributed to an individual retirement plan as provided in section 408(d)(3)(A)(i) (determined by substituting "120th day" for "60th day" in such section), except that

(i) section 408(d)(3)(B) shall not be applied to such contribution

(ii) such amount shall not be taken into account in determining whether section 408(d)(3)(B) applies to any other amount.

(9)   Special rule for rollovers to section 457 plans
For purposes of this subsection , a distribution from an eligible deferred compensation plan (as defined in section 457(b)) of an eligible employer described in section 457(e)(1)(A) shall be treated as a distribution from a qualified retirement plan described in 4974(c)(1) to the extent that such distribution is attributable to an amount transferred to an eligible deferred compensation plan from a qualified retirement plan (as defined in section 4974(c)).

(u)   Treatment of annuity contracts not held by natural persons

(1)   In general
If any annuity contract is held by a person who is not a natural person

(A)   such contract shall not be treated as an annuity contract for purposes of this subtitle (other than subchapter L)

(B)   the income on the contract for any taxable year of the policyholder shall be treated as ordinary income received or accrued by the owner during such taxable year.

For purposes of this paragraph, holding by a trust or other entity as an agent for a natural person shall not be taken into account.

(2)   Income on the contract

(A)   In general. For purposes of paragraph (1), the term *income on the contract* means, with respect to any taxable year of the policyholder, the excess of

(i)   the sum of the net surrender value of the contract as of the close of the taxable year plus all distributions under the contract received during the taxable year or any prior taxable year, reduced by

(ii)   the sum of the amount of net premiums under the contract for the taxable year and prior taxable years and amounts includible in gross income for prior taxable years with respect to such contract under this subsection.

Where necessary to prevent the avoidance of this subsection, the Secretary may substitute "fair market value of the contract" for "net surrender value of the contract" each place it appears in the preceding sentence.

(B)   Net premiums. For purposes of this paragraph, the term *net premiums* means the amount of premiums paid under the contract reduced by any policyholder dividends.

(3)   Exceptions
This subsection shall not apply to any annuity contract which

(A)   is acquired by the estate of a decedent by reason of the death of the decedent

(B)   is held under a plan described in section 401(a) or 403(a), under a program described in section 403(b), or under an individual retirement plan

(C)   is a qualified funding asset (as defined in section 130(d) but without regard to whether there is a qualified assignment)

(D)   is purchased by an employer upon the termination of a plan described in section 401(a) or 403(a) and is held by the employer until all amounts under such contract are distributed to the employee for whom such contract was purchased or the employee's beneficiary

(E)   is an immediate annuity

(4)   Immediate annuity
For purposes of this subsection, the term "immediate annuity" means an annuity

(A)   which is purchased with a single premium or annuity consideration

(B)   the annuity starting date (as defined in subsection (c)(4)) of which commences no later than 1 year from the date of the purchase of the annuity

(C)   which provides for a series of substantially equal periodic payments (to be made not less frequently than annually) during the annuity period

(v)   10-percent additional tax for taxable distributions from modified endowment contracts

(1)   Imposition of additional tax
If any taxpayer receives any amount under a modified endowment contract (as defined in section 7702A), the taxpayer's tax under this chapter for the taxable year in which such amount is received shall be increased by an amount equal to 10 percent of the portion of such amount which is includible in gross income.

(2)   Subsection not to apply to certain distributions
Paragraph (1) shall not apply to any distribution

(A)   made on or after the date on which the taxpayer attains age 59 ½

(B)   which is attributable to the taxpayer's becoming disabled (within the meaning of subsection (m)(7))

(C)   which is part of a series of substantially equal periodic payments (not less frequently than annually) made for the life (or life expectancy) of the taxpayer or the joint lives (or joint life expectancies) of such taxpayer and his or her beneficiary

(w) Application of basis rules to nonresident aliens

(1) In general
Notwithstanding any other provision of this section, for purposes of determining the portion of any distribution which is includible in gross income of a distributee who is a citizen or resident of the United States, the investment in the contract shall not include any applicable nontaxable contributions or applicable nontaxable earnings.

(2) Applicable nontaxable contribution
For purposes of this subsection, the term *applicable nontaxable contribution* means any employer or employee contribution—

(A) which was made with respect to compensation

(i)   for labor or personal services performed by an employee who, at the time the labor or services were performed, was a nonresident alien for purposes of the laws of the United States in effect at such time, and

(ii)   which is treated as from sources without the United States, and

(B) which was not subject to income tax (and would have been subject to income tax if paid as cash compensation when the services were rendered) under the laws of the United States or any foreign country.

(3)   Applicable nontaxable earnings
For purposes of this subsection, the term *applicable nontaxable earnings* means earnings

(A) which are paid or accrued with respect to any employer or employee contribution which was made with respect to compensation for labor or personal services performed by an employee,

(B) with respect to which the employee was at the time the earnings were paid or accrued a nonresident alien for purposes of the laws of the United States, and

(C) which were not subject to income tax under the laws of the United States or any foreign country.

(4) Regulations

The Secretary shall prescribe such regulations as may be necessary to carry out the provisions of this subsection, including regulations treating contributions and earnings as not subject to tax under the laws of any foreign country where appropriate to carry out the purposes of this subsection.

(x) Cross reference

For limitation on adjustments to basis of annuity contracts sold, see section 1021.

§ 1035 Certain exchanges of insurance policies

(a) General rules

No gain or loss shall be recognized on the exchange of

(1) a contract of life insurance for another contract of life insurance or for an endowment or annuity contract

(2) a contract of endowment insurance (A) for another contract of endowment insurance which provides for regular payments beginning at a date not later than the date payments would have begun under the contract exchanged, or (B) for an annuity contract

(3) an annuity contract for an annuity contract.

(b) Definitions

For the purpose of this section

(1) Endowment contract

A contract of endowment insurance is a contract with an insurance company which depends in part on the life expectancy of the insured but which may be payable in full in a single payment during his or her life.

(2) Annuity contract

An annuity contract is a contract to which paragraph (1) applies but which may be payable during the life of the annuitant only in installments.

(3)   Life insurance contract
A contract of life insurance is a contract to which paragraph (1) applies but which is not ordinarily payable in full during the life of the insured.

(c)   Exchanges involving foreign persons
To the extent provided in regulations, subsection (a) shall not apply to any exchange having the effect of transferring property to any person other than a United States person.

(d)   Cross references

(1)   For rules relating to recognition of gain or loss where an exchange is not solely in kind, see subsections (b) and (c) of section 1031.

(2)   For rules relating to the basis of property acquired in an exchange described in subsection (a), see subsection (d) of section 1031.

§ 2039 Annuities

(a)   General
The gross estate shall include the value of an annuity or other payment receivable by any beneficiary by reason of surviving the decedent under any form of contract or agreement entered into after March 3, 1931 (other than as insurance under policies on the life of the decedent), if, under such contract or agreement, an annuity or other payment was payable to the decedent, or the decedent possessed the right to receive such annuity or payment, either alone or in conjunction with another for his or her life or for any period not ascertainable without reference to his or her death or for any period which does not in fact end before his or her death.

(b)   Amount includible
Subsection (a) shall apply to only such part of the value of the annuity or other payment receivable under such contract or agreement as is proportionate to that part of the purchase price therefor contributed by the decedent. For purposes of this section, any contribution by the decedent's employer or former employer to the purchase price of such contract or agreement (whether or not to an employee's trust or fund forming part of a pension, annuity, retirement, bonus, or profit sharing plan) shall be considered to be contributed by the decedent if made by reason of his or her employment.

2002 Regulations

Effective with RMDs taken on or after January 1, 2003, the tables shown below must be used to determine the respective Single Life and Joint Life tables according to the age(s) of the recipient(s).

Under IRS regulations that went into effect in 2002, distributions from a qualified plan or IRA can be calculated by dividing the account owner's balance by the applicable distribution period determined from the table below. For example, a 71-year-old with $100,000 in his or her account as of December 31 of the previous year would divide this balance by 26.5 to arrive at an RMD of $3,774.

TABLE I
RMD Uniform Lifetime Table—Distribution Period
(For Use by Unmarried Owners, Married Owners Whose Spouses Are Not More Than 10 Years Younger, and Married Owners Whose Spouses Are Not the Sole Beneficiaries of Their IRAs)

Age of Employee	Distribution Period	Age of Employee	Distribution Period
70	27.4	93	9.6
71	26.5	94	9.1
72	25.6	95	8.6
73	24.7	96	8.1
74	23.8	97	7.6
75	22.9	98	7.1
76	22.0	99	6.7
77	21.2	100	6.3
78	20.3	101	5.9
79	19.5	102	5.5
80	18.7	103	5.2
81	17.9	104	4.9
82	17.1	105	4.5
83	16.3	106	4.2
84	15.5	107	3.9
85	14.8	108	3.7
86	14.1	109	3.4
87	13.4	110	3.1
88	12.7	111	2.9
89	12.0	112	2.6
90	11.4	113	2.4
91	10.8	114	2.1
92	10.2	115+	1.9

TABLE II
Joint Life and Last Survivor Expectancy Table*
For Use by Owners Whose Spouses Are More Than 10 Years Younger and Are Not Their Sole Beneficiaries
Ages 70–77

Ages	70	71	72	73	74	75	76	77
35	48.7	48.7	48.7	48.6	48.6	48.6	48.6	48.6
36	47.8	47.7	47.7	47.7	47.7	47.7	47.6	47.6
37	46.8	46.8	46.8	46.7	46.7	46.7	46.7	46.7
38	45.9	45.9	45.8	45.8	45.8	45.7	45.7	45.7
39	44.9	44.9	44.9	44.8	44.8	44.8	44.8	44.8
40	44.0	44.0	43.9	43.9	43.9	43.8	43.8	43.8
41	43.1	43.0	43.0	43.0	42.9	42.9	42.9	42.9
42	42.2	42.1	42.1	42.0	42.0	42.0	41.9	41.9
43	41.3	41.2	41.1	41.1	41.1	41.0	41.0	41.0
44	40.3	40.3	40.2	40.2	40.1	40.1	40.1	40.0
45	39.4	39.4	39.3	39.3	39.2	39.2	39.1	39.1
46	38.6	38.5	38.4	38.4	38.3	38.3	38.2	38.2
47	37.7	37.6	37.5	37.5	37.4	37.4	37.3	37.3
48	36.8	36.7	36.6	36.6	36.5	36.5	36.4	36.4
49	35.9	35.9	35.8	35.7	35.6	35.6	35.5	35.5
50	35.1	35.0	34.9	34.8	34.8	34.7	34.6	34.6
51	34.3	34.2	34.1	34.0	33.9	33.8	33.8	33.7
52	33.4	33.3	33.2	33.1	33.0	33.0	32.9	32.8
53	32.6	32.5	32.4	32.3	32.2	32.1	32.0	32.0
54	31.8	31.7	31.6	31.5	31.4	31.3	31.2	31.1
55	31.1	30.9	30.8	30.6	30.5	30.4	30.3	30.2
56	30.3	30.1	30.0	29.8	29.7	29.6	29.5	29.4
57	29.5	29.4	29.2	29.1	28.9	28.8	28.7	28.6
58	28.8	28.6	28.4	28.3	28.1	28.0	27.9	27.8
59	28.1	27.9	27.7	27.5	27.4	27.2	27.1	27.0
60		27.2	27.0	26.8	26.6	26.5	26.3	26.2
61			26.3	26.1	25.9	25.7	25.6	25.4
62				25.4	25.2	25.0	24.8	24.7
63					24.5	24.3	24.1	23.9
64						23.6	23.4	23.2
65							22.7	22.5
66								21.8

* Use this table to figure your required minimum distribution only if your spouse is your sole beneficiary and is more than 10 years younger than you. Find your age (as of your birthday for the year you are making the computation) on the horizontal line and your spousal beneficiary's age in the vertical column. For example, if you are age 74 and your spousal beneficiary is 63, the life expectancy factor is 24.5. If your age or your spouse's age is not shown here, refer to IRS Publication 590.

TABLE II (Cont'd)
Joint Life and Last Survivor Expectancy Table*
For Use by Owners Whose Spouses Are More Than 10 Years Younger and Are Not Their Sole Beneficiaries
Ages 78–85

Ages	78	79	80	81	82	83	84	85
35	48.6	48.6	48.5	48.5	48.5	48.5	48.5	48.5
36	47.6	47.6	47.6	47.6	47.6	47.6	47.6	47.5
37	46.6	46.6	46.6	46.6	46.6	46.6	46.6	46.6
38	45.7	45.7	45.7	45.7	45.6	45.6	45.6	45.6
39	44.7	44.7	44.7	44.7	44.7	44.7	44.7	44.7
40	43.8	43.8	43.7	43.7	43.7	43.7	43.7	43.7
41	42.8	42.8	42.8	42.8	42.8	42.8	42.7	42.7
42	41.9	41.9	41.8	41.8	41.8	41.8	41.8	41.8
43	40.9	40.9	40.9	40.9	40.9	40.9	40.8	40.8
44	40.0	40.0	40.0	39.9	39.9	39.9	39.9	39.9
45	39.1	39.1	39.0	39.0	39.0	39.0	39.0	38.9
46	38.2	38.1	38.1	38.1	38.1	38.0	38.0	38.0
47	37.2	37.2	37.2	37.2	37.1	37.1	37.1	37.1
48	36.3	36.3	36.3	36.2	36.2	36.2	36.2	36.2
49	35.4	35.4	35.4	35.3	35.3	35.3	35.3	35.2
50	34.5	34.5	34.5	34.4	34.4	34.4	34.3	34.3
51	33.6	33.6	33.6	33.5	33.5	33.5	33.4	33.4
52	32.8	32.7	32.7	32.6	32.6	32.6	32.5	32.5
53	31.9	31.8	31.8	31.8	31.7	31.7	31.7	31.6
54	31.0	31.0	30.9	30.9	30.8	30.8	30.8	30.7
55	30.2	30.1	30.1	30.0	30.0	29.9	29.9	29.9
56	29.3	29.3	29.2	29.2	29.1	29.1	29.0	29.0
57	28.5	28.4	28.4	28.3	28.3	28.2	28.2	28.1
58	27.7	27.6	27.5	27.5	27.4	27.4	27.3	27.3
59	26.9	26.8	26.7	26.6	26.6	26.5	26.5	26.4
60	26.1	26.0	25.9	25.8	25.8	25.7	25.6	25.6
61	25.3	25.2	25.1	25.0	24.9	24.9	24.8	24.8
62	24.6	24.4	24.3	24.2	24.1	24.1	24.0	23.9
63	23.8	23.7	23.6	23.4	23.4	23.3	23.2	23.1
64	23.1	22.9	22.8	22.7	22.6	22.5	22.4	22.3
65	22.4	22.2	22.1	21.9	21.8	21.7	21.6	21.6
66	21.7	21.5	21.3	21.2	21.1	21.0	20.9	20.8
67	21.0	20.8	20.6	20.5	20.4	20.2	20.1	20.1
68		20.1	20.0	19.8	19.7	19.5	19.4	19.3
69			19.3	19.1	19.0	18.8	18.7	18.6
70				18.5	18.3	18.2	18.0	17.9
71					17.7	17.5	17.4	17.3
72						16.9	16.7	16.6
73							16.1	16.0
74								15.4

* Use this table to figure your required minimum distribution only if your spouse is your sole beneficiary and is more than 10 years younger than you. Find your age (as of your birthday for the year you are making the computation) on the horizontal line and your spousal beneficiary's age in the vertical column. For example, if you are age 74 and your spousal beneficiary is 63, the life expectancy factor is 24.5. If your age or your spouse's age is not shown here, refer to IRS Publication 590.

TABLE III
Single Life Table—Life Expectancy

Age	Life Expectancy	Age	Life Expectancy	Age	Life Expectancy	Age	Life Expectancy
0	82.4	29	54.3	58	27	87	6.7
1	81.6	30	53.3	59	26.1	88	6.3
2	80.6	31	52.4	60	25.2	89	5.9
3	79.7	32	51.4	61	24.4	90	5.5
4	78.7	33	50.4	62	23.5	91	5.2
5	77.7	34	49.4	63	22.7	92	4.9
6	76.7	35	48.5	64	21.8	93	4.6
7	75.8	36	47.5	65	21	94	4.3
8	74.8	37	46.5	66	20.2	95	4.1
9	73.8	38	45.6	67	19.4	96	3.8
10	72.8	39	44.6	68	18.6	97	3.6
11	71.8	40	43.6	69	17.8	98	3.4
12	70.8	41	42.7	70	17	99	3.1
13	69.9	42	41.7	71	16.3	100	2.9
14	68.9	43	40.7	72	15.5	101	2.7
15	67.9	44	39.8	73	14.8	102	2.5
16	66.9	45	38.8	74	14.1	103	2.3
17	66	46	37.9	75	13.4	104	2.1
18	65	47	37	76	12.7	105	1.9
19	64	48	36	77	12.1	106	1.7
20	63	49	35.1	78	11.4	107	1.5
21	62.1	50	34.2	79	10.8	108	1.4
22	61.1	51	33.3	80	10.2	109	1.2
23	60.1	52	32.3	81	9.7	110	1.1
24	59.1	53	31.4	82	9.1	111+	1
25	58.2	54	30.5	83	8.6		
26	57.2	55	29.6	84	8.1		
27	56.2	56	28.7	85	7.6		
28	55.3	57	27.9	86	7.1		

Glossary

A-B trust • a trust that divides the deceased's property into two parts, according to the grantor's will. The marital Part A trust is designed to hold assets that qualify for the marital deduction. The nonmarital Part B trust is designed to preserve the full estate tax credit for the grantor spouse.

accumulation units • what a policyowner is credited with when he or she invests a portion of the premium in the subaccounts of a variable annuity. The value of the accumulation units will vary depending on the investment performance of the underlying subaccounts.

accumulation value • the dollar amount of the value of the annuity. The accumulation value is the amount in the annuity prior to the imposition of surrender charges.

active listening • a method of listening in which the agent demonstrates his or her understanding of the prospect's perspective and can state in the prospect's own words what the prospect has said and meant to communicate

additional markets for annuities • market segments for annuity products involving specialized financial-needs-based concepts, including structured settlements, business planning, charitable planning, college funding, and estate planning

advance medical directive • either a durable power of attorney for health care or a living will, which lets the physician and other health-care providers know the kind of medical care an individual wants, or does not want, if he or she becomes incapacitated

age-based • an effective way to segment the annuities market by age

age-based market segment • one of three market segments for annuity products as follows: (1) prospects who see retirement as a distant goal (those under age 45), (2) prospects who see retirement as a more immediate concern (those ages 45 to 64), and (3) prospects who are enjoying retirement or semiretirement (those age 65 and older)

age 70 ½ IRS penalty tax • a tax imposed by the Internal Revenue Service when minimum distributions from qualified plans and individual retirement accounts are not distributed as mandated. The penalty tax is equal to 50 percent of the amount that was required to be distributed but was not.

alternative funding services • financing alternatives to annuities used in retirement that include Social Security, pensions, personal savings, and employment

annual contract charge • an annual fee charged against the account value of fixed-interest annuities and variable annuities

annual reset • indexing method for indexed annuities that provides growth by locking in the previous year's anniversary value. It compares the positive change in the index from the beginning of the policy year to the end of the policy year.

annuitant • the measuring life for deferred and immediate annuities who must be a living person and cannot be a nonnatural entity

annuitization • the process by which a deferred annuity is transformed into a guaranteed payout stream (for example, a life income with 10 years period certain). However, the amount of the income payments is not guaranteed with variable income annuities.

annuity • the annual payment of an allowance or income; the right to receive this payment or the obligation to make this payment; an investment on which a person receives fixed payments for a lifetime or a specified number of years; a contract or agreement under which one or more persons receive periodic payments in return for prior set payments made by themselves or another (as an employer)

annuity disclosure • a disclosure document recommended by the NAIC to be given to an individual prior to purchasing an annuity. The NAIC adopted a model regulation in 1999 that recommends the specific information that should be disclosed in the document.

approach • the step in the selling/planning process that involves asking the prospect for an appointment. An approach can be done face to face or via the telephone.

asset allocation • the process of developing a diversification strategy that allocates premiums to various asset classes to build an overall portfolio consistent with the investor's risk tolerance and long-term goals

asset fee • the amount assessed by an insurance company on indexed annuities. The fee is applied against the growth in the index and reduces the amount of interest the insurer credits to the annuity. *See also* margin and spread.

assumed investment return (AIR) • an interest rate used to determine the amount of initial income from a variable immediate annuity

automatic rebalancing • readjusting a portfolio back to the original asset allocation among the subaccounts after growth has occurred. Many variable annuities offer this service.

averaging • a term used with indexed annuities in which the indexed points are averaged together over a daily basis or a monthly basis rather than using the actual value of the ending index on one specified date

Baby Boomer Generation • population segment born between 1946 and 1964. Many members of this generation are educating their children and taking care of aging parents. Because of this dual role, they are sometimes referred to as the sandwiched generation.

back-end load • a fee imposed by the insurance company when withdrawals or surrenders are taken from a deferred annuity. These fees are generally imposed only during a fixed period of time beginning with the issuance of the annuity (also called a contingent deferred sales charge). *See also* surrender charge.

beneficiary • the person or entity entitled to receive the proceeds of an annuity upon the death of the annuitant

benefit • what the buyer receives as a result of a feature—that is, what the product does for the buyer and why he or she wants it

bonus interest rate • an interest rate sometimes added on top of the first-year interest rate of a fixed-interest deferred annuity. The duration of the bonus interest is usually one year.

broker-dealer • a person who engages in the business of effecting transactions in securities for the account of others, or who is engaged in the business of buying and selling securities for his or her own account. Broker-dealers must become members of the NASD.

building prestige • a preapproach strategy in which an advisor implements a personal public relations campaign designed to build and maintain a good reputation within a target market and the community at large

buying signals • obvious verbal and nonverbal signals that indicate acceptance or rejection of what an advisor is selling

cap rate • a term used with indexed annuities that defines the maximum interest rate that may be credited to the policy for the defined time period

center of influence • an influential person who knows an advisor, has a favorable opinion of the advisor, and agrees to introduce or recommend him or her to others

charitable gift annuity • a type of charitable gift in which a donor gives an asset to a charity in exchange for a lifetime income. A charitable gift annuity is not an annuity sold by an insurance company.

charitable remainder trust • a type of charitable gift in which a donor gives assets to a trust in exchange for an annual income stated as a percentage of trust assets. Upon death, the charity receives the balance of the trust assets.

contract term • a term used with deferred annuities to describe the length of time during which the particular index is measured

cost basis • the amount of premiums a policyowner paid into an annuity

creditor protection • the concept that some annuities can be protected from attachment by the policyowner's creditors. The level of protection varies from state to state; not all states protect annuities from creditors.

death benefit • the amount of proceeds from an annuity that are payable to the beneficiary upon the death of the annuitant

deductive approach • an approach to the personal information-gathering process that starts with a thorough and lengthy fact-finding form that broadly covers all the prospect's financial needs. The process requires quantifying a prospect's financial planning needs, prioritizing them, and then selling the prospect the appropriate product or products that address the highest priority of need.

deferred annuity • a type of policy offered by an insurance company in which a person deposits a lump sum or a series of payments into a contract without determining a specified point in time when, or if, the policy will be annuitized into an income stream

designated beneficiary • a legal concept that applies to an individual named as the beneficiary of a qualified annuity. A designated beneficiary must be a person and cannot be a trust, estate, or corporation. It does not have the same meaning as a typical beneficiary. For example, a corporation can be named as beneficiary, but for purposes of distribution options at the death of the annuitant, the corporation is not a "designated beneficiary."

direct mail • a preapproach strategy that involves sending a letter or postcard to a prospect. Some direct-mail strategies involve a giveaway (or premium offer).

discovery agreement • a verbal or written mutual agreement between the advisor and the prospect to work together to address the prospect's expressed financial goals. It is formulated at or after the conclusion of the initial fact-finding interview.

diversification • a risk-management technique in which the investor does not put all his or her money into one investment but, instead, invests across asset categories to take advantage of the relationships among different investments that tend to have highly opposite fluctuation sensitivities in order to minimize risk

dollar cost averaging • the consistent investment of equal periodic payments into a diversified equity-based investment over an extended period of time. It is also defined as depositing regularly scheduled additional premiums into a flexible-premium deferred annuity.

durable power of attorney • a document signed by one person (the principal) authorizing another person (the attorney-in-fact) to act on behalf of the signer. The word *durable* indicates that the power stays in effect in the event that the signer becomes incapacitated.

effective communication • important interviewing skills such as knowing how and when to ask appropriate types of questions, being an active and empathetic listener, and being able to explain financial needs and insurance products to prospects

enhance earnings benefit • optional death benefit rider available in variable deferred annuity contracts that helps to offset the federal income taxes payable by beneficiaries upon the death of the contract owner by providing them with an additional lump-sum amount usually equal to a percentage of the contract's earnings (e.g., 40%).

exclusion ratio • the ratio or percentage applied to an immediate annuity payment to determine how much of the payment is excluded from income taxation

existing clients • a prospecting source for annuity products consisting of people with whom the advisor has an established professional relationship because they have already purchased at least one financial product

expected return • a factor in the calculation of the exclusion ratio for immediate annuities. The expected return is the total amount of payments the policyowner can expect to receive from the immediate annuity. The total investment is divided by the expected return to produce the exclusion ratio.

fact finder • a self-contained discovery document for gathering facts, figures, and feelings from prospects that is designed to quantify and qualify their need for financial products

feature • a characteristic about a product—what it is and what it does

Financial Industry Regulatory Authority (FINRA) • the entity responsible for regulating the securities industry and enforcing the rules of the SEC. Broker-dealers must become members of FINRA.

fixed-amount annuity • a type of immediate annuity in which the policyowner declares the amount of the payment desired, given the lump-sum premium, and the insurance company establishes the specific time frame during which the specified amount of income will be paid

fixed-interest deferred annuity • tax-deferred annuity in which the issuing insurance company guarantees the principal deposited into it against loss, along with a guaranteed compound interest rate that will be credited to the cash value for the benefit of the contract owner. Generally the insurer offers the annuity owner a guaranteed interest rate for a certain period of time, after which a periodically declared current compound interest rate will apply to the policy's cash value until some specified future maturity date.

fixed-period annuity • a type of immediate annuity in which the payments to the policyowner are payable for a finite period of time. At the end of the time period, the payments cease. The policyowner declares the length of time desired, given the lump-sum premium, and the insurance company establishes the dollar amount of payments for the specified time frame.

flexible-premium annuity • a type of deferred annuity in which the policy allows the owner to make additional contributions beyond the initial premium

flexible-premium deferred annuity • a type of deferred annuity in which the policyowner may deposit more than one premium

401(k) plan • a type of qualified profit-sharing plan offered by employers to their employees

403(b) plan • a type of qualified retirement plan for public school employees and 501(c)(3) organizations. *See also* tax-sheltered annuity.

free-corridor amount • an amount of money the policyowner can withdraw from the annuity each year during the surrender-charge period without the imposition of a surrender penalty. It is commonly equal to 10 percent of the annuity's value.

free-look period • a feature of annuity policies that offers the purchaser a specified period of time during which the purchaser may return the policy to the insurer for a full refund for any reason. In most states, the free-look period is 10 days from the date the policy is delivered to the customer.

free-window period • limited number of days at the end of the contract term in an equity-indexed annuity during which it can be renewed for another contract term, exchanged for another type of annuity such as a fixed or variable annuity, annuitized and the annuitant can begin to receive the benefits under one of the available settlement options, or partially or completely surrendered without incurring company surrender charges

front-end load • a term applied mostly to variable annuities that describes a fee charged against the initial premium paid into a deferred annuity

fund expense • an asset-based fee for management operations of the various subaccounts in a variable annuity. It is charged for the expense of paying fund managers and the fund's operating expenses.

general account • the investment option in a variable annuity that guarantees the owner's principal and a stated level of interest earnings. It can also be referred to as the guaranteed account.

general power of attorney • a document signed by one person (the principal) authorizing another person (the attorney-in-fact) to act on behalf of the signer. A general power is effective as long as the person granting the power remains in good health, but it becomes legally ineffective in cases of mental incompetence or medical incapacity.

generation • an age-based segmentation of the general population developed by demographers. It is based on the theory that the general population's psyche and behavior are shaped by significant life experiences, such as the way people are raised, national and world events, wars, the social and economic climate of the times, and so forth.

Generation X • population segment born between 1965 and 1981. They are the children of Baby Boomers or the younger members of the Silent Generation.

guaranteed lifetime withdrawal benefit • a benefit available in variable deferred annuities that guarantees that a certain percentage of the amount invested (typically 4 percent to 6 percent) can be withdrawn each year for as long as the contract holder lives, regardless of market performance.

guaranteed minimum accumulation benefit • a benefit available in variable deferred annuities that guarantees that the value of the annuity can be stepped up to a certain amount on a specified date, whether or not the contract owner annuitizes

guaranteed minimum interest rate • the lowest interest rate established in a deferred annuity that the insurance company promises it will always pay. Traditionally 3 percent has been the guaranteed minimum interest rate, but recently, states are lowering this amount due to the prolonged time frame of low interest rates during which insurance companies have been operating.

guaranteed minimum income benefit • a benefit offered in variable deferred annuities that increases the owner's investment by some compounded percentage—typically between 3 percent and 6 percent. At the end of a specified period, the increased amount may be used to turn the contract into an immediate annuity.

guaranteed minimum return of premium benefit • a benefit offered in variable deferred annuities that guarantees that the owner may take back the premium after a specified number of years if the investment is more than the account value

guaranteed minimum withdrawal benefit • a benefit available in variable deferred annuities that guarantees the systematic withdrawal of a certain percentage (usually 5 percent to 7 percent) of premiums annually until premiums are completely recovered, regardless of market performance.

health care power of attorney • a signed and witnessed legal document by one person that designates another person (the health care proxy) to make important medical decisions about his or her care in the event that the signer becomes incapacitated

high water mark • a crediting method used with indexed annuities in which the growth in the index is credited by comparing the index point at the end of each policy year to the last highest anniversary point within each contract term. If the current point is higher, then interest is credited from the last highest point to the current point.

immediate annuity • a type of annuity in which the policyowner pays a lump sum of money to the insurance company in exchange for a guaranteed stream of income. The length of time the income stream is payable varies with the specific type of payout requested by the policyowner.

index • a measure of a particular group of securities' performance

index average • the number that reflects the average earnings of a particular index

indexed annuity • a type of deferred annuity in which the interest earnings are tied to an index usually outside the control of the insurance company. Usually the index is an equity index, but it can be a bond index. Indexed annuities were introduced in 1995.

individual retirement account (IRA) • a type of retirement plan established by individuals that has limited contribution amounts. Distributions from IRAs are generally fully taxable.

inductive approach • the converse of the deductive approach to information gathering. It starts with a dominant or single need, then broadens into a full-blown comprehensive financial-need analysis where several financial-planning needs are identified and prioritized.

interest rate guarantee period • the length of time during which the insurance company will promise the payment of a specified amount of interest earnings

investment objectives • financial goals the client wishes to accomplish by purchasing a particular investment product. These may include safety of principal, tax reduction, asset appreciation strategies, the need for liquidity, generation of current income, and preservation of purchasing power. A client's time horizon and tolerance to exposure to financial risks are factors the advisor must also consider in recommending products to achieve the desired financial goals.

investment risk • the inherent exposure to loss of principal, interest, or dividends; capital gain; purchasing power; tax advantages; other investment opportunities; or any other financial advantage that a client is exposed to by purchasing financial products

joint and survivor annuity • a type of immediate annuity payout in which the policyowner and another person chosen by the policyowner are the measuring lives over which the annuity payments are made. The annuity payments will continue in full or in a reduced amount as specified in the contract upon the death of the first annuitant and will cease upon the death of the second annuitant.

joint and survivor life annuity with period certain • a type of immediate annuity payout in which the policyowner and another person chosen by the policyowner are the measuring lives over which the annuity payments are made. The annuity payments will continue until the death of the last annuitant, with a minimum payment period, generally 5, 10, 15, 20, 25, or 30 years.

joint and survivor life annuity with installment or cash refund • a type of immediate annuity payout in which the policyowner and another person chosen by the policyowner are the measuring lives over which the annuity payments are made. Under the installment-refund option, the insurance company will refund the remaining balance of the deposit by continuing payments to the named beneficiary after the second annuitant's death until the full deposit is returned. Under the cash-refund option, the insurer will refund the discounted present value of the remaining payments in a lump sum.

joint and survivor life annuity with percent of premium death benefit • a type of immediate annuity payout in which the policyowner and another person chosen by the policyowner are the measuring lives over which the annuity payments are made. The annuity payments will continue in full upon the death of the first annuitant, and at the surviving annuitant's death, a specified percentage of the initial premium payment selected at the time of purchase (i.e., 25 percent or 50 percent) will be paid to a designated beneficiary in a single sum.

joint annuitants • a deferred or immediate annuity that names two annuitants over whose lives the payments will be made

joint owners • a deferred or immediate annuity that names two owners of the policy. Each owner has equal rights to the policy. Both owners must agree to all policy transactions to be effective.

life annuity with period certain • a type of immediate annuity in which the insurance company will pay the policyowner payments for the entire life of the annuitant. In the event the annuitant dies before the end of a specified period (5, 10, 15, 20, 25, or 30 years) beginning with the issuance of the policy, the insurance company will continue payments to the named beneficiary for the rest of that period.

life-only annuity • a type of immediate annuity in which the insurance company will pay the policyowner payments for the entire life of the annuitant. Upon the death of the annuitant, payments will cease, regardless of the length of time the annuitant actually lived.

life annuity with cash refund • a type of immediate annuity in which the insurance company will pay the policyowner payments for the entire life of the annuitant. In the event the policyowner dies before receiving back in payments the amount of premium paid, the insurance company will pay the difference between the dollar amount of the original premium and the total payments paid prior to death in a lump-sum payment to the beneficiary.

life annuity with installment refund • a type of immediate annuity in which the insurance company will pay the policyowner payments for the entire life of the annuitant. In the event the policyowner dies before receiving back in payments the dollar amount of the premium originally paid, the insurance company will continue payments to the named beneficiary until the dollar amount of the original premium has been paid.

life annuity with percent of premium death benefit • a type of immediate annuity in which the insurance company will pay the policyowner payments for the entire life of the annuitant. Upon the death of the annuitant, a specified percentage of the initial premium payment selected at the time of purchase (i.e., 25 percent or 50 percent) will be paid to a designated beneficiary in a single sum.

lists • a prospecting source that contains the names of prospects within a target market or market segment who will likely have an interest in annuity products

living will • a legal document that describes the types of medical treatment an individual chooses to accept or reject. The purpose of a living will is to let others know a person's medical wishes when he or she is terminally ill or in a vegetative state and unable to communicate.

long-term care benefit rider • a policy rider that gives the owner of a deferred annuity contract access to cash values (usually up to 50 percent of annuity cash values without a surrender change) if the annuitant, up to a maximum specified age, has to enter a long-term care facility

margin • a fee assessed by an insurance company with indexed annuities. This fee is applied against the growth in the index and reduces the amount of interest the insurer credits to the annuity. *See also* asset fee and spread.

market conduct • a term relating to insurance companies' and agents' activities in the sale of its products. State insurance departments regulate insurance companies on the basis of their market conduct to make sure that consumers are treated fairly.

market segment • an identifiable group of people with common characteristics and needs

market value adjustment • an increase or decrease in the annuity's value, depending on the overall level of interest rates in the United States economy relative to the interest rate in the specific annuity. If the policy's interest rate is 8 percent and the market is earning only 4 percent, the policy's values would be adjusted upward under this feature if the owner surrenders early.

maturity date • the date in deferred annuity policies at which point the policy terminates and is payable in full to the policyowner, usually when the annuitant is age 85 or 90.

minimum distribution rules • see "required mimimum distributions"

mortality and expense charge (M&E) • asset-based charge against the investment subaccounts in a variable annuity

National Association of Insurance Commissioners (NAIC) • the entity that provides a forum for creating uniform insurance laws and regulations. The NAIC is comprised of the state insurance commissioners, the District of Columbia, and four U.S. territories.

networking • the process of communication and sharing ideas and prospects with others whose work does not compete with the participating advisor

nonnatural person • a trust, business, corporation, estate, or other legal entity that is not a living person

nonqualified annuity • a particular type of annuity classification defined by the type of funds invested in the annuity. Nonqualified funds are those that have already been subject to income tax by the taxpayer. The opposite of a nonqualified annuity is a qualified annuity in which the premiums are funded with money that has not been taxed to the policyowner.

nonqualified retirement planning • a market segment for annuities involving either (1) the deposit of after-tax premiums into tax-favored deferred annuities for the purpose of accumulating dollars for retirement, or (2) the deposit of after-tax premiums into immediate annuities for the purpose of providing a stream of income during retirement

nonverbal signals • gestures, bodily movements, or facial expressions, such as leaning forward, listening attentively, making eye contact, nodding, showing appreciation, or participating, that indicate acceptance or rejection of a person or an idea

objections, four categories of • resistance to purchasing annuity products that falls into one of four general categories: no need, no money, no hurry, and no confidence

options • an investment used by insurance companies when investing equity-indexed annuity premiums. Investing in options allows the insurance company to meet its obligations to pay interest earnings based on outside indexes. By buying options, the insurer owns the right to any gain in the index. The cost of options can vary widely.

owner • the person or legal entity who enters into the annuity contract with the insurance company and who has all the legal rights to the contract, including the right to name the beneficiary and the right to withdraw policy values

partial Sec. 1035 exchange • a term used with deferred annuities when a policyowner takes a portion of the cash values from an existing deferred annuity and transfers it directly to a new annuity policy purchased from another insurance company

partial surrender • an amount taken from the cash values of a deferred annuity by the policyowner prior to the maturity date of the policy. *See also* withdrawal.

participation rate • a term used with indexed annuities to describe the percentage of the growth in a particular index that will be credited to the annuity values. Participation rates are generally 70 percent to 100 percent.

pension plan • a type of retirement plan offered by employers to their employees

percentage change • the change in the index to which an indexed annuity's performance will be measured, starting from the beginning of the contract term to the end of the contract term, expressed as a percentage. For example, if the S&P 500 Index stands at 1,000 at the beginning of the term and it rises to 1,150, there is a 15 percent change.

pivot approach • making the transition from a successful or unsuccessful sale or discussion of one product and asking for an appointment to discuss another financial or insurance need and product

pivoting • a suggestion to the prospect that he or she consider alternative products when the prospect does not qualify for an annuity

point-to-point • a type of indexing method with indexed annuities which credits interest earnings by measuring from one particular index point to a second particular index point

pre-59 ½ IRS penalty tax • a 10 percent IRS penalty tax assessed against annuity owners who take withdrawals or surrenders from their policies prior to age 59 ½ and do not fall within one of the exceptions to the rule. The tax is assessed against the amount of the withdrawal that is subject to ordinary income tax.

preapproach • any method or strategy used to create awareness of the advisor and interest in his or her products so that prospects are preconditioned to meet with the advisor and buy the products. Examples of methods include direct mail, building prestige, and a professional brochure.

preliminary discovery agreement • a verbal mutual agreement between the advisor and the prospect to work together to construct a plan to address the prospect's expressed financial goals. This agreement comes after the prospect has been properly qualified and prior to completing the fact-finding segment of an interview.

premium bonus • a dollar amount of money sometimes available on indexed annuities that is applied on top of the amount of premiums paid by the policyowner. The addition of a premium bonus will often increase the surrender charges in the policy and/or the length of the surrender-charge period.

private annuity • a contract between two people in which one person transfers assets to the other in exchange for lifetime income. It is often used to transfer assets from one generation to the next in the context of estate planning. It is not a product sold by an insurance company.

professional brochure • a printed introductory preapproach piece that includes self-promotional information such as the advisor's name and contact information, a mission statement, a short biography, credentials (designations, experience, and so forth), services, and products

prospecting • continuous, systematic process of identifying individuals who are potentially qualified and willing to purchase the products and services an advisor provides

prospecting sources • existing clients, referrals, centers of influence, networking, seminars, and lists. Seminars, which are a prospecting and marketing source, are of particular significance in the annuities market.

prospectus • a document required in the sale of variable annuities that outlines the fees and expenses charged in the policy, the product features, and the investment options. The SEC regulates the contents of the prospectus, as well as at what point it is given to the potential purchaser.

qualified annuity • a particular type of annuity classification defined by the type of funds invested in the annuity. Qualified funds are those that have not yet been subject to income tax by the taxpayer. Qualified annuities include

IRAs, SEP IRAs, tax-sheltered annuities, SIMPLE IRAs, pension plans, and profit-sharing plans. The opposite of a qualified annuity is a nonqualified annuity in which the premiums are funded with money that has already been taxed to the policyowner.

qualified prospects • people who meet the following criteria: They (1) need and value your products and services, (2) can afford to pay for your products and services, (3) are insurable or financially suitable, and (4) can be approached by you on a favorable basis.

qualified retirement planning • a market segment for annuities involving either (1) the deposit of pretax premiums into tax-favored deferred annuities for the purpose of accumulating dollars for retirement, or (2) the deposit of tax-qualified premiums into immediate annuities for the purpose of providing a stream of income during retirement. This involves the sale of IRAs, SIMPLE plans, SEPs, tax-sheltered annuities, and a variety of other employer-sponsored qualified retirement plans.

ratcheting • the term for indexed annuities that defines how the measuring point for the particular index is determined each year. It compares the positive change in the index from the beginning of the policy year to the end of the policy year. *See also* annual reset.

referral • a person who has been suggested by another person as a prospect who may be interested in the products and services an advisor provides. Referrals are also known as referred leads and can come from clients, prospects, centers of influence, and even nonprospects.

renewal interest rate • the interest rate declared in fixed-interest deferred annuities that follows the initial interest rate guarantee period. The policyowner has no input on what interest rate will be credited in the renewal periods.

required beginning date • the date on which the participant of a qualified annuity needs to begin taking required minimum distributions. The date is generally April 1 following the year the participant reaches age 70 ½. For some individuals, it is the later of the above date or the date the person actually retires.

required minimum distributions • the dollar amount of funds that must be withdrawn from qualified annuities when owners reach their required beginning date. The failure of a participant to withdraw the minimum distribution will result in an IRS penalty tax of 50 percent of the amount that should have been withdrawn but was not.

retirement planning fact finder • a comprehensive questionnaire that is designed for the discovery of personal data and retirement goals, quantitative data, and retirement income sources from a prospect. It also includes a worksheet and interest tables used to calculate the amount of any additional retirement income needed.

rising floor death benefit • a death benefit in a variable deferred annuity in which the benefit is equal to the larger of the account value or the premiums paid plus interest

risk management • a technique used to balance the risks of an individual's various investment decisions one against the other. One of the best ways to manage risk is through financial diversification. Risk management through diversification offers an opportunity for clients with low risk tolerance to balance loss of principal concerns against needs for capital appreciation.

risk tolerance • the degree to which one is willing to accept exposure of his or her financial resources to one or more types of investment risk

rollover • the process of moving a qualified plan or IRA distribution to an IRA account within 60 days. A rollover can be transacted only once a year.

rollover IRA • a tax-qualified investment vehicle that accepts funds from either IRAs or other qualified retirement plans

Roth IRA • a type of individual retirement account that offers limited after-tax contributions but offers tax-free retirement income

SARSEP (salary reduction simplified employee pension) • a type of qualified retirement plan in which employees had the ability to defer a portion of their salary to the plan. This type of plan is no longer offered.

Sec. 1035 exchange • the transaction in which an annuity's cash values are exchanged by surrendering one annuity for a new annuity, usually with a different insurance company. The process can happen without the policyowner being subject to any income taxes on the gain in the original annuity contract. IRC Sec. 1035 is the code section that allows this transaction.

Securities and Exchange Commission (SEC) • the entity that oversees and regulates the U.S. securities markets. It is concerned with the accurate disclosure of information to investors.

security • a type of investment regulated by the Securities and Exchange Commission. Fixed-interest deferred annuities are exempted from regulation as securities, but variable annuities are not.

segmenting • the process of finding groups of prospects with common needs and characteristics

seminar • a prospecting method in which the financial advisor, alone or as part of a team of professional advisors, conducts an educational and motivational meeting for a group of people who are interested in a particular topic

seminar checklist • a comprehensive list of items that summarizes the details and logistics necessary to conduct a successful seminar

Senior Protection in Annuity Transactions Model Regulation • a model regulation adopted by the National Association of Insurance Commissioners in 2003 to set standards and procedures for recommendations of annuity products to consumers age 65 and older

SEP IRA (simplified employee pension) • a qualified retirement plan for business owners or self-employed persons

separate account • the investment option of the variable annuity that houses the various subaccounts. These assets are segregated from the insurance company's other assets, hence the term "separate" account. The variable annuity is made up of two accounts: the separate account and the general account.

Silent Generation • population segment born prior to 1946, sometimes referred to as the GI, Swing, or Mature Generation

SIMPLE IRA • a type of qualified retirement plan introduced in 1997 for employers with 100 or fewer employees

single-premium annuity • a type of annuity, deferred or immediate, in which the policyowner can make only one premium at the point of policy issue. No additional premiums can be deposited into a single-premium annuity.

single-premium deferred annuity • a type of deferred annuity, whether fixed or variable or equity indexed, in which the policyowner can make only one premium at the point of policy issue. No additional premiums can be deposited into a single-premium deferred annuity.

social style • predictable patterns of behavior that people display in assertive/responsive situations. Understanding and responding appropriately to the characteristics of each social style enables the advisor to establish rapport with a prospect who has that style.

solvency • financial stability. State insurance departments are concerned with the financial solvency of the insurance companies operating within their state's borders.

spousal IRA • an individual retirement account in which a working spouse makes the contribution on behalf of a nonworking spouse

spousal rollover • an IRA established by the spouse of a deceased person funded with monies from the deceased person's qualified retirement account or IRA

spousal Roth IRA • a Roth IRA account in which a working spouse makes the contribution on behalf of a nonworking spouse

spread • the difference between the earnings an insurance company makes on the premium dollars it invests and the amount of interest earnings the insurance company credits to the policyowner for those same premium dollars. Generally insurance companies intend to earn at least a 2 percent spread on premiums they invest.

Spread is also referred to as the amount assessed by an insurance company with indexed annuities. The fee is applied against the growth in the index and reduces the amount of interest the insurer credits to the annuity. *See also* asset fee and margin.

springing durable power of attorney • a document signed by one person (the principal) authorizing another person (the attorney-in-fact) to act on behalf of the signer. A springing durable power becomes operative only when a specified event occurs, such as the physical or mental incapacity of the principal.

state guaranty association • a nonprofit association created in each of the 50 states designed to cover the losses of policyowners' funds if the insurance companies become insolvent

state insurance department • the entity in each of the 50 states that regulates insurance activity within the borders of the particular state

stepped-up death benefit • a death benefit in a variable deferred annuity in which the benefit is updated on specific policy anniversary dates by the policy value as of that date, if higher. Step-up dates can occur every year or at specified intervals, depending on the policy's design (also referred to as a ratcheted death benefit).

stretch IRA • a concept, not a particular type of annuity policy, in which beneficiaries of IRA accounts can avoid a lump-sum death benefit and take only the required minimum distributions

structured settlement • lifetime financial support that is composed of periodic payments instead of, or in addition to, a single lump-sum payment awarded by a court to an injured party or throughout the minority of dependent heirs. These annuity contracts are specifically tailored to meet financial needs of the claimants who are the injured or wronged parties. The periodic payments of income are received tax free by the claimant during his or her life and by the claimant's beneficiaries thereafter for the balance of any guarantee period.

subaccounts • similar to mutual funds, accounts that are part of the separate account of a variable annuity contract. The subaccounts offer investment funds into which the policyowner allocates his or her premiums.

substantially equal periodic payments (SEPPs) • the series of withdrawals an annuity owner can take from a deferred annuity policy prior to the owner's age 59 ½ without being assessed a 10 percent IRS penalty tax

suitability • a concept of appropriateness that has been required in the sale of variable annuities but that has not been required in the sale of fixed or indexed annuities until 2003. Suitability was addressed in 2003 in the sale of both fixed and variable annuities through the NAIC's adoption of the Senior Protection in Annuity Transactions Model Regulation.

surrender • the complete withdrawal of a deferred annuity policy by the owner. A surrender is distinguished from the payment of a death benefit if the annuitant dies or from the payment of the annuity values when the policy matures.

surrender charge • a fee imposed by the insurance company for withdrawals or partial surrenders taken from a deferred annuity policy during the surrender-charge period, usually during the first 7 to 10 years from the issuance of the policy. The fee is expressed as a percentage of the amount withdrawn or surrendered.

surrender-charge period • the length of time from the issuance of a deferred annuity during which the insurance company will impose a fee for amounts withdrawn or surrendered. Surrender-charge periods usually last for 7 to 10 years.

surrender value • the portion of the deferred annuity contract that is available to the policyowner upon a complete redemption of the policy. During the early years of an annuity, the surrender value is less than the accumulation value. The difference is due to the surrender charge imposed by the insurance company.

target market • a market segment that is large enough so that the advisor does not run out of prospects and that has a communication system that will facilitate the process of identifying prospects

tax deferral • the feature of deferred annuity policies that allows the cash values to grow each year without the policyowner having to pay income tax each year on the growth. Instead, the policyowner is not subject to tax until the annuity values are withdrawn or surrendered.

tax-sheltered annuity (TSA) • a type of qualified retirement plan for public school employees and 501(c)(3) organizations; also called a 403(b) plan. *See also* 403(b) plan.

telephone approach • use of the telephone to set an appointment with a prospect

terminal illness rider • a policy rider that may be offered on deferred annuity contracts where a certain amount of the annuity's cash values can be accessed without the imposition of surrender charges if the policyowner (or annuitant, depending on the specific language of the rider) suffers from a terminal illness

total expense ratio • the combination of the mortality and expense charge with the fund expenses in a variable annuity. The average total expense ratio is 2.356 percent.

transfer• the process by which qualified annuity funds are moved from one policy to another without the policyowner being subject to income taxes on the policy. It is similar to the IRC Sec. 1035 exchange allowed on nonqualified annuities. Annuity owners can transfer their qualified plan policies on an unlimited basis.

trust • a legal agreement that contains instructions to the trustee from the grantor regarding what can and cannot be done with the trust property. The four components of a trust are the corpus, grantor, trustee, and beneficiary.

variable deferred annuity • a specific type of annuity that is considered a security and in which the risk of loss is shifted away from the insurance company to the policyowner. A variable annuity allows purchasers to participate in the investment of their annuity funds by determining how their contributions will be invested among a series of accounts.

variable immediate annuity • a stream of income payments payable to the annuity owner by an insurance company in which the payments vary with the investment experience of the underlying investment vehicle.

withdrawal • an amount of money taken from a deferred annuity contract before the annuity reaches the maturity date. *See also* partial surrender.

Answers to Review Questions and Self-Test Questions

Chapter 1

Answers to Review Questions

1-1. The *American Heritage Dictionary* and *Webster's Third New International Dictionary* define annuity as follows:
- the annual payment of an allowance or income
- the right to receive this payment or the obligation to make this payment
- an investment on which a person receives fixed payments for a lifetime or a specified number of years
- a contract or agreement under which one or more persons receive periodic payments in return for prior set payments made by themselves or another (as an employer)

1-2. The distinction between qualified and nonqualified funds within annuities is as follows:
- Nonqualified annuities are annuity contracts into which investors put their after-tax funds.
- Qualified annuities are funded with pretax (or before-tax) funds.

1-3. The primary objective of an annuity contract is to pay financial benefits to the persons who receive the annuity payments during their lifetimes. Annuitization is the surest way to provide systematic payments from a specific sum of money over a specified period, or for the duration of a single life or the lives of two people; this is because the payments are guaranteed by the insurance company.

1-4. The four classifications of annuities are
- single-premium or flexible-premium annuities
- immediate or deferred annuities
- qualified or nonqualified annuities
- fixed-interest, indexed, or variable deferred annuities

1.5 Immediate annuities are contracts with immediate payments or those with payments that begin within one year of the contract date. Deferred annuities are future-pay contracts with payments that begin at some later date beyond the first contract year.

1-6. The tax-deferral feature that is a part of all annuity contracts is redundant when dealing with qualified money that already enjoys that advantage. As a result, when the decision is made to invest qualified money in annuities, it should be because of the features that annuity contracts offer, rather than for tax deferral.

1-7. The eight steps in the selling/planning process are as follows:
- Identify the prospect.
- Approach the prospect.

- Meet with the prospect.
- Gather information and establish goals.
- Analyze the information.
- Develop and present the plan.
- Implement the plan.
- Service the plan.

1-8. Medical advancements have increased life expectancy. The average life expectancy in 1900 was 47 years; in 2000 it reached 76.9 years. That is a 29.6-year increase in the average life expectancy. Perhaps more significantly, people who survive to age 65 can expect to live to age 83; in 1900 they could expect to live only to age 68.

1-9. Six sources for obtaining annuity prospects are
- existing clients
- referrals from clients/prospects
- centers of influence (COI)
- networking
- seminars
- lists

1-10. The three age-based market segments are
- under age 45 (providers)
- ages 45 to 64 (preretirees)
- ages 65 and older (retirees)

Answers to Self-Test Questions

1-1. D
1-2. B
1-3. B
1-4. B
1-5. B
1-6. A
1-7. C
1-8. C
1-9. A
1-10. A

Chapter 2

Answers to Review Questions

2-1. As retirement planning tools, nonqualified deferred annuities offer clients these important features:
- income tax deferral
- probate avoidance
- guaranteed lifetime income at annuitization

- limited liquidity using free-corridor amounts
- the ability to take partial surrenders without having to surrender the entire annuity
- flexibility in making contributions as needed
- no limits on the amount of premiums that can be invested
- surrender charges that discourage clients from withdrawing funds prior to retirement age
- low cost (typically annuities do not charge an annual fee, but if they do, it is a relatively modest fee)

2-2. The stretch IRA is a marketing concept that allows beneficiaries of IRAs to avoid taking a lump-sum death benefit by instead taking only the required minimum distribution and correspondingly avoiding a huge income tax liability. Instead, the beneficiary can stretch out the required distributions from the death benefit over a long period of time, usually over the life expectancy of the beneficiary.

Stretching out the proceeds simultaneously stretches out the income tax liability. At the same time, it allows the remaining balance to continue to grow on a tax-deferred basis. The end result is that, over time, the beneficiary ends up with a much larger inheritance than he or she would have had if the IRA were taken as a lump-sum distribution at the time of death.

2-3. The most beneficial aspect of the Roth IRA is that if certain conditions are met, all the funds withdrawn from the Roth IRA by the participant or the surviving spouse are completely income tax free. Unlike their traditional IRA counterpart for which distributions are almost always 100 percent taxable, Roth IRA distributions can provide tax-free retirement income.

Furthermore, "qualified distributions" from Roth IRAs are not included in the recipient's gross income for federal income tax purposes, regardless of whether or not the recipient is the participant or a beneficiary.

2-4. Even though a charitable gift annuity is not an annuity available from an insurance company, there is a market for the sale of an immediate annuity with a charitable gift annuity. A charitable organization may "reinsure" its financial obligation to the donor by purchasing an immediate annuity. The charitable organization purchases the immediate annuity on the life of the donor. It is the owner and beneficiary. The insurance company pays the immediate annuity to the charity that, in turn, pays the donor. The benefit to the charity is that no matter how long the donor lives, it will not be a financial hardship to the charity.

2-5. A special type of charitable trust called a net income with make-up charitable remainder trust, or NIMCRUT for short, allows the deferral of income from the charitable remainder trust until some later date. Because of the special nature of this type of charitable trust, it is the most ideal charitable trust to invest in a deferred annuity.

2-6. When a beneficiary inherits nonqualified deferred annuity death benefits, the beneficiary must pay income taxes on any gain in the annuity. Therefore the beneficiary does not receive the proceeds on an income-tax-free basis like life insurance normally is received or a stepped-up cost basis like mutual funds or shares of stock are received. In addition, the annuity is included in the estate for estate tax purposes.

2-7. Three methods for preapproaching prospects are

- direct mail—a letter or postcard that preconditions prospects to be receptive when you call them

- building prestige—establishing a reputation that allows you to approach prospects on a favorable basis
- professional brochure—a 4-inch by 9-inch promotional piece, for example, that introduces and describes you

2-8. The four components of an effective telephone script are
- a greeting—making a good first impression
- creating interest—motivating the prospect to see you
- closing for the appointment—the reason you are calling
- the conclusion—reconfirming the appointment and affirming your desire to meet the prospect

2-9. Seminars enable you to
- use time efficiently. Seminars are an opportunity to educate and motivate many prospects at once in a group setting.
- meet prospects in a nonthreatening way. Seminars allow you to demonstrate your knowledge of the financial problems prospects face and to present the solutions that you can offer.
- identify qualified prospects. Answers to questions on a feedback questionnaire can give you insight into prospects' concerns and needs before you meet them for follow-up appointments.
- prequalify prospects. Although you initiate the seminar by inviting the prospects, they confirm their interest by attending, which creates a much better prospect pool than a cold-call list.

Answers to Self-Test Questions

2-1. B
2-2. D
2-3. B
2-4. B
2-5. C
2-6. D
2-7. C
2-8. B
2-8. D
2-9. D

Chapter 3

Answers to Review Questions

3-1. A single-premium deferred annuity is a fixed-interest annuity contract that accepts a single deposit with a current interest rate that is guaranteed to some future date. At that time, the insurance company will offer a new interest rate for the next period of time. The policy's maturity may be at a date after the end of the interest guarantee period such as age 90.

A flexible-premium deferred annuity is a tax-deferred fixed-interest annuity contract that accepts periodic premiums and typically offers a guaranteed minimum interest plus excess interest, reflecting the general interest rate marketplace for a shorter period of time. The time period for the surrender charge may be measured from the original date of the contract or from the date of each deposit, referred to as a rolling surrender charge. The existence of a rolling surrender charge, however, means that the contract owner has to consider the risk this puts on each future deposit into the annuity contract.

3-2. Tax deferral for money in an annuity contract is granted by the government under tax law. This concept allows for the accumulation of money in a deferred annuity contract to be free of taxation until the funds within it are withdrawn. Therefore paying income taxes on the earnings does not happen every year, nor does it reduce the funds that a contract owner would otherwise have available to invest.

3-3. A bonus interest rate is an additional amount of interest granted to new purchasers of deferred annuities and typically credited at the end of the first year. It is paid in addition to the normal stated current interest rate, which is usually based on the amount of dollars paid into the contract in its first year. A premium bonus is applied to the premium when it goes into the contract, not added later to the current interest rate paid on dollars after they were deposited into the contract.

3-4. Market value adjustments are features added to some deferred annuities to discourage surrenders prior to the expiration of their initial contractually guaranteed current interest rate. The MVA is an increase or decrease in the annuity's value, depending on the level of the general economy's interest rates relative to the interest rates of the contract from which the withdrawal is taken. The MVA works in the annuity contract in a manner similar to the way individual bond prices fluctuate. For example, if a contract owner has a deferred annuity with a contractually guaranteed interest rate of 8 percent for a term of 7 years, and similar contracts after 3 years into the term are being issued with 4 percent interest rates, the contract owner can expect some gain upon early surrender before the 7-year term has expired. This is because the surrender will relieve the insurance company from its 8 percent obligation in a market where interest rates have decreased to 4 percent. On the other hand, if the opposite occurred and the existing contractual obligation was for 4 percent in a current interest rate market of 8 percent, the contract owner can expect a negative MVA and therefore will receive a smaller surrender value.

3-5. A partial surrender is a withdrawal provision found in deferred annuity contracts whereby the policyowner is allowed limited withdrawal of funds prior to the maturity of the contract. A full surrender is a provision found in deferred annuity contracts whereby the policyowner is allowed total withdrawal of funds prior to the maturity of the contract, which results in its termination.

3-6. A free corridor is some maximum amount of money that a contract owner can withdraw from a deferred annuity contract each year without incurring a surrender charge. If a contract owner elects to make an early withdrawal of just part of the funds in an annuity contract before the end of the surrender-charge period, there is likely to be a free-corridor amount that he or she can withdraw without any charge. Usually this amount is about 10 percent of the last year's accumulation value or 10 percent of the initial premium paid.

3-7. Qualified deferred annuity contracts generally carry a maximum issue age of 70 although nonqualified deferred annuities will be issued to age 85 or 90. The reason for the qualified funds' limitation is based on the minimum distribution requirements for qualified annuity contracts. The tax code requires that qualified plans distribute a certain percentage of the account after the owner reaches age 70 ½. The insurance company does not want to accept new policies of funds at the same time the policyowner will be forced to take immediate distributions. The distribution requirement goes against the fundamental principle of the insurance companies' desire to have a long-term investment from the policyowner.

3-8. A critical area for a prospective purchaser of a fixed-interest deferred annuity to consider is the interest rate the company declares it will pay when the initial current interest rate guarantee period is over. Some insurance companies and banks attract attention with higher first-year "teaser" interest rates at which they may give up some of their spread or profit. Later, when the rates are up for renewal, they lower renewal rates to increase their spread. Prospects should know if the rate for the second year will be competitive with what other fixed-interest deferred annuities are paying at that time. A problem that can crop up with fixed-interest deferred annuities is that renewal interest rates, especially in an economic environment of decreasing interest rate periods, may be less than what some other companies may be offering or less than what most people desire.

3-9. The main purpose of the initial interview in a two-interview sales approach is to build the foundation for a collaborative relationship with the prospect, not to make a sale.

3-10. The four social styles and the characteristic that best explains what a prospect with a particular style is motivated by are
   - driver—motivated by a desire for power
   - expressive—motivated by a desire for recognition
   - amiable—motivated by a desire for approval
   - analytical—motivated by a desire for respect

3-11. The steps involved in the retirement planning process are to
   - assist the prospect in forming goals and objectives
   - help the prospect identify existing resources to meet the goals and objectives
   - analyze the gap between the goals and objectives and the existing resources
   - devise a plan to bridge the resource gap
   - implement the plan
   - monitor the plan

3-12. Sales presentation tools and techniques that the advisor can use to help explain the need for annuities are
   - visual materials to help focus attention
   - third-party substantiation brochures, fact sheets, and testimonials
   - statistical evidence using charts and graphs to show the cost of retirement funding in light of increasing longevity in the United States today
   - real-life stories and case histories of people who have benefited from annuities

3-13. Some prospects fail to qualify for an annuity during the fact-finding interview because they
   - are hostile or uncooperative

- have insufficient funds
- are unsuitable
- are shopping for a better deal

Answers to Self-Test Questions

3-1. B
3-2. D
3-3. D
3-4. C
3-5. C
3-6. C
3-7. C
3-8. C
3-9. C
3-10. C

Chapter 4

Answers to Review Questions

4-1. An indexed annuity, or equity-indexed annuity, is a unique form of deferred annuity that offers a middle ground between a fixed-interest deferred annuity and a variable deferred annuity. It pays interest not on what the insurance company declares but rather on the perfomance of an outside index of securities. It also provides a guaranteed minimum return. Thus it offers its owner the potential for greater upside accumulation that is characteristic of a variable deferred annuity while simultaneously protecting against the loss of principal, which is a feature of fixed-interest deferred annuities.

4-2. A recent review of the indexed annuity marketplace shows the following indexes are used for interest-crediting purposes:
- S&P 500 Index®
- S&P Midcap 400®
- Dow Jones Industrial Average®
- Russell 2000® Index
- Lehman Brothers U.S. Treasury Index®
- Lehman Brothers Aggregate Bond Index
- Merrill Lynch All Convertibles Index
- NASDAQ 100 Index®
- various international indexes

4-3. The three principal types of indexing methods for crediting interest to EIAs are the annual reset design, point-to-point design, and high water mark design.

4-4. Every dollar the client pays in premium for an indexed annuity has to be split into three pieces. First, the expenses are deducted. Second, the portion of the dollar required to provide the guarantee (for example, 90 percent of the principal will earn 3 percent) is invested. Finally, what is left over is used to purchase options on the index. These options are securities that an insurance company purchases, using a portion of the premium it collects from the sale of an indexed annuity to back the interest-earning obligation it has to pay to the contract owners. By buying options, the insurance company owns the right to any gain in the index during the policy period. If the option is profitable to the company, it will have the needed profit to pass on to the annuity policy.

4-5. The insurance company may place a cap or upper limit on the amount of interest the equity-indexed annuity can earn. The cap is the absolute maximum interest rate the annuity will earn, and it is usually expressed as a percentage. For example, assume the cap rate is 10 percent, the index earns 20 percent, the asset fee is 2 percent, and the participation rate is 100 percent. Although the credited rate is 18 percent (20% − 2% x 100%), the cap rate will prevail, and 10 percent will be the maximum amount of interest credited to the equity-indexed annuity. Like asset fees and participation rates, caps are adjustable by the insurance company.

4-6. Averaging is an interest-crediting strategy used in an equity-indexed annuity to bring up the value of returns in negatively moving indexes and bring down the value of returns in positively moving indexes. Some indexed annuities average an index's value either daily or monthly rather than using the actual value of the index on a specified date. Because averaging can reduce the amount of index-linked interest, it reduces the insurance company's risk and therefore its cost.

4-7. The guaranteed minimum interest rate is the contractually stated percentage rate that will be credited to an indexed annuity during a year or over the term of the contract. The owner has the assurance of knowing that the money within the contract will earn the higher of the indexed earnings percentage or the guaranteed minimum interest rate each year or within the contract term period. Furthermore, as in a fixed-interest deferred annuity, there is no chance of "negative interest rates" causing an erosion of the principal. This guaranteed minimum interest rate is what allows the equity-indexed annuity to be considered a fixed annuity rather than a securities product.

When a policyowner decides to surrender the policy, generally the insurance company determines which of the two account values is higher, and this is what the client receives, minus any applicable surrender charges. Note, however, that not all indexed policies will credit guaranteed interest if the client surrenders before the end of the contract term.

4-8. Indexed annuities are generally considered fixed annuity products. Most are not registered with the SEC despite the fact that they reference equity indexes to determine how much interest the policies earn. They do not pay equity returns; they pay interest. The interest they pay is measured by the positive change in the index or the guaranteed interest rate, whichever is higher.

4-9. A formal retirement planning fact finder can be divided into these four distinct components:
- personal data and retirement goals
- quantitative date
- retirement income sources
- calculations and interest tables

4-10. The implied contract that represents mutual consent between you and the prospect to continue to work together is the discovery agreement. It is a verbal or written agreement that acknowledges a willingness to work together toward seeking financial solutions that address the retirement planning concerns discussed throughout the interview within the framework of the prospect's budget.

Answers to Self-Test Questions

4-1. C
4-2. A
4-3. A
4-4. A
4-5. B
4-6. B
4-7. C
4-8. A
4-9. D
4-10. D

Chapter 5

Answers to Review Questions

5-1. The prospectus is a document that provides the complete details of a variable annuity product, including investment features, options, fees, other costs, death benefits, and payout options. Any potential buyer of a variable annuity must be given a prospectus, as required by the Financial Industry Regulatory Authority (FINRA) and the Securities and Exchange Commission.

5-2. Fixed-interest deferred annuities are nonsecurities insurance products and are therefore regulated by the state departments of insurance in the states where they are sold. Unlike fixed-interest deferred annuities, variable deferred annuities are considered securities and are registered products. In addition to state insurance department regulation, they are regulated by the SEC. They may be sold only by salespeople who are properly licensed by the state and as registered representatives licensed by FINRA.

5-3. In a variable deferred annuity, the general account guarantees principal and some minimum fixed interest rate—usually between 1 percent and 3 percent. A separate account is composed of various subaccounts from which the contract owner can select investment options that match his or her investment objectives and risk tolerance. Variable annuity contract owners can continually adjust their investment choices as their circumstances change.

5-4. Dollar cost averaging is the consistent investment of equal periodic payments into a diversified equity-based investment over an extended period of time. With each consistent investment, the number of shares or units purchased will vary with the share price. In some months, the investor will purchase more shares or units than in other months. With this systematic investment approach, the goal is, over time, to invest with a lower average cost per unit than the average price per unit paid.

5-5. A dollar-for-dollar reduction of death benefit is just that: When the policyowner withdraws $10,000 from a deferred annuity policy, the death benefit is reduced by $10,000.

The alternative to a dollar-for-dollar reduction is a pro rata reduction. A pro rata reduction causes a decrease in the death benefit by the percentage that the withdrawal is to the death benefit. For example, suppose a policy starts out with a premium of $100,000, but now the death benefit has grown to $300,000 even though the policy cash value has tumbled back to $100,000. At this point, the policyowner chooses to withdraw $50,000. A dollar-for-dollar reduction decreases the death benefit to $250,000 ($300,000 − $50,000 = $250,000). A pro rata reduction is determined by the ratio of the withdrawal over the account value ($50,000 ÷ $100,000). The withdrawal drops the death benefit by 50 percent to $150,000 (50% x $300,000 = $150,000).

5-6.   A front-end load is deducted as a percentage from money coming into the contract. It is often seen as a disadvantage to the client because less of the contract owner's money is put to work in the contract.

A back-end load is also called a surrender charge or contingent deferred sales charge. This charge is assessed at the time of a withdrawal from a variable annuity as a percentage of the amount withdrawn according to a contractually defined schedule.

5-7.   The charges commonly found in deferred variable annuities consist of
- either front-end loads charged against premiums remitted or back-end loads charged against withdrawals taken
- annual administrative contract charges
- insurance expenses, often referred to as M&E charges (for mortality and expense), which are asset-based charges (including administrative and distribution costs) against the investment subaccounts in a variable annuity
- the fund expense, which is an asset-based fee for management operations of the various subaccounts

5-8.   The four types of death benefit guarantees available in variable deferred annuities are
- account value or premiums paid death benefit
- rising floor death benefit
- stepped-up or ratchet death benefit
- enhanced earnings benefit

5-9.   An annuity recommendation can be developed according to the prospect's financial goals and the following policy classification criteria:
- how premiums are paid—single- or flexible-premium annuity
- when annuity payments begin—deferred or immediate annuity
- how annuity funds are invested—fixed, indexed, or variable annuity

5-10. The key areas to evaluate when comparing the competition with your company and the annuity products it offers are
- financial strength
- reputation
- value
- interest rate stability
- company and advisor service
- differences in policies

Answers to Self-Test Questions

5-1. A
5-2. D
5-3. B
5-4. B
5-5. B
5-6. A
5-7. A
5-8. B
5-9. D
5-10. D

Chapter 6

Answers to Review Questions

6-1. The payment of the fixed-amount or fixed-period immediate annuity is issued to the annuity owner in a fixed amount for the duration of the payout period. In a fixed-amount annuity, the purchaser pays a premium and selects the periodic payment amount the insurance company is to pay. The company informs the purchaser how long it will be able to pay the stipulated amount. If the annuitant dies before the funds in the annuity have been paid, the remainder is generally paid to the annuitant's beneficiary.

   In a fixed-period annuity, the purchaser pays a premium and selects the period of time the insurance company is to make the periodic payments. The company calculates the payment amount and informs the consumer what that amount will be. If the annuitant dies during the distribution period, benefits continue to the annuitant's beneficiary until the end of the distribution period.

6-2. A straight life annuity (commonly called a life-only annuity) is the least expensive type of life-contingent annuity. It provides the largest possible payment based on a given deposit. It is low in cost because there is a high risk of loss of money. The risk is that if the annuitant dies prior to the time that an amount equal to the original deposit in the annuity has been repaid, the balance of the deposit is forfeited to the insurance company.

6-3. Life with period certain is a life-contingent annuity in which the purchaser requests that if the annuitant's death occurs before a certain number of years have passed, payments are to continue until they reach the end of the specified period. Payments continue for life, however, if the annuitant survives longer than the specified period.

   Suppose Jean, age 71, purchases a life and 10 year certain immediate annuity with a $100,000 deposit. The insurance company offers to pay $1,000 per month for Jean's lifetime with the guarantee that if she should die before the end of 10 years—for example, in 7 years—the $1,000 per-month payment will be made to her named beneficiary until the end of the 10th year. If Jean lives longer than 10 years, the payments will continue for as long as she lives.

6-4. The risk to the annuity owner with a variable immediate annuity is that the payments can decrease as well as increase. Therefore the contract owner accepts the interest rate risk from the insurance company that would not exist in a fixed immediate annuity with guaranteed level payments.

6-5.   A joint and survivor annuity pays income for the lives of two individuals. After the death of the first annuitant, the insurance company continues to make full payments until the death of the second annuitant. Variations of this form of payout can provide for higher payments while both annuitants are living, with reduced income payments to the survivor of, for example, 75 percent, 66.6 percent, or 50 percent. Upon the second death, payments cease, and no death benefit is available to any named beneficiary.

The joint and survivor life annuity with period certain protects against the early termination of payments if both annuitants die early. The insurance company is instructed to continue payments until the death of the last to die, with a minimum payout period—generally 5, 10, 15, 20, 25, or 30 years.

The joint and survivor life annuity with installment or cash refund protects against the early termination of payments due to the death of both or all annuitants. Under the installment refund option, the insurance company is instructed to refund the remaining balance of the deposit by continuing payments to the named beneficiary after the death of all annuitants until the full deposit is returned. If the cash refund option is selected, the lump-sum payout will be the discounted present value of the remaining payments.

This joint and survivor life annuity with percent of premium death benefit pays a lifetime income jointly to two annuitants and also guarantees that at the surviving annuitant's death, a specified percentage of the initial premium payment selected at the time of purchase (i.e., 25 percent or 50 percent) will be paid to a designated beneficiary in a single sum.

6-6.   When shopping for immediate annuity rates, the advisor and the potential purchaser need to (1) look at the strength and financial stability of the insurance company guaranteeing the payments, and (2) compare the dollar amount of the payments among companies.

6-7.   A policy feature is a characteristic of the policy itself—what it is and what it does. A feature is a fact about the policy. On the other hand, a policy benefit is what the owner gets as a result of the feature. It is what the policy does for the owner and usually why he or she wants it. Features produce benefits.

6-8.   It is important to have the prospect's participation and involvement in the selling/planning process for several reasons:

- It helps the prospect feel responsible for solving his or her own problems.
- It helps the advisor know whether he or she is on target with the presentation.
- It builds agreement one step at a time.
- It helps to clarify any misunderstandings by either party.
- It helps lead to a logical and successful close—a conclusion to buy.
- It provides opportunities to deal with objections before asking the prospect to buy.

6-9.   Examples of nonverbal buying signals are

- leaning forward
- listening attentively
- making good eye contact
- nodding, showing appreciation
- smiling

6-10.   Three things to put into focus when taking a problem-solving approach to handling a prospect's objections are
    - building trust and rapport with prospects
    - dealing with the needs involved, not the personalities
    - instilling a sense of urgency to act now

6-11.   Two three-step techniques for responding to prospect resistance are as follows:
    - Acknowledge a concern, clarify it, and then resolve it.
    - Use the words *feel, felt,* and *found* in three successive sentences as demonstrated below:
        - I understand how you *feel.*
        - Many of my prospects have *felt* the same way.
        - Until they *found* that . . . (state a benefit or explain how the plan was a good solution for their situation).

6-12.   The four general categories of objections to purchasing annuity products are
    - no need
    - no money
    - no hurry
    - no confidence

Answers to Self-Test Questions

6-1.   A
6-2.   D
6-3.   C
6-4.   A
6-5.   C
6-6.   A
6-7.   C
6-8.   D
6-9.   D
6-10.   D

Chapter 7

Answers to Self-Test Questions

7-1.   A tax problem can arise when an annuity is issued with three different individuals as owner, annuitant, and beneficiary. The court in *Goodman v. Commissioner* (156 F.2d 218 (2nd Cir. 1946)) held that at the annuitant's death, the owner is deemed to have made a taxable gift to the beneficiary for the amount of the death benefit. The logic behind this is that since the owner could have named anybody in the world as the beneficiary, it must be a gift from the owner to the beneficiary.

7-2.   Amounts borrowed from a deferred annuity issued after August 13, 1982, are considered taxable income to the owner to the extent of gain in the policy. This also applies to annuities used as a pledge or as part of an assignment. This is true even if the owner does not technically withdraw any funds from the annuity. Furthermore, the 10 percent IRS penalty tax will apply if the owner is under age 59 ½.

7-3. The IRS provides tax relief to the purchasers of deferred annuities, life insurance, and endowment policies if the purchaser wants to move funds from one insurance company to another. The tax code allows this transaction without making it a taxable event.

The tax-free-exchange rules under IRC Sec. 1035 state that a life insurance policy can be exchanged for a life insurance policy, a deferred annuity policy can be exchanged for a deferred annuity policy, and a life insurance policy can be exchanged for an annuity policy. It does not matter what type of deferred annuity is under consideration as long as it is a nonqualified deferred annuity. It can be variable, fixed, or equity indexed. The same is true for life insurance.

However, an annuity cannot be exchanged on a tax-free basis for a life insurance policy. This is because the IRS does not want a taxpayer to exchange a potentially taxable asset— such as a deferred annuity—for a potentially tax-free asset—such as life insurance. However, it allows the taxpayer to move from a tax-free asset to a taxable asset.

7-4. The following exceptions to the 10 percent penalty exist under IRC Sec. 72(q) for distributions taken from a nonqualified annuity prior to the policyowner's age 59 ½:

- payments made if the taxpayer is age 59 ½ or older
- any payment made on or after the death of the participant (or the primary annuitant if the holder is a nonnatural person). This means that beneficiaries of deceased persons under the age of 59 ½ are not subject to the penalty tax if they receive the death benefit in a lump sum.
- a payment attributable to the taxpayer's becoming disabled
- any payment allocated to premiums paid before August 14, 1982, including earnings on pre-August 1982 premiums
- any payments under a qualified funding asset (that is, any annuity policy issued by a licensed insurance company that is purchased as a result of a liability to make periodic payments for damages, by suit or agreement, or on account of personal physical injury or sickness)
- any payment made under an immediate annuity (one that is purchased with the starting date no later than one year from issue). If the taxpayer purchases an immediate annuity, it is not subject to the 10 percent penalty tax.
- any payment that is part of a series of substantially equal periodic payments (SEPP) made for the life or life expectancy of the taxpayer or the joint lives or joint life expectancies of the taxpayer and the taxpayer's designated beneficiary. The IRS has approved three methods to determine substantially equal periodic payments: (1) the life expectancy method (required minimum distribution), (2) the fixed amortization method, and (3) the fixed annuitization method. However, the distribution schedule cannot be altered for the later of five years or the taxpayer's reaching age 59 ½ without the taxpayer's having to pay back penalty taxes plus interest.

7-5. Qualified annuities have their own set of rules with respect to transferring qualified funds from one account to another on an income-tax-free basis:

- 60-day rule—A participant has 60 days in which to take a qualified plan or IRA distribution and place those funds into a rollover IRA account. Rollovers can be done once a year.
- trustee-to-trustee transfer—An IRA holder can move funds from one IRA to another an unlimited number of times during a year without being in violation of the 60-day rule as long as the transfer is completed on a trustee-to-trustee basis. This means that one financial institution must directly transfer the funds to the new financial institution without the funds ever going into the hands of the participant.

7-6. When qualified plan holders reach age 70 ½, or retirement age if later, the tax code provides that the participant must begin to take distributions from the account. For IRA holders, only age 70 ½ is used.

The first distribution must be taken by April 1 following the year in which the participant turns age 70 ½ or retires, if applicable. This date is technically referred to as the required beginning date.

7-7. When the owner of an IRA reaches the required beginning date (on April 1 of the year after the year in which he or she reaches age 70 ½), the owner must begin to take required minimum distributions from these accounts as prescribed by the IRS. The dollar amount of the distribution is determined by using the RMD Uniform Lifetime Table. This table is used by all participants except participants who have named their spouse as sole beneficiary, and the spouse is more than 10 years younger than the participant. A second table, the Joint and Last Survivor Expectancy Table, may be used to determine the minimum distributions in that situation.

The penalty tax for a participant who does not take the required minimum distribution is 50 percent of the amount that should have been distributed but was not.

7-8. If the participant dies prior to the required beginning date, a spouse beneficiary must begin to receive payments by the later of
- the end of the year after the year in which the participant died or
- the end of the year in which the deceased would have turned age 70 ½

or the spouse can roll over the account into his or her own name.

If the participant dies after the required beginning date, the spouse beneficiary has these choices:
- to continue on with the annuity as the new owner and annuitant at the death of the participant
- to take a lump sum or choose a settlement option

7-9. The advisor must take the following steps to complete the application:
- Obtain all the information requested, leaving no questions unanswered.
- Complete the application in the applicant's presence.
- Record accurately all information as provided by the applicant.
- Obtain necessary signatures.
- Complete a suitability form for variable annuities.

- Provide the applicant with all receipts, disclosure documentation, and the appropriate annuity buyer's guide according to the laws of the state and the requirements of the insurer.

7-10. The objectives of the delivery interview are to
- reinforce the buying decision
- review the policy
- build the advisor-client relationship
- obtain the required forms
- develop other sales opportunities

7-11. The important aspects for servicing existing clients are as follows:
- regular communications with the client to maintain and build the professional relationship
- annual or other periodic reviews to see that retirement funding objectives reflect the current and possibly changing needs of the client
- any processing of beneficiary or asset allocation changes within a variable annuity that should be assisted and monitored

7-12. a. The tremendous financial and personal risk exposure that long-term care poses must be a serious consideration in every retirement plan. A retirement plan that does not address this issue would have to be considered incomplete. To fail to take into account circumstances that could leave a person and his or her family impoverished would be a breach of your professional duties. A secure retirement depends not only on accumulating sufficient assets but also on protecting those assets from the potentially devastating effects of LTC. Therefore you need to help your clients eliminate the uncertainty of who will pay for this care.

   The need for long-term care insurance can result in joint selling opportunities that involve the sale of an immediate annuity in conjunction with long-term care insurance for the purpose of funding LTC.

b. The goal of estate planning is to fulfill the wishes of the individual regarding the disposition of property during life and, ultimately, the disposition of property at death. Because of the enormous potential costs of funding retirement, a person's assets may be severely depleted or his or retirement lifestyle compromised if not planned for appropriately.

   Immediate annuities and estate concerns are inextricably intertwined, as both are concerned with the preservation of assets. Deferred annuities enhance the value of financial assets within a person's estate through the deferral of taxation on wealth accumulation prior to and subsequent to retirement, and through the reduction of income taxation on Social Security retirement benefits.

Answers to Self-Test Questions

7-1. A
7-2. B
7-3. B
7-4. A
7-5. C
7-6. C

7-7. A
7-8. B
7-9. D
7-10. C

Chapter 8

Answers to Review Questions

8-1. State insurance departments regulate the financial aspects of insurance companies. Therefore states must be concerned with financial solvency of their insurers. They want assurance the insurance companies have enough money invested to cover their policyholders. Making sure their insurance companies stay solvent to pay claims is of primary importance to state regulators.

　　　Insurance departments supervise the sales and marketing practices of both insurance companies and advisors. The goal is to make sure consumers are treated fairly. In fact, each state insurance department's number one priority is the protection of its insurance consumers.

8-2. Generally an advisor who is selling an annuity must be licensed in the particular state where the application is written. This may or may not be the state of residence for the policyowner. Advisors may be licensed in more than one state to sell insurance. Typically an advisor will carry a resident license in his or her home state and then may have additional nonresident licenses in other states.

　　　The advisor must also obtain an appointment from one or more companies. This appointment is what allows the advisor to sell a particular insurance company's products. During the appointment process, the insurance company will verify the existence of the advisor's insurance license and will most likely perform both financial and criminal background checks. If an advisor sells for several insurance companies, he or she will have several appointments.

8-3. Recently state legislatures have lowered the minimum guaranteed interest rate for newly issued fixed-interest deferred annuities. Before now, 3 percent had been the standard minimum interest rate guarantee. The reason for the legislative rate decrease is the low-interest-rate environment in which insurance companies conducted business during the early years of this century. Most insurance companies cannot maintain a 3 percent guarantee for such a prolonged decreased interest rate period. To address these market conditions, legislators allowed a decrease in the guaranteed minimum interest rate so that companies could compete in the insurance market and still maintain some level of profitability.

8-4. Even though guaranty associations exist in each state to protect policyowners, the insurance departments prohibit advisors from discussing the guaranty fund as part of their sales presentations. One reason for this is cited in the Life and Health Insurance Association Model Act, Sec. 19D, 1999, that is recommended in the following Guaranty Association disclaimer to the states:

　　　"The State Life and Health Insurance Guaranty Association provides coverage of claims under some types of policies if the insurer becomes impaired or insolvent. Coverage may not be available for your policy. Even if coverage is provided, there are significant limits and exclusions. Coverage is always conditioned on residence in this state. Other conditions may also preclude coverage."

Another reason is that guaranty associations cover only the cash values accumulated by fixed annuity policyowners.

8-5. The National Association of Insurance Commissioners serves as the forum for creating uniform insurance laws and regulations among the states. Comprised of the state insurance commissioners from all 50 states, the District of Columbia, and four U.S. territories, it has helped coordinate regulation among the states since 1871. NAIC commissioners discuss issues of common concern and align their oversight of the insurance industry.

The NAIC has been responsible for passing many model laws. It has no binding authority on the individual states but functions merely as an advisory board.

8-6. The Securities and Exchange Commission is the overseer and regulator of U.S. securities markets. The SEC protects investors and helps maintain the operation of the securities markets. It monitors the stock exchange, broker-dealers, investment advisors, and mutual fund companies. The SEC is concerned with the accurate disclosure of information to investors.

The National Association of Securities Dealers was a self-regulatory organization created in 1938 that was previously responsible for regulating the securities industry in the United States.

Created in July 2007 through the consolidation of the NASD and the member regulation, enforcement and arbitration functions of the New York Stock Exchange, The Financial Industry Regulatory Authority (FINRA) is dedicated to investor protection and market integrity through effective and efficient regulation and complementary compliance and technology-based services.

FINRA is the largest nongovernmental regulator for all securities firms doing business in the United States. All told, FINRA accomplishes its oversight of the securities industry by registering, educating, and testing member firms and their staffs, as well as by creating and enforcing rules.

FINRA enforces the rules of the SEC and self-regulates broker-dealers subject to SEC oversight. Broker-dealers must become FINRA members. FINRA provides the NASD rules of conduct for sellers of variable annuities, including suitability requirements.

8-7. In order to sell variable annuities, an advisor must be a registered representative with FINRA. To become a registered representative, an individual must become affiliated with a broker-dealer, submit an application to FINRA, and pass the appropriate FINRA Series examination. The Series 6 is the Investment Company/Variable Contracts Representative examination that enables registered representatives to sell variable annuity products and, in some states, mutual funds as well. Many states also require a state securities exam called Series 63. The Series 63 exam is the Uniform Securities Agent State Law Examination, which is required by most states in conjunction with either the Series 6 or Series 7 in order to sell the respective securities products permitted with these registrations.

FINRA also administers a two-part mandatory continuing education training program that registered representatives must complete in order to maintain their registration status. The program consists of a Regulatory Element and a Firm Element.

8-8. Because the issue of creditor protection is controlled by state law, each policyowner must consult legal counsel in his or her state to determine the level of creditor protection for the policyowner's annuity holdings. Financial advisors should not give advice to their clients regarding creditor protection of annuities and should refer their clients to legal counsel.

Answers to Self-Test Questions

8-1. A
8-2. D
8-3. C
8-4. A
8-5. C
8-6. C
8-7. C
8-8. B
8-9. D
8-10. C

Index

THE AMERICAN COLLEGE
ALUMNI
ASSOCIATION

Your Bridge to a Lifetime of Professional Achievement

We encourage you to take advantage of knowing more about The Alumni Association. Together we can create a stronger community and explore new opportunities for professional success.

Call us at (610) 526-1200

e-mail: russell.figueira@theamericancollege.edu